GLOBAL GOVERNANCE OF FINANCIAL SYSTEMS

Finance and the Economy

A CERF Series edited by John Eatwell

The Cambridge Endowment for Research in Finance (CERF) was founded in 2001 as an independent research center at the University of Cambridge. It is dedicated to developing an enhanced understanding of the evolution and behavior of financial markets and institutions, notably in their role as major determinants of economic behavior and performance. CERF promotes theoretical, quantitative, and historical studies, crossing conventional disciplinary boundaries to bring together research groups of economists, mathematicians, lawyers, historians, computer scientists, and market practitioners. Particular attention is paid to the analysis of the impact of financial market activity on the formulation of public policy. The CERF series of publications on Finance and the Economy embodies new research in these areas.

Identifying International Financial Contagion
Edited by Mardi Dungey and Demosthenes N. Tambakis

Global Governance of Financial Systems: The International Regulation of Systemic Risk
Kern Alexander, Rahul Dhumale, and John Eatwell

GLOBAL GOVERNANCE
OF FINANCIAL SYSTEMS

The International Regulation
of Systemic Risk

Kern Alexander
Rahul Dhumale
John Eatwell

UNIVERSITY PRESS

2006

OXFORD
UNIVERSITY PRESS

Oxford University Press, Inc., publishes works that further
Oxford University's objective of excellence
in research, scholarship, and education.

Oxford   New York
Auckland   Cape Town   Dar es Salaam   Hong Kong   Karachi
Kuala Lumpur   Madrid   Melbourne   Mexico City   Nairobi
New Delhi   Shanghai   Taipei   Toronto

With offices in
Argentina   Austria   Brazil   Chile   Czech Republic   France   Greece
Guatemala   Hungary   Italy   Japan   Poland   Portugal   Singapore
South Korea   Switzerland   Thailand   Turkey   Ukraine   Vietnam

Published by Oxford University Press, Inc.
198 Madison Avenue, New York, New York 10016

Oxford is a registered trademark of Oxford University Press

www.oup.com

Library of Congress Cataloging-in-Publication Data
Alexander, Kern, [date]
Global governance of financial systems: the international regulation of systemic risk / Kern
Alexander, Rahul Dhumale, John Eatwell.
p.   cm.
Includes bibliographical references and index.
ISBN-13 978-0-19-516698-9
ISBN 0-19-516698-1
1. Financial services industry—Law and legislation.   2. Financial services industry—State
supervision.   I. Dhumale, Rahul.   II. Eatwell, John.   III. Title.
K1066.A9154   2004
346'.082—dc22   2003064714

9 8 7 6 5 4 3 2 1

Printed in the United States of America
on acid-free paper

Preface

This book was written while all three of us were working at Cambridge University (before Dhumale left for the Federal Reserve Bank of New York). We were brought together under the aegis of a research project entitled "A World Financial Authority," directed by John Eatwell, of Queens' College, Cambridge, and Lance Taylor, of the New School for Social Research, New York. We are very grateful to the Ford Foundation for funding the project. We are also grateful to colleagues at the Centre for Business Research at the University of Cambridge and at the Cambridge Endowment for Research in Finance for the stimulating conversation and the active dissension that helped hone our ideas. Although most chapters have been separately drafted, we are collectively responsible for them.

Over the past thirty years, innovation in international financial regulation has followed on the coattails of financial crises, some of which have resulted in significant losses in employment and reductions in standards of living. We hope that the ideas in this book will contribute to the development of a more robust financial architecture and build in preparation for the financial storms that are a persistent feature of international financial markets.

The views expressed in this book are entirely those of the authors and should not be attributed in any manner to the Federal Reserve Bank of New York or the Federal Reserve System.

Kern Alexander
Rahul Dhumale
John Eatwell

Contents

GLOBAL GOVERNANCE OF FINANCIAL SYSTEMS

Introduction

The financial crises that in recent years have spread through East Asia, Russia, Turkey, and Latin America, and from these countries to the United States and other Organization for Economic Cooperation and Development (OECD) countries, have led to renewed calls for reform of the "international financial architecture" that would involve institutional and legal changes for international financial markets. Since the collapse of the Bretton Woods system in the early 1970s, there have been more than one hundred financial crises, while a majority of the members of the International Monetary Fund have suffered some degree of banking fragility and distress. Many experts agree that adequate regulation at the domestic and international level has not accompanied the liberalization of financial markets and, in particular, of short-term capital flows. It is a serious defect of the current system that the development of international financial regulation—especially with respect to banking supervision and payment system regulation—has occurred only haphazardly and principally in response to the series of financial crises that began in the mid-1970s. Indeed, unlike the many other books that have attributed the cause of financial crises to weak domestic banking systems and to inadequate regulation and corporate governance structures, this book argues that reforms at the domestic level will be inadequate if not accompanied by major institutional and legal reforms at the international level. The analysis to support this argument in the book draws heavily on the relationship between microeconomic risk taking and the macroeconomic propagation of financial crises.

Since the liberalization of international financial markets in the mid-

1970s, international financial crises have assumed a form unfamiliar since the 1930s: their origins have been increasingly found within the private sector. For many years after the Second World War, economic crises were associated with mistakes in government macroeconomic policies. The interwar world was quite different. In the 1920s and 1930s, crises were typically generated in the private sector: failures by institutions such as that of the Credit Anstalt in 1931 reverberated through the financial system to produce a general economic collapse. The removal of the extensive system of domestic and international financial and monetary controls that characterized the post–World War II world before 1971 has resurrected the prewar origins of crises in microeconomic *as well as* macroeconomic circumstances.

Nonetheless, even where crises have microeconomic origins, an important macroeconomic component remains. The negative externalities associated with financial risk taking by individuals and firms are not spread solely through the microeconomic connections of trade (as is typically the case, for example, with environmental externalities). A major component of financial externalities is macroeconomic. The reason derives from the fact that while commodity markets (including the "market" for dirty smoke) involve the pricing of flows of goods and services, financial markets involve the pricing of stocks of financial assets. Moreover, the price of a financial asset depends on expectations about its future price, as well as expectations about its future liquidity and rate of return. Consequently, expectations play an extraordinary role in the determination of the prices of financial assets, and shared expectations are a potent source of macroeconomic contagion. A wave of pessimism can result in a *general* fall in the prices of financial assets as the demand for liquidity rises, or a rise in the general rate of interest or a collapse of the exchange rate.

Of course, the relationship between microeconomic risk taking and macroeconomic contagion is not a peculiarity of international markets. Exactly the same story may be told about domestic financial markets. International markets simply add a number of extra dimensions. And the liberalization of financial markets in the 1970s and 1980s also posed major new institutional and policy questions as domestic regulation was dismantled and the domain of the newly liberalized international market exceeded the jurisdiction of national regulators. Deregulation thus had two components: the removal of preexisting regulations and controls and the migration of the market out-with national juridical boundaries and hence out-with national controls. The subsequent attempt to recover some regulatory control on an international scale has had only limited success.

Successful financial regulation, particularly in the attempted management of "systemic risk," must be based on a coherent understanding of the relationship between microeconomic risk, macroeconomic contagion, and macroeconomic consequences.

There is another important dimension of economic policy in which microeconomic regulation and macroeconomic policy are linked. To a considerable extent, regulatory rules define the relationship between the stock of financial assets and overall liquidity. In other words, they define the monetary transmission mechanism. The procyclical impact of regulation has been a topic of recent debate. Yet, despite their potentially major impact, regulatory rules have not yet been incorporated into the broader fabric of monetary policy, and certainly not into any countercyclical policy.

An understanding of the need for regulation, of the impact of regulation, and of the limits of regulation therefore requires an analysis of the relationship between microeconomic actions and the behavior of the macroeconomy. Yet it is exactly this analysis that appears at the moment to be absent from the discussion of international financial regulation and to play little role, if any, in considerations of the future of the international financial "architecture." In part, this is because of the need to concentrate on the microeconomic "nuts and bolts" of regulation and supervision. But, more fundamentally, it derives from the lack of a generally accepted, let alone satisfactory, macroeconomic theory or microfoundations of macroeconomics.

In much of financial theory, it is assumed that the "real" economy is characterized by a tendency toward, or even presence at, a Walrasian equilibrium: all markets clear, including the labor market, at an equilibrium set of prices. Financial markets play no role in the determination of this equilibrium; they may only temporarily disrupt it by introducing financial rigidities or instabilities such as overshooting.

However, a more realistic view encompasses a totally different relationship between financial markets and real output and employment. Financial factors determine the ability of individuals, firms, and governments to spend and hence determine aggregate demand, output, and employment. Financial factors are "imperfections," resulting in disequilibria or overshooting; they are at the very core of the determination of overall economic performance. This view has significant consequences for an understanding of the relationship between financial variables and the behavior of the economy as a whole. Instead of finance being imposed as an awkward imperfection upon the general equilibrium equations that determine output and employment, it is the financial markets that determine the liquidity of the economy and hence permit spending decisions to be implemented. It is the appropriate spending decisions that then determine the overall level of output.

The key spending decisions include expenditure by firms, spending by the state, and debt-financed expenditure by households. In all cases, finance does not simply provide the option for spending or not spending. The possibility of financial disruption or of severe financial imbalances can lead to a diminution (even a disappearance) of liquidity and hence to the disruption of spending or the absence of spending.

In this respect, the pricing of financial assets is the key to the availability of liquidity and hence of the ability to spend. Markets for the stocks of financial assets are driven by supply (virtually fixed) and demand (heavily influenced by the *expectation* of future market conditions).

The key to economic performance is thus the availability of liquidity and the desire to spend.

Both of these factors may be influenced by "real variables." For example, the technological changes that created the Internet in turn precipitated the expectation that investments in dotcom companies would yield substantial returns and sharply increased the availability of liquidity for dot-com investments. The excess of liquidity that flowed into dot-com markets (a classic financial bubble) when contrasted with the paucity of realized returns in turn precipitated the collapse in price of dotcom stocks as liquidity vanished.

An important role is played by innovation in the financial sector itself. Developments in information technology and the creation of new financial instruments have significantly increased the availability of liquidity. The increase in the supply of liquidity in turn increases the volume of lending as financial institutions are eager to secure returns to their enhanced lending abilities. And with that increased lending goes the potential for increased risk.

That risk feeds into the other fundamental characteristic of financial markets—that value can disappear in an instant, as the price of assets adjusts to new information or to new beliefs about what average opinion believes average opinion to be. This disappearance of financial value then precipitates a disappearance of the value of real assets as a result of the impact of reduced spending on real asset returns.

This was particularly well characterized by Keynes in his portrayal of the Beauty Contest (Keynes, 1936, chapter 12). He was not referring to a 1930s equivalent of Miss World, in which "expert" judges decide a winner. He had in mind a competition that was at the time very popular in down-market British Sunday newspapers. Readers were asked to rank pictures of young women in the order that they believed would correspond to the average preferences of the papers' readers as a group. So, in order to win, the player should not express his or her own preferences, or even try to estimate the genuine preferences of average opinion. Instead, the successful player should anticipate "what average opinion expects average opinion to be." In the same way, the key to success in the financial markets is not what the individual investor considers to be the virtues or otherwise of any particular financial asset, or even what the mass of investors actually believes are virtues of that financial asset. The successful investor is concerned to establish what everyone else in the market will believe everyone believes.

For substantial periods of time, markets may be stabilized by convention: everyone believes that everyone else believes that the economy is sound and financial markets are fundamentally stable. But if convention is questioned or, worst of all, shattered by a significant change in beliefs, then the values of financial assets may soar to great heights or collapse to nothing. Average opinion is reinforced by labeling these beliefs "fundamentals," as if they were revealed truths.

For many years it was believed that the U.K. balance of payments was a "fundamental." Any deficit in the current account would result in selling pressure on the pound sterling, as the markets followed their beliefs. In the past decade, opinion has changed; the current account is no longer a "fundamental," so deficits no longer produce the reaction they once did. A "fundamental" is what average opinion believes to be fundamental. Of course, this is not to say that some characteristics of the real economy will not eventually overwhelm even the most stubborn beliefs. Belief in the profitability of the stock of a nonexistent silver mine will eventually be punctured by the evident lack of any silver. Belief in the sustainability of a large and persistent current account deficit may eventually be punctured by the accumulation of debt and debt interest that that deficit entails. The reversal of average opinion can then be frighteningly sudden.

So long as the market follows what average opinion believes average opinion to be, then anyone who bucks the trend will lose money. Anyone who invests for the long term against the conventional short-term wisdom will require extraordinary confidence in his or her predictions, as short-term losses pile up.

Average opinion has its own history. It is heavily influenced by fashionable theories and by the exercise of the financial powers of national governments, particularly the more economically powerful ones. The recent history of capital market liberalization has coincided with a swing in the balance of intellectual influence from a postwar theory of economic policy that urged national governments to limit international capital movements to the present-day theory that encourages free capital movements and the abdication of national regulatory powers. So financial stability is largely a matter of convention. Convention may be stable for long periods. But even stable conventions may contain the seeds of their own destruction. When stock markets are rising rapidly, it quickly becomes the convention that they will rise forever. When convention breaks down, financial markets become very unstable. Convention is peculiarly vulnerable when there is a shift in the balance of risk. Just such a shift took place in the early 1970s, when foreign exchange risk was privatized.

The dangers of high-risk financial investments are apparently reduced if those investments are highly liquid. A market that operates as a beauty contest is likely to be highly unstable and prone to occasional severe loss of liquidity as all opinion tends to shift in the same direction. Everyone wants to sell at the same time, and nobody wants to buy. The operation of the beauty contest destroys the liquidity that would encourage risk taking. Increased instability may well therefore result in systematic changes in the behavior of both public and private sectors, as decision makers become ever more risk-averse. Although these changes may succeed in reducing instability, they do so only at the cost of less risk taking, less investment, and medium-term deterioration in overall economic performance.

The potential instability of financial markets is based on the possibility of switching funds into and out of investments. Swings of convention translate into sharp fluctuations in asset prices that in turn reinforce the swings in confidence. In the circumstances, it might be thought desirable to limit the ability of investors to make such switches. If investors were locked into long-term investments, then markets would not be plagued by boom-and-bust waves of buying and selling. But here lies an important paradox. Without liquidity, without the ability to sell and recover cash invested, many investors would be simply unwilling to take risks at all. Although it is true that when the opinion of the whole market swings one way, liquidity vanishes, nonetheless the individual investor tends to believe that his or her investment is liquid and that he or she will sell out in time. The ability to exit from an investment by selling a financial asset is, at the same time, a necessary foundation for investment in a market economy *and* the source of the instability that can undermine investment, output, and employment.

The microeconomic analysis of financial markets can therefore be the starting point of an understanding of overall macroeconomic performance. What is necessary is to link that microeconomic analysis to a macroeconomic model via the impact of financial variables on overall spending behavior.

This then provides the framework within which to examine the impact of regulatory proposals, and particularly the relationship among financial institutions, financial innovation, and systemic risk. Analyzing the impact of regulation in this context will ensure that regulation is seen as having macroeconomic consequences; indeed, many regulatory goals may be more readily achieved at the macro rather than at the micro level. For example, it is well known that Korean regulators have, since 1998, been eager to reduce the foreign exchange, or forex, exposure of Korean companies. This has been achieved primarily by the enforcement of regulatory requirements for the risk analysis of balance sheets. The same goal might well have been attained, far less onerously, by introducing macroeconomic controls on financial flows.

But the key point is, of course, that a large component of systemic risk derives from macroeconomic contagion, and thus an understanding of the behavior of financial markets and the interrelationship between those markets and macroeconomic performance must be central to any coherent program of regulatory reform, domestic or international. That program of regulatory reform, if it is to succeed, must therefore be grounded in a comprehensive framework of international law and a coherent economic analysis of regulatory issues. This book attempts that dual task.

The first part of this study (chapters 1 to 6) analyzes the international institutional and legal framework for regulating systemic risk in global financial markets. Recent financial crises suggest that current international efforts to regulate financial systems lack coherence and legitimacy and fail to effectively manage systemic risk. The discussion in chapter 1 covers the nature of systemic risk in the international financial system and the dilemmas that face national regulators who seek to protect their economies from the ravages of financial contagion and payment system breakdown. The concept of global governance is addressed, along with a history of the recent demise of the Bretton Woods system, which has been followed by lower rates of economic growth in most countries and by increased volatility and risk in the global financial system.

The evolution of international standard setting in financial markets is assessed in chapter 2 by examining the characteristics of the various international bodies, such as the Basel Committee on Banking Supervision and the International Organization of Securities Commissions, that are involved in international standard setting. The work of these committees must be considered in parallel with the implementation efforts of the IMF and, potentially, the World Trade Organization (WTO). Decision making in these bodies and organizations is almost invariably dominated by the G10 rich countries. It therefore lacks political legitimacy and accountability in the international community because many countries outside this group have, by and large, not played a role in influencing the development of international financial norms.

The international legal framework of financial regulation is outlined in chapters 3 and 4. Multilateral treaty organizations govern important areas of the international financial system. In chapter 3 the role of international organizations and treaties in regulating financial markets is discussed. For example, the Articles of Agreement of the International Monetary Fund empower the IMF to oversee the international monetary system to ensure its effective operation. To accomplish this, the IMF exercises treaty-sanctioned surveillance powers over member states' exchange rate policies, and it has recently begun using these powers to assess member states' compliance with international standards. The IMF often works in conjunction with the World Bank in overseeing the design and implementation of economic restructuring programs and the legal and regulatory framework of financial systems. The third major international organization involved in financial sector issues is the World Trade Organization. The WTO's General Agreement on Trade in Services plays a growing role in financial sector issues by creating obligations for its member countries to liberalize cross-border trade in financial services based on the principles of most-favored nation, national treatment, and market access. Although the WTO plays no role in setting domestic financial regulatory standards, the free-trade principles of the GATS may influence how domestic regulators implement international standards of financial regulation. This chapter explores the roles of these international organizations in financial standard setting and their impact on issues related to systemic risk.

Regional treaty arrangements have also played an important role in influencing the development of international financial regulation. The European Union (EU) financial regulatory system has essentially been based on the principle of home country control and mutual recognition based on minimum standards. This allows firms to operate with a passport that enables them to trade in other host EU member states subject to their home country regulation. EU directives and regulations contain minimum harmonized standards in many areas, including, inter alia, capital adequacy for banks and financial firms, prospectuses for initial public offerings, market abuse and insider dealing, and money laundering. Although much of EU financial legislation has become increasingly prescriptive, the principle of subsidiarity allows member states some discretion to implement standards according to their domestic legal and regulatory frameworks. Some experts view the EU regulatory framework as a model to be used for a global approach to regulating financial markets in which states would be subject to demanding standards but would have a margin of discretion in respect of implementation. Moreover, the role of the European Central Bank in overseeing the eurozone payment system will be mentioned as an important development in payment system regulation along with some unresolved issues regarding the scope of the ECB to engage in prudential supervision in order to protect the payment system.

These international organizations and their formal treaty frameworks are in stark contrast to the informal international bodies such as the Basel Committee on Banking Supervision, which have no legal status as international organizations and no "hard" law-making powers. They serve as forums where leading developed-country financial regulators and supervisors deliberate and exchange information on a voluntary basis with a view to establishing legally nonbinding international standards, rules, and codes of conduct to reduce systemic risk in the international financial system.

The important role played by international soft law in developing international principles of banking supervision and financial regulation is examined in chapter 4. International soft law is defined as legally nonbinding standards, principles, and rules that influence and shape state behavior but do not fit into the traditional categories of public international law of legally binding general custom of states and bilateral or multilateral treaties. For too long, international lawyers have clung to obsolete notions of public international law that do not adequately explain many legally relevant areas of state practice and policy. This chapter suggests that international soft law in its various dimensions can contribute to an understanding of the development of legally relevant international financial norms and how they govern state regulatory practice.

Although international soft law is viewed as a more flexible mechanism by which to regulate vital and technical areas of interstate relations, its Achilles' heel lies in its implementation and enforcement in national jurisdictions. In chapter 5, therefore, the argument is made for a particular institutional approach to ensure that an effective international financial regulatory regime can be implemented and enforced in domestic systems. To accomplish this, attention should be given to various official and market incentives to induce state regulators to adopt and implement international standards, but within the framework of rules and procedures of each national jurisdiction. Exclusive reliance, however, on national regulatory approaches might result in disparate impacts across countries, which might be difficult to reconcile with the objective of harmonized or uniform international standards. Indeed, the lack of harmonization in applying and interpreting international standards could result in significant divergence among national legal systems, thus creating obstacles to the efficient performance of financial transactions in global markets. This is where market incentives in a global financial market can play a role in reducing the discrepancies among national regulations. Liberalized capital markets will permit capital to flow to its most efficient and profitable use, and this will likely occur in those jurisdictions with the most efficient regulatory regimes, those that emphasize financial transparency, sound banking supervision, and robust corporate governance standards.

There is some consideration of various proposals for improving the institutional framework of international financial regulation that would involve a treaty-based global governance council represented (directly or indirectly) by all states that would review proposed international standards of financial regulation. The proposal for a "Governing Council" is considered, along with the feasibility of delegating standard-setting authority to informal bodies of financial supervisors, such as the Basel Committee. We suggest that informal bodies would maintain many of their responsibilities over specific issue areas that reflect their expertise (i.e., IAIS and insurance), but these bodies would have to expand their membership to include regulators from emerging economies, with a view eventually to reaching universal membership. Moreover, these bodies would participate in a broad consultation process in which they would exchange their recommendations and proposed standards with other bodies and organizations (i.e., IMF and WTO). These various sets of standards would be submitted to a global governance committee that would have ultimate authority to adopt them as legally binding principles with adequate exceptions and provisos for states to implement them differently when justified by economic and legal circumstances.

The book's second part has been motivated mainly by the interests of financial regulators and the institutions that they regulate. Much government activity involves the motivation of private interests to further the public good. When government seeks to limit the level of systemic risk within the financial environment, many of its actions affect the incentives of private financial institutions. This problem has been evident in various aspects of international financial regulation, which chapters 6–10 consider in detail.

In chapter 6 we pose the question whether there is even a role for incentive-based regulation to reduce systemic risk. In chapters 7–10 we analyze these very problems by examining the nature of systemic risk in different cases. A common theme that runs throughout this volume and is further highlighted in the following chapters is the importance of setting appropriate standards in order to gain the most from an incentive-based approach to financial regulation. Chapter 7 begins with consideration of the current debate over settlement systems and the need for minimum standards in national payment systems to foster greater harmonization at an international level. The efficacy of capital adequacy requirements in the recent Asian financial crisis is the focus of the next chapter. Clearly, one of the important lessons from this crisis is the establishment of clear analytical links between microeconomic risk taking and macroeconomic outcomes. The discussion then turns to an analysis of some of the suggested solutions as recommended by the Basel Committee and others international bodies, namely the use of internal ratings and private agency credit assessments in the recently released Basel II proposals, as well as the use of subordinated debt as a tool to enhance market discipline. Finally, the discussion turns to the idea that national financial markets may vary according to their legal system, institutional structures, business customs, and practices. Uniform international financial regulatory standards may not have the same impact on all financial systems, which may result in different types of systemic risk. Although financial markets are seamless, their structures are not homogenous. Thus, in chapter 10 we set out a list of specific standards of corporate governance as advocated by various international bodies and describe their specific relevance to financial institutions.

Finally, chapter 11 presents a summary of the main themes of the preceding chapters in an assessment of the main contemporary measures designed to create a "new international financial architecture." These measures have in the past thirty years taken a number of turns, stimulated by the "fear factor" that accompanies international financial crises. Today, the reliance on market forces as a complement to regulatory measures is a prominent theme. But, if the market is to be relied upon to overcome the inefficiencies created by externalities, then not only must measures be incentive compatible; they must also serve to "complete" markets when markets fail. And they must achieve this not only in normal times but in the face of the extreme events associated with an international financial crisis.

The defining issues of our day are globalization and interdependence, and the challenge of managing financial globalization requires institutional structures of international financial regulation that are efficient, accountable, and legitimate. The collapse of WTO negotiations at Cancun highlighted the concerns of developing countries with the existing pace of globalization and its impact on economic development and financial markets. It has been asserted that the global governance process is dysfunctional because the institutional structure of international financial regulation has not kept pace with developments in financial markets. Policymakers are torn between the pressures of multinational banks to liberalize financial markets and the dangers of exposing their economies to the rough edges of international capitalism, which often results in economic dislocation and, for many countries, lower levels of economic growth and development. This book attempts an ambitious task of analyzing some of the key issues of financial regulation with respect to the problem of systemic risk in financial systems and the need to devise global governance structures that can efficiently regulate financial markets while adhering to principles of accountability and efficiency.

1

Managing Systemic Risk

The Rationale for International Financial Regulation

The deregulation and liberalization of domestic financial markets, combined with advances in technology, has resulted in a substantial increase in cross-border trade in financial services and portfolio capital flows. The changing structure of global financial markets not only has created more opportunities for profits but also has introduced a higher level of risk in financial transactions that may impact systemic stability (Crockett, 2000). In the post–Bretton Woods era, banks and financial institutions have adopted innovative financial instruments to diversify earnings and to hedge against credit and market risk. This has led to increased international banking activity and to the rise of multifunctional universal banks. These developments have led to more efficient allocation of savings and investment and to deeper liquidity in financial markets, thus producing beneficial results for economic growth and development. But they have also made financial institutions more interdependent and thus more exposed to systemic risk that can arise from bank failures and to volatility in international portfolio capital flows. Recent financial crises in the 1990s suggest that these factors have destabilized financial systems, thus undermining national economic growth and social stability. These are the forces of financial globalization that lend urgency to efforts to strengthen the institutional framework of international financial regulation.[1] This book addresses some of the major issues involved in establishing international regulatory norms for banks and payment systems. It argues that optimal international regulatory structures require an institutional framework of standard setting and rule-making that satisfies principles of global governance. We define global governance of financial systems to involve three main principles: *effectiveness* in devising efficient regulatory standards and rules, *accountability* in the decision-making structure and chain of command, and *legitimacy*, meaning that those subject to international regulatory standards have participated in some meaningful way in their development.

Governance is a multifaceted term that takes on a variety of meanings across disciplines, and we apply it in the context of interstate relations whereby policymakers are confronted with the challenge of making international banking regulation more effective, accountable, and legitimate. In particular, this involves controlling systemic risk and the threat it poses to financial stability. Systemic risk often occurs because banks have an incentive to underprice financial risk, which can lead to too much of it being created in the financial system. High levels of financial risk can lead to bank failures, which can spread quickly by means of the interbank payment system to other banks in other financial systems and thereby cause an international banking or financial crisis. The primary role of international banking regulation therefore should be to promote the efficient pricing of financial risk in all financial systems and to ensure that regulators focus not only on the amount of risk created by individual financial institutions but also on the aggregate amount of risk created by all financial institutions in global financial markets. To achieve this, the existing institutional framework of international financial regulation should be restructured to provide more effective standard setting, surveillance, and coordination among national regulators. This would entail national regulators and supervisory authorities acting through international organizations and standard-setting bodies to devise more effective and efficient standards of prudential regulation and to coordinate the implementation and enforcement of such standards in national jurisdictions. The existing institutional framework of international financial regulation has failed to accomplish these objectives because it lacks coherence and a sense of clear objectives in addressing the causes of financial fragility in international banking markets. This book argues that further institutional and legal consolidation should occur at the international level but that states should retain ultimate authority to select and implement certain standards that are suitable for their economic systems.

Part I of this book sets forth the international response to the problem of systemic risk in global financial markets by analysing the institutional structure of international financial regulation and whether it adheres to the relevant principles of global governance for international financial policymaking. Building on the work of Eatwell and Taylor (2000), we argue that the institutional design and scope of international financial regulation should be linked, in some way, to the level of integration in global financial markets. In other words, the domain of the regulator should be the same as the domain of the financial market. Specifically, the degree of integration in global banking markets should play an important role in influencing the institutional design and scope of international banking regulation.

Although substantial integration has occurred in global banking and capital markets, considerable fragmentation still exists, thus supporting the view that the optimal institutional structure should combine a layered framework with divided responsibilities between international, regional, and national authorities. In reality, however, the institutional structure of international banking regulation is controlled by the world's richest countries (the G10) and the standards they produce often reflect the needs and interests of developed country financial systems. Countries outside the G10 are increasingly finding themselves subject to banking regulation standards promulgated by exclusive international standard-setting bodies and implemented through IMF and World Bank assistance programs. This global regime is ill suited to address the economic needs of many financial systems of non-G10 countries. We argue therefore that efforts to reform international financial regulation must adhere to principles of global governance.

Part I also addresses the emerging international legal framework of financial regulation that increasingly requires states to adopt certain regulatory measures to improve the management of systemic risk. We argue that the efficient regulation of systemic risk in global financial markets requires a multilateral framework treaty that sets broad standards of good regulatory practice, which states will be generally obliged to observe. The responsibility for adopting more detailed regulatory rules and procedures will be delegated to expert international bodies whose membership will be composed of national regulators who are representative of most of the world's economies and financial systems.

THE ROLE OF INSTITUTIONS

As a theoretical backdrop for understanding the role of regulation in international finance, it is necessary to understand the role of institutions in economic growth and development (North, 1990). Institutions are generally defined as regularities in social behavior that are agreed to by all members in a society (Axelrod, 1984). Institutions may also specify certain behavior in recurrent circumstances and may be enforced by external authorities or by self-regulatory bodies (Allegret and Dulbecco, 2002). Institutional practices may derive from rules, norms, and routines that can either be required by law or be the result of voluntary custom. Economic institutions arise to address problems of market failure and coordination problems between market participants. Common rules of interaction and decision making are often needed to reduce economic uncertainty. Indeed, private agents use institutions to collect information and knowledge and to coordinate their actions with other agents. At the international level, states and substate actors create institutions as orientation points to exchange information and to solve coordination problems. International institutions have been defined as a set of rules that govern the ways in which states should cooperate and compete with each other by prescribing acceptable and unacceptable state behavior and practices (Kahler, 1995: 3–10).

Financial liberalization and deregulation have created many opportunities for economic growth but have also burdened the global economy with a great many financial crises over the past thirty years. The international response to the growing number of financial crises has usually involved the actions of an array of international public- and private-sector bodies that are involved in setting standards and rules to govern financial markets. These international financial institutions (IFIs) have concluded various international agreements that have taken a number of forms including informally negotiated, nonbinding agreements between financial regulators all the way to international treaties between sovereign states with detailed procedures for dispute resolution and enforcement. Other agreements have been negotiated by private sector bodies that cover model financial contracts and codes of conduct (ISDA, 2002). Many experts view the growing number of these international agreements and institutional arrangements as responses to increasing fragility in the global financial system. Moreover, the plethora of international institutions that address issues of financial stability have raised the concern that international standard setting is not governed adequately by principles of global governance.[2]

THE CONCEPT OF GLOBAL GOVERNANCE

The term "governance" derives from the ancient Latin term *gubernator*, which denotes helmsmanship and navigation. In modern international relations parlance, most scholars understand governance as the establishment and operation of a set of rules of conduct that define practices, assign roles, and guide interaction in order to address collective problems (Young, 2000). Others define governance as "the process and institutions, both formal and informal, that guide and restrain the collective activities of groups" (Keohane and Nye, 2000: 12). These processes and rules of conduct create informal institutional frameworks that shape and constrain state behavior. They may also influence the behavior of states as they interact in more formal international institutions. International institutions can take the form of international economic organizations or less formal international standard-setting bodies. In both cases, the interaction of states and substate actors in international economic institutions can be analyzed within the principal-agent framework (Drazen, 2002).

The principal-agent framework forms the basis for evaluating whether state activities within international institutions conform with principles of global governance.[3] This framework analyses the decision-making process and the line of authority that runs from states as principals to international institutions as agents. It requires an analysis of the decision-making process of institutions to determine whether it is accountable to those parties (state and substate actors) that are subject to its standards. It also considers the effectiveness of the decision-making process in generating efficient standards of economic governance for *both* the global economy and national economies. More specialized studies have referred to "common agency" models that see states not as unitary actors but rather as collections of heterogeneous groups within states that exercise different levels of influence on international organizations and other states (Tirole, 2002).

International relations scholars refer to international governance systems as regimes, which are commonly defined as "norms, rules, and procedures agreed to in order to regulate an issue area" (Haas, 1980). According to international regime theory, states jealousy guard their sovereignty against other states and seek to promote their perceived national interests by adopting measures to enhance their political and economic security. International regimes usually involve states sharing a common view of certain rules of conduct, which are often formalized, and sometimes enforced by states acting individually or in concert with other states. This approach has traditionally studied the concept of governance through the lens of state actors by focusing on the creation and operation of rules in interstate relations.

In contrast, the term "global governance" covers not only those phenomena but also situations where the creators and operators of rules are nonstate actors, working across state boundaries and at different levels of the international system. This concept of global governance contrasts with the narrower view of *international governance* implied in regime analysis, which focuses primarily on interstate relations. Global governance is more broadly conceived, referring to the creation and operation of rules at other levels involving transnational and subnational actors, while still recognizing the important role that states play in the international system (Rosenau, 1995). Others view global governance critically as a threat to traditional public international law because it uses law merely as an instrument to achieve policy objectives defined by rich and powerful states (Koskenniemi, 2004). Although global governance of financial systems encompasses the role of private-sector bodies and nonstate actors, the aspect of it that deals with financial stability and systemic risk involves a public regulatory concern that is most optimally dealt with by state bodies. This is true because financial stability is a global public good (Wyplosz, 1999). The very definition of a public good means that it will never be adequately provided by the market without regulatory intervention. Our analysis of global governance and financial regulation therefore primarily involves the role of public-sector actors, with some input from private-sector bodies, acting through international financial institutions to develop standards and rules to promote financial stability.

Financial Systems

Before we proceed further, we would like to clarify what we mean by a "financial system." A large number of studies have examined the nature and characteristics of financial systems. Allen and Gale (2000) have provided the most comprehensive study, evaluating the various types of financial systems under the broad categories of bank-led systems, stock market–based systems, and hybrid systems that rely more or less equally on bank and capital market finance. In their analysis, they also classified the various types of financial systems along national jurisdictional boundaries. For instance, the United States was classified as a financial system that relies to a large extent on capital-market finance, whereas Germany was classified as a financial system that relies, by and large, on bank-led finance. Although these classifications are useful for comparing the various financial structures of *national* financial systems, we would like to set forth a more flexible definition of a financial system that does not focus solely on national jurisdictional boundaries but also takes account of the increasingly global nature of international finance. Our definition would define a financial system, in part, on the basis of measures of integration between and within national jurisdictional boundaries. Indeed, if a particular national jurisdiction exhibited high levels of integration in its major financial sectors, it would qualify as a financial system. In contrast, if a country was economically integrated and exhibited high levels of financial integration with a group of other countries, this grouping of states might also qualify as a financial system.

Under this approach, the definition of a financial system depends crucially on the specific measures used to demonstrate financial integration. Some studies have emphasized quantity-based measures, such as the IMF's aggregate data on cross-border trade in financial services, that are consistent with the notion that such cross-border trade is growing (Organization for Economic Cooperation and Development, 1999). Other quantitative data measure the number of foreign banks and foreign bank assets present in a domestic market, while still other studies use portfolio composition of investment funds, that is, the share of foreign assets in total assets or share of assets held by foreign institutions. Other studies use price-based measures that show, for example, differentials in bank charges for cross-country credit transfers (Adam et al., 2002). Others have used an index of capital mobility that measures the size of capital flows or a price approach that relies on the law of one price or covered interest parity differentials (Adam et al., 2002). Although it is not the task of this work to evaluate the various measures of financial integration, it is our contention that an adequate understanding of the limits and scope of international financial regulation must be grounded in an understanding of the nature of financial markets and the extent of their integration.

We should also add that the definition of a financial system should also depend on existing institutional structures of legislation and regulation. The legislation governing particular financial markets can be transnational, national, or subnational. In the United States, most insurance regulation is conducted by states with varying requirements across jurisdictions. In Canada, securities markets are governed and regulated by provincial regulatory authorities. In the European Union, an increasing array of EU legislation and regulations and a growing institutional structure of European regulators are increasingly controlling Europe's financial regulatory framework. The definition of a financial system should therefore also include the existing institutional design and scope of financial regulation. It is therefore important to note the two important factors for determining a financial system: (1) the extent of integration of the relevant financial sectors, and (2) the scope and design of financial regulation and legislation.

THE RATIONALE FOR INTERNATIONAL FINANCIAL REGULATION

The Bretton Woods Era

In the late stages of World War II, postwar economic planners met at Bretton Woods, New Hampshire, and concluded several agreements to rebuild the global economic order. These agreements became known as the Bretton Woods agreements, which formed the basis for the creation of the International Monetary Fund (IMF, or Fund) and the International Bank for Reconstruction and Development (World Bank). The main objective of these international organizations was to avoid the economic mistakes of the interwar years that included the experience with floating exchange rates in the 1920s and the competitive devaluations of the 1930s. To address this, the IMF's Articles of Agreement required all countries that were members of the Fund to maintain official par values for their currencies. These par value currency exchange rates could only be changed with IMF approval to correct a "fundamental disequilibrium" in a country's balance of payments.[4] Moreover, member states agreed to make their currencies convertible, which permitted the resumption of international trade by allowing nonresidents to exchange surpluses in one currency to import goods priced in another currency at the par value exchange rate.

The IMF assisted member countries experiencing short-term payment imbalances by providing them with loans denominated in reserve currencies. The Fund determined the amount loaned on the basis of a complex formula that considered a country's subscription quota to the IMF. Member countries normally were not allowed to borrow reserve currencies from the Fund in excess of their subscribed quotas unless specifically approved by the IMF. In deciding whether to approve such requests, the IMF exercised discretionary authority and often based its decision on a member's compliance with broader IMF economic policies (Kenen, 2002).

The IMF system of exchange rate management addressed trade imbalances of member countries by requiring members to draw on their Fund subscriptions to finance their imbalances until equilibrium was restored. A member country might allow its nationals to purchase foreign exchange in order to pay for imports of goods and services, or to make foreign direct or portfolio investments. A country that ran a persistent trade and capital account imbalance would eventually exhaust the initial 25 percent tranche of its subscription of reserve currencies and would thus be forced to seek financial assistance from the IMF or subject itself to a sharp correction in its external position. IMF members therefore had an incentive to restrict foreign exchange speculation that might drive the value of their currencies outside their par values. This led many countries to adopt or maintain capital controls, which improved their ability to manage foreign exchange risk in their financial systems.

The Bretton Woods exchange rate management regime had the effect of reducing volatility in currency markets, which led to improved macroeconomic growth and to a period of relative financial stability in most Organization for Economic Cooperation and Development (OECD) countries. This was in contrast to the "hot money" flows and competitive devaluations by leading economies during the 1930s. Although financial crises occurred during this period, they were predominantly of macroeconomic origin, disrupting the microeconomy: high inflation rates undermining confidence in monetary policy, or persistent current account deficits undermining confidence in the exchange rate. The Bretton Woods framework sought to avoid the economic disaster of the interwar period when microeconomic instability spread like contagion through the financial sector and destabilized the macroeconomy.[5] Those lessons were now embodied in appropriate policies and institutions. Important among these institutions were powerful regulatory structures and interventionist central banks dedicated to the reduction of systemic risk.

Although the Bretton Woods exchange rate regime was largely not in effect during the transition period 1947–1959 (which allowed U.S. postwar reconstruction programs to be implemented), currency convertibility as a policy had been adopted by the G10 industrial countries by the early 1960s. During this period, the IMF played an important role in advising its members to adopt adequate regulatory frameworks to manage foreign exchange risk while making their currencies convertible to promote international trade. By the early 1960s, reserve countries and most IMF members had adopted powerful national regulatory regimes to manage exchange rate policy, thus reducing systemic instability. For example, the U.S. government imposed strict regulations on domestic money markets with the adoption of an interest equalization tax, which had the effect of reducing the incentive of U.S. investors to invest in Euro dollar instruments. The national monetary authorities of developed Western states were dedicated to a policy of maintaining the fixed exchange rate system. The collapse of the Bretton Woods system, however, in 1971, resulted in the privatization of foreign exchange risk, and the consequent necessary dismantling of international and domestic financial regulation threatened to recreate the unstable prewar environment (Eatwell and Taylor, 2000).

As international barriers to financial flows disappeared, national regulators, and national central banks, were trapped in increasingly irrelevant national boundaries. The domain of banks, investment houses, insurance companies, and pension funds increasingly became international.

In a rapid return to the prewar norm, it was a microeconomic failure (of the Herstatt Bank, in 1974) that threatened severe disruption of the U.S. clearing system and hence of the U.S. macroeconomy. Similarly, in recent years, the Asian crisis also stemmed primarily from failures in the private sector reverberating through the macroeconomy.

THE END OF BRETTON WOODS AND THE PRIVATIZATION OF FOREIGN EXCHANGE RISK

The elimination of the Bretton Woods fixed-exchange rate parity with gold took place in August 1971, when President Nixon closed the gold window. This began a series of events that resulted in the virtual floating of the major reserve currencies against the U.S. dollar. This resulted in the privatization of foreign exchange risk, which created the need for banks to adopt hedging strategies involving the diversification of assets into multiple currencies and the creation of portfolios held in foreign and offshore jurisdictions. This shifted foreign exchange risk onto the private sector, which in turn put pressure on governments to liberalize their national controls on cross-border capital flows and to deregulate banking practices so that banks could spread their risks to foreign assets and diversify their business. As more and more states began to liberalize and deregulate their financial sectors in the late twentieth century, national financial systems became increasingly vulnerable to increased systemic risk and to a growing number of financial crises.

The first major banking collapse that resulted from the privatization of foreign exchange risk and that focused the attention of the international financial community on the need for enhanced international banking supervision occurred in 1974 and involved major banks from Great Britain, West Germany, and the United States. In June 1974, West German authorities closed the Herstatt Bankhaus (Herstatt) following losses from foreign exchange dealings that threatened severe disruption of the U.S. clearance system (Dale, 1984), while U.K. authorities closed the British-Israel Bank of London for insolvency problems (Kapstein, 1989). The closure of Herstatt and British-Israel Bank of London exposed major weaknesses in the international banking system. Shortly thereafter, the Franklin National Bank, in the United States, collapsed under the combined weight of bad management in the volatile domestic wholesale deposit base, excessive speculation in international foreign exchange markets, and over-ambitious efforts to expand (Dale, 1992). To prevent the crisis from spreading, the U.S. Federal Reserve intervened by guaranteeing the bank's failed short-term foreign exchange commitments. It has been argued that these banking collapses occurred because of the lack of adequate regulatory standards to protect against foreign exchange risk (Eatwell and Taylor, 2000).

During the 1980s and 1990s, a market-led global financial system emerged in which the volume of financial assets, the sophistication of international financial transactions, and advances in computer and tele-communications technology increased dramatically. By contrast, no corresponding institutional framework or regulatory response was developed on the international level to provide effective and efficient regulation of globalized financial markets. Unlike during the Bretton Woods era, the current international financial order has led to recurring financial crises and overall declines in rates of economic growth and investment in the OECD countries (Eatwell and Taylor, 2002). In response, governments have attempted to recover some of the regulatory controls that they exercised during the Bretton Woods era. For example, leading developed states have established various international bodies to improve the supervision of financial institutions involved in banking, securities, and insurance. These bodies have agreed on various sets of principles and rules, establishing what are now agreed to be generally accepted international standards of prudential supervision. Notwithstanding these efforts, the financial and currency crises of the 1990s demonstrate the inadequacies of the current international regime of financial regulation. They led the leading industrial states to create, in 1999, the Financial Stability Forum, which meets twice a year to examine potential threats to the international financial system.

The current loosely assembled regulatory and institutional framework for supervising international financial markets lacks coherence and political legitimacy and requires more concerted efforts to manage systemic risk. Indeed, the British Chancellor of the Exchequer, Gordon Brown, recognized the need for more concerted efforts at international regulation of financial markets when he stated, "[B]ecause today's financial markets are global, we need not only proper national supervision, but also a fundamental reform—global financial regulation" (Brown, 1999). Accordingly, the leading industrial states have responded to these events by proposing a set of policy initiatives designed to increase the efficiency, stability, and transparency of international financial markets (Group of Ten, 1996; Group of 22, 1998). Although these proposals for a new international financial architecture remain vague and subject to much dispute, there is a growing consensus that a coherent institutional framework must be established to administer and facilitate the implementation of international standards. Before we describe and analyze the current institutional structure of international financial regulation, it is necessary to discuss the major rationale for "global financial regulation."

THE PROBLEM OF SYSTEMIC RISK

The problem of systemic risk has become an issue of great importance for public policymakers, bank regulators, and central banks, especially following the 1998 Asian financial crisis and the Russian and Latin American crises of the late 1990s. Although there is no one generally accepted definition of systemic risk, it can arise from problems with payment and settlement systems or from some type of financial failure that induces a macroeconomic crisis (Dow, 2000). Some studies have identified the systemic risk inherent in international banking to include (1) global systemic risk—the risk that the world's entire banking system may collapse in response to one significant bank failure; (2) safety and solvency risks that arise from imprudent lending and trading activity; and (3) risks to depositors through the lack of adequate bank insurance (Cranston, 1996). This study defines systemic risk as arising from the mispricing of risk in financial markets, which often means that risk is underpriced in relation to its cost and that the underpricing of risk results in too much of it being created in financial markets. Often, those private actors who create financial risk do not internalize its full cost, leading to excessive risk that may take the form of substantial exposures accumulated by banks and derivative-dealing houses in foreign exchange markets and in speculating in financial instruments whose values depend on variations in interest rates in different markets. Overexposures to risk may precipitate a financial crisis that may result in bank runs and/or a collapsed currency. These are the excessive costs of risk that can be shifted onto society at large as a negative externality, in much the same way as the cost of pollution (in terms of health and environmental damage) is shifted onto society at large as a result of the underpricing of certain modes of production that create pollution. Systemic risk is therefore a negative externality that imposes costs on society at large because financial firms fail to price into their speculative activities the full costs associated with their risky behavior (Eatwell and Taylor, 2000).

High levels of systemic risk can lead to bank failures, which can pose a threat to the overall financial system and to the broader economy. Bank failures can threaten systemic stability because of the following: (1) many banks play an important role in the payments and clearing systems; (2) banks are credit institutions that generally hold illiquid assets and liquid liabilities, the latter of which are usually cash deposits that may be recalled on demand, with the potential for a bank run; and (3) the interconnections between banks in their wholesale operations make them vulnerable to contagion, in which one bank's failure can have a domino effect on other banks. To manage systemic risk, national regulators have relied on various ex ante and ex post measures. Some ex ante measures include capital adequacy requirements, large exposure limits, and limitations on lending. Ex post measures include deposit insurance and the lender-of-last-resort function. These regulatory measures compose the main framework of bank prudential regulation.

Prudential regulation of banks seeks to contain the following risks: credit risk, concentration risk, market risk, settlement risk, liquidity risk, and operational risk. Credit risk has been defined as "the potential that a bank borrower or counterparty will fail to meet its obligations in accordance with agreed terms" (Basel Committee on Banking Supervision, 2000a). Concentration risk concerns so-called hot money flows into and out of a bank or financial system that can undermine stability and liquidity, especially in less sophisticated and smaller financial systems. Market risk represents broader linkages in the market whereby fluctuations in the prices of financial instruments can affect movements in interest rates, equity prices, or the prices of other traded instruments. Settlement risk applies to all forms of derivatives, but, because of the relative size of the foreign exchange market, it is most prevalent among foreign exchange market participants (BCBS, 2000b). The Basel Committee has acknowledged two types of liquidity risk: (1) market liquidity risk, and (2) funding liquidity risk (BCBS, 2001a). Market liquidity risk concerns a party's ability to liquidate a position. This depends on a number of factors, including the market for the product, the size of the position, and possibly the creditworthiness of the party's counterparty. Funding liquidity risk is a different issue that focuses on the ability to fund a position. Operational risks is a residual category known as "other risks" that covers a broad area including (but not limited to) fraud, legal negligence, misconduct, and technology failure.

Although the taking of risks is a large part of what financial institutions do, prices in financial markets reflect only the private calculation of risk, and so tend to underprice the risk—or the cost—of investments faced by society at large. This underpricing of risks in financial markets creates a negative externality caused by excessive risk-taking that may result in a financial crisis. The regulator's task is to internalize the negative externality of risk, ensuring that investors take into account the risks their activities impose on society. This may be accomplished through either of two approaches: (1) by requiring firms to internalize the costs of the risks they take by, for example, requiring them to adhere to capital adequacy standards or certain risk management practices, or (2) by the direct regulation of a firm's activities. In this way, the financial regulator seeks to require businesses to behave as if they took systemic risk into account, which should reduce the occurrence of systemic breakdown in financial markets. Although effective regulation can make a significant contribution in reducing normal systemic risk, it can never protect firms and markets from abnormal market risk. Even the best regulatory standards and risk management practices may sometimes be overwhelmed by exceptional market turbulence. However, by building confidence in the maintenance of market stability in normal times, it likely reduces the chance of abnormal market risk.

In addition, banks have increasingly recognized that traditional methods of risk management have become obsolete and that new measures are needed to assess the risk of new financial instruments. The objective of reducing risk in complex financial markets has led banks to use innovative financial instruments to diversify earnings among several countries so that, in any given year, an inadequate *investment* outcome in one country may be offset by a positive investment outcome in another country. This need to reduce risk by expanding cross-border financial services has also resulted in the establishment of complex organizations, known as financial conglomerates (Adams, 1999; Walker, 2001). An international financial conglomerate is an integrated group of companies that offers a broad range of financial services. While financial conglomerates offer the benefits of diversified assets, risks, and sources of earnings, their structure poses several problems for regulators. Comprehensive supervision of financial conglomerates requires that supervisors develop standards that address the degree of transparency[6] within the organization and the placement of overall supervisory responsibility with a particular regulator. Moreover, the interrelationship of various divisions within a multinational conglomerate increases the likelihood that the default or liquidation of an affiliate in one jurisdiction will spread to other affiliates or controlled entities in other jurisdictions. To prevent systemic risk from occurring on the international level, national regulatory authorities should establish effective corporate governance standards that address the principal-agent problem and transparency issues for banks that operate within multinational financial conglomerates.

The lack of a coherent international regime to provide standards for the risk-taking activities of financial institutions has exposed financial systems to an increased risk of systemic failure. Indeed, increasing linkages among the world's financial markets have led to a significant expansion in the number, size, and types of activities, and in the organizational complexity of multinational financial institutions. Although these cross-border linkages generally bring efficiency to world capital markets, the increasing scope of international banking activity has highlighted the difficulty of ensuring effective supervision and may, in some cases, increase systemic risk, whereby losses between banks in different jurisdictions or between subsidiaries and affiliates within the multinational group can affect the entire financial system. It has become a major objective of many national policymakers therefore to strengthen the safety and soundness of the banking and financial sectors by ensuring the effective management of systemic risk.

EXTRATERRITORIAL REGULATION AND SYSTEMIC RISK

In the absence of effective international financial regulation, states may take regulatory measures to control systemic risk that have extraterritorial effects and in some cases offend the jurisdictional principles of other legal systems. As a general matter, state regulatory practice in G10 countries has evolved to permit extraterritorial economic regulation of foreign conduct in situations where the conduct in question has effects on the territory or economy of the regulating state.[7] This effects doctrine provides the jurisdictional link that allows financial regulators to adopt regulatory rules or to take measures to control extraterritorial sources of systemic risk. For instance, a host country regulator could require a foreign bank, as a condition for operating in the host jurisdiction, to demonstrate that its global operations are well capitalized and well managed according to the legal requirements of the host jurisdiction. The regulatory requirements of the host jurisdiction, however, may depart from, or be contrary to, the requirements of the foreign bank's home jurisdiction. This may result in a conflict of regulatory requirements and thus lead to inefficiencies in the regulation of the bank's cross-border activities and unnecessary barriers and burdens for entry to financial markets.

The U.S. Financial Services Modernization Act of 1999 requires that all foreign banks that seek to be licensed as Financial Holding Companies (FHC) under U.S. law demonstrate to U.S. regulators that their global operations are well capitalized and well managed.[8] The well-capitalized requirement provides that the bank subsidiaries of the FHC meet the numerical capital requirements on a risk basis and leverage basis.[9] Foreign banks seeking FHC status must satisfy risk-based capital standards on a global basis. The Federal Reserve exercises ultimate authority over whether the foreign bank's global operations are well capitalized, notwithstanding the views of the foreign bank's home supervisor. Similarly, the Federal Reserve exercises extraterritorial authority regarding the law's requirement that the foreign bank be well managed. In this regard, the U.S. regulator has the authority to evaluate *both* the foreign bank's management of its U.S. operations and its management of its global operations. The Board has ultimate authority to decide if the global operations of the bank are managed satisfactorily. In making this determination, it may take account of the home supervisor's rating or evaluation, but it is not required to accept the home supervisor's conclusions.

Once the foreign bank obtains FHC status, the Federal Reserve can revoke the status, after notification and hearing, on the grounds that it is no longer satisfied that the bank is well managed or well capitalized in its global operations. The broad discretion of the U.S. regulator to determine whether the foreign bank is well managed or well capitalized may lead to situations where the Board revokes the bank's license to operate as a FHC on the basis of rumors concerning the bank's operations anywhere in the world, notwithstanding the views of the foreign bank's home supervisor. This may potentially lead to a bank run or to the withdrawal of the bank's credit lines by other banks in foreign jurisdictions. In this scenario, the exercise of unilateral and extraterritorial authority by the U.S. regulator can threaten systemic stability and possibly precipitate a financial crisis.

In addition, the U.S. Patriot Act of 2001 contains many provisions that create extraterritorial subject matter jurisdiction over foreign banks and their customers if they use or maintain U.S. dollar accounts with U.S. correspondent banks. The purpose of the Patriot Act is to address the financial risks arising from international money laundering and terrorist financing. U.S. financial institutions that maintain correspondent or interbank payable through accounts with foreign banks are now required to ensure that the foreign banks (even those with no physical presence in the

United States) take appropriate customer due diligence measures, in accordance with U.S. law, to identify and verify the identity of the foreign bank's customers.[10] Moreover, foreign banks that utilize correspondent or payable through accounts with U.S. banks must ensure that the accounts are not used by non-U.S. shell banks that are based in poorly regulated jurisdictions.

Moreover, section 327 of the Act requires the Federal Reserve to take account of a foreign bank's antimoney-laundering practices, including its overseas practices, and the adequacy of the regulations of its home jurisdiction before deciding whether to permit the foreign bank to acquire or to merge with a U.S. financial institution. This also applies to foreign banks that are proposing to establish initial or additional U.S. branches, agencies, representative offices, or bank subsidiaries. U.S. regulators may "contact pertinent foreign host country supervisors as appropriate to obtain information about an applicant's anti-money laundering activities at its overseas branches or bank subsidiaries," but they exercise final authority in deciding the adequacy of the foreign practices or regulatory system (Federal Reserve, 2002).

These examples of U.S. unilateral and extraterritorial banking regulation truly demonstrate the essence of the extraterritoriality problem and the need for global rules to govern the jurisdictional authority of financial regulators. Indeed, the efficient regulation of international banking activity requires conflict of jurisdictions rules that allocate jurisdictional authority among national regulators according to principles of home-host country control. Chapter 2 discusses the Basel Committee's approach in this area, and chapter 5 suggests how this might be applied in a reformed international regulatory regime. It is important that any set of rules address regulatory gaps (e.g., offshore financial centers) and how to resolve overlapping jurisdictional claims between competing regulators. The essential requirement would be that all states adhere to uniform rules and principles for the allocation of jurisdictional authority to regulate cross-border banking or financial activity.

Financial Crises in the 1990s

In recent years, financial markets have been particularly vulnerable to the effects of cross-border and cross-asset transfers and flows, leaving some markets, especially emerging markets, susceptible to higher short-term volatilities as a result of economic shocks. Indeed, when cross-border capital flows transmit economic shocks, it is often referred to as contagion. Generally, contagion may take two forms: (1) economic contagion that occurs through trade and investment flows, and (2) financial contagion that arises from changing risk appetite among investors, which can lead to reverse capital flows away from emerging markets to the more secure investments of developed countries (i.e., U.S. government Treasury bills). Sometimes the economic shock of contagion can be so strong that it can threaten to undermine the more liquid financial markets of developed countries, such as occurred in the East Asian financial crisis of 1997 and the Russian default and devaluation of 1998 (Bank for International Settlements, 2001b).

Most economists agree that a major cause of these financial crises was the dramatic increase in portfolio capital flows that had begun to flow to developing countries and emerging markets in the 1990s, mainly in the form of sovereign and corporate debt and, to a lesser degree, in equity purchases by foreign investors. The G10 paid little attention to the effect that liberalization of the capital account was having on developing and emerging economies, other than to argue that the massive inflows of capital that these countries were receiving was providing a solid basis for future economic growth. No regard was given to the potential of a banking or currency crisis if foreign investors decided not to roll over their short-term investments and to repatriate their capital. Indeed, the so-called Washington consensus (strongly supported by then-U.S. Treasury secretary Robert Rubin and the IMF) supported the view that capital account liberalization would promote financial stability by leading to increased capital flows, thereby improving conditions for economic growth and development. Whenever a financial crisis did occur, as with the Mexican peso crisis in December 1994, the U.S. and IMF response of providing a bailout had the effect of guaranteeing the investments of New York and London banks that would otherwise have lost substantial sums.

Many economists criticized the U.S./IMF bailout of Mexico in early 1995 on the grounds that it would increase moral hazard by allowing foreign banks and other investors to believe that their risky emerging market investments would be effectively guaranteed by the United States and/or the IMF if a financial crisis were to occur. In the late 1990s, a vast literature accumulated that examined some of the causes and policy implications of the economic and financial downturn that occurred in east Asia in the late 1990s (Eatwell and Taylor, 2000). In the same period, the Russian government defaulted on most of its U.S.-denominated debt, in August 1998, which triggered much instability in international capital markets as investors began rebalancing most of their portfolios away from emerging-market issues. These events, along with the near-bankruptcy of Long-Term Capital Management (LTCM), revealed the substantial threat posed by unregulated hedge funds and offshore financial centers to financial stability.[11]

As banking becomes more international and deregulated, national regulatory authorities remain the prime supervisors monitoring cross-border banking activities. Expanded and diversified international banking operations require adherence to a common core of supervisory and regulatory standards recognized by the world's major financial regulators. These core international standards require effective international supervision to reduce systemic risk. Moreover, the institutional framework of international financial regulation has not kept pace with globalized financial markets. The effective control of systemic risk requires a global supervisory regime that performs certain essential ex ante and ex post regulatory functions. Ex ante functions include, inter alia, the generation of norms and rules of prudential supervision, surveillance of financial institutions and markets, and coordinating enforcement by national authorities of international regulatory standards. The main ex post functions could potentially include some type of lender-of-last-resort function and a global regime of deposit insurance.

Ex Post Regulatory Measures and the Too-Big-to-Fail Doctrine

Essentially, banks borrow money short-term from depositors and lend it long-term, often to companies and other business enterprises. The bank performs an intermediary function that is integral to the operation of the economy. Moreover, banks are key players in the payment system, as interbank loans provide banks with liquidity and serve as collateral or lending to other banks. This is why most countries have some type of lender-of-last-resort policy (LOLR) and/or deposit insurance scheme (Freixas et al., 1999). In the case of LOLR, large banks are often supported with liquidity by the central bank in order to prevent the bank failure from spreading to other banks. In the case of deposit insurance, governments may provide guarantees for a bank's short-term liabilities to depositors and other creditors. These schemes often lead to agency costs that arise from asymmetries of information between depositors and banks and between the regulator and the banks. For instance, deposit insurance and limited liability may lead bank management to engage in excessive risky activity because the manager is protected from most of the downside of risk but has an incentive to gamble for success by pursuing risky investment strategies. This moral hazard can result in excessive financial risk taking that can produce systemic risk.[12]

The Too-Big-to-Fail doctrine often plays a role in the LOLR function of a central bank. This can induce moral hazard on the part of large financial institutions and their counterparties by incentivizing them to take on more risk because of the belief that they will be protected from failure by the central bank. In this way, the LOLR function is a form of insurance that can lead bank managers and owners to be less diligent than necessary in managing their credit and market risk exposure.

The historic example of the too-big-to-fail doctrine occurred in 1890 when the Bank of England organized a bailout of Barings after its default on its highly leveraged portfolio of loans to the Argentinian government. More recently, during the Latin American sovereign debt crisis of the 1980s, U.S. bank regulators were confronted with the too-big-to-fail problem when major U.S. banks, including Citibank and Chase Manhattan, were threatened with substantial losses because of their excessive lending to many Latin American governments. With the U.S. banking system facing substantial losses, U.S. authorities orchestrated a major bailout, with the support of the IMF and the World Bank, that resulted in additional loans for the defaulted governments so that they could resume payments to their bank creditors. U.S. banking regulators again intervened to prevent major U.S. banks from suffering substantial losses when the Federal Reserve, in September 1998, coordinated several U.S. banks' bailout of the overleveraged hedge fund LTCM after it had suffered enormous losses in the aftermath of the Russian government's bond default.

In these cases, regulators used their discretion to decide whether a bank's losses are such that a bailout of some type is necessary to maintain financial stability. In other cases, the regulators may exercise their discretion to let a bank fail if its collapse does not pose a threat to the financial system. This occurred in 1995, when the Bank of England decided to allow Barings to fail after it had suffered devastating losses as a result of the fraudulent trades of a rogue trader who had incurred $580 million in losses in betting on futures contracts linked to the Nikkei 225 stock index. The criteria that regulators or central banks use to decide which banks will be saved and which will not is not entirely clear and vary from crisis to crisis. This is appropriate given the need to reduce the moral hazard problem, but in the case of large systemically relevant financial institutions, there may be a presumption that they will be bailed out in the event of a financial crisis. This creates an incentive for financial institutions to underprice risk, thereby undermining systemic stability. Moreover, the cross-border operations of most large banks create coordination problems for central banks in determining which authority should take the lead—both administratively and financially—in resolving a banking crisis.

FINANCIAL CRIME: A SYSTEMIC THREAT TO FINANCIAL STABILITY

Money laundering is a form of financial crime that can threaten the systemic stability of banking systems. Money laundering and financial crime distract economic decision making away from lawful conduct to activities that are motivated by criminal objectives. When it involves the banking system and securities markets, it can create liquidity risks for banks and investment firms viewed as too risky to be lent to because of their criminal affiliations. It can also undermine stability for a country's financial system by affecting currency markets and causing a sharp markdown on the assets of financial institutions with operations in high-risk jurisdictions.

The main types of financial risk posed by money laundering are reputational risk, concentration risk, and operational risk. Reputational risk can undermine a bank's ability to raise capital, while concentration risks can involve substantial flows of criminally derived funds in and out of a financial system that can undermine systemic stability. Such concentration risks can especially undermine the stability of emerging market and developing country economies. Moreover, operational risk can arise because of financial fraud. Effective management controls and internal risk management procedures are necessary for reducing operational risk. Senior management must exercise direct lines of control and responsibility over individuals within financial firms who exercise key functions. The collapse of Barings, in 1995, and substantial losses suffered by Allied Irish Bank, in 2002, because of the fraudulent acts of a rogue trader in their U.S. subsidiary are examples of financial fraud that arise because of poor operational controls over individuals who exercise key functions.

In the post-September 11 environment, most countries, led by the United States, have enacted legislation that redefines money laundering to include any type of financial assistance for terrorist organizations (Alexander, 2002). Moreover, many countries now define money laundering to involve any type of facilitation or assistance to corrupt public officials that involves performing financial transactions or providing advice regarding the use of the proceeds of public corruption. Chapter 3 discusses how the Financial Action Task Force has addressed the risks posed by financial crime.

CONCLUSION

The health of the global financial system has been undermined by the mispricing of risk in financial markets, which can create the externality of systemic risk that can be transmitted quickly into different financial systems because of sophisticated technological linkages between financial systems and because of the extensive global reach of many major financial institutions. This chapter has argued that the efficient management of systemic risk in financial markets requires effective international standards of financial regulation that encourage the efficient pricing of risk and the effective supervision of a bank's international activitives. Although liberalization and deregulation have created many economic benefits, they have resulted in increased financial fragility. Existing national regimes are inadequate to regulate the extraterritorial nature of systemic risk that arises from the cross-border trade of financial services and associated payments, cross-border portfolio capital flows, and the increasing scope of activities of multifunctional financial institutions and conglomerates. Therefore, a more effective international regime is needed to devise international standards and to monitor their implementation and enforcement.

The establishment of international financial bodies and their efforts to set international standards and improve national regulatory regimes are responses to the growing problem of how to regulate risk taking in financial markets. The globalization of financial markets has resulted in increased integration of financial systems, especially in the banking sector, where financial conglomerates play a significant role in facilitating cross-border capital flows and in spreading risk across borders. Although many of these activities are efforts to hedge against risk with a view to reducing expected losses and thus promote financial stability, the formulas and methodologies used to price such risk are inexact and often result in the underpricing of risk. This may create more risk than is optimal for financial markets. Since the collapse of Bretton Woods, international regulatory efforts have been haphazard responses to specific crises that threaten the stability of the global financial system. The standard setting processes of these international bodies are usually informal exercises that are often dominated by the world's richest countries (the G10) with little or no input from developing and emerging-market countries. Moreover, the informal and secretive nature of the decision-making process raises issues of *accountability* in decision making and standard setting. Indeed, the great virtue of G10 decision making was once viewed as its discretionary flexibility, but those were in the days when their decisions applied only to G10 countries, whereas today G10 standards are recognized by the IMF and the World Bank in their various conditionality and surveillance programs. Moreover, international capital markets often rely on these standards as market signals that inform their decisions whether to invest in certain countries. Thus, the global impact of G10 international standard setting raises issues regarding the *legitimacy* of the standards, especially when countries subject to the standards have not been allowed to participate in any meaningful way in their development. We argue throughout this book that global governance of financial systems requires *effectiveness* in decision making, especially regarding expertise and logistics, *accountability* in ensuring that decision making is transparent and provides clear lines of authority between those who make decisions and those who are subject to them, and *legitimacy* concerning the degree of ownership and influence that countries have in setting international standards. A more detailed analysis of the institutional structure of these international bodies and their principles and standards of international financial regulation is presented in chapter 2.

2

Global Governance and International Standard Setting

As global financial markets become integrated, regulators must take account of how cross-border activities and capital flows affect the pricing of financial risk. Market failure may occur because of systemic risk, which is difficult for states, acting on their own, to manage effectively because of high transaction costs. To overcome this, states form international financial institutions (IFIs) to manage systemic and other types of financial risk in global markets. States act as rational agents in using IFIs to solve the collective action problem. The IFIs have become the main instrument through which states act to reduce the occurrence of financial crises. They perform this function by serving as focal points for states in exchanging information about other states's preferences, intentions, and motivations. This leads to increased cooperation and coordination among national regulators in developing international standards and rules to promote the efficient pricing of financial risk.

Effective decision making in the IFIs requires that states have strong links and confidence in one another. Developing these linkages and mutual confidence depends on a common set of guiding principles that takes the form of international standards and rules of regulatory practice. Because the adoption of international standards and rules of financial regulation can significantly impact a nation's economic growth and political sovereignty, it is necessary that the decision-making structure and process satisfy the core principles of global governance. This means that IFI decision making should be accountable both procedurally and substantively. It also means that the standard-setting process should be legitimate in the sense that all countries and economies subject to these standards exercise a certain degree of participation in the standard-setting process.

IFI standard setting involves a number of public- and private-sector bodies that adopt international agreements that govern the activities of financial regulators and market participants. These international agreements are generally divided into three categories (White, 2000): (1) model contracts or agreements to facilitate cross-border financial transactions, usually in securities (i.e., ISDA Master Agreement) or technical standards to facilitate payments between banks; (2) interstate agreements to promote cross-border competition in banking and financial services (i.e., WTO's General Agreement on Trade in Services and OECD's Codes of Liberalization); and (3) agreements to enhance and maintain financial stability through the efficient management of systemic risk. This chapter addresses the latter category as it relates to IFI standard setting and principles of global governance.

THE INTERNATIONAL FINANCIAL INSTITUTIONS—AN OVERVIEW

The G10 developed countries[1] have undertaken various international efforts to control and manage the problem of systemic risk in globalized financial markets. Specifically, several committees of central bankers and leading financial regulators have met at the Bank for International Settlements in Basel, Switzerland, and have developed voluntary, legally nonbinding international standards and rules of prudential supervision for the regulation of financial institutions, payment systems, and foreign exchange markets.[2] The best known is the Basel Committee on Banking Regulation and Supervisory Practices (Basel Committee), founded in 1974, which consists of the central bankers and bank regulators of the thirteen G10 countries. The Basel Committee seeks to create common standards of banking oversight by adopting international standards of prudential supervision covering such issues as capital adequacy and consolidated supervision of a bank's cross-border operations. The Committee on Payment and Settlement Systems sets standards to support the continued functioning of payment and settlement systems. The oldest Bank for International Settlements (BIS) committee is the Committee on Global Financial Systems (formerly the Euro-currency Standing Committee), which was formed in 1962 to monitor and assess the operations of the then newly established Euro currency markets and today deals with broader issues of financial stability. Significantly, these committees have no formal mandate and operate through informal consensus to adopt international standards of best practice for the regulation of monetary and financial matters.

The Basel Committee's capital adequacy standards and rules on consolidated supervision were intended originally to apply only to credit institutions based in G10 countries and with international operations. This changed in 1998, when the Basel Committee stated its intent to amend the

Capital Accord and to make it applicable to all countries in which banks conduct cross-border operations. The secretive manner in which the BIS committees meet and conduct consultations has generally been considered a strength in the effectiveness of its governance structure because it allows flexible and quick responses to rapid developments in financial markets. In recent years, however, the decision-making structure has been criticized on the grounds of procedural accountability and broader issues of political legitimacy, as discussed later.

Other international supervisory bodies have played a key role in developing international standards and rules for the regulation of financial markets. The International Organization of Securities Commissioners (IOSCO), comprising the world's leading securities commissioners, has adopted standards with respect to disclosure, insider dealing, and capital adequacy for securities firms that have fostered a similar type of convergence in standard setting in the world's leading securities markets. Similarly, the International Association of Insurance Supervisors (IAIS) first met in 1994 and consists of representatives from more than 160 of the world's insurance regulators with a view to developing international standards of insurance regulation in respect to disclosure, managing reserves, and consumer protection.[3] In the area of money laundering and terrorist financing, the Financial Action Task Force (FATF) has attained a high-profile role in setting international standards (so-called Recommendations) of disclosure and transparency for banks and other financial service providers in order to combat financial crime. In contrast, IOSCO and the IAIS have been less prominent than the Basel Committee or FATF in setting international standards of financial supervision, but they have become increasingly influential because of their growing membership, which enjoys near universal support and the recognition of their standards by the IMF and the World Bank in their surveillance programs.

Although these international standards are considered to be "gentlemen's agreements" with no legally binding effect, they are increasingly viewed as important mechanisms for promoting convergence and harmonization of national financial law and regulation. Moreover, the international reach of these standards has spread to many countries and jurisdictions that have not been given the opportunity to participate in the standard-setting process. This has been done mainly through IMF and World Bank conditionality and surveillance programs. The standard setting of the BIS committees and FATF raise the most concern with respect to the accountability of the decision-making process and the legitimacy of the standards adopted. In contrast, IOSCO and IAIS have made progress by expanding the scope of their membership, improving decision-making processes, and enhancing participation by countries affected by the standards.

THE BASEL COMMITTEE ON BANKING REGULATION AND SUPERVISORY PRACTICES

The Basel Committee is probably the most influential international financial standard-setting body. It exercises either direct or indirect influence over the development of banking law and regulation for most countries. It is because of its influence and importance as an international norm builder that its governance structure merits close examination regarding its decision-making process and the impact of its regulatory standards on global financial markets and economic growth. The Committee has produced a number of important international agreements that regulate the amount of capital that banks must set against their risk-based assets and the allocation of jurisdictional responsibility for bank regulators in overseeing the global operations of banks. Its activities have usually been kept away from the fanfare of high politics, but its recent efforts to amend the 1988 Capital Accord and to extend its application to all countries where international banks operate has attracted significant critical comment and brought its work under close scrutiny by leading policymakers and regulators. The proposals to amend the Capital Accord, known as Basel II, have been criticized as favoring large multinational banks at the expense of small and medium-size banks and as inappropriate for the supervisory regimes of developing and emerging market countries (Ward, 2002). Moreover, its capital calculations seek to price financial risk based on the bank's individual risk exposure, rather than on the total risk created by all banks in the financial system. A major contention of this study is that some of the flaws in Basel II can be attributed, in part, to the flawed decision-making structure of the Committee and its recent efforts to impose its standards on non-G10 countries who have played little, if any, role in promulgating the Accord.

The Institutional Structure

The Basel Committee is composed of the G10 central bank governors and national bank regulators who meet periodically at the Bank for International Settlements in Basel to negotiate and agree international banking norms.[4] The Basel Committee works informally and operates by consensus. Its decision-making process is secretive and relies substantially on personal contacts. The Committee's decisions are legally nonbinding in an international law sense and place a great deal of emphasis on decentralized implementation and informal monitoring of member compliance. The Committee's informal decision-making process has been viewed as effective for its members because of its absence of formal procedure (Jackson, 2000b). The Committee has sought to extend its informal network with banking regulators outside the G10 through various consultation groups.[5] Most recently, it has conducted seminars and consultations with banking regulators from more than 100 countries as part of the consultation process for amending the Capital Accord.

As stated, monitoring noncompliance has generally been a decentralized task that is the responsibility of member states themselves, and not international organizations, such as the BIS, or other international bodies (Norton, 1995). Nonetheless, the Committee monitors and reviews the Basel framework with a view to achieving greater uniformity in its implementation and convergence in substantive standards. Moreover, the Committee claims to have a mandate from a communiqué issued by the G7 Heads of State in 1997 that encourages emerging economies to adopt "strong prudential standards" and "effective supervisory structures." The Committee has interpreted the G7 communiqué as authority for it to devise global capital standards and other core principles of prudential regulation for all countries where international banks operate. To ensure that its standards are adopted, the Committee expects the IMF and the World Bank to play a surveillance role in overseeing member-state adherence through its various conditionality and economic restructuring programs. The extended application of the Basel Committee's standards to non-G10 countries has raised questions regarding the accountability of its decision-making structure and the suitability of its standards for developing and emerging market economies. In addition, because most G10 countries are members of the European Union, they are required by EU law to implement the Capital Accord into domestic law. The only G10 countries that are not required by local law to implement the Capital Accord are Canada, Japan, and the United States.[6]

The Capital Accord

The 1988 Capital Accord's[7] original purpose was to prevent the erosion of bank capital ratios as a result of aggressive competition for market share by the leading banks during the 1980s. The Accord also sought to harmonize the different levels and approaches to measuring capital among the G10 countries. In adopting the 1988 Accord, banking regulators wanted to establish an international minimum standard that would create a level playing field for banks operating in the G10 countries; banking regulators wanted capital requirements to reflect accurately the true risks that faced banks in a deregulated and internationally competitive market. The 1988 Capital Accord required banks actively engaged in international transactions to hold capital equal to at least 8 percent of their risk-weighted assets. This capital adequacy standard was intended to prevent banks from increasing their exposure to credit risk by imprudently incurring greater leverage.

Internal Risk Management Models

In the early 1990s, national supervisors began to complain that the category of risk-weighted assets against which capital charges were calculated was focused on narrowly defined measures of credit risk. This did not take into account other sources of financial risk, such as market, liquidity, and operational risks, all of which increased with the growth of banks' trading and derivative books. In 1996, the Basel Committee responded by adopting an amendment to the Capital Accord that expanded the asset category against which banks calculate their capital adequacy to include not only credit risk but also market risk (BCBS, 1995).[8] The approach allows banks, for the first time, to use their internal risk-management models to determine regulatory capital requirements for market risk. Instead of adhering to a detailed framework for computing risk exposures (for reporting purposes) and capital requirements, banks are able, under certain conditions, to use their own models—the ones they use for day-to-day trading and risk management—to determine an important component of their regulatory capital requirements. In particular, the Basel Committee recommends that banks that opt for internal models measure market risk using value-at-risk as the standard measure for risk exposures. Value-at-risk relies on historical data to provide an estimate of the maximum loss in the value of a portfolio or the portfolios of various firms over a given time period with a certain level of confidence. This level of confidence is represented by the probability that the actual value of a particular capital account will not decline beneath a specified minimum value over a period of time at a given probability. Value-at-risk also refers to the requirement of closer involvement with the banks under supervisory control and formal risk assessments using appropriate evaluation factors. The Basel Committee adopted the value-at-risk model in 1997, and it has been enacted into law by the G10 national regulators.

Implementing the Basel Accord

Many non-G10 countries have incorporated the Basel standards into their regulatory framework for a variety of reasons, including to strengthen the soundness of their commercial banks, to raise their credit rating in international financial markets, and to achieve a universally recognized international standard. The International Monetary Fund and the World Bank have also required many countries to demonstrate adherence or a realistic effort to implement the Basel Accord in order to qualify for financial assistance and as part of IMF Financial Sector Assessment programs and World Bank Financial Sector Adjustment programs. Also, all G10 countries require foreign banks to demonstrate that their home country regulators have adopted the Capital Accord and other international agreements as a condition for obtaining a bank license. Moreover, as discussed in Chapter 4, international reputation and market signals are also important in creating incentives for non-G10 countries to adopt the Capital Accord. Many non-G10 countries (including developing countries) have found it necessary to require their banks to adopt similar capital adequacy standards in order to attract foreign investment, as well as to stand on equal footing with international banks in global financial markets.

BASEL II

The aim of Basel II is to make the regulatory capital held by banks more sensitive to the economic risks that banks face. Basel II contains three mutually reinforcing pillars that constitute the framework for assessing capital adequacy.

The first pillar is the minimum regulatory capital charge that includes both the standardized approach (adopted in the 1988 Accord with subsequent amendments) and a revised internal ratings–based approach. The revised standardized approach provides enhanced, though limited, sensitivity to various risk categories. The internal ratings–based approach represents a fundamental shift in the Committee's view on regulatory capital by allowing large banks to utilize sophisticated internal credit risk models to reduce their regulatory capital.

Pillar I would maintain the 1988 Accord's 8 percent capital adequacy ratio, but it would change how the risk weights to the capital ratio are determined. It would do so by replacing its system of credit-risk weightings, which relies on the work of public regulatory agencies, with a system of external credit assessments to determine risk weights.[9] These external credit assessments would largely be conducted by private bodies or firms that would provide credit-risk assessments of both private and sovereign borrowers. The use of private ratings bodies raises the important issue of whether private assessors and monitors have the appropriate incentives (discussed in Chapter 6).

The second pillar is supervisory review, "intended to ensure that not only banks have adequate capital to support all the risks in their business, but also to encourage banks to develop and use better risk management techniques in monitoring and managing these risks." (BCBS, 2001a) This pillar encourages supervisors to assess banks' internal approaches to capital allocation and internal assessments of capital adequacy. Subject to the discretion of national regulators, it provides an opportunity for the supervisor to indicate where such approaches do not appear sufficient and to play a proactive role with bank management in improving risk calculation methods. This pillar also provides for the regulator to assist the bank in devising various internal control frameworks and corporate governance structures that would enhance the evaluation of risk within the bank.

The third pillar recognizes that market discipline has the potential to reinforce capital regulation and other supervisory efforts to ensure the safety and soundness of the banking system. It proposes widespread disclosure standards that add more transparency to the risk and capital position of banks.[10]

Pillar I would permit some sophisticated banks to use their own internal ratings of loans as a basis for calculating capital adequacy ratios.[11] Some of the important issues regarding the IRB approach are discussed in Chapter 8, such as the accounting methods for valuing bank assets, the ability of large banks to utilize their own data to calculate capital adequacy, and the possible effects on competition between large and small banks.

Pillar II increases the degree to which supervisors can exercise discretion and hence is vulnerable to regulatory failure (Ward, 2002). If this discretion is not used for the public good, then regulation will be ineffective. In many countries, banks and regulators have more opportunity and incentive to extract benefits at public cost because institutions that limit rent-seeking are weak. This is of particular concern in developing countries where regulatory independence and accountability have little institutional or legal support.

Pillar III sets forth market discipline standards that many economists have criticized as procyclical. Rather, Basel II should impose countercyclical requirements, such as higher capital charges during boom times and lower ones during a market downturn.

Finally, because the Basel Committee has stated that Basel II will apply to "all countries where international banks operate," it fails to take account of the differences in economic and financial structure of developing countries. Developing countries experience greater macroeconomic volatility and greater volatility in financial flows and thus are more vulnerable to external shocks. The procyclical effect of Basel II would have a disproportionate impact on developing countries and thereby undermine economic development (Ward, 2002). Finally, the increased risk sensitivity of Basel II does not provide an incentive-compatible framework in which bankers are incentivized to assume more of the costs of the risk they create. For example, increasing the level of personal liability for bank owners should be used as a disincentive to reduce the social cost of risk taking.

Flawed Decision Making and Institutional Structure

The Basel Committee is composed of the central bank governors and national bank regulators of the G10 countries, which are the thirteen richest developed countries in terms of per-capita income. Because of the Herstatt and Franklin National Bank collapses in the 1970s, the Committee was initially concerned with the threat of systemic risk arising from banks and payment systems in G10 countries. As more countries began to liberalize their foreign exchange controls in the 1980s and to deregulate their financial sectors, the Committee became more concerned with the regulatory and supervisory practices of non-G10 countries. Following the financial crises of the late 1990s, the Committee began to interact more with, and to seek the views of, large and systemically important developing countries in such forums as the G22 and G24. Also, during this period, the IMF and World Bank were encouraging member states to adopt the Capital Accord and other principles of prudential supervision through surveillance and technical assistance programs. In addition, the effect of increased liberalization of the capital account, combined with pressures from foreign direct and portfolio investors, led many national regulators to adopt Basel and other IFI standards in order to prevent foreign capital flows from shifting out of their countries. As a result, by 1998, over one hundred and twenty countries either claimed to have adopted the Capital Accord or were in the process of doing so.

The decision-making process of the Basel Committee has been criticized for serious deficiencies in accountability and legitimacy for those countries and economies subject to its standards. Some of the problems with the existing decision-making process are that its internal operations and deliberations are not disclosed to the public and that the increasing number of countries subject to its standards play no meaningful role in influencing their development. In previous years, when the Committee was seeking to address problems that were of concern only to G10 regulators, secrecy and informality were viewed as hallmarks of effective decision making. Today, however, the global impact of the Committee's standard setting has called into question the legitimacy of its decision-making structures. Although the Committee has sought to involve policy makers and regulators from non-G10 countries in various aspects of the standard-setting process, the actual decision making remains controlled by the G10 countries. The New Accord should be of serious concern to all countries and their banking regulators because the Committee's decision making now exercises substantial influence over the development of international banking norms that apply to all countries. Indeed, the Committee has interpreted its broader mandate as providing authority for it to extend its international standards and principles to all countries where international banks operate. Its efforts to create common and uniform standards that would apply throughout the global financial system have met with resistance from many large developing countries and emerging economies that contend that they should not have to adopt standards which they played little role in developing.[12]

The Committee has traditionally represented the world's most systemically important financial markets. But, in recent years, in light of the Asia crisis and the problems facing Latin American financial markets, there has been a growing recognition that some non-G10 countries that represent systemically relevant financial systems should be represented on the committee (Griffith-Jones and Persaud, 2003). The Basel Committee has recognized the problem by establishing a Core Principles Liaison Group composed of thirteen non-G10 countries, including Brazil, China, India, and Russia, to consult regarding core principles on banking supervision, as well as capital adequacy standards. Nevertheless, although these thirteen non-G10 countries are often consulted about the possible impact of the Capital Accord on their economies, they have no seat on the Committee and therefore do not exercise direct influence on the standard-setting process. Given the Committee's mandate to establish international standards, one may question the legitimacy of such a mandate if it was intended to authorize the Committee, an exclusive G10 committee, to set standards for countries outside the G10.

Accountability The Committee's decision-making process has been criticized for lacking clear lines of accountability and for failing to ensure that its members actually implement the standards it approves. Technical definitions of accountability in the financial regulatory arena have focused on the obligation owed by the person exercising authority to another person for whom such authority is being exercised. This usually requires that the person who exercises authority provide some type of justification or explanation for his or her actions or decisions to the person on whose behalf the actions were taken (Lastra and Shams, 2001). For the bank supervisor, accountability in prudential regulation requires the regulator to provide an account and explanation of its actions to the relevant government authority and, more broadly, to members of the public.[13] The public may also include regulated firms that should be consulted and kept informed of proposed changes to regulation. There must be clear lines of authority that show where the regulator derives its authority and to which stakeholder interests it is accountable.

Moreover, the regulator's exercise of authority should be measured for performance against some criteria of assessment (Lastra, 1996). These criteria may be stated in statute or in regulation. The complexity of banking and financial regulation makes it very difficult to establish standards against which to measure the regulator's performance. The term "performance accountability" has been used in banking regulation to suggest that regulatory effectiveness and accountability can be measured but only against explicit legislative objectives that involve single goals that are narrowly defined; if there are multiple goals, they should be clearly defined and prioritized (Lastra and Shams, 2001).

In addition, transparency has become an important aspect of accountability in international economic organizations and standard-setting bodies. Market failures can arise because of asymmetries of information that result from poor disclosure standards and reporting requirements. But it should be emphasized that the benefits of transparency for the regulator depend on the availability and relevance of the information. The relevance of the information depends on the way it is presented; that is, it must be accurate, comprehensive, and not misleading. For instance, too much information may not help regulators in setting meaningful standards or rules requiring banks to manage financial risk in a more efficient manner. Rather, regulators should emphasize not so much the quantity of information but its relevance in informing investors about financial risk. Moreover, regulators should have discretion to balance the amount of information they release to the market against proprietary information that should remain undisclosed to the public in certain circumstances where its release might induce a financial panic or bank run or otherwise provide some banks with an unfair competitive advantage.

The Basel Committee's decentralized approach to implementation has resulted in uneven implementation and enforcement of its standards. For instance, throughout the 1990s, Japan suffered from a major banking crisis that derived in part from a collapse of its capital markets. This resulted in the value of Japanese banking assets plummeting, leading Japanese regulators to relax capital adequacy and loan classification standards. This type of regulatory forbearance is generally viewed as a necessary countercyclical response to a banking or financial crisis. Many developing countries and emerging market economies, however, often do not have the discretion to pursue such policies under IMF and World Bank conditionality and restructuring programs. Rather, these countries are required, as a condition of financial and technical assistance, to implement stringent banking sector reforms in accordance with standards set by the Basel Committee and other IFIs. It is suggested that the present international regulatory framework lacks accountability and legitimacy because it allows G10 countries to disregard the standards they expressly adopt in international fora, such as the Basel Committee, whenever they deem it desirable to do so, while requiring non-G10 countries to implement such standards and to adhere to them in accordance with programs monitored by the IMF and World Bank.

The absence of a clear and transparent decision-making procedure in the Basel Committee undermines its accountability. Indeed, the decision-making process itself is not disclosed, nor are the minutes of meetings made publicly available. On the other hand, however, it should be recognized that the standard-setting process often involves the exchange of sensitive information, and regulators need the flexibility and discretion to give honest and frank assessments of country regulatory policies without having such information released publicly. Full disclosure of all negotiations may deter regulators from making candid assessments of reform proposals and thereby undermine the efficacy of the standard-setting process. Moreover, in times of crisis, effective decision making may require regulators and officials to meet at short notice and out of the public eye in order to make emergency decisions that may have a substantial effect in averting a full-blown crisis. Safeguards are necessary, therefore, to prevent the unnecessary disclosure of sensitive financial market information during regulatory negotiations and proceedings. Effective standard setting requires a certain level of secrecy and discretion in order for regulators to make difficult decisions, especially in times of crisis. Nevertheless, accountability requires that the process for such decision making be made clear in advance and that lines of authority for decision making also be clear and indicate how states can participate in setting standards, with the understanding that their role may be limited in times of emergency.

Legitimacy The Capital Accord and other BIS committee standards are undoubtedly perceived today as international standards of best practice with broad adherence by most countries of the world. The real weaknesses with Basel II, however, demonstrate that international financial standards can be bad economic policy not only for the rich G10 countries who adopt them but also for the great majority of countries that are pressured to adopt them by international economic organizations and by foreign investors. This raises issues of political legitimacy regarding the international standard-setting process and what role countries should play in influencing the development of standards to which they are subject. Although there is a vast literature on concepts of legitimacy, we adopt this term with respect to the notion of ownership of policy development. That is, in international economic relations, the legitimacy of international standards and rules that regulate state behavior, especially in the area of financial regulation, should be determined, in part, by the extent to which all states that are subject to such standards have an opportunity to participate in their development. Because states have different levels of power and influence in international relations, we do not equate the opportunity to participate with actual influence. But we do argue that international economic decision making should be structured in a way that allows politically and economically weaker states—especially developing countries—to exercise meaningful influence over the formation of international economic norms. There is no strict formula that prescribes the exact degree of participation or influence that states should have in international economic rule making. This may vary depending on the subject area to be regulated, and it may involve delegation of authority to other states or international organizations in certain circumstances.

The basic principle of legitimacy in international policymaking should involve the recognition that states that are subject to international norms of economic regulation should have the opportunity to participate and influence the development and maintenance of such standards. By playing a role in influencing the development of such standards, states have the opportunity to make changes or adjustments that take account of their different economic and legal structures. This type of involvement gives a greater degree of ownership over the standards and possibly fosters a certain political willingness to implement and enforce the standards in good faith. In the case of Basel II, if more countries outside the G10 had played a meaningful role in influencing the amendments to the Capital Accord, it would have probably contained more safeguards to reduce macroeconomic volatility in developing countries and competitive distortions between large banks from developed countries and smaller, less sophisticated financial institutions in developing countries.

Indeed, by applying principles of legitimacy to international decision making, the substantive standards of financial regulation devised by IFIs might be improved significantly in a way that enhances financial stability for both individual countries and the global financial system. This would require that the Basel Committee expand its membership to include more non-G10 countries, especially large, systemically relevant developing countries, such as Brazil, India, China, and South Africa. Today, the Accord is the result of G10 decision making and appears to work for the benefit of large banks based in the G10 and to the detriment of regulators, financial institutions and borrowers in non-G10 countries. The principle of legitimacy is a core element of devising an efficient and equitable structure of global governance.

In the case of Basel II, some of the weaknesses of the proposed amendments to the Capital Accord can be attributed in part to the Committee's intention that it be applied to *all countries* where international banks operate. Pillar I allows large sophisticated multinational banks to calculate their own capital charges on the basis of historical data and within general parameters set by the supervisor. It creates competitive distortions for small and medium-size banks that do not have the elaborate internal controls and data collection capabilities, and it undermines macroeconomic growth in many developing countries because the riskier profile of their borrowers requires higher capital charges. It focuses on processes, rather than on credit outcomes, and so is procyclical, rather than countercyclical in a Keynesian sense. This exacerbates economic and financial cycles and results in much higher volatility in developing countries.

Pillar II provides broad discretion for supervisors to approve various risk management procedures and practices for banks and presumes a high level of expertise and political independence for the supervisor that does not exist in many developing, and some developed, countries. In other words, Pillar II does not protect against regulatory capture or government failure. Pillar III places too much emphasis on the role of export credit-rating agencies to assess the credit-worthiness of sovereign and private debtors and has a particularly pernicious impact on government and corporate borrowing in countries outside the OECD. Also, it fails to treat favorably alternative methods of credit provision, such as microfinance, which is seen as an especially beneficial form of finance for developing countries. It also ignores the proven benefits of diversification (Persaud, 2002).

In summary, many of these defects can be blamed in part on the Committee's composition and decision-making process and structure. As an international body that exercises significant influence over the development of banking regulation, its decision-making procedures fail to conform to accepted principles of accountability and legitimacy. The decision-making process is too secretive and lacks transparency. Moreover, it is subject to disproportionate influence by private-sector banks that are based in the countries on the Committee. To date, there are no proposals for reform, although it is becoming increasingly accepted that lack of accountability and legitimacy in the decision-making process has resulted in lower quality standards of banking regulation for most countries. Indeed, by expanding the number of countries involved in the standard-setting process, the Committee might improve immeasurably the quality of the regulatory standards in terms of improving long-term financial development. On the other hand, expanding the number of countries in the decision-making process may create logistical problems and undermine the Committee's effectiveness. However, a carefully negotiated multilateral framework to establish a more effective and legitimate decision-making process is not beyond the realm of practical policy.

ALLOCATING CROSS-BORDER REGULATORY AUTHORITY

Consolidated Supervision

The allocation of jurisdictional authority to regulate the cross-border activities of banks is an issue of major concern for the Basel Committee. In fact, the original raison d'etre of the Committee was to establish principles of cooperation for home and host state supervisors in overseeing the international activities of banks (BCBS, 1975). The 1975 Basel Concordat established several important principles, including that home country and host country supervisors shall share supervisory responsibilities for all banks operating in host countries. Under this approach, the host authority takes primary responsibility for the adequacy of the foreign bank's liquidity, while the home country assumes primary responsibility for regulating the solvency of home country banks' global operations. Finally, home and host country regulators are encouraged to cooperate in the exchange of information and, in certain circumstances, to remove legal restraints on the transfer of confidential financial information if such information is considered necessary for effective supervision or regulation. At the time these principles of home-host country control were adopted, they were intended to be applied only to G10 regulatory authorities.

The 1975 Concordat was amended in 1983 in response to the Latin American sovereign debt crisis and to the collapse and insolvency of the Italian bank Banco Ambrosiano, which had operated and managed several foreign subsidiaries that were utilized for various corrupt practices and financial crime in connection with the Italian mafia. The Italian bank regulators had justified their failure to oversee the bank's foreign operations on the grounds that it was beyond their jurisdictional authority because the questionable practices took place in subsidiaries established in Luxembourg and several offshore jurisdictions, even though these subsidiaries were effectively controlled and managed by the Italian holding company. The Basel Committee sought to remedy these jurisdictional gaps by amending the Concordat to ensure that consolidated supervision could occur on a transnational basis. The agreement was approved in 1983 and was entitled "Principles for the Supervision of Banks' Foreign Establishments" (BCBS, 1983).

The Revised Concordat established new principles for the allocation of bank regulatory responsibilities between home and host authorities. Its main objective was to ensure that the foreign operations of all banks based in G10 countries would not escape from the principle of "consolidated supervision." Consolidated supervision provides that home country regulators shall have responsibility for ensuring that the global operations of home country banks are sound regarding credit risk exposure, quality of assets, and the capital adequacy of the banking group's total global business. Significantly, the Revised Concordat also contained the principle of "dual key supervision," which provides that G10 regulatory authorities shall assess the ability of other national authorities to supervise and carry out their respective responsibilities. For instance, where a host country determines that a home country has inadequate supervision, the Revised Concordat proposes two options: (1) the host country could deny entry approval to an institution based in an inadequately regulated jurisdiction, or (2) the host country could impose specific conditions on the conduct of foreign banks based in inadequately regulated jurisdictions. Although the Revised Concordat was intended to apply only to G10 countries, G10 regulators were encouraged to evaluate all home country regulatory regimes of foreign banks seeking licences to operate in G10 countries. This had the effect of imposing G10 banking regulatory standards and performance criteria on non-G10 country regulators without any assessment of the appropriateness of those standards for non-G10 jurisdictions. Another omission of the Concordat was its failure to define precisely when an international bank was registered with a particular jurisdiction for purposes of home country control. This became a major supervisory gap in the case of the Bank of Credit and Commerce International.

The BCCI Case and the Challenge of Supervising Financial Conglomerates

Although the Revised Concordat was amended with supplemental standards in 1990 to address some of the gaps in supervising the global operations of G10 banks, serious problems in implementation continued to plague G10 regulators. Of particular significance was the failure of some regulators to provide adequate supervisory oversight of major financial institutions that operated in their jurisdictions but that were incorporated in other jurisdictions. This occurred in the case of the Bank of England in its efforts to supervise the London branch operations of the Bank of Credit and Commerce International (BCCI). BCCI had operated for many years with its principal place of business in London. From its London offices, it administered a complicated global web of affiliates and holding companies registered in Luxembourg and the Cayman Islands to perpetrate fraud, money laundering, and public corruption on a massive scale. U.S. regulators and law enforcement authorities exposed BCCI's fraudulent machinations and convicted it for multiple corporate criminal offenses in 1990.

Shortly thereafter, in 1991, the Bank of England closed down BCCI's U.K. subsidiary. Bank of England officials justified their failure to close BCCI earlier by arguing that under U.K. law it was not the home country supervisor because BCCI was wholly owned by a Luxembourg holding company and that therefore the Bank of England had no responsibility for overseeing BCCI's global activities, which were administered mainly from its London office.[14] U.K. officials argued furthermore that it was the responsibility of Luxembourg to act as home country supervisor and to be responsible for overseeing its global activities, even though BCCI had few or no operations in Luxembourg. As a result, the regulatory forbearance shown by the Bank of England and the absence of any kind of credible regulation by Luxembourg authorities, combined with the regulatory failure of other jurisdictions (including the United States), enabled BCCI to evade supervision by both home and host country regulators (Bingham Report, 1993).

The BCCI scandal provided the impetus for the Basel Committee to reexamine its principles on consolidated supervision. This led to its 1992 Report on Minimum Standards for the Supervision of International Banking Groups and Their Cross-Border Establishments.[15] In many ways, the Minimum Standards report reiterates earlier standards contained in the Revised Concordat. For instance, it restates the general principle of consolidated supervision: that all international banking groups should be supervised adequately by a home country regulator. It also reaffirms the host country's prerogative set forth in the Revised Concordat to impose restrictive measures on entry by foreign banks, including prohibitions or revocations of foreign bank licences, if the host country determines that the home country of the foreign bank does not comply with international prudential norms, including the minimum standards.

The Minimum Standards report adds new requirements to the Revised Concordat by encouraging both home and host country supervisors to agree in advance to the creation of cross-border banking establishments. It also encourages national authorities to ensure that regulators have the power to gather information from the cross-border banking establishments of banks or banking groups for which they are the home country supervisors. Basically, there should be very few restrictions on the cross-border transfer of sensitive information within the banking group.

The standards are generally accepted today as conflict of jurisdiction rules that reflect international norms of consolidated supervision for the cross-border activities of banking and financial groups. Practically, the standards not only emphasize the need for consolidated supervision but also recommend that the host country regulators ensure that the home country receives consolidated financial statements of the bank's global operations. The Minimum Standards report further urges that the home country's regulators have the means to satisfy themselves as to the completeness and validity of all financial reports. In addition, the host country's regulators should assure themselves that the home country's regulators have the authority to prevent banks under their jurisdiction from establishing organizational structures that circumvent supervision.

SUPERVISORY STRUCTURES FOR FINANCIAL CONGLOMERATES

The BCCI case highlights many of the supervisory challenges posed by the transnational operations of financial conglomerates.[16] International financial conglomerates today are providing an array of products and services, including not only the traditional offerings of loans and deposits, but also, inter alia, insurance, investment services, and tax and estate planning. These modern financial institutions conduct diversified operations across borders to diversify their earnings and enhance profits. The liberalization of restrictions on capital flows across national borders has increased international lending and deposit-taking activities.[17]

In 1996, the Basel Committee, IOSCO, and the IAIS created the Joint Forum on Financial Conglomerates[18] to devise standards for the effective regulation of financial conglomerates that operate in different jurisdictions and in different financial services sectors. The Joint Forum has issued a number of proposals that seek to improve coordination between regulators. Specifically, it has proposed that a lead regulator be appointed for each conglomerate, determined by the conglomerate's overall activities. In mixed conglomerates with financial and other activities, it is proposed that the financial divisions of the group have separate legal personality and separate management structures in order to prevent "contagion" or the spread of financial risk within the group. In February 1999, the Forum issued a final paper proposing measurement techniques and principles for assessing the capital adequacy of financial conglomerates on a group-wide basis (BCBS Joint Forum, 1999). The expanding activities of conglomerates and the ease by which they can shift high-risk activities into poorly regulated jurisdictions pose a threat to financial stability and raise important issues regarding the role of international regulation and what type of institutional structure is necessary to oversee their operations. The Basel Committee has addressed this issue in the context of Basel II by adopting high-level principles to allocate jurisdictional responsibilities between home and host regulators to ensure that financial conglomerates cannot evade the requirements of Basel II by shifting their operations to lightly regulated jurisdictions.

The High-Level Principles for Implementing Basel II

The effective implementation of Basel II requires increased cooperation and coordination between home and host country regulators, especially for complex financial conglomerates or groups. The New Accord strongly encourages home and host supervisors to cooperate in ensuring that the new capital rules apply to each level of the banking group, which means that they have to do a Pillar I capital adequacy assessment and a Pillar II assessment of internal controls and risk management practices for each affiliate and subsidiary within the banking group.[19] To accomplish this, the principles of consolidated supervision require a bank to obtain the approval of *both* the home and host supervisors before it can expand its operations into the host jurisdiction. Such approval would be based on the bank's compliance with Basel II at each level of its global operations, including its compliance with any host country requirements regarding Pillars 1 and 2 for the bank's subsidiaries or branches operating in the host jurisdiction. This framework is similar to how the home-host country principle applies under the Capital Accord's 1996 Market Risk Amendment, which holds that a bank should obtain the approval of the home and host supervisors before it can use its own calculations for market risk capital in its operations in the host jurisdiction. Basel II utilizes this approach by requiring banks, before expanding cross-borders, to obtain the approval of both the home and the host supervisors regarding Basel II compliance. Under this approach, host supervisors are expected to ensure that the local operations of the foreign-owned subsidiary or branch comply with Basel II on either an individual or subconsolidated basis.

Basel II's expectation that host jurisdictions apply Basel II to the local operations of multinational banking groups means that Basel II applies to multiple jurisdictions and that many host countries that played little or no role in developing Basel II are subject to its regulatory requirements. Moreover, the choice of capital measurement approaches that banks and supervisors can agree to under Pillar 1 and the discretionary powers of supervisors under Pillar 2 may result in disparities across jurisdictions in how the New Accord is implemented. This may result in contradictory and duplicative requirements for banks in different jurisdictions. For instance, because national supervisors have discretion in deciding which capital adequacy approach—Standardized, Foundation, or Advanced—to adopt for individual banks or banking groups, conflicts may arise between home and host supervisors regarding the particular approach to use for the cross-border operations of certain banks. The Committee attempted to address these problems by issuing, in August 2003, a set of "High-Level Principles" of consolidated supervision to be applied under Basel II.

The High-Level Principles reaffirm the existing conflict of jurisdiction rules set forth in the Revised Concordat and in the 1992 Minimum Rules for allocating regulatory authority between home and host country supervisors on a consolidated basis, while recognizing the existing legal responsibilities of supervisors to regulate their domestic financial institutions (Principle 1). Principle 1 holds that Basel II should build on the existing framework of consolidated supervision to achieve effective implementation for all countries where banking groups operate. To accomplish this, supervisors are expected to increase cooperation through enhanced channels of information exchange with safeguards for confidentiality and provide mutual recognition of supervisory standards. The Committee envisions that this will lead to convergence of standards, which will ultimately lead to "equivalence of regulatory and supervisory systems" (BCBS Joint Forum, 1999).

In carrying out its responsibilities, the home supervisor may enlist the support of the host supervisor (especially in the case where the bank has major operations in the host country) to collect data or to make assessments of the bank's capital adequacy and overall compliance with Basel II. This is especially important when the home supervisor is strongly encouraged to delegate some Pillar 2 oversight to the host supervisor in situations where the banking group has significant operations in the host country (Principle 2). In the case where the home and host supervisors have adopted different approaches for implementing Basel II, the home country's approach prevails for the consolidated supervision of the global banking group. In performing this function, however, the home supervisor should seek assistance from the host supervisor regarding the collection of data and analysis especially in situations where the bank or banking group has significant operations in the host jurisdiction. For the home supervisor to implement Pillar 2 on a global basis, it is necessary for it to seek information from the host on the types of processes and internal controls the host has applied to the banking group's local operations. It is necessary therefore that the existing framework of information exchange and cooperation and coordination as set forth under the Revised Concordat be adhered to by supervisors in overseeing the bank's internal controls and operations in the host jurisdiction.

Despite the primary role of the home supervisor in overseeing the consolidated operations of the bank's global business, Principle 3 reaffirms the sovereign authority of the host country to impose legal and regulatory requirements on foreign-owned banks that operate in subsidiary form in the host jurisdiction.[20] This may result in the host country applying different approaches for calculating capital adequacy under Pillar 1 or different supervisory review processes under Pillar 2. Principle 3 stresses, though, that the host supervisor should be encouraged to accept the methods and approval processes that the home supervisor has approved for the bank's consolidated global operations. But host supervisors retain discretion to reject certain approaches that the home supervisor has approved at the group level if the application of such approaches to the local subsidiary would violate local law or regulation or if the host supervisor makes a determination that the home supervisor is incapable of providing effective consolidated supervision on a global basis.

Principle 4 recognizes that the home country supervisor should take the lead in developing practical measures of cooperation with host supervisors that have responsibility for overseeing major operations of the banking group. Supervisors have traditionally relied upon informal arrangements for the exchange of information and coordinating supervisory practices.[21] Recent financial crises have made it necessary to develop more formal arrangements, many of which have taken the form of bilateral Memoranda of Understanding (MOUs) and mutual legal assistance treaties (MLATs). MOUs are usually legally nonbinding bilateral agreements that set forth general principles of cooperation and coordination in the exchange of information along with suggested procedures for investigations and enforcement. Because they are not legally binding, there is no formal requirement for the supervisor to disclose information or to assist investigations. In contrast, MLATs are legally binding treaties that create obligations for supervisors to exchange information on banks, firms, and individuals and even to assist in investigations and enforcement actions undertaken by other authorities.[22] Implementing Basel II requires further consolidated efforts to establish effective bilateral and multilateral mechanisms for the exchange of information and assistance in investigations and enforcement. This creates opportunities for increased synergies among regulators and supervisors in overseeing the international operations of banks. Improved coordination among supervisors may also allow banks to avoid duplicative compliance costs and to realize greater operational efficiencies at the international level.

Moreover, the role of the home supervisor would be to coordinate measures of practical cooperation with host supervisors where the banking group has "material operations" (Principle 4). This would involve the home supervisor's communicating with senior management of the banking group regarding their various compliance strategies and informing the host supervisors accordingly. This may require more formalized lines of communication between the home and the host supervisors and increased coordination to supplement existing arrangements in MOUs or MLATs. Existing bilateral arrangements may therefore need to be revised to enhance the quality of information sharing among supervisors and to provide adequate surveillance of the bank's cross-border activities. Indeed, bilateral agreements should provide supervisors with relevant information, which may vary according to the level and type of operations the bank has in the host country.

In addition, the New Accord increases the responsibility of the home supervisor to provide initial approvals and validation of advanced approaches used by large banks to set their capital levels for their global operations. For instance, the home supervisor would have to approve the particular measurement approach for calculating capital adequacy for credit, market and operational risk.[23] Principle 5 seeks to reduce compliance costs for both banks and supervisors by urging supervisors not to perform "redundant and uncoordinated approval and validation work." It is necessary, therefore, for home and host supervisors to coordinate their validation and approval processes. For instance, supervisors would need to agree on whether to apply particular measurement approaches at the group level or at the level of the individual entity. Principle 5 recognizes that the decision to adopt a specific capital measurement approach and validation process at the entity or group level should depend primarily on the organizational and management structure of the banking group. For example, if the banking group's risk management approach is centralized at the group level and there is little variation in the techniques used to manage risk throughout the group, it is more appropriate for the home supervisor to apply a capital measurement approach at the group level. In contrast, where there is limited integration in decision making at the group level or where the techniques to calculate capital vary significantly across subsidiaries within the group, the host supervisor should play a more prominent role in influencing the capital approach used by the subsidiary in the host country. Other factors are also important, such as the availability of data and legal restrictions on the application of group approaches to local branches and subsidiaries. The main principle concerns reducing compliance costs for banks and conserving supervisory resources by avoiding redundant approval and validation work by individual supervisors.

To achieve the stated objectives in an efficient and effective manner, Principle 6 urges home and host supervisors to agree to a plan for communicating the allocation of responsibilities among the home and host supervisors to banks with significant cross-border operations. These should be individualized plans that apply to the largest and most sophisticated banking and financial groups. The degree of detail in each plan should reflect the particular circumstances of the banking group. The home supervisor normally takes the lead role in formulating such a plan for a banking group that is based or has its principal operations in its jurisdiction. Each plan should include input from host supervisors regarding the group's operations in the host country. Although this principle applies to all banks with international operations, it has particular relevance for the most sophisticated and complex banking and financial groups. The home and host supervisors should act together in communicating each plan to the most senior managers and directors of the banking group. The plan should also emphasize that existing legal responsibilities of the home and host supervisors should remain unchanged.

Although the New Accord does not alter the legal responsibilities of national supervisors, the emphasis on "equivalence" of regulatory and supervisory standards and the expectation that all host states apply Basel II to the local operations of foreign banks dramatically changes the supervisory and regulatory practices and the legal regulation of banking in many jurisdictions. Given the shortcomings of the Basel II regime, as discussed earlier, the implication that it may be applied indirectly in host countries through the principle of consolidated supervision may have the effect of increasing systemic risk in many jurisdictions, especially for developing and emerging market countries. Moreover, although it seeks to respect national legal principles regarding the confidentiality of information held by the supervisor, the enhanced framework for cooperation and coordination in the exchange of information and for surveillance and investigations may undermine the local autonomy of non-G10 regulators to utilize alternative capital adequacy standards in their countries.

The Basel Committee has become the most influential international financial standard-setting body. Its once-narrow focus on the G10 countries has now expanded to include all jurisdictions where international banking activity occurs. The original 1988 Accord had a tremendous impact on the world's leading financial systems by changing the national legal and regulatory requirements for bank capital adequacy. Most experts note that the Capital Accord resulted in U.S. banks adding $20 to $25 billion to their capital reserves in the 1990s, while Japanese banks added an estimated $40–$45 billion and French banks added $15 billion over the same period. Although higher levels of capital enhanced the soundness of many countries' banking systems, it has become evident that such standards can have procyclical effects that exacerbate volatility and economic cycles. Indeed, recent economic studies have demonstrated that inflexible capital adequacy standards can so restrict credit in a economic downturn that it makes it more difficult for an economy to pull itself out of recession. (Borio and Lowe, 2001; Turner, 2002).

The Basel Standards also serve as a reference point for future work in association with other international financial bodies that cover regulatory standards in the areas of securities, insurance, and accounting. For example, the Basel Committee, IOSCO, and IAIS have worked with the International Accounting Standards Board (IASB) to establish international accounting standards. The Basel Committee has also worked with the Financial Action Task Force in developing minimum standards of disclosure and transparency for financial intermediaries in order to reduce financial crime (FATF, 2000a). The Basel Committee and IOSCO have agreed on converging capital adequacy standards for financial institutions conducting securities activities in derivatives (BCBS and IOSCO, 1995). IOSCO has also sought to formulate capital adequacy ratios for securities firms to match those already existing for banks under the Basel Accords (IOSCO, 1989, 1998). The Committee will continue to exert substantial influence over the development of international banking and financial norms and therefore it is necessary that its decision-making procedures adhere to basic principles of accountability and legitimacy.

REGULATING SECURITIES MARKETS: THE INTERNATIONAL ORGANIZATION OF SECURITIES COMMISSIONS

Banks are no longer the major institutions in the process of intermediation. In the past decade, nonbank financial institutions, including securities firms, financial companies, and insurance companies, have joined the intermediation process in most major financial markets (Litan & Rauch, 1997). As a result, regulators have become concerned with the type of financial risk posed by nonbank financial firms.

Securities Firms and Systemic Risk

The traditional view held that securities firms posed little systemic risk because their funding structure was more secure than that of banks. Assets held by securities firms are more liquid than those held by banks because they benefit from higher levels of collateralization and liquidity. In contrast, most banks suffer from substantial mismatches in duration between assets and liabilities, which, in the case of a bank run, can lead to failure with a contagion effect for other banks. In contrast, securities firms' trading books usually contain liquid, tradable assets for which the duration between assets and liabilities is more evenly matched. In the case of default, most securities firms can exit markets easily by trading down their exposures and leaving creditors and other claimants with limited losses. As a result, the negative externality to the financial sector is limited, and therefore there would be little justification for a lender of last resort. Accordingly, prudential regulation of the securities industry has been more concerned with conduct of business rules (e.g., antifraud and consumer protection) than with capital adequacy requirements.

Moreover, securities firms were viewed as posing much less systemic risk than banks in settlement and payment systems because they do not (as banks do) ordinarily fulfil the function of settling payments. In contrast, a bank failure might cripple a settlement and payment system if it has large overnight exposures to other banks in the interbank payment system. While it was recognized that a large investment bank's failure could significantly disrupt financial markets, an orderly wind-down with little systemic effect is possible because of the liquid assets and secured funding structure of most nonbank securities firms.

This lower level of concern regarding the risk posed by securities firms to the broader financial system began to change in the late 1980s after the October 1987 U.S. stock market crash, after which the U.S. Federal Reserve injected liquidity into the U.S. banking system in order to stabilize what had become a major asset price collapse. Later, in the aftermath of the Russian default and the LTCM collapse, many regulators expressed new interest in regulating securities firms with a view to managing and controlling systemic risk. The view taken was that some securities firms could become highly leveraged by taking large positions in portfolios of derivatives in which the underlying assets had maturities significantly different from those of the firm's liabilities. In this case, a securities firm could be exposed to a selloff or refusal by wholesale investors to provide more capital, potentially resulting in a default with large losses to other firms and banks. This could have systemic implications, especially for firms with large exposures to portfolios of derivative instruments that contain nonstandard terms. But major liquidity problems could exist where the portfolio even contained instruments with uniform or standardized terms, as in the case of Barings, because most investors would seek to abandon their positions.

In this situation, contagion can occur because the trading books of many banks have substantial exposures to other securities firms through the repurchase and foreign exchange markets. Because many large investment banks are members of clearing and settlement systems, this might have direct effect on banking institutions and possibly result in Herstatt risk. Moreover, a sharp downturn in financial markets might eliminate most or all of any collateral position for derivative traders and lead to margin calls that could exacerbate the problem further. Consequently, this type of financial risk can have a systemic effect, as was demonstrated with the Russian bond default in 1998 and the LTCM collapse.

The regulation of systemic risk in securities markets has become an important concern for the leading securities regulators and has been recognized by international standard-setting bodies as a major objective of international regulation. Moreover, the events of September 11, 2001, show that clearing and settlement and payment systems can be disabled because of terrorist attacks and other emergency situations. To this end, the International Organization of Securities Commissioners (IOSCO) has played an important role as the world's leading international body of securities regulators.[24] IOSCO was established in 1983 as a forum where the world's securities regulators could meet, discuss, and agree on policies and best practices for regulating securities markets.

IOSCO states that the three core objectives for securities regulation are: (1) protecting investors; (2) ensuring that markets are fair, efficient and transparent; and (3) reducing systemic risk (IOSCO, 1998).[25] It is true that these objectives are closely related and, in some instances, overlap, as the requirement of fair, transparent, and efficient markets also implicates issues of investor protection and financial stability. To accomplish its objectives, IOSCO's members commit themselves to the following: (1) to cooperate in order to maintain fair and efficient markets; (2) to exchange information designed to further the development of domestic markets; (3) to establish standards and effective surveillance of international securities transactions; and (4) to provide mutual assistance for enforcement (IOSCO, 1999). Further, accurate information and data often requires effective mechanisms of surveillance and compliance programs that allow market participants to assess the extent of counterparty risk.

Capital Adequacy and Securities Firms

IOSCO published a report in 1989 that addressed the issue of systemic risk and stability of financial markets by recommending methodologies for measuring credit, liquidity, and market risk and for determining the amount of capital to be charged against such risk. It recognizes that regulatory capital should be determined, in part, by the types of activities that securities firms undertake (IOSCO, 1998a, 1998b). IOSCO recognizes, in Resolution 18 of its Principles, that capital adequacy standards enhance confidence in financial markets and should be designed to allow a firm to wind down its losses in the event of a large adverse market downturn in a relatively short period without loss to customers or the customers' of other firms and without disrupting the orderly functioning of financial markets. This means that capital adequacy standards should be formulated to allow supervisory authorities time to intervene to facilitate an orderly wind down and to ensure against contagion and systemic risk.

Regulatory capital should be matched against risk that arises from activities of unlicensed and off-balance-sheet affiliates, and regulation should consider the need for information about these affiliates and subsidiaries. IOSCO's VAR model provides a test for determining capital adequacy that allows securities firms to evaluate the riskiness of their assets on the basis of historical data of credit-worthiness, as well as in relation to the type and amount of business undertaken by the firm.

Institutional Structure

IOSCO is not a formal international organization as such because it was not formed by treaty or interstate agreement.[26] In 2000, the secretariat was relocated from Montreal to Madrid. As of 2004, its membership comprised regulatory agencies with responsibility for securities and futures regulation from more than 180 jurisdictions.[27] IOSCO members fall into one of three categories: ordinary, associate, and affiliate. Ordinary members exercise one vote each at general meetings and on the committees on which they serve. Associate members exercise no right to vote and cannot serve on committees, except for the President's Committee. Affiliate members are usually self-regulatory organizations (SROs), such as stock exchanges or industry self-regulatory bodies, and have no right to vote and cannot serve on any of the leading committees (IOSCO, 2000b).

IOSCO's President's Committee meets each year at the organization's annual meeting and is composed of the heads of all member securities and futures agencies. The Committee's membership is geographically, politically, and economically diverse. It is empowered by IOSCO's bylaws to take all necessary measures to achieve the purposes of the organization and exercises ultimate authority whether to accept or reject the proposals of other committees.[28] The Executive Committee oversees IOSCO's operations and presently has nineteen agency representatives elected for two-year terms and has representatives from each regional standing committee.[29] The Executive Committee meets periodically during the year and "takes all decisions necessary to achieve the purpose of the Organization" in accordance with the guidelines set by the President's Committee. It also reviews and approves the proposals for adopting international standards and principles.

The Executive Committee has established two important working committees: the Technical Committee and the Emerging Markets Committee. The Technical Committee was established in 1987 and consists of fifteen representatives from the regulatory agencies with jurisdiction over the most developed securities markets. The Committee has emerged as IOSCO's most influential committee, reviewing the major regulatory issues and proposing standards that impact most of the world's securities markets. Its work is divided into five subject areas: multinational disclosure and accounting, regulation of secondary markets, regulation of market intermediaries, enforcement and exchange of information, and investment management. The Committee has established several working parties to analyze and make proposals in these subject areas. For instance, the Working Party on Multinational Disclosure and Accounting reviews the accounting standards of the international accounting standards board. It has an overall objective of recommending that national authorities approve a comprehensive body of accounting standards that could be used to facilitate multinational offerings and listings.

Moreover, the Technical Committee has endorsed the need for a common approach for adopting a capital adequacy assessment methodology for securities firms. This approach is based on minimum capital requirements, market risk-based capital requirements, and a standard definition of capital that reflects varying market practices. Moreover, it states that the objectives of capital adequacy standards should be to foster confidence in the financial system; allow firms to absorb losses and, if necessary, wind down their business without losses to their customers or to customers of other securities firms; and provide a reasonable, if finite, limitation on excessive expansion by securities firms in order to minimize the possibility of customer losses and disruption of markets.

The Technical Committee does most of the important standard-setting work. Most of its members are regulators from G10 countries, and their main activity involves the examination of regulatory issues and standards that affect the world's most liquid and sophisticated financial markets. All proposals of the Technical Committee are submitted first to the Emerging Markets Committee, then to the Executive Committee, and finally to the President's committee. All IOSCO members have the opportunity to comment on and propose changes to Technical Committee proposals, but most of the practical bargaining and shaping of issues takes place in the Committee. This means that the members of the Technical Committee play the central role in the standard-setting process and exert a disproportionate influence over the development of international securities regulatory standards.

On the basis of the foregoing, IOSCO's institutional structure and decision-making process can be criticized on the grounds of accountability and legitimacy. The decision-making structure lacks transparency because all committee meetings are not open to outside observers, including IOSCO members who are not members of the particular committee.[30] Moreover, the Technical Committee has assumed a disproportionate amount of influence relative to other committees within IOSCO's decision-making structure. It appears that the Committee's influence derives in part from the expertise of its membership and staff and the important issues it addresses that concern the regulation of the world's leading financial markets. Because of the important impact that these markets have on less sophisticated markets, it may be necessary to change the composition of the Committee so that it provides more representation from developing countries and emerging economies. Nevertheless, in the current structure, each member has the opportunity to voice its concerns on all proposals and to vote against their adoption in the President's Committee. IOSCO has a broader and more diverse membership and therefore is more legitimate in its institutional structure because it provides the regulators of most jurisdictions with the opportunity—either directly or indirectly—to influence the standard-setting process. This is not the case with other international financial bodies, such as the BIS Committees and the Financial Action Task Force.

Mutual Assistance

The Preamble to IOSCO's bylaws emphasizes the importance of international cooperation and coordination in the regulation and enforcement of securities laws by stating:

> Securities authorities resolve to cooperate together to ensure a better regulation of the Markets, on the domestic as well as on the international level, in order to maintain just, efficient and sound markets. (IOSCO, 1999)[31]

To this end, IOSCO has adopted various principles and standards to facilitate the cross-border exchange of information to assist investigations and enforcement. The 1986 Resolution Concerning Mutual Assistance called upon all securities authorities to provide assistance on a reciprocal basis to those seeking information related to market oversight and protection of each nation's markets against fraudulent securities transactions (IOSCO, 1986). Later, in 1991, IOSCO adopted a resolution entitled "Principles for Memoranda of Understanding" (MOU), which contains the basic principles for exchange of information and disclosure that securities regulators should implement in their national regulatory codes. The IOSCO MOU principles contributed to a substantial body of state practice that provided the basis for negotiations that led, in 2002, to the adoption of a comprehensive IOSCO Memorandum of Understanding that reinforced preexisting principles and clarified some of the procedures for seeking mutual assistance in investigations and enforcement. The model IOSCO MOU has now been implemented, or is in the process of being implemented, by all of IOSCO's membership.

In addition, IOSCO has addressed some of the concerns that have arisen from the corporate scandals of the late 1990s and early 2000s. Indeed, corporate governance reform must be premised on the notion that full disclosure of information material to investors is necessary to ensure efficient markets and to protect investors. Full disclosure, however, will not be achieved without improved accounting and auditing standards that meet internationally accepted standards (IOSCO, 2000b).[32] The Technical Committee has addressed corporate governance reform by publishing several reports and proposing a set of principles that were approved by the President's committee in May 2003. The principles address reporting requirements for public companies and principles of auditor independence and oversight. Moreover, the threat of market abuse and fraud continues to plague most financial markets, with an increasing number of high-profile cases. As a result, the Technical Committee has created a task force to examine the major issues and make recommendations (IOSCO,

2004). Investors should be protected from misleading, fraudulent, or manipulative conduct, which may take the form of insider dealing, front running, or trading ahead of customers.

Although, in its early years, IOSCO was not as successful as the Basel Committee and FATF in achieving generally accepted international standards among its members, it has made significant progress in recent years in reaching agreement on a number of important areas, including international accounting standards for securities offerings and value-at-risk models to measure capital adequacy for securities firms. Despite the criticisms regarding its institutional structure and decision-making process, it has expanded its membership beyond its initial grouping of developed country regulators to include most developing countries and emerging market jurisdictions. It will play an important role in any future reforms of the international financial regulatory regime.

INTERNATIONAL ASSOCIATION OF INSURANCE SUPERVISORS (IAIS)

Insurance markets pose a special challenge to regulators. Significant asymmetries of information exist between the purchaser and the seller of insurance. For instance, the purchaser of insurance often knows more about the riskiness of its activities than the seller knows. This creates moral hazard that undermines the capacity of the insurance company to price the underlying risk in an efficient manner. Also, the limited liability structure of insurance companies makes them prone to excessive risk taking. The investment structure of insurance companies is such that the amount of funds under management far exceed the amount invested by shareholders. This produces a gearing effect that, combined with the limited liability structure of most insurance firms, incentivizes management to engage in excessive risk taking (Spencer, 2000).

The operations of insurance companies are increasingly global, and the nature of their business is to diversify and spread risk. This creates problems for regulators because insurance firms are able to transfer risk to other insurance companies operating in less-well-regulated jurisdictions. It is vital, therefore, that the operations of insurance companies and in particular their risk management practices be subject to adequate regulation and possibly minimum international standards of supervision. The International Association of Insurance Supervisors (IAIS) plays the important role of coordinating work of national regulators and setting minimum standards of supervisory practice for most of the world's insurance regulators. IAIS was initially established in 1994 as a private nonprofit corporation to promote the exchange and sharing of views regarding best regulatory practices in the insurance industry.[33] It has quickly evolved to become an important international standard-setting body with a broad membership that includes national regulators and supervisors from more than 160 jurisdictions as well as more than seventy observers from the insurance and professional sectors.[34]

Although the IAIS's original objectives did not include setting international standards, it has become a major IFI, with responsibility for the insurance sector. The impetus for this was the 1999 Tietmeyer proposal for a Financial Stability Forum, which stated that the primary role of the IAIS should be that of a supervisory rule-setting body and that there should be intensified cooperation and coordination with national financial authorities, international financial regulatory organizations, and international financial bodies charged with monitoring and fostering the implementation of standards.[35] The IAIS has developed international core principles and regulatory standards to cover most areas of insurance practice and in recent years has focused on issues of systemic risk and financial stability by publishing solvency and reinsurance standards and best practices for risk management. It has also promoted cooperation and coordination among regulators by adopting a model bilateral agreement on exchange of information and implementation. The IAIS coordinates its standard setting with other IFIs, such as the Basel Committee and IOSCO.

Institutional Structure

The IAIS's highest decision-making body is the General Meeting, which takes place once a year at the IAIS Annual Conference. The General Meeting has responsibility for approving all proposed principles and standards. All members of the IAIS are entitled to attend the general meeting and to vote on all proposed resolutions, including all principles, standards, and guidance papers. Members may vote on a one-member, one-vote basis for most proposals, except for the election of the Executive Committee, the approval of the annual budget, changes to the bylaws, or the relocation of the General Secretariat, in which cases each country receives only one vote.[36] The General Meeting may also obtain reports of the IAIS committees and elect members to those committees, change the bylaws, and approve the annual report and financial statement of the association.

The Executive Committee exercises authority over all organizational decisions. It is composed of fifteen members from different regions around the world.[37] They serve for two-year terms and are elected at the General Meeting. The Executive Committee generally "takes all decisions necessary to achieve the objectives of the Association in accordance with the directions given by the Association in General Meeting."[38] The Executive Committee oversees three committees: Technical, Budget, and Emerging Markets. The Technical Committee has the main responsibility for developing and submitting to the General Meeting all proposals for international principles and standards. The Technical Committee often relies on the assistance of various working parties, which are often delegated responsibility for examining and making recommendations regarding specific issue areas.

Unlike other IFIs, the IAIS also accepts applications from private parties to be IAIS observers. IAIS observers often come from the private sector and include most major insurance companies and some law firms but can also include government organizations with an interest in insurance supervision, even if "the organisation is not directly responsible for insurance law or its administration," and "any other person or body nominated by the Executive Committee."[39] Observers may participate in IAIS functions but may not vote or serve on the Executive Committee.

The IAIS's governing document is a set of bylaws that "do not impose legal obligations on members or the countries which they represent" (IAIS, 1999b) and that may be amended by a majority vote of the General Meeting. The Association is financed by membership dues, and its work is conducted through a committee system.[40] The internal operations of the IAIS are conducted in secret and its deliberations are not released to the public unless there is a two-thirds vote of the members at a General Meeting.

The IAIS has fared better in terms of its accountability to its members and the legitimacy of its standards than other IFIs. Its broad membership covers a range of developed and developing countries with different degrees of economic sophistication. The one-member, one-vote principle and the openness of its committee system and working groups suggest that most members have an opportunity to play a significant role in standard setting. Once proposals or documents are reviewed by the relevant working group, they are sent for consultation to the broader membership, including observers, which may propose revisions. The proposals are then submitted to the Technical Committee, which must approve the proposal before it can be sent on to the Executive Committee for final endorsement. At each stage of review, a different group of regulators has the opportunity to influence the standard-setting process. Although the most influential regulators are from the developed countries, the increasing political sophistication and expertise of a growing number of developing country regulators has resulted in a more balanced dialogue regarding the key issues related to implementation and the impact of new regulations on the economy.[41]

Standard Setting

Although in its early years the IAIS made little progress in adopting harmonized international standards of insurance regulation, its first set of supervisory principles was published in 1997. In 1999, the IMF and the World Bank criticized these principles in their financial sector country reports on the grounds that they provided an inadequate framework of insurance regulation and supervision for most countries. The IAIS responded, in 2000, by agreeing to new core principles of insurance supervision, which became known as the Insurance Core Principles (ICP). The ICPs were immediately utilized by the IMF and the World Bank as reference points in their financial-sector assessment programs and thus played an important role in influencing the development of insurance regulation in many member countries.

Many IAIS member countries began implementing the ICPs and were scrutinized for compliance by IMF and World Bank surveillance programs. The IMF/World Bank surveillance revealed that the ICPs contained a number of gaps and weaknesses that made it difficult for countries to implement them. This led the IAIS to conduct a comprehensive study of its standards and principles, which resulted in substantial amendments to the ICPs that took effect in 2003 (IAIS, 2003b). The revised ICPs contain twenty-eight principles that cover all aspects of the supervisory framework. They extend the original principles to include enhanced standards for transparency and disclosure, groupwide supervision, winding-up requirements, and antimoney-laundering and terrorist-financing standards. Unlike the Basel Accord and other IFI standards, the revised ICPs have been praised by most countries "as a joint product of jurisdictions from around the world and from both developed and emerging economies" (IAIS, 2003c). Indeed, these principles are written in a way that addresses many of the concerns of both developed and developing countries and therefore have attained a higher degree of legitimacy than, for instance, the principles adopted by the Basel Committee. Moreover, the enthusiastic reception of the principles by most countries means that they will be implemented with a degree of vigor that is absent from most other IFI implementation efforts.

The revised ICPs brought about important changes to solvency limits, capital adequacy, and the regulation of reinsurance companies. Specifically, IAIS standard setting in respect of solvency requirements is based on the concern that insurers that are inadequately capitalized can threaten financial stability. IAIS standard setting for solvency requirements also includes capital adequacy standards for insurers. Unlike the Basel Accord's capital adequacy standards for banks, there has been no minimum internationally agreed-upon standards by which insurance regulators may assess the capital adequacy and solvency of insurance firms. Presently, most countries and major jurisdictions have different solvency requirements. For instance, the EU solvency ratios are different from the risk-based approach of the U.S. states, and the Japanese solvency margin system differs from both the EU and the U.S. systems.

Any assessment of solvency and capital adequacy standards in the insurance sector must first recognize that capital adequacy requirements are only one part of the solvency margin system for insurance companies. Unlike the banking sector, the major risks in the insurance sector are found in *both* the assets and the liabilities. For instance, a major liability risk for insurance firms is the underestimation of future payments to claimants. Moreover, the mismatch in duration between assets and liabilities is different for insurance firms than for banks. The asset side of the insurance firm's book is normally shorter term than its liability side, creating a mismatch in the risk exposure to assets and liabilities that, in times of financial crisis, could lead to a dramatic fall in asset values and an increase in the number of claims or liabilities faced by the firm. The IAIS addressed many of these issues in its 2002 "Principles on Capital Adequacy and Solvency," which seeks to find a middle ground in devising solvency requirements that place realistic values on the firm's assets and liabilities.

The IAIS seeks to promote convergence between different solvency systems and coordinates its efforts with the European Commission and other IFIs, such as the Basel Committee and the World Bank. The IAIS's analysis of solvency requirements and capital adequacy standards is ongoing and was addressed in a 2004 paper that analyzes how investment risk management affects insolvency risk (IAIS, 2004). This work supports in principle the three-pillar approach of Basel II and the principles in the EU Solvency II Directive, but it recognizes the difficulty of translating these standards into precise requirements for countries with different economic and legal systems. Accordingly, it seeks to achieve the overall objective of developing efficient standards of insurance regulation for the effective management of systemic risk in a way that suits the particular economic needs and legal requirements of different jurisdictions.

Reinsurance The regulation of reinsurance firms has emerged as a major issue in light of the rapidly growing credit risk transfer market and its implications for financial stability. The two main areas of development are *standard setting* and *enhancing disclosure and transparency* for reinsurance firms. Regarding standard setting, the IAIS has addressed the issue of supervisory standards on reinsurance by setting standards for the evaluation of reinsurance cover and for reinsurance companies.[42] Standard setting for reinsurance cover applies to the reinsurance cover of primary insurers and covers the policies and procedures that primary insurers should maintain and the supervisory approaches for assessing the adequacy of reinsurance cover.

The other approach involves the supervision of reinsurers. The IAIS follows the 2002 principles[43] that state that all reinsurers should be subject to regulation and supervision by their home country and that each home country regulator should be evaluated and subject to some form of accreditation for its supervisory practices. These proposals are important because many jurisdictions have traditionally not subjected reinsurance companies to supervision or regulation.

On the basis of these principles, the IAIS issued the standard on supervision for reinsurers in October 2003. It focuses on issues and requirements of supervision that are different from those that apply to direct insurers. It provides guidance regarding how reinsurers should be supervised in areas such as investment and liquidity, economic capital, corporate governance, and exchange of information.

In addition, IAIS is reviewing whether to adopt the principle of mutual recognition for reinsurance supervision. This would require that the home

supervisor have primary responsibility for overseeing the global operations of the reinsurance firm. It would be expected to communicate
and coordinate its activities with supervisors in other jurisdictions where
the reinsurer operates. It is premised on the notion that home country
control will lead to competition between jurisdictions that will result in a
convergence on the most efficient form of regulation and will foster a
climate of trust between supervisors and between supervisors and the
industry. Although it seeks to avoid overlapping regulatory requirements,
this approach can be criticized on the grounds that it may lead to regulatory arbitrage and a race to the bottom in reinsurance regulation standards

Mutual Assistance

One of the IAIS's early functions was as a forum for information
exchange.[44] Its most significant effort along those lines was its approval
of the "Recommendation Concerning Mutual Assistance, Cooperation,
and Sharing of Information" (IAIS, 1995). The Recommendation outlined
cooperative efforts for information exchanges, which built on the mandate
in the IAIS bylaws that each member "cooperate together to maintain just
and efficient insurance markets for the benefit and protection of policyholders" and "to exchange information on their respective experiences in
order to promote the development of domestic insurance markets."[45]

The Recommendation required signatories "to provide assistance on a
reciprocal basis . . . for the prudential supervision of the insurance industry and obtaining information and documents related to market oversight
or protection of each other's markets against fraudulent insurance transactions" (IAIS, 1995). The signatories have also committed themselves to
"the recommendation of legislation" to implement the exchange of material information.[46] The provisions of the Recommendation were incorporated into a model memorandum of understanding approved by the
IAIS in 1997 (IAIS, 1997), which contains legally nonbinding provisions
that address the main practical issues relating to cross-border surveillance
and enforcement of insurance regulation. The MOU, along with the revised ICP, has played an important part in fostering the IAIS's role as an
international financial supervisor.

Although the IAIS's original objectives were limited to serving as a
forum for the exchange of information and experiences for supervisors
across all jurisdictions, its recent efforts in promulgating international core
principles and measurement standards for solvency and capital adequacy
have marked a new role for it as an international financial standard-setting
body. Moreover, the growing threat of credit risk transfer to financial stability has made IAIS's standard setting for reinsurance and reinsurance
firms an important area of international financial regulation. The IAIS has
had far more success that other IFIs in developing accountable decision-
making structures within the organization, and it has achieved a high
degree of legitimacy for its international standards because of its wide-

ranging consultation process and the participation of regulators from most affected jurisdictions and countries.

THE FINANCIAL ACTION TASK FORCE

The International Monetary Fund's Executive Board has called money laundering "a problem of global concern" that threatens to undermine the stability and integrity of financial markets (IMF, 2001a). Most major jurisdictions define money laundering as any financial transaction that involves the proceeds of an underlying criminal offense. It is difficult to quantify the amount of criminal profits that enter into the international financial system each year, but reports estimate the amount to be in excess of hundreds of billions of dollars per year.[47] The scope of money-laundering activity extends beyond the proceeds of drug trafficking to include all types of economic crime that can permeate and impact the stability of banking, securities, and insurance markets. The threat posed by money laundering is not diminished by its very lucrative nature, which provides strong incentives for it to persist and to transform itself within the financial system. Indeed, an example of the changing way through which money laundering can threaten the banking system is demonstrated by the use of alternative payment systems, such as smart cards and Internet banking. The increasing use of electronic money and other banking payment networks by economic criminals to transfer the proceeds of their ill-gotten gains poses a major regulatory concern.

Offshore financial centers also pose a major regulatory concern because they often lack adequate regulation and present numerous obstacles to customer identification. This undermines the efforts of other countries to implement and enforce antimoney-laundering laws. Indeed, increasing integration of financial systems has led to a dramatic increase in the number of jurisdictions offering financial services without appropriate control or regulation and protected by strict bank secrecy. The proliferation of these countries and territories has exacerbated the problem of regulatory arbitrage between these offshore centers and well-regulated jurisdictions. These poorly regulated jurisdictions contribute to worsening standards of risk management by financial institutions.

The Financial Action Task Force (FATF) is the only international body dedicated solely to attacking financial crime.[48] FATF was established in 1989 by the leaders of the G7 states,[49] in recognition of the threat posed to financial stability by money laundering. FATF's original mandate was broadly defined to cooperate in cross-border antimoney-laundering efforts and to adopt standards that would lead states to take the necessary legal and regulatory measures to prevent the use of their financial systems for criminal purposes (FATF, 1990). FATF recognizes that money laundering and other types of financial crime pose a threat to the systemic stability of financial systems. Accordingly, it has focused its antimoney-laundering efforts not only on drug traffickers and economic criminals but also on financial institutions and third-party professionals because of the ease with which criminal groups have used them to facilitate and transmit the proceeds of their illicit activities.

Forty Recommendations

The Forty Recommendations and the Eight Special Recommendations on Terrorist Financing constitute international minimum standards in the fight against money laundering and terrorist financing. Although not legally binding, the so-called Recommendations are mandatory for all OECD and non-OECD countries with noncomplying countries subject to potential sanctions. The original Forty Recommendations, adopted in 1990, were designed to prevent the misuse of financial systems by drug traffickers. The Recommendations were revised in 1996 to address evolving money laundering practices and to extend antimoney-laundering efforts to a broader range of offenses. The 1996 Recommendations were revised around three themes: (1) requiring national legal systems to expand their controls against money laundering; (2) focusing on the role of financial institutions and other third parties that facilitate criminal activity; and (3) strengthening international cooperation and countermeasures against noncompliant jurisdictions (FATF, 1996a). The Recommendations were revised again and renumbered in 2003 with the primary objective of prescribing a range of actions to address the increased use of legal persons to disguise the ownership and control of the proceeds of crime. The Forty Recommendations have been adopted by over more than 130 countries and serve as the international antimoney-laundering standard.

Although the 1990 FATF recommendations are stated as voluntary codes of good practice, they have become effectively mandatory for all countries and territories (Norgren, 2003).[50] For example, all member states must criminalize money laundering and require their own financial institutions to implement vigilant "know your customer" procedures and other forms of transparency. Recommendations 5–10 provide detailed customer due diligence guidelines to enable financial institutions to identify the individuals who own and control bank accounts and to verify the source of all funds.[51] Recommendation 12 extends the customer due diligence and record-keeping requirements to nonfinancial businesses and professions. For instance, businesses and individuals that handle large cash transactions, such as casinos, real estate agents, dealers in precious metals and stones, lawyers, accountants, and trust and company service providers must engage in customer due diligence background checks and report suspicious transactions to the relevant authority.[52] These requirements are far-reaching and extend beyond the reporting and disclosure standards of the 1996 Recommendations.

Financial institutions should also undertake additional measures in relation to cross-border correspondent banking and similar transactions. For instance, regulators should ensure that banks collect sufficient information about the foreign banks and their customers with whom they provide correspondent banking and interbank payment services (Recommendation 7). This information should allow the correspondent bank to ascertain the identity of the ultimate beneficiary of accounts or transactions. States are also required not to allow their banks to provide services to shell banks that have no physical place of operation.

Recommendations 13–16 set out the procedures for suspicious transaction reporting for banks and nonfinancial businesses and professions. Banks and nonfinancial businesses should pay special attention to all complex, unusual, or large transactions and all unusual patterns of transactions that have no apparent economic or lawful purpose. Banks should utilize risk control policies and procedures, employee training, and external audits to scrutinize suspicious transactions and operations. They should examine the background and design of such transactions to the extent possible and reduce their findings to writing in order to assist the relevant authorities (Recommendation 15). If financial institutions suspect that funds are connected to criminal activity, they should be allowed or required to report promptly any suspicions to the competent authorities.

Recommendations 35–40 seek to promote international cooperation in the investigation and enforcement of antimoney-laundering standards. Countries should provide the widest possible range of mutual legal assistance with respect to investigations of money laundering and terrorist financing. Cross-border enforcement should also take the form of executing compulsory process, asset seizures, and extraditions. As discussed later, FATF has a unique institutional structure that allows teams of national regulators to conduct surveillance and oversee other countries' compliance with the FATF recommendations.

Institutional Structure and Sanctions

FATF's primary purposes are to develop international standards to combat money laundering and to coordinate legislative and enforcement efforts (FATF, 1996a; OECD, 1996a). FATF's secretariat is located at the Organization for Economic Cooperation and Development (OECD) in Paris, and its membership consists of all OECD members.[53]

In 1996, FATF adopted a formalized policy for sanctioning members that fail to comply with the Forty Recommendations (FATF, 1996b). The FATF sanctions policy consists of a series of graduated steps designed to pressure members to enact the necessary reforms to achieve compliance. Initial steps include the issuance of a letter from the FATF president to the noncomplying government and the dispatch of a special delegation led by the FATF president to the subject country. More serious measures include invocation of FATF Recommendation 21, which authorizes FATF to urge financial institutions worldwide to closely scrutinize business relations and transactions with persons, companies, and financial institutions domiciled in the subject country (FATF, 1990). The ultimate sanction is expulsion from membership in the organization (FATF, 1996a).

FATF has never expelled a member. It has invoked Recommendation

21, the most severe sanction outside of expulsion, on two occasions. The first case involved the government of Turkey. In October 1996, after exhausting all other efforts to encourage the government of Turkey to pass legislation criminalizing money laundering and to take other steps necessary to adhere to the Forty Recommendations, FATF issued a press release advising financial institutions to scrutinize transactions with persons or businesses domiciled in Turkey (FATF, 1996b). The public shame created by the statement and Turkey's political objectives to become a member of the European Community led Turkey to enact a law making money laundering a criminal offense and to implement other mandatory FATF standards (FATF 1996c).

Similarly, FATF began an investigation of Austrian bank secrecy laws in 1999. At the time of the FATF investigation, Austria was already under investigation by European Commission for breaches of the EU money-laundering directive. In February, 2000, FATF threatened the ultimate sanction against Austria—suspension from the OECD—unless it fulfilled two conditions: (1) issuance of a clear statement announcing that all necessary steps to eliminate the system of anonymous passbook accounts in accordance with the Forty Recommendations would be taken by June 2002; and (2) introduction and support of legislation to prohibit the opening of anonymous passbook accounts and to eliminate existing anonymous accounts.

The Austrian government responded in June 2000 by stating that it would conform completely to the FATF demands (OECD, 2000). Shortly thereafter, the Austrian Parliament adopted an amendment to the Banking Act that required the elimination of anonymous passbook savings accounts by 2005. Upon Austria's compliance with FATF demands, FATF's threat of suspension from the OECD was lifted.

While FATF has no authority to sanction the governments of nonmember states, it may apply Recommendation 21 to financial institutions operating in nonmember jurisdictions that have not complied with FATF standards. For example, it may require its member states to impose restrictions on financial institutions that operate in noncomplying offshore jurisdiction. FATF threatened this course of action in the case of the government of the Seychelles, which had enacted a law designed to facilitate money laundering (OECD, 1996b). The law in question, the Economic Development Act (EDA), granted immunity from criminal prosecution to investors who placed $10 million or more in approved investment schemes and protected their assets from compulsory acquisition or sequestration. An exception to this immunity existed only for acts of violence or drug trafficking in the Seychelles itself. FATF's warning to the Seychelles attracted international attention and prompted many governments to advise their financial institutions not to do business in the Seychelles. The mounting pressure forced the small jurisdiction to capitulate to FATF demands and led it to rescind the offending legislation.

Designating Noncooperative Jurisdictions

FATF relies on a process to identify jurisdictions that are not cooperating in taking measures against money laundering and terrorist financing. This process involves the use of twenty-five criteria to identify detrimental rules and practices that impede international cooperation in the fight against money laundering. The essential issues identified by the criteria are:

- Loopholes in financial regulations that allow no, or inadequate supervision of financial institutions, weak licensing or customer identification requirements, excessive financial secrecy provisions, or lack of suspicious transaction reporting systems;
- Weak commercial regulations, including the identification of beneficial ownership and the registration procedures of business entities;
- Obstacles to international cooperation, regarding both administrative and judicial levels;
- Inadequate resources for preventing, detecting and repressing money laundering activities. (FATF, 2000a)

As part of the review process, FATF has established four regional groups to begin reviews of a number of jurisdictions, both within and outside the FATF membership. The reviews involve the gathering of all relevant information, including laws and regulations, as well as any mutual evaluation reports, self-assessment surveys, or progress reports. The information derived from these reviews will be analyzed with respect to the twenty-five criteria, and a draft report will be prepared and sent to the jurisdictions concerned for comment. Once the reports are completed, FATF will consider further steps to encourage constructive antimoney-laundering action, including the publication of a list of noncooperative jurisdictions.

In June 2000, the Financial Action Task Force completed its first comprehensive review process and published the names of fifteen noncooperative countries and territories (NCCTs) that had failed to take adequate legal, regulatory, and administrative measures against money laundering.[54] FATF threatened to impose sanctions against these jurisdictions unless they made substantial progress within a year toward enacting legislation to prohibit money laundering and took effective measures to implement such legislation by, for example, requiring all financial institutions operating within their territories to comply with the disclosure, transparency, and "know thy customer" guidelines set forth in the FATF Recommendations.[55]

In June 2001, FATF published the results of its first compliance review of NCCTs. Several countries were removed from the NCCT list because they had adopted the necessary legislation and implementation measures to comply with the FATF Recommendations. The compliance review, however, exposed weaknesses and serious deficiencies in other jurisdictions that justified adding several new countries to the NCCT list. The FATF reviews are ongoing and involve FATF regional groupings and FATF-affiliated bodies, such as the Caribbean Financial Action Task Force, in mutual evaluations of members and nonmembers, as well as in compliance reviews of jurisdictions allegedly in breach of standards. A key area of FATF compliance review now involves terrorist financing, which involves the funding of terrorist acts and third-party assistance to terrorists by professionals, businesses, and financial institutions.

FATF has proved itself to be a powerful force for shaping and developing international norms against money laundering and terrorist financing (Gilmore, 2003). Its decision-making structure is formalized to a greater extent than that of the other IFIs, and its delegation of oversight to regional groupings that conduct mutual evaluations of other members' legal and regulatory policies provides an important peer review mechanism for assessing compliance with FATF standards. FATF's policy and regulatory focus, however, has always been the issues that confront regulators and market participants in sophisticated, developed countries. This is understandable, given that FATF is an OECD body whose membership by and large represents developed countries. But FATF's decision to extend the application of its Forty Plus Eight Recommendations to "all countries and territories" raises concerns regarding the accountability and legitimacy of the standard-setting process.

More than 130 countries have endorsed the FATF Forty Recommendations, but only the 33 members of FATF played a direct role in devising the standards. When revising the Forty Recommendations, in 2003, FATF undertook an extensive review that involved not only FATF members but also nonmember countries and territories and other affected parties and market participants. It is not clear, however, how extensively non-FATF members were consulted, or to what extent they were allowed to participate in the final decision making that determined the content of the standards. It is clear that final approval of the standards lay solely with the represented members of FATF and that all non-FATF jurisdiction are now required to comply with the revised Forty Recommendations and the eight recommendations on terrorist financing. In fact, the IMF and the World Bank have recognized the FATF standards as international benchmarks to be applied in their financial sector assessment and adjustment programs. Therefore, as with the Basel Accord, FATF standards are being devised by mostly developed countries to be applied (with the help of the IMF and the World Bank) to all countries and territories. This raises important questions of accountability and legitimacy, as well as questions regarding the economic efficiency of applying these standards to undeveloped economies.

The lack of meaningful participation by non-FATF members in the revision of the Forty Recommendations calls into question the legitimacy of the standards adopted. The strict reporting requirements and disclosure standards for banks and third-party professional advisers will dramatically increase the costs of doing business in the financial sector. They may have the effect of weakening many financial systems by driving liquidity out of the formal market and into the underground economy. The costs of compliance will be higher for banks in developing countries because of their inadequate data and market infrastructure.[56] This will undermine the crucial role that banks are expected to play in generating economic growth in developing countries and emerging economies. Similarly, the stringent reporting requirements for companies seeking to obtain loans or to raise capital on exchanges may lead them to withdraw from the capital markets. Moreover, the strict reporting requirements for lawyers and accountants may lead to infringements of personal rights, especially in countries without a tradition of respecting political and civil rights. By and large, the requirements will increase the costs of financial services and impose disproportionate compliance costs for financial firms that have limited operations and are based in less-developed markets. Large banks from developed countries will benefit because their economies of scale allow them to internalize more easily the substantial compliance costs.

Although FATF decision making is more transparent than that of other IFIs, the consultation process and negotiations over standard setting should be subject to improved procedures that alert all affected parties to when meetings are to take place and the agenda. Presently, FATF members are informed, but there is no consistent procedure for notifying non-FATF countries and interested parties, other than for them to consult the Web site.

In the post-September 11 environment, FATF has been engaged in intense assessments of antiterrorist financing regulations for all countries and territories. FATF has worked closely with the United Nations Security Council to ensure that Resolution 1373, which requires the freezing of assets of designated terrorists, is implemented in all jurisdictions. FATF has also monitored compliance with the UN Convention on the Suppression of Financing of Terrorism and has incorporated most of its requirements into the revised Forty Recommendations that took effect in 2003.

Overall, FATF has demonstrated that it is probably the most effective international standard-setting body for implementing and enforcing its standards. It has reacted quickly to the evolving threat of financial crime and terrorist financing by revising the Forty Recommendations and by adopting separate recommendations to deal with terrorism. FATF also has been successful in achieving widespread adherence to its standards by more than 130 countries and territories. For example, mandatory suspicious-transaction reporting procedures for banks and nonbank financial businesses are required in all FATF jurisdictions, as well as many non-FATF jurisdictions. Countries that are compliant with FATF requirements are encouraged to require that their financial institutions not do business with noncooperating jurisdictions and even to require higher, more costly disclosure from institutions that operate in so-called black-listed jurisdictions.

The major criticism of FATF concerns the accountability and legitimacy of its decision-making and standard-setting process. The absence of any real participation by non-FATF jurisdictions in standard setting under-mines the legitimacy of the Forty Recommendations and the eight terrorist financing recommendations. We suggest that further consideration be given to the economic consequences of implementing these standards in both FATF and non-FATF countries. Moreover, the imposition of FATF countermeasures against noncooperative jurisdictions may violate inter-national trade law.

FINANCIAL CRISES IN THE 1990S AND BEYOND

A further important development came in response to the Mexican peso crisis of 1994. In response, the G7 governments agreed, at their Halifax summit, in 1995, that the regulation of international financial markets should not be left to the G10 but should be on the agenda of intergovern-mental discussions. Not much was achieved in concrete terms until the East Asian financial crises of 1997–1998 and the Russian bond default crisis of 1998, occurring as it did after a period of extreme volatility em-anating from Asia, brought home to G7 governments that their economies are not immune from contagion arising from emerging economies. The response was the creation of the Financial Stability Forum and the estab-lishment of the World Bank-IMF Financial Sector Assessment Program (FSAP) under the direction of the joint Bank-Fund Financial Sector Liaison Committee (FSLC).

The 1997 East Asian financial crises and the 1998 Russian bond crisis exposed continuing gaps in the international regulatory system, particu-larly with regard to inadequacies in the quality of risk assessment and a lack of understanding of the interrelationship of microeconomic weakness of banks and financial institutions and macroeconomic risk. On the basis of the recommendation of the Tietmeyer Report,[35] the G7 financial policy officials (central bank governors, finance ministries, and supervisory au-thorities) decided unanimously, in February 1999, to establish the Finan-cial Stability Forum in order to strengthen international cooperation and coordination in the area of financial market supervision and surveillance. The FSF meets semiannually and comprises thirty-nine members consist-ing of the G10 countries (plus Russia), the IMF, the World Bank, the OECD, the IOSCO, IAIS, and Basel Committee states, and other international and regional groupings (e.g., the European Union). The Tietmeyer Report em-phasized that existing gaps in the international regulatory regime should be addressed by existing rules and procedures of international financial bodies and that no new regulatory infrastructure should be created to duplicate work that is already done or under way by such bodies or or-ganizations. The Tietmeyer Report expressed strong support for a process of coordination between the activities of the different international bodies but did not see a need for additional rules and institutions to address issues that were already being addressed in the existing framework. Moreover, it recommended that the FSF set priorities for addressing particular issues that threaten financial stability and noted that this would be facilitated by a timely exchange of information with other international bodies and forums.

At the FSF's first meeting, in Washington, D.C., in April 1999, FSF members were asked to give their views regarding potential threats to the financial system.[58] Representatives of national authorities agreed that the FSF should not deal with country by country situations but rather should focus on the nature of systemic risk in the international financial system and on what measures should be adopted for its efficient regulation. FSF members agreed to conduct an analysis of specific vulnerabilities in financial systems and not to undertake macroeconomic policy assessment, because that was viewed as duplicating existing work by the IMF and BIS committees. Specific areas of particular interest to the FSF include assessment of the market risk posed by highly leveraged institutions, regulation in offshore centers, potential inconsistencies in supervisory regulation, technical deficiencies in the implementation of core principles, and early warning systems for future crises. Moreover, the FSF has created working groups to address such issues as highly leveraged institutions, offshore regulation, and short-term capital flows. Further, it has published a compendium that contains existing standards of best regulatory practice that have already been set forth by the BIS committees, IOSCO, and IAIS.

The FSF agreed at its 2000 meeting that more use should be made of official and market incentives to foster implementation of supervisory and regulatory standards. It views technical assistance as key in achieving implementation of core principles. The FSF also has examined the implications of e-finance for supervision, regulation, and market operations by establishing a contact group of relevant international bodies and key national regulators to monitor developments in this area.

Despite its success in serving as a forum where interested parties can meet and examine important issues that affect financial stability, the FSF is not much more than a "talking shop." It exercises no regulatory authority and has no mandate to generate standards, even on a voluntary basis, as other international bodies (e.g., BIS committees and IOSCO) have done. It serves a facilitative function of bringing interested regulators together under the auspices of the BIS secretariat to keep the issue of financial stability on the public agenda. Although it has shed light on important issues that affect financial stability (HLIs and offshore regulation), it has failed to fill the current gaps in the international regulatory system.

The FSF has brought together on the one hand the political and the supervisory authorities and on the other hand the regulatory authorities and the macroeconomic policymakers. So, on the operational side, the supervisors are meeting with the politicians and treasury staff who can get things done. On the economic side, it brings together regulation and macroeconomic policy, a vital and until now missing component of effective international regulation. At the moment, while it has produced some excellent reports, the FSF is a think tank with nowhere to go. It is not at all clear what action will follow the reports, or, indeed, who will act. Having suffered a fright in 1998, the policymakers in national treasuries are retreating from the sort of collaborative view of the world that the establishment of the FSF seemed to foreshadow.

The BIS committees, IOSCO, IAIS, and FATF have been in the forefront in devising international legal and regulatory standards for the effective regulation of systemic risk in financial markets. Most of the work of these bodies and organizations has been in direct response to the dramatic increase in volatility and instability in financial markets that has weakened economic systems in the post–Bretton Woods era. Increased levels of systemic risk and contagion have been transmitted through financial markets by the forces of liberalization, deregulation, and technological advances. This has led to a dramatic growth in multinational banking and financial institutions and in the diversity of products and services they provide, acting through various exchanges and markets. International banking has thus developed from a relatively unimportant sideline activity of a few major institutions to an important financial activity that accounts for a significant portion of the assets of a number of large banks. Similar changes have occurred in the international securities and insurance markets. The value of transactions in stocks, bonds, and derivative instruments involving parties who reside in different countries increased dramatically in the 1990s and early 2000s (IOSCO, 2003a). Similarly, credit risk transfer in the insurance sector has taken on a substantial cross-border dimension (IAIS, 2003).

As more financial transactions involve transnational elements, however, the ability of financial institutions to avoid rigorous regulatory standards by migrating to poorly regulated jurisdictions has become a concern. This is why minimum international standards of banking and financial regulation are needed to prevent regulatory gaps from developing in the international financial system. But international standards should be sensitive to market developments and should not hinder liquidity or innovation in financial markets. Therefore, it is necessary to develop a certain degree of competition between various jurisdictions to produce market-driven standards that nevertheless address the objective of controlling systemic risk.

CONCLUSION

Financial stability is a global public good that states seek to promote in their regulatory policies. In promoting financial stability for the global economy, states form international institutions to overcome the collective action problems of managing financial risk in their own economies. In doing so, states are confronted with a range of obstacles, including trans-action costs, which are reduced by their working together through IFIs to promote and coordinate their policy objectives. As discussed in chapter 1, the underpricing of financial risk can lead to a systemic financial crisis that can spread through the banking sectors and payment systems of many countries and engulf the broader international economy in a mac-roeconomic shock. A major objective of financial regulation, therefore, is to control systemic risk by promoting the efficient pricing of capital and financial products. In globalized financial markets, regulators can achieve this only by having access to information from other regulators and by having the ability to coordinate the implementation and enforcement of regulatory standards at the international level. The IFIs have played the main role in this area by reducing collective action costs in order to pro-mote the objective of financial stability.

The Basel Committee, along with other BIS committees, and IOSCO, IAIS, and FATF are international financial bodies established to promote financial stability by minimizing the negative consequences of various types of financial risk. The scope of operations of the IFIs has steadily increased since 1975, usually in response to crises (Eatwell and Taylor, 2000, chap. 6). The consensual and informal approach of the Basel Com-mittee IOSCO and IAIS in developing nonbinding standards and rules for regulating international financial markets has generally been viewed as a success in fostering cooperation and coordination among the regulators of advanced economies. The application of these standards by the IMF and the World Bank and their incorporation into EU law shows their importance as international financial norms and the need to coordinate supervisory and regulatory practices in order to ensure their efficient and equitable application to all countries.

Concern has been expressed, however, about the accountability and legitimacy of the IFIs' decision-making structures. Specifically, their de-cision making often lacks transparency and clear lines of authority. More-over, most states that are subject to these international standards do not feel a sense of ownership because they did not participate in the deliber-ations and decision-making process and were not consulted regarding implementation.

Moreover, as a matter of economic policy, these standards may not be appropriate for the financial markets of many emerging and developing countries that are undergoing tremendous economic change. These coun-tries may require different standards to suit their various stages of eco-nomic development. The financial crises of the late 1990s have reinforced this view, in part because the economic restructuring programs imposed by the IMF on recipient countries in most cases exacerbated the financial crises while bringing few, if any, benefits for long-term economic devel-opment (Stiglitz, 2000). Moreover, the lack of coherence and fragmentation in IFI standard setting and its increasing global impact on non-G10 coun-tries has raised the question whether the informal procedures of the Basel

Committee and other IFIs should be reassessed and supplemented by a more concerted regulatory coordination by national authorities under the auspices of the Financial Stability Forum (FSF) (Giovanoli, 2000: 25–27).

The informal approaches discussed in this chapter for setting international standards of financial regulation are only part of a broader international regulatory regime, which is also composed of multilateral and regional treaty frameworks that create binding obligations on nation-states in particular areas of monetary and financial affairs. Indeed, recent efforts by the IMF, the World Bank, and the WTO suggest that a more formal legal framework is developing for the supervision of international financial markets. A reformed global governance structure will be necessary therefore to maximize the benefits of state coordination in this area. Chapter 3 explores the existing international legal framework for financial regulation.

3

The International Legal Framework
for International Financial Regulation

As discussed in chapter 2, various international bodies have influenced the development of international financial regulation; the most important of these are the Basel Committee on Banking Supervision, the International Organization of Securities Commissions, the International Association of Insurance Supervisors, and the Financial Action Task Force. These international bodies are concerned primarily with establishing international standards of prudential supervision in order to address the causes of financial instability that have resulted from liberalization and deregulation of financial markets. These bodies have no legal status as international organizations and otherwise have no legal capacities to promulgate "hard" law. They serve as forums at which leading developed country financial regulators and some emerging market regulators meet and exchange information on a voluntary basis with a view to establishing legally nonbinding international standards, rules, and codes of conduct to reduce systemic risk in the international financial system. The establishment of the Financial Stability Forum is recognition that the loosely coordinated efforts of these bodies should be more concerted and focused on addressing specific issues that threaten financial stability.

This chapter assesses the current international legal framework that governs international monetary and financial relations. These issue areas are related in important ways to the overall objective of regulating systemic risk in the international financial system. The international economic organizations with responsibility in these areas are the International Monetary Fund (IMF, or Fund), the International Bank for Reconstruction and Development (World Bank), and the World Trade Organization (WTO). These three international organizations form the great triumvirate of international economic policymaking. They have played an important role in facilitating collective action among states to address market failures and capital market imperfections at the international level.

This chapter also examines the two major regional trade agreements that govern cross-border trade in financial services and capital flows. The European Community's treaty regime and legislative framework and the North American Free Trade Agreement (NAFTA) provide two different types of regional governance arrangements for the regulation of financial systems. The EU has made significant progress in promoting harmonization through the principles of home country control and mutual recognition of state regulatory practices. By contrast, NAFTA's legal and institutional framework for financial regulation remains relatively undeveloped because of the unwillingness of its members to cede supervisory authority to a regional body. Moreover, as with the WTO, it is unlikely that NAFTA dispute settlement tribunals will interpret the agreement as superseding the domestic authority of host states to regulate their financial markets.

Binding international legal obligations arise under customary international law and in relation to bilateral and multilateral treaty agreements. Traditionally, public international law played little, if any, role in influencing the development of standards and rules of international financial regulation. In recent years, however, public international law's role has grown as the responsibilities of the IMF, the World Bank, and the WTO have expanded and become increasingly relevant in a legal sense to the development of adequate financial regulatory regimes and increased competition for trade in financial services. Multilateral treaties now govern important areas of the international financial system. For example, the Articles of Agreement of the International Monetary Fund empower the IMF to oversee the international monetary system in order to ensure its effective operations. To accomplish this, the IMF exercises surveillance over the exchange rate policies of its member states. The Articles of Agreement of the World Bank seek to promote economic development by making loans that are conditioned on members undertaking macroeconomic adjustment programs along with institutional reforms that include promoting the rule of law, improving public- and private-sector accountability, including good governance in all its forms, and reducing corruption and financial crime. Moreover, the World Trade Organization's General Agreement on Trade in Services promotes the liberalization of cross-border trade in financial services by requiring member states to reduce barriers to trade in financial services according to a specific schedule of negotiated commitments.

Regional treaty arrangements have also played an important role in establishing principles and rules of international financial regulation. Specifically, the European Community adopted the principle of mutual recognition of home country regulatory standards based on minimum standards of prudential regulation for banking and financial firms operating across EU member states. Moreover, the European Central Bank presides over the European System of Central Banks, which is responsible for monetary policy for eurozone countries and for payments systems regulation for all EU member states. By contrast, the North American Free Trade Agreement regulates financial services based on the principle of host-country control with no minimum standards of prudential supervision for the NAFTA trade area.

INTERNATIONAL ECONOMIC ORGANIZATIONS— THEIR ROLE AND FUNCTION

As discussed in chapter 1, international financial institutions (IFIs) have been established to achieve certain collective benefits by coordinating specific areas of national regulatory policy. International economic organizations also play an important role in the global economy by facilitating collective action among states to promote stronger economic growth and enhanced financial stability. Indeed, Keynes observed during the planning of the Bretton Woods institutions that international economic organizations and institutions were necessary to allow states to address economic problems, such as currency instability and long-term economic growth and development. In today's globalized economy, the coordination benefits achieved by states acting through international economic organizations allow them to overcome the high transaction costs of unilaterally pursuing their own economic and regulatory objectives. For instance, the World Bank seeks to address imperfections in international capital markets by using its own good credit to obtain capital from western investors and to lend that money to developing countries at competitive rates which would not otherwise be available. This facilitative role allows more private capital to find efficient uses in developing countries and thus promote economic growth and development (Stiglitz, 1999). Similarly, the IMF has played a facilitative role by addressing market failures that arise from liquidity constraints that result from the unwillingness of private investors to provide short-term loans to IMF member states that would otherwise not have access to capital and loans.

To understand how international economic organizations govern and set standards for their member states to regulate monetary and financial affairs, it is necessary to discuss their legal framework and how they differ from international financial supervisory bodies. International economic organizations are composed entirely or mainly of states and usually are established by treaty or agreement.[1] They possess legal personality and may assert or be subject to legally cognizable claims under public international law (Restatement 1987 ss 221-223).[2] The three international organizations examined in this chapter have different institutional structures that reflect in part the differences in their purposes and objectives. For instance, the WTO is a member-driven organization with more than

145 members (including the European Community) and a small secretariat that provides administrative and research services. The executive bodies of the WTO are the Ministerial Conference and General Council, which have authority to make nonbinding interpretations of the WTO Agreements and to set the agenda for member negotiations. The relevant WTO Agreement for trade in financial services is the General Agreement on Trade in Services (GATS), which seeks to reduce discriminatory barriers to international trade in services.[3]

The IMF and World Bank are similar in their institutional structures, but different in their overriding objectives. The Fund's main purpose is to provide short-term financing for countries experiencing balance-of-payments imbalances and to assist countries experiencing economic difficulties in making macroeconomic adjustments. The World Bank's main purpose is to make long-term loans for economic development in less-developed countries and to promote sustainable growth programs that reduce poverty and improve living standards. The Fund and the World Bank were both established by founding treaties in 1944 as the pillars of the Bretton Woods institutions,[4] and they are each governed by Articles of Agreement. The Fund and the World Bank share the same membership of more than 185 countries. Unlike in recent years, the Fund has primarily been concerned with short-term payment imbalances and exchange rates, while the World Bank's scope of operations has expanded significantly to include not only the broader issues of macroeconomic growth and development but also microeconomic reforms that focus on firm pricing and resource allocation, legal and regulatory reform, labor conditions, social services delivery, and civil society.

The treaties that established these international organizations are binding on their respective member states but contain different types of obligations and methods of enforcement. The WTO's Dispute Settlement Understanding provides detailed procedures for members that wish to bring claims against other members for alleged violations of obligations under the WTO Agreements. The bulk of rights and obligations created by the WTO Agreements generally run *horizontally* between members and can be enforced only by members, and not by the WTO itself, while a limited number of rights and obligations flow between the WTO itself and its member states and concern such matters as participation in the trade policy review mechanism and the payment of organizational dues (Hudec, 1999). In contrast, the rights and obligations that are created under the Articles of Agreement of the IMF ("Fund") and the World Bank are *vertical* in nature because they largely run between the Fund and the World Bank and their respective member states (Siegal, 2002). The *vertical* structure of rights and obligations in these organizations creates a hierarchical framework in which member states incur obligations directly to the Fund and the World Bank and not to each other. For example, Article IV of the Fund Agreement obliges member states to maintain certain exchange rate arrangements vis-à-vis the currencies of other members. Moreover, Fund members may incur additional obligations to the IMF in return for financial assistance that forms part of an economic restructuring or currency stability program. World Bank financial sector adjustment programs also involve conditionality in which members are provided loans for economic adjustment in return for undertaking certain financial and regulatory reforms, that is, privatization and competition laws (Stiglitz, 1999). As discussed later, the institutional structure of these international organizations significantly influences their decision-making processes with respect to developing standards of economic governance and financial regulation and therefore constitutes a global governance concern.

By contrast, international financial supervisory bodies are not established by multilateral or bilateral treaties or agreements and have no legal personality under international law. They are therefore not subject to the rights, privileges, immunities, and duties accorded to international organizations under public international law (Restatement s 221 cmt C). As discussed in chapter 2, they are created informally through the tacit consent of states or through more formal methods, such as bylaws or incorporation in a particular jurisdiction. These bodies have less formal institutional structures and fewer manifestations of administrative bureaucracy. Unlike most international organizations, international supervisory and standard-setting bodies generally do not require their members to possess all the attributes of statehood to qualify as members. For instance, most U.S. states are members of the IOSCO and the IAIS, while many offshore financial centers that are not independent states in their own right are members of various regional financial bodies, such as the Caribbean Financial Action Task Force.

The regulatory standards and rules adopted by international supervisory bodies create no legally binding obligations under international law. This legally nonbinding international framework of rules and principles can create what some scholars refer to as international soft law, which covers a variety of principles, standards, and norms that influence state behavior but without having any binding authority as such to which nonadherence would result in the imposition of state responsibility.

Under international law, a state party's violation of a treaty or other agreement establishing an international organization may result in that state providing redress to the international organization or an interested state party. In contrast, noncompliance by a state with nonbinding principles and rules adopted by international supervisory bodies does not invoke state responsibility for breach.[5] International norms thus constituted do not result in international legal obligations for which state parties or international organizations may seek redress.

As discussed in chapter 2, international supervisory bodies have promulgated most of the relevant international standards and rules that have been adopted by most leading states and emerging economies to regulate their financial markets and to reduce systemic risk. Although such international standards and rules do not serve as traditional forms of public international law as defined by the Statute of the International Court of Justice,[6] they are international norms nonetheless that directly influence state regulatory practice and policy. Moreover, as discussed later, they have also become potential reference points for various multilateral and regional treaties that regulate cross-border trade in financial services. They also serve as official international benchmarks to measure compliance with IMF and World Bank conditionality and restructuring programs. The work of these specialist international bodies is reviewed and approved at the most senior levels of government—by finance ministers, central banks, and the relevant legislative committees—before being implemented into national law and administrative practice.[7] They have become important manifestations of state regulatory practice and policy and therefore cannot be dismissed as irrelevant in an international legal and policy sense.

The following sections analyze the institutional and legal structure of these important international and regional treaty frameworks and organizations and show how they affect the regulation of systemic risk.

THE INTERNATIONAL MONETARY FUND: PROMOTING MONETARY STABILITY

The IMF possesses the attributes of an international organization, as defined under public international law. The functions and powers of the IMF are defined by a multilateral treaty, the Articles of Agreement, which became effective in 1947. The IMF's initial role was to promote monetary stability in order to foster international trade and economic reconstruction in war-ravaged member countries. Article I of the Articles of Agreement provided the IMF with a mandate to promote international monetary cooperation, facilitate the growth of world trade, promote exchange rate stability, and create a multilateral system of payments. The Fund sought to address the exchange-rate risk problem by creating a system of fixed, but adjustable, exchange rates in which several reserve currencies, led by the U.S. dollar, were pegged or fixed to one another at predetermined rates and linked to gold at a specified value.[8] Under the Agreement, the Fund was authorized to conduct surveillance over the exchange rate policies of its members (Article IV, sec. 3) and to oversee adherence by members of their exchange rate obligations (Article IV, sec. 1). The rationale for the fixed exchange rate system was that the competitive currency devaluations of the 1930s had damaged economies and had exacerbated the depression. It was the Fund's responsibility therefore to monitor this system of fixed exchange rates and to provide short-term liquidity to members having balance-of-payments difficulties. If a member's imbalance reflected a fundamental disequilibrium, which was interpreted by the Fund to be an unsustainable payment imbalance, the exchange rate could be altered with IMF approval.

The IMF also sought to address another important economic problem of the inter-war years, which was the financial instability created by cross-border capital flows. Indeed, Keynes had divided capital movements into three categories: "investment," "speculative," and "refugee" (Moggridge, 1980, vol. xxv: 53, 87, 130, 185). He defined cross-border "investment" capital to be foreign direct investment and other "productive" capital movements that were necessary to facilitate payments for international transactions in goods and services. Cross-border investment capital was beneficial for an economy because it utilized productive resources and helped maintain equilibrium in the balance of payments. In contrast, "speculative" capital was essentially portfolio investments that were not directly related to productive resources or international trade, while "refugee" capital was political in nature and sought refuge from tyrannical regimes. Both types of capital flows had a tenuous connection to a country's economic fundamentals and often created or exacerbated imbalances in international payments by allowing, for example, refugee capital from countries with adverse trade balances to flee to countries with trade surpluses. According to Keynes, this exacerbated international imbalances and undermined economic growth and financial stability (Ibid.: 130).

During negotiations in the early 1940s, Keynes argued that an international economic organization should have jurisdiction to regulate cross-border capital flows (Ibid.: 134–35). Indeed, it was the conventional view at the Bretton Woods conference that unfettered capital flows were undesirable and that some type of regulatory controls should be imposed. The issue was to what extent should the IMF exercise jurisdiction over cross-border capital flows in the international economy. Keynes's view was that the IMF should play a large role, while the U.S. delegation, led by Harry Dexter White, took the view that vesting too much authority in the IMF would infringe on national sovereignty and undermine the efficient development of financial markets (Ibid.: 149). Keynes and White eventually agreed on a plan in which the IMF would exercise limited authority over cross-border capital flows, but only to the extent that such capital flows were being used to finance payments for current international transactions. This became known as Article VIII convertibility in which states were restricted from imposing "restrictions" on the convertibility of foreign currency used to pay for current international transactions (e.g., international trade in goods or services).[9] This obligation applied only to *payments for current transactions*, and not to the *underlying transactions* themselves.

For example, a state could maintain import tariffs or quotas that were otherwise permitted under international law so long as the import restrictions applied to the products or services in question and not to the payments for such imports. In other words, what the state was prohibited from doing was imposing restrictions on the convertibility of foreign currency used to pay for imports if such imports were otherwise being lawfully imported into the country.

The scope of the Article VIII convertibility obligation is broad because the IMF Agreement defines "payments for current transactions" to cover a number of payments that would technically be defined by economists as payments for transactions in the capital (not the current) account. For instance, Article XXX(d) provides the definition of "payments for current transactions" to mean "payments which are not for the purpose of transferring capital" and includes, *without limitation*:

(1) "All payments due in connection with foreign trade, other current business, including services, and normal short-term banking and credit facilities;
(2) Payments due as interest on loans and as net income from other investments;
(3) Payments of moderate amount of amortization of loans or for depreciation of direct investments; and
(4) Moderate remittances for family living expenses."

Paragraph 1 defines "normal short-term banking and credit facilities" to be current transactions. This would apply to bank letters of credit, standby guarantees, and trade finance. Paragraph 2 extends the definition to interest payments on loans, including bonds and other debt instruments, and income from equity investments, possibly capital gains income. Paragraph 3 covers payments for amortizing loans or for the depreciation of investments. The payments in paragraphs 2 and 3, normally classified in the capital account, are treated as payments for current transactions. This broad definition of payments for current international transactions sweeps into the current account a number of capital account transactions that might otherwise be restricted by regulatory authorities. It was Keynes's idea that the definition of payments for current transactions should be broad enough to include the capital transactions that were necessary to promote "productive or useful" investment, and not for speculative or refugee capital.

Article XIV, however, allowed a transition period for states during which they did not have to assume the convertibility obligation for a limited period upon joining the IMF.[10] The duration of this transition period had to be negotiated with the IMF and renewed on an annual basis.[11] Once a state came to an agreement with the Fund to assume the convertibility obligation, it could not depart from its obligation without IMF approval.

Most IMF members today have assumed the convertibility obligation. This means that under Keynes's notion of "investment capital" they are generally free to make payments for current international trade in goods or services and other related transactions. Under Article VI, however, states retain authority to impose capital restrictions and "such controls as are necessary to regulate international capital movements." This means that states may still prohibit or restrict capital flows that do not fall into the definition of "payments for current transactions." Article VI (3) explicitly provides for this by stating that each member "may exercise such controls as necessary to regulate international capital movements." This means that states that have assumed the Article VIII convertibility obligation may still retain or impose controls on capital transfers, such as portfolio investments and other speculative capital, which compose most of today's global financial flows.

The Articles of Agreement became an institutional embodiment of a system of rules and principles to regulate foreign exchange convertibility within a framework of stable exchange rates and expanded international trade. The Articles did not confer jurisdiction on the Fund to impose controls on the capital account, as states were generally allowed to maintain controls so long as they were not restricting payments for current transactions. But the fixed-exchange-rate regime imposed rigid rules on states that required them to make adjustments in the current and capital accounts to offset any macroeconomic imbalances. As a practical matter, this meant that capital would flow to another country only to redress imbalances in the current and capital accounts, and not for speculative or political reasons. In cases where the IMF was called upon to disburse short-term loans to cure a persistent disequilibrium in a member's current account, it would negotiate with the borrowing country concerning the necessary macroeconomic adjustments or, in extreme cases, agree to a currency realignment. This had the effect of controlling and reducing systemic risk because members did not have an incentive to run big imbalances in the current account nor to permit destabilizing capital flows.

The legal framework in the Articles that allowed member states to control and regulate cross-border capital flows to secure the fixed exchange rate system and thus to maintain financial stability on the foreign exchange markets has been amended over the years. In 1978, the Second Amendment to the IMF Agreement was adopted, which made significant changes to the Fund's surveillance powers under Article IV and oversight of members' currency arrangements.[12] The Second Amendment essentially codified the post–Bretton Woods floating exchange rate system and expanded the IMF's scope of operations through surveillance and conditionality.

Surveillance

After the adoption of the Second Amendment, the IMF dramatically increased its involvement in advising member countries regarding economic restructuring, privatizing state economic activity, and overseeing implementation of international financial standards. The Fund exercises these functions on the basis of its Article IV surveillance powers and Article V conditionality powers. Regarding surveillance, Article I, section 1, refers to the establishment of a "machinery for consultation and collaboration on international monetary problems." This consultation process is known as "surveillance." The legal basis for surveillance can be found in Article IV (3), entitled "Surveillance over Exchange Arrangements." In recent years, surveillance has consisted of Financial Sector Assessment Programs (FSAPs) and other IMF programs to collect information and statistics regarding the financial health of member countries. IMF surveillance generally extends only to members' exchange rate policies and obligations under the Agreement and to any other areas expressly provided for in the Agreement.[13] However, it should be emphasized that IMF powers in this area are mainly for analyzing information and providing advice. Members are not obliged to accept IMF advice, nor are they necessarily bound to participate in surveillance operations.

There are two main types of surveillance. First, multilateral surveillance is conducted by analyzing interactions of national economic policies with other economies and the broader global economy. The IMF produces this analysis with its publication, *World Economic Outlook*, which provides a macroeconomic analysis of a country's policies.[14] In 1996, responding to the Mexican currency crisis, the IMF adopted a systematic standard for presenting the data of each of its members in a way that would be relevant for determining the vulnerabilities of that member in its banking and capital markets. This is known as the Special Data Dissemination Standard, and it involves the IMF monitoring borrowers' compliance with international regulatory standards in areas such as banking supervision, financial crime, and securities and insurance regulation (Bordo and James, 1999: 11).

Second, there is bilateral Article IV surveillance, based on regular consultations with member countries. In the 1990s, Article IV consultations began to occur for most members on an annual basis through FSAPs and other consultations. Under FSAPs, IMF staff prepare an annual report on a member's economic development and financial sector stability. These reports are published only with the member's consent.[15] Today, the IMF publishes the results of consultations in a paper (with the consent of the member country) as a "Public Information Notice."

In addition, the Second Amendment of 1978 changed Article IV (1) to increase the IMF's surveillance role to include capital flows. Specifically, Article IV (1) now states "that the essential purpose of the international monetary system is to provide a framework that facilitates the exchange of goods, services, and *capital* [italics added] among countries." The extension of IMF surveillance authority over capital movements has led to a host of financial sector reports that analyze capital market developments and evaluate the impact of global capital flows on financial sectors stability.[16]

Conditionality

Since its inception, the IMF has always exercised a certain degree of oversight of member economies, and in cases where countries drew on their IMF quotas (or exceeded their quotas), the Fund often insisted that the money be used for making macroeconomic and fiscal policy adjustments so that the member's economy could be brought back into equilibrium. This was the beginning of conditionality that involved the IMF in requiring limited adjustments to a member's economy as a condition for drawing on its quota. The legal basis for conditionality can be found in the adequate safeguards provision of Article V section 3(a), which provides

that the Fund may adopt policies for special balance-of-payments problems that will assist members in a manner that is consistent with the
Agreement and that will establish "safeguards" for the temporary use of
the Fund's resources. Moreover, Article (3)(b)-(f) provides some of the
specific requirements of Fund conditionality programs. For instance, the
Fund may condition a member's use of Fund resources on activities that
comply with the objectives and requirements of the Agreement (para. i),
and on a member's attesting that the use of Fund resources is necessitated
by imbalances in the member's balance of payments or inadequacies in
its reserves (para. ii).

In the 1970s, Article V (3)(a) and (b) provided authority for the IMF to
extend the scope of its conditionality programs to include disbursing
funds to countries for problems that went beyond mere current-account
imbalances to more fundamental problems of macroeconomic reform. In
1974, the Fund instituted its first payment facility, the Extended Fund
Facility (EFF), which provided medium term loans to countries willing to
undertake macroeconomic reforms. The EFF loan programs were the first
explicit Fund conditionality programs in which the recipient countries
were monitored to ensure that they adopted Fund reforms and were making progress toward solving their balance-of-payments problem within a
given period.

Moreover, as a legal matter, many experts agree that Fund conditionality can cover only a member's activities related to its obligations under
the Agreement (Holder, 1999). This means that the IMF cannot require a
member to undertake certain economic policies as part of conditionality
unless the Fund itself exercises jurisdiction over the particular policy or
issue in question. For instance, the Fund may prohibit multiple-currency
practices by a member as part of a conditionality program because the
Agreement restricts these practices. On the other hand, the IMF cannot
require a member to liberalize its capital account as part of conditionality
because the IMF does not exercise direct jurisdiction over the use of capital
controls by a member, unless it is mandated by some other Fund power.
For instance, a member may be required to impose controls on capital
inflows as part of a conditionality program to ensure that public-sector
agencies implement fiscal reforms and do not borrow excessively from
foreign lenders (Article VI, sec. 1).

Enforcement and Article VIII (2)(b)

The Fund provides two methods—direct and indirect—for the enforcement of obligations and rights under the Agreement. First, Article XXVI
(2)(a) reaffirms the vertical nature of the rights and obligations that run
between the IMF and its member states by providing the Fund with authority to declare that a member has failed to fulfill "any of its obligations"
under the Agreement and thereby is ineligible to use the Fund's general
resources.[17] If the member persists in the breach of its obligations beyond
a reasonable period following the IMF's declaration of ineligibility, the

Fund, by a 70 percent majority vote of its Executive Board, may suspend its voting rights and eventually require the member to withdraw from IMF membership.[18] These are the most draconian sanctions the Fund can impose under the Agreement. They can be applied, for instance, to a member that has obtained financing from the Fund but that has failed to implement some of the specific requirements of an IMF macroeconomic adjustment program. They can also be applied to a member that imposes exchange restrictions in violation of its Article VIII convertibility obligation. Although the IMF has never imposed these sanctions, some observers argue that they have a deterrent effect on poorer countries that are undergoing Fund supervised economic and financial restructuring programs. As with IMF conditionality programs, the fear of IMF sanctions falls disproportionately on poorer members, which are more likely to draw on Fund financial support than richer developed countries (e.g., Japan) that do not rely on the IMF when experiencing economic or financial problems.

The Fund Agreement also provides an indirect enforcement technique to induce members to adhere to their foreign exchange obligations. This is found in Article VIII (2)(b), which provides that:

> Exchange contracts which involve the currency of any member and which are contrary to the exchange control regulations of that member maintained or imposed consistently with this Agreement shall be unenforceable in the territories of any member.

Article VIII (2)(b) has created much controversy in legal circles and has been subject to considerable commentary and litigation (Mann, 1992). Its text has remained unchanged since it was adopted as part of the original Articles of Agreement in 1947. It requires the courts or administrative agencies of any IMF member not to enforce exchange contracts involving the currency of a member if performance of the contract would violate the exchange control regulations of that member state. At first glance, it appears to be a sweeping prohibition on enforcing exchange contracts that violate the currency control regulations (including capital controls) of a member state that are consistent with the IMF Agreement. Indeed, the eminent former IMF legal adviser Joseph Gold took that view by arguing that it was necessary to prevent contracting parties from circumventing a member's lawfully maintained controls on capital (Gold, 1979). Indeed, the *travaux preparatoires* of the Bretton Woods negotiations appear to suggest that the provision was originally designed to reinforce the fixed-exchange-rate par-value system by reducing the incentives for parties to enter into official or black market foreign exchange contracts and to uphold the capital controls of members maintained under Article VI.

Another interpretation, recognized by German courts, holds that Article VIII (2)(b) can be considered only in the context of Article VIII (2)(a), which, as discussed earlier, prohibits a member from restricting the making of payments or transfers *for current international transactions*. This interpretation holds that the exchange contract is unenforceable under Article VIII (2)(b) *only* if it violates the member's exchange restrictions on current transactions. This means that Article VIII (2)(b) would not render unenforceable exchange contracts that violated the capital control regulations of a member, unless the contracts also involved a violation of the member's exchange restrictions on current transactions. U.S. courts have taken a different approach by focusing narrowly on whether the contract itself is an "exchange contract." For instance, in *J. Zeevi and Sons Ltd. v. Grindlays Bank (Uganda) Limited*,[19] the New York State Court of Appeals rejected the defendant's argument that plaintiff's enforcement of a contract based on a letter of credit would cause it to violate the exchange control laws of Uganda in breach of Article VIII (2)(b) of the Articles of Agreement. In its decision, the court focused on the meaning of "exchange contract" and held that a bank letter of credit was not a exchange contract and therefore did not fall under the scope of Article VIII(2)(b). This decision reinforced previous U.S. court rulings that rejected efforts to extend the coverage of Article VIII (2)(b) to contracts that are not exchange contracts but that involve payments or transfers in violation of a member's capital control regulations.[20]

Although the lack of judicial consensus regarding the scope and extent of Article VIII (2)(b) has undermined its effectiveness as a means for enforcing a state's IMF exchange control obligations, the basic principle it espouses—that the doctrine of illegality of contracts can be used to render a contract unenforceable if performance of the contract violates a treaty obligation—can be used in other international agreements to regulate financial markets. If such a provision were included in an international financial agreement and its content and scope of application could be clearly defined by state parties and recognized by their judicial and administrative tribunals, it could provide an important disincentive for parties to enter into contracts whose performance would violate financial controls required by international agreements. For example, any such provision in an international agreement would need to specify whether it covers only exchange contracts or all contracts that might fall under the jurisdiction of a country's capital controls. The effectiveness of such a provision will depend on the precision of its drafting and the ability of state parties to ensure that courts and tribunals will interpret it in a substantially similar way and to give it effect as between private parties. This type of indirect approach to enforcing international financial regulation could potentially be more effective than formal methods of regulatory oversight conducted by national authorities and international organizations.

Institutional Structure

The IMF has become a universal international organization, its membership having grown from the original 44 states that met at Bretton Woods in 1944 to over 185 countries today. The IMF is managed by a Board of

Governors who are normally the finance ministers or central bank governors of their respective countries. The vote of each governor on the Board is weighted according to a formula based on the amount of the country's shareholding or "quota" in the Fund. Most important decisions that involve such things as the currency calculation for special drawing rights (SDRs), the subscription amount for a particular voting quota, the allocation of voting rights, or major financial assistance programs are taken by supermajority votes of 85 percent of the weighted voting. Member states' voting power is based on the relative size of their quota. The United States has the largest quota of 17.78 percent, which allows it to veto most important Fund decisions. A change to a member's quota can take place only with a supermajority 85 percent vote of the Fund's members.[21] The Articles of Agreement provide that the Board may undertake a general review of the allocation of quotas every five years, but any changes must be approved by a supermajority vote.[22]

The Board of Governors delegates the analysis of policy recommendations for the Fund to the International Monetary and Financial Affairs Committee (IMFAC), which is composed of 24 governors who meet twice a year and have responsibility for reporting and making recommendations to the Board of Governors on issues related to the management and functioning of the international monetary system and on proposals to amend the Articles of Agreement.

An Executive Board supervises the Fund's daily operations. Membership of the Executive Board is composed of countries that are grouped into constituencies, which elect 24 executive directors as members of the Board, with the exception that the five largest IMF members—the United States, Germany, Japan, France, and the United Kingdom—have their own executive directors. The Executive Board appoints a managing director, who oversees a large staff of more than 2,500 employees who are recruited from all member countries, but without any quotas as to nationality.

In the post–Bretton Woods era, the IMF has assumed a role that goes beyond its original mandate to provide exchange-rate stability to countries experiencing short-term payments difficulties. Indeed, by the mid-1970s, IMF membership had grown significantly to include most of the world's noncommunist states. Many of these countries were relatively underdeveloped economically and suffered disproportionately from the economic shocks of that period, including oil price rises and currency volatility arising from the privatization of foreign exchange risk. Many of the new IMF members of recent years are making the transition from state planning and communism and are therefore particularly vulnerable to the financial crises that have plagued the global economy. Moreover, many of these countries are dependent on the IMF for advice regarding international standards of good regulatory practice and for financing for various reforms in their economic and financial sectors. Although these countries are subject to surveillance and conditionality regarding their adherence to various international standards, they exercise little, if any, influence over the determination of standards that apply to them. The lack of transparency in Fund decision making and evaluation regarding the design of financial-sector programs and the limited input of recipient countries regarding how and to what extent these standards should be applied in these countries raises a number of concerns with respect to accountability and legitimacy.[23]

Returning to Its Original Mission

As discussed earlier, the IMF's role has greatly expanded from its original Bretton Woods tasks of maintaining a pegged, but adjustable, exchange rate system and of allowing members to draw on their quotas during periods of short-term payment difficulties. It has taken on a broader role of setting standards for the management of systemic risk. Today, the IMF has adopted an array of programs to assist countries in managing financial crises in emerging markets, providing long-term lending assistance to developing and emerging countries, advising on banking and macroeconomic reform, and collecting and disseminating economic data for its member countries.

Critics of the IMF's expanded role note that the financial crises of the 1990s are unlike the crises of the 1930s, when there was no international lender of last resort to provide capital, or to facilitate private-sector lending, during times of economic and financial market distress. By contrast, the financial crises of recent years have "involved not too little but too much lending, particularly short-term lending that proved to be highly volatile" (International Financial Institutions Advisory Committee to the United States Congress [Meltzer Report], 2000). Indeed, it is argued that the frequency and the severity of recent financial crises raise doubts about the effectiveness of IMF crisis management policies and the expanded role that the IMF has assumed in managing broader issues of financial stability that have not been traditionally within its remit. Moreover, it has failed to place enough emphasis on the role of incentives to induce private actors to act more efficiently by reducing their risk exposures. Too little emphasis has been given to strengthening regulatory structures, and there has been too much reliance on expensive rescue operations. Overall, the IMF's short-term crisis management operations are too expensive, make insufficient use of incentives for private investors and institutions, reacts too slowly to crises, and often provide incorrect advice, and its efforts to influence policy and practice are too intrusive.

A view has emerged that the expanded role of the IMF, in which it involves itself in such a comprehensive way in financial crises and gives advice on the regulation and governance of financial markets, has failed to accomplish the overall objective of effectively managing systemic risk. One reason is that the absence of an effective regulator on the international level has created a void that the IMF has had no choice but to fill when financial crises do occur; in this view, any shortcomings in its policy prescriptions are due not to aggrandizement of regulatory prerogative but to

inadequate regulatory coordination with other international bodies that
have traditionally supervised these areas. In fact, the U.S. Congress's
Commission examining the role of the IMF in the international financial
architecture has proposed that the IMF return to its traditional responsibility of providing short-term credits to members experiencing temporary
balance-of-payment difficulties and providing only limited short-term liquidity support (that is, short-term funds) to solvent member governments when financial markets close (International Financial Institutions
Advisory Committee to the United States Congress [Meltzer Report], 2000:
4).[24]

Jurisdiction over Capital Controls

As discussed earlier, the Fund has no general authority to regulate cross-
border capital flows, except in limited circumstances involving the exercise of its express powers. Under the Bretton Woods system, cross-border
portfolio capital flows were restricted by fixed exchange rates, which were
considered essential to avoiding the competitive devaluations and low
levels of international trade that were hallmarks of the 1930s international
financial system. Capital flows were thus viewed negatively and generally
discouraged by the official community, with the result that various forms
of exchange controls were maintained in many developed countries until
the 1980s. As discussed in chapter 1, capital flows gradually increased as
regulatory restraints on foreign exchange trading were gradually circumvented thanks to advances in technology that facilitated the rise of Euro-
markets and offshore financial centers. By the mid-1990s, the conventional
wisdom appeared to suggest that regulatory controls on capital flows led
to financial instability and distorted economic growth. Accordingly, debate ensued at the IMF over whether the IMF should take jurisdiction
over its members' regulation of cross-border capital flows with the objective of reducing and eventually eliminating such controls.

The International Financial and Monetary Committee[25] (IFMC) of the
Board of Governors examined this issue and proposed to the Board of
Governors, in 1997, that the IMF amend the Articles of Agreement to
divest its members of jurisdiction over capital controls. The IFMC issued
a communiqué that emphasized that an open and liberal system of capital
movements was beneficial to the world economy. It considered the Fund
uniquely placed to promote the orderly liberalization of capital movements and to play a central role in this effort. It, therefore, agreed that the
Fund's Articles should be amended to make the promotion of capital account liberalization a specific purpose of the Fund and to give the Fund
appropriate jurisdiction over capital movements; the scope of such jurisdiction would need to be carefully defined, and sufficient flexibility
should be allowed through transitional provisions and approval policies
(IMF, 1997b).

Later, on September 21, 1997, the IFMC Committee reiterated its view
that an open and liberal system of capital movements, supported by

sound macroeconomic policies and strong financial systems, enhances economic welfare and prosperity in the world economy. The Committee adopted the "Statement on the Liberalization of Capital Movements under An Amendment of the Fund's Articles" and considered that an amendment of the Fund's Articles would provide the most effective means of promoting an orderly liberalization of capital movements consistent with the Fund's role in the international monetary system. The statement provides as follows:

> It is time to add a new chapter to the Bretton Woods Agreement. Private capital flows have become much more important to the international monetary system, and an increasingly open and liberal system has proved to be highly beneficial to the world economy. By facilitating the flow of savings to their most productive uses, capital movements increase investment, growth and prosperity. Provided it is introduced in an orderly manner, and backed both by adequate national policies and a solid multilateral system for surveillance and financial support, the liberalization of capital flows is an essential element of an efficient international monetary system in this age of globalization.

However, the 1998 Asian financial crises and Russian bond default resulted in a radical reassessment of the merits of liberalizing capital flows. In particular, evidence from the Asian crises suggested that liberalizing capital flows can often result in increased financial fragility (Singh, 1999). This led the IFMC to reexamine the merits of full convertibility of the capital account and to temper its once enthusiastic support for liberalization of capital flows. On October 4, 1998, the Interim Committee stated:

> As regards capital movements, the preconditions for a successful opening of national markets must be carefully ascertained and created. It is essential to prevent participation in global capital markets from beginning a channel or a source of financial instability, with the attendant risk of negative spillovers onto the rest of the world economy. The opening of the capital account must be carried out in an orderly, gradual, and well-sequenced manner, keeping its pace in line with the strengthening of countries' ability to sustain its consequences. The Committee underscored the crucial importance in this regard of solid domestic financial systems and of an effective prudential framework.

On April 27, 1999, the IFMC reaffirmed its position of October 1998 by encouraging the Fund to continue its work in analyzing the effects of capital account liberalization on economic growth and financial stability issues and in particular to assess the experience of countries that have used capital controls and what role, if any, the Fund should play in promoting "an orderly and well-supported approach to capital account liberalization."[26] The IMF continues to explore its role in this area, and its experience in regulating cross-border payments and transfers and monitoring capital flows suggests that it might have an institutional advantage in leading reform efforts in this area.

Collective Action Clauses and Sovereign Debt Restructuring

The Argentinian debt crisis that began in 2001 has raised important issues regarding sovereign debt crises and how they affect financial stability. Indeed, private lenders often forget that many states pose significant credit risk and it is necessary to price that risk efficiently in capital markets. The role of international economic organizations should be to create a legal and regulatory framework that creates the correct incentives for lenders to efficiently price sovereign risk. Unfortunately, many of the IMF bailout policies in recent years have contributed to moral hazard on the part of both sovereign debtors and private lenders, which has had the effect of increasing overall financial fragility for many emerging market and developing countries and reducing their access to private foreign capital. In 2002, the IMF Executive Board considered and rejected a proposal to establish a sovereign debt restructuring mechanism that would have allowed a country in arrears on its private sector debt to declare a U.S.-style Chapter 11 stay of action against the enforcement of creditor claims while the country underwent a "debt workout" or payment restructuring. Under the proposal, a country's restructuring of its private sector debt would have occurred under Fund supervision and would have involved negotiations with creditors over repayment terms that could have potentially involved substantial reductions in the principal owed and contractual rate of interest. Proponents argued that SDRM would have allowed countries experiencing a public debt crisis to restructure onerous repayment terms and to avoid slipping further into crisis, while opponents led by the U.S. Treasury argued that SDRM would result in much higher spreads on emerging market and developing country debt and make it more difficult for countries to obtain affordable financing in the international capital markets.

Rather than SDRM, collective action clauses in sovereign bond contracts have emerged as the mechanism for allowing sovereign borrowers to renegotiate their debts in the event of payment problems. Since the 1960s, most sovereign bond contracts had been governed by New York law and usually contained clauses that required a bond issuer (the debtor) to obtain unanimous consent from all bondholders (creditors) before a payment restructuring of the contractual terms of the debt could be agreed. New York law bond contracts made it difficult for sovereign debtors to restructure repayment terms because a single (or small group) creditor had an incentive not to cooperate in debt renegotiations and to hold out for a better deal at the expense of creditors who were negotiating in good faith. By contrast, English law bond contracts have contained collective action clauses (CACs) that allow the issuers of bonds to restructure the repayment terms of the principal and interest on the debt if they can persuade the creditors who hold a super majority of the value of any class of creditor claims to agree to a restructuring of the repayment terms. CACs offer a flexible mechanism for debtors and creditors to renegotiate repayment terms and provide an incentive for all creditors to participate in restructuring negotiations and not to free ride on the willingness of other creditors to renegotiate their claims. CACs today are used in a majority of both English and New York bond contracts and represent a flexible market-based approach to addressing the problems faced by countries undergoing economic and financial crises and in need of sovereign debt restructuring.

THE WORLD BANK

The World Bank is part of the "World Bank Group," which is composed of the Bank, the International Development Association (IDA), the International Finance Corporation (IFC), the Multilateral Investment Guarantee Agency (MIGA), and the International Center for the Settlement of Investment Disputes (ICSID).[27] The Bank's Articles of Agreement set forth three general purposes: to assist in economic reconstruction and development; to promote private foreign investment; and to increase international trade, economic growth, and overall living standards. In pursuit of its objectives, however, the Bank is prohibited from interfering in the political affairs of its member countries (Article 4(10)) and must make its lending decisions on the basis of economic factors, such as considerations of efficiency and the economic viability of particular projects. As with the IMF, the Bank's conditionality and surveillance powers are confined to its scope of operations and to the treaty obligations of its member countries. Because it has a broader role in promoting economic growth and development than the Fund, its scope of surveillance and conditionality requirements are broader and thus can influence the development of domestic regulatory regimes within member countries in need of financial assistance. Although the Bank's Articles do not provide it with the authority to regulate capital movements, its overall purpose to advise members to adopt programs of sustainable economic growth and development and to put capital to "productive purposes" suggests that it might have some role to play in developing a soft and hard infrastructure to regulate finance.

The Bank's initial mandate in the late 1940s was to provide loans for postwar economic reconstruction and to provide guarantees for certain private investment. In the 1950s and 1960s, it played a sort of lender-of-last-resort role for foreign direct investment projects and infrastructure loans to Asian, Latin American, and Middle Eastern countries. During this period, a number of regional banks were established under Bank auspices to promote Bank lending and economic development programs in the developing world.[28] In the late 1970s and 1980s, the economic conditions of many developing countries worsened because of oil price shocks and the increased number of financial crises, which led many developing countries to run huge balance-of-payments deficits and suffer from high inflation. The Bank responded by offering two types of financial assistance programs that provided short-term emergency loans in return for broad economic policy commitments by the borrowing country. The first program provided structural adjustment loans (SALs) that were short-term disbursements to governments in return for macroeconomic policy reforms. The second program provided sectoral adjustment loans (SECALs) that focused more on microeconomic reforms in the private sector by directly assisting private-sector firms and governments in establishing regulatory agencies to promote competition and privatization. These structural adjustment programs were the first Bank conditionality programs. Moreover, under these programs, the Bank now lends much more than it actually guarantees for foreign investors.

In the 1980s, Bank and IMF structural adjustment programs began to converge in terms of the duration of short-term loans and the types of economic adjustment programs borrowing countries were expected to undertake. Bank and Fund programs were similar to the extent that they emphasized institutional reforms in the areas of market practices, regulation, and fiscal policy. Newburg (2000) observes, however, that "there were few signs of co-operation and cross-conditionality" between Bank and Fund programs. It was not until the early 1990s that the Bank and the Fund embarked on a concerted effort to coordinate their efforts to advise borrowing countries, especially postcommunist transition economies, on implementing adjustment programs based on neoclassical economic theory. These so-called reforms emphasized the privatization of most state-owned enterprises, the adoption of transplanted Western commercial codes, and a general retrenchment of the state's economic and social role. By the late 1990s, it became apparent that Bank/Fund adjustment programs in postcommunist countries, such as Russia, had failed abysmally to achieve their objective of sustainable economic growth and institutional reform. Moreover, in many developing countries in Africa and Latin America, Bank adjustment programs had failed to bring about economic growth and sustainable development with the result that a "crisis of governance" was declared regarding Bank programs; there was a general recognition that sweeping new institutional reforms were needed if countries were to attain their economic development objectives.

The Bank responded to these criticisms and extended the scope of its economic adjustment programs to take into account noneconomic factors that nevertheless influence the development of economic institutions. Instead of rolling back the state's role in the economy, the Bank now views the state as necessary for providing an institutional and regulatory framework to promote efficient economic growth. This framework involves the development of legal institutions with an independent judiciary, expert state regulators to monitor macroeconomic developments, and an emphasis on human rights (including property rights), along with the development of social infrastructure. This has become known as the "new conditionality," or the so-called governance agenda, that provides the principles and guidelines for countries undergoing economic restructuring and serves as the basis for the requirements or conditions that borrowing countries are expected to fulfil as part of the Bank's financial-sector adjustment programs.

The extent of the "new conditionality" or governance agenda and its influence on the development of institutional, legal, and regulatory structures in member countries have led to questions as to whether the Bank has exceeded its competence under Article 4(10) by interfering in the internal affairs of member countries. Indeed, former Bank general counsel Shihata addressed this concern in a report that advised the Bank to be cautious regarding the types of programs it recommended for countries, especially in the areas of rule of law, the judiciary, economic regulation, and broader institutional reforms of the state, because they may breach the Bank's obligation under Article 4 not to interfere in domestic political affairs of member states (Tung, 2003). The challenge posed by Article 4(10) to the implementation of the new governance agenda will raise important legal and economic development issues in the future.

The Bank's Accountability Programs—Inspection Panels

The Bank has been subject to tremendous criticism over the years on the ground that its development programs do not accomplish their stated economic, social, and environmental objectives and that adequate accountability mechanisms do not exist to provide clear lines of communication between the intended beneficiaries of projects and Bank and country officials charged with implementation. This has weakened confidence and support for the various infrastructure projects the Bank has advocated. In response to pressure from the U.S. Congress and from nongovernmental organizations in both developed and developing countries, the Bank adopted a public accountability mechanism, in 1993, that established inspection panels to hear complaints from individuals directly affected by Bank programs and to assess the effectiveness of Bank infrastructure projects and investments. The Bank Inspection Panel process has become the most important institutional reform for accountability in the Bank's history. Indeed, Bank president James Wolfensohn has called the Inspection Panel a "bold experiment in transparency and accountability" that has benefited all interested parties.

The Inspection Panel's jurisdiction, however, does not extend to the Bank's conditional lending for financial-sector adjustment programs and economic restructuring programs. The Bank's Board of Governors rejected any extension of the inspection panels to noninfrastructural lending, such as microeconomic reforms, regulatory and supervisory restructuring, and institutions and law reform. Although these programs are the fastest-growing areas of the Bank's lending, they are not subject to the Bank's accountability mechanism.[29] Nevertheless, it can be argued that, by approving the creation of the panels, the Bank's Board of Directors recognized the importance of public accountability as a concept of global governance for international economic organizations and that this does not preclude the future application of some type of accountability mechanism for financial-sector reforms.

INTERNATIONAL TRADE IN FINANCIAL SERVICES: THE GENERAL AGREEMENT ON TRADE IN SERVICES AND THE LIBERALIZATION OF TRADE IN FINANCIAL SERVICES

The World Trade Organization

The World Trade Organization was created in 1995 as an international organization that serves as a forum for intensive negotiations to obtain binding commitments from members to reduce barriers to international trade.[30] The WTO treaty framework contains several binding agreements that cover international trade in goods, services, and intellectual property and a Dispute Settlement Understanding that provides a mechanism for binding dispute resolution for members. The General Agreement on Trade in Services (GATS) applies to cross-border trade in services, including financial services as set forth in the GATS Annex on Financial Services. The GATS provides a set of flexible rules for members to negotiate specific liberalization commitments in all areas of services trade on the basis of the principles of national treatment and market access. The impact of the GATS on international financial standard setting has been negligible because the Annex on Financial Services contains an exception allowing broad discretion for member states to take regulatory measures for a prudential reason that may restrict cross-border trade in financial services. The relevant WTO Committees have so far not attempted to interpret the scope of this so-called prudential exception, and it has not been subject to dispute resolution. Moreover, GATS jurisdiction generally does not extend to a state's regulation of capital flows (except in narrow circumstances discussed below) and therefore has limited impact on issues related to systemic risk. Nevertheless, the GATS provides a framework of principles designed to support the objective of nondiscrimination in cross-border trade in services and this has important implications for domestic regulation in the financial sector.

Under the WTO Marrakesh Agreement, the Ministerial Conference and the General Council have exclusive authority to adopt interpretive decisions of the various WTO agreements.[31] The Ministerial Conference conducts a plenary meeting every two years at which the political leaders of WTO member states meet to set goals and objectives and to approve the work of the General Council. The General Council is composed mainly of trade diplomats from all WTO members, and they meet monthly to prepare the groundwork for the Ministerial Conferences. The Council also serves as the Trade Policy Review Body and the Dispute Settlement Body. It also has the authority to make interpretative decisions of the various WTO multilateral and plurilateral agreements. It also can set the agenda and policy programs for the three WTO Trade Councils that deal respectively with trade in goods, services, and intellectual property. The Council delegates authority to these Trade Councils to examine proposals by members on trade issues, negotiating procedures, and the division of responsibilities among WTO Committees. It also influences which members will be involved in vetting meetings where WTO policy and negotiation procedures are examined.

For instance, in the area of trade in services, the WTO Council on Trade in Services has responsibility for issuing legally nonbinding interpretations of the GATS and its various annexes and may fulfill this function by acting upon the recommendations of various WTO committees that examine particular services sectors. Regarding trade in financial services, the Committee on Trade in Financial Services may make recommendations to the Council on Trade in Services regarding proposed standards and interpretations of the GATS and any communications by members.

The internationalization of financial services has meant that a country's prudential regulatory and supervisory regime should promote not only safe and sound banking practices but also financial innovation and deepening of capital markets. Some studies suggest that increased competition among financial intermediaries promotes more efficient pricing of financial risk and enhanced liquidity in capital markets (Kono & Schuknecht, 1998: 2–4). Moreover, a 1995 World Bank study showed that national efforts to liberalize stock markets strengthened the overall condition of financial intermediaries operating in those jurisdictions (Demirgu, Kunt, and Levine, 1996: 291). This view holds that stock market development is strongly correlated to the development and stability of financial intermediaries if the information generated by stock markets is relevant for the pricing of risk.

The GATS regime is premised on the notion that enhanced competition in financial services will lead to healthier financial institutions and improved financial products for consumers and investors (Kono et al., 1997). It seeks to do this by eliminating discriminatory regulatory practices and reducing obstacles to cross-border trade in financial services. Domestic regulators are permitted discretion to impose regulatory controls for a prudential purpose that may restrict cross-border trade in financial services and capital flows. Such prudential regulatory controls, however, cannot be taken to avoid commitments and obligations under the GATS. Despite the broad scope for prudential controls, the negotiating posture of many member states is firmly focused on gaining access to other members' markets by offering access to one's own market on a most-favored-nation basis.

The General Agreement on Trade in Services

The relevance of the GATS for financial sector issues lies mainly in its disciplines governing cross-border trade in financial services and its principles for domestic regulation. The GATS contains two main parts: (1) a framework agreement that consists of principles, rules, and disciplines to be applied to trade in services, and various annexes, including one on financial services; and (2) a detailed list of WTO members' schedules of specific commitments to liberalize their services sectors and MFN exemptions. The GATS also incorporates by reference the Understanding on Commitments in Financial Services that allows members to opt for a different and more robust set of national treatment commitments that are applicable to all WTO members.[32]

The jurisdictional scope of the GATS is broad, as it applies to all "measures by Members affecting trade in services," which include any law, regulation, rule, procedure, or administrative action taken by "central, regional, or local governments or authorities" and any measure taken by "non-governmental bodies" that exercise delegated powers from state governments or authorities.[33] In financial regulation, this would cover all state laws, regulations, and administrative acts involving the regulation and supervision of the financial sector, including the adoption of any measures taken by self-regulatory bodies, such as stock exchanges, clearing and settlement systems, or professional standards bodies, that were based on conferred or delegated state authority.

The Annex on Financial Services extends the scope of the GATS by defining "financial services" broadly to include "any service of a financial nature offered by a financial service supplier of a Member."[34] The Annex goes on to define financial services to include "insurance and all insurance-related services" and "[b]anking and other financial services.[35] Indeed, in the banking and securities sectors, the definition has broad application covering:

> [A]cceptance of deposits, lending of all types, financial leasing, payment services, guarantees and commitments, trading money market instruments, foreign exchange, derivatives, exchange rate and interest rate instruments, securities and other financial assets, money brokering, asset management, settlement and clearing services for financial assets, provision of financial information, advisory or intermediation services, and insurance services. (GATS Annex on Financial Services)

An important exception, however, exists for "services supplied in the exercise of governmental authority."[36] This includes *any* service not provided on a commercial basis or in competition with other suppliers. Regarding state financial policy, this would cover the activities of central banks and other monetary authorities, statutory social security and public pension plans, and public entities that use government financial services.[37] For instance, the GATS does not apply to how a member state regulates its central bank regarding monetary policy or open market operations.

The broad scope of the GATS and Annex on Financial Services does not apply to a state's regulation of capital flows and related issues of capital account liberalization, unless the member's capital controls derogate from its specific commitments (except when justified under the balance of payments exception). For example, a member may not restrict capital flows that are necessary to make payment for cross-border trade in services if such services are subject to market access or national treatment commitments. As a general matter, however, the jurisdictional scope of the GATS does not cover the liberalization of capital movements (Hoekman & Kostecki, 2002).

The Modes of Supply The GATS applies to *both* cross-border service flows and the supply of services abroad by natural persons or through commercial establishment. Part I of the GATS defines trade in services as taking the form of four modes of supplying services: cross-border trade, consumption abroad, commercial presence, and presence of natural persons.[38] The most relevant for analyzing cross-border trade in financial services are cross-border service flows and commercial presence. Cross-border supply is defined to cover services flowing from the territory of one member state into the territory of another member state (e.g., banking or insurance conducted via telecommunications or e-mail). Commercial presence implies that a service supplier of one member establishes a territorial presence, including through ownership or lease of premises, in another member's territory in order to provide a service (e.g., establishing a bank branch office, brokerage office, or agencies to deliver legal services or communications). This latter mode of supplying services has been described as the most important, but it also raises the most difficult issues for host governments regarding regulatory issues and future liberalization of markets.

As defined earlier, cross-border trade in financial services covers a number of areas, including instances when a service provider based in one country offers financial services in another or the provider seeks the right of establishment through a branch or subsidiary in another country. The type of establishment may be significant in a regulatory context, as many jurisdictions impose additional regulatory requirements on subsidiaries as opposed to branches.[39]

Part II sets forth the "general obligations and principles" of the GATS, which apply to all members and to most services. The two main general principles of Part II are most-favored-nation status and transparency. For example, Article II of the GATS contains the most-favored-nation principle that provides, in relevant part, that "with respect to any measure covered by this Agreement, each Member shall accord immediately and unconditionally to services and service suppliers of any other Member treatment no less favorable than it accords to like services and service suppliers of any other country."[40] The MFN principle is meant to eliminate discriminatory treatment among services and service suppliers in the international trading system. It is subject to important exceptions, however, for regional economic agreements[41] and for exemptions listed by members when they join the WTO, which are permitted for a period not to exceed 10 years.[42]

Some experts have observed that the GATS's most-favored-nation principle may prohibit certain informal international and bilateral agreements that are based on reciprocity and mutual recognition (Marchetti, 2003).

For instance, the Basel Committee's principles of consolidated supervision and home–host-country control may conflict with the MFN principle because it permits Basel Committee members to assess the adequacy of a foreign bank's home-country regulatory regime as a condition for allowing it to operate in the host country's markets. U.S. banking law follows this approach under the Financial Services Modernization Act of 1999, which requires the Federal Reserve to impose more onerous reporting requirements and capital reserves on foreign banks seeking to establish a financial holding company under U.S. law if the foreign bank's home regulator does not comply with the Capital Accord. Moreover, in the area of money laundering and financial crime, the U.S. Patriot Act requires foreign banks whose home jurisdictions do not comply with the FATF Forty Recommendations on money laundering and the Eight Recommendations on terrorist financing to be subject to more extensive U.S. regulatory scrutiny and information disclosure as a condition for participating in the U.S. correspondent banking market. The Patriot Act also authorizes the U.S. attorney general and Treasury secretary to take special measures against jurisdictions that do not comply with FATF or Basel Committee standards on money laundering, which may include sanctions or requirements that U.S. banks meet additional reporting requirements before they can undertake any type of financial transactions with banks based in those jurisdictions. These unilateral measures and international agreements may not comply with the GATS MFN principle.

The second basic principle of the GATS is that of transparency.[43] Indeed, a major obstacle to doing business in a foreign country often involves a lack of information regarding the relevant laws and regulations of a particular jurisdiction. This problem has particular importance for trade in services because many of the relevant foreign trade restrictions take the form of domestic regulations. Accordingly, laws and regulations must be transparent, setting forth clear standards so that foreign traders can discern exactly what conditions must be fulfilled in order to conduct trade. To this end, the GATS requires each member to publish promptly "all relevant measures of general application" that affect operation of the agreement.[44] It should also be noted that no exemptions or exceptions apply for the transparency requirement.

Part III contains the rules and disciplines for national treatment and market access. Unlike the general obligations of most-favored-nation and transparency, the national treatment and market access principles are specific commitments that are negotiated by members. A member does not incur a market access or national treatment obligation unless it expressly consents to such an obligation for a particular sector or subsector of its financial services industry. This is known as a positive-list approach, which means that a member incurs national treatment and market access obligations only if it expressly undertakes a specific commitment for a designated sector or subsector and mode of supply and to the extent that no limitations are imposed by the member. In contrast, a negative-list approach would allow a country to avail itself of restrictions and limitations in applying national treatment and market access principles only if the country in question specifically lists those restrictions and/or limitations in its schedules of specific commitments. The positive-list approach as set forth in the GATS provides more autonomy and flexibility for countries in negotiating their commitments and has particular benefit for developing countries that may lack the necessary expertise to understand which limitations or restrictions to list under the negative-list approach.

The negotiations and scheduling of commitments for cross-border trade in services began in the Uruguay Round where members had negotiated schedules of specific commitments for market access and national treatment. When the negotiations concluded in 1994, the members agreed to a "standstill" that meant they could not rescind or restrict their commitments in the future. These schedules of commitments became the basis for future negotiations that have resulted in further commitments for most members to liberalize trade in services. These commitments are minimum standards of treatment and do not preclude members from taking autonomous measures to liberalize their markets in both scheduled and unscheduled sectors. In fact, most WTO members provide much greater access to their financial services sectors on both a market access and national treatment basis than what they have committed themselves to do in their schedules of commitments. Indeed, the disparity between the level of liberalization in most members' schedules of commitments and the degree of liberalization they actually provide has become so great that GATS liberalization commitments are a poor indicator of the extent of openness in international financial services markets.

The GATS national treatment principle requires a member to "accord to services and services suppliers of any other Member . . . treatment no less favorable than that it accords to its own like services and service suppliers."[45] This is a negotiated commitment that applies only to those sectors and modes of supply for which a negotiated commitment has been expressly undertaken and only to the extent the member has not imposed a limitation in the schedule. The GATS provides that "treatment no less favorable" means both de jure and de facto treatment.[46] For instance, even though a member may accord de jure equal treatment (formally identical treatment) to foreign services or service suppliers, if such identical treatment results in a modification of competitive conditions in favor of a domestic service provider, it will violate the national treatment principle (Marchetti, 2003).

The national treatment principle seeks to ensure that foreigners are afforded equivalent opportunities to compete, while members are not under any obligation to guarantee success in the marketplace (Arup, 1999). Moreover, formally differential treatment of foreign service providers can sometimes be justified under the national treatment principle if a host regulator has greater concern regarding the ability of foreign firms to satisfy host-state regulatory objectives. Thus, extra regulatory measures im-

posed against foreigners may be required to ensure that regulatory objectives are met. In the banking sector, a host regulator may seek to impose
more stringent capitalization requirements than host-state banks are required to meet or may require that foreign banks establish subsidiaries
and a physical presence in the host-state's territory as a condition for
obtaining access to the host state's payment system or to sell financial
products to host-state consumers.

The market access principle contained in Article XVI signifies the importance of trade liberalization as an objective in the GATS and the need
to reduce both discriminatory and nondiscriminatory barriers to trade in
services. Article XVI sets out six measures that restrict market access and
that a member cannot impose on a sector that is subject to a specific commitment unless the restrictive measure has been listed in the member's
schedule. These six elements cover a number of market access restrictions
that include limiting the number of service suppliers in a particular sector
or limiting the number of persons that may be employed in a particular
sector or by a particular supplier.[47]

For the two modes of service—cross-border supply and commercial
presence—two specific disciplines apply. If a member undertakes a commitment with respect to the cross-border supply of services (*mode 1*), it
may not restrict capital flows that are an essential part of that service
(Article XVI, n.8). Similarly, if a member has undertaken a commitment
to permit the commercial presence of a service provider in the territory
of another member, it may not restrict any related transfers of capital into
that territory (ibid). The rules and disciplines that apply to the principles
of national treatment and market access are by far the most significant in
influencing the particular types of liberalization commitments a member
undertakes. These provisions have implications for a member's regulation
of cross-border capital flows and may affect existing obligations of IMF
members that have not yet assumed Article VIII (2) status under the Fund
agreement.

Domestic Regulation of Financial Services Significant barriers to cross-border
trade in services can arise from the requirements of domestic regulation.
Under the GATS, domestic regulation takes the form of licensing requirements and technical standards that do not constitute unlawful trade barriers but that nevertheless pose obstacles to market access and result in
excessively burdensome compliance costs that nullify the benefits that
derive from a member's liberalization commitments. To address these barriers, Article VI prohibits members that have undertaken market access
commitments from maintaining technical standards and licensing requirements that form unnecessary trade barriers (Article VI: 4). For instance, a
member must ensure that its qualification and licensing requirements *and*
technical standards and procedures are based on transparent and objective
criteria and are not unnecessarily burdensome for accomplishing a valid
regulatory objective (ibid).

In the case of a bank, licensing requirements may take the form of fit and proper standards for senior management and board members, while technical standards may take the form of capital adequacy standards. Under Article XVI, these do not constitute restrictions on market access, but they may violate Article VI if they are not based on transparent and objective criteria and are more burdensome than necessary to accomplish a valid regulatory objective. Moreover, where a member's capital adequacy requirements are higher for foreign banks than for domestic ones, the national treatment principle may be contravened, unless the member has scheduled the limitations on national treatment in its schedule of commitments or the discriminatory measure in question was taken for a prudential reason and thus falls within the prudential exception. However, even if the minimum capital standards are not discriminatory as applied between foreign and domestic banks, they must still comply with the disciplines of Article VI's domestic regulation requirements. Article VI disciplines raise important issues regarding the nature and scope of domestic regulation and could potentially serve as a point of convergence for future regulatory practices in the financial sector.

Regarding monetary stability, Article XII of the GATS allows a state to impose restrictions on cross-border trade in services that are necessary to safeguard the balance of payments.[48] This would permit members in serious balance-of-payments difficulties, or those threatened by such difficulties, to restrict trade in services for which they have undertaken commitments. Such restrictions may be utilized by developing countries or countries in transition if such measures are necessary to maintain a level of reserves adequate for the prudential management of their economies. These restrictions, however, must not discriminate among members, cause unnecessary damage to the trading interests of other members, or be unnecessarily restrictive, and must be phased out as the situation improves. Although the restrictions may focus on a particular sector, they must not be used or maintained as a protectionist trade barrier. Restrictions adopted pursuant to Article XII must be reviewed periodically by the WTO Balance of Payments Committee. And a member may not restrict international transfers and payments for current transactions (except as permitted by Article XII) if to do so would violate the members' specific services commitments.

The Prudential Carve-Out

During negotiations over the GATS in the Uruguay Round, it was generally accepted that the financial services industry should be given special treatment because of the systemic impact that banks, insurance companies, and other providers of finance can have on the economy (Dobson and Jacquet, 1998). It was therefore important to allow member-state regulators broad authority to take regulatory and supervisory measures that were necessary for the efficient oversight of the financial sector.

The WTO's emphasis on liberalization of financial markets creates a potential conflict with national financial regulators to apply standards of prudential oversight and regulation to the activities of financial institutions operating in their markets. The WTO negotiators sought to reconcile these differences by providing for a so-called prudential carve-out in the Annex on Financial Services that provides:

> Notwithstanding any other provision of the Agreement, a member shall not be prevented from taking measures for prudential reasons, including for the protection of investors, depositors, policyholders, or persons to whom a fiduciary duty is owed by a financial service supplier, or to ensure the integrity and stability of the financial system. Where such measures do not conform with the provisions of the Agreement, they shall not be used as a means of avoiding the Member's commitments or obligations under the Agreement.

The prudential carve-out allows states to impose regulatory barriers to trade in financial services if such measures are adopted for "prudential reasons" *or* to "ensure the integrity and stability of the financial system." The definition of "prudential reasons" includes the protection of investors, depositors, policyholders, or persons to whom a financial service supplier owes a fiduciary duty. No guidance is provided, however, regarding the types of regulatory standards and rules that would be necessary to accomplish these prudential objectives. Similarly, it is not clear what measures would be necessary to ensure the integrity and stability of the financial system. It appears to suggest that States will be allowed to impose regulatory barriers on cross-border trade in financial services only if such measures are adopted for "prudential reasons" and not to circumvent a member's specific commitments and general obligations under the GATS. It is not clear what standards of prudential regulation could withstand a challenge in a dispute settlement proceeding. Some observers suggest that a dispute panel might use generally accepted international standards of prudential supervision as a benchmark for determining whether a member's regulatory controls comply with the GATS. This may result in using the Basel Capital Accord and other core principles of banking supervision as reference points for assessing whether a member's regulatory restrictions on financial services trade are justified for prudential reasons. The objection to using the Capital Accord or other core principles to determine GATS compliance would be that standard-setting in the Basel Committee lacks accountability and legitimacy because its decision-making process is closed to non-G10 countries. This is also the case with other IFIs, such as the Financial Action Task Force, that suffer from defects in institutional design similar to those of the Basel Committee.

Paragraph 3 of the Annex seeks to promote harmonization of prudential regulatory practices by encouraging members to negotiate and recognize the prudential regulatory standards of other members with a view to promoting convergence in regulatory standards. The objective is to make it more difficult to deviate from generally accepted regulatory practices or to depart from a member's general obligations and specific commitments. Specifically, paragraph 3, entitled "Recognition," allows a member to recognize the prudential measures of any other member in determining how the member's measures relating to financial services shall be applied.[49] This provision states that "such recognition, which may be achieved through harmonization or otherwise, may be based upon an agreement or arrangement with the country concerned or may be accorded autonomously." Further, paragraph 3(b) states that if a member is a party to such an agreement:

> [it] shall afford adequate opportunity for other interested Members to negotiate their accession to such agreements or arrangements, or to negotiate comparable ones with it, under circumstances in which there would be equivalent regulation, oversight, implementation of such regulation, and, if appropriate, procedures concerning the sharing of information between the parties to the agreement or arrangement.[50]

Paragraph 3 (a) and (b) seeks to facilitate bilateral and multilateral agreements or arrangements among members that would work on the basis of mutual recognition but with an obligation not to exclude other members that commit to adopt regulatory standards substantially in compliance with the standards agreed to—either bilaterally or multilaterally—between any members. This mutual recognition framework seeks to encourage members to negotiate a prudential minimum standard or common denominator for banking and financial institutions that operates on an international basis.[51] In theory, this would create a "level playing field," promoting competition objectives by allowing comparative advantage to shape the development of international trade in financial services. In practice, no negotiations to enter such agreements have taken place. Although the principle of promoting harmonized prudential standards among WTO members is an attractive proposition for those who espouse the merits of regulatory competition, the lack of progress by members toward agreement in this area demonstrates that this will probably not serve as an effective mechanism for developing efficient and accountable standards of prudential regulation in global financial markets.

To address some of the uncertainties surrounding this issue, the WTO Council for Trade in Services has provided the Committee on Trade in Financial Services with a mandate to discuss issues related to establishing GATS-compliant standards of domestic financial regulation. The Committee, however, has made little, if any, progress in this area. For instance, the Committee has addressed, but only to a limited extent, the desirability of defining the scope of the prudential exception; various ideas have been mentioned, including the feasibility of establishing an international standard of prudential regulation,[52] but no formal action has taken place. Although the Committee's terms of reference are broad and include the possibility of making proposals to the Council regarding all issues related to trade in financial services, the Committee has been underutilized in this respect, and it is unknown at this time whether any members will, in the near future, make any formal proposals to clarify the "prudential exception." Nevertheless, the issue is assuming increasing importance, especially in today's turbulent global financial markets, because states are confronted with the contradictory pressures to keep domestic financial markets open to foreign capital and financial services in accord with their international obligations while also having to decide which regulatory measures to take for prudential objectives, even though they may result in restrictions on trade in financial services.[53]

Dispute Resolution The WTO Dispute Settlement Understanding provides a dispute resolution process (DSP) by which members may commence proceedings before a panel of experts to determine whether another member's trade restrictions violate obligations under the WTO Agreements. DSP panels are ad hoc and rely on a legalistic approach to interpreting WTO agreements and determining compensation for breach.[54] The DSP could potentially be used to interpret whether a member's financial regulatory measures fall within the prudential exception. The ad hoc and legalistic nature of DSP adjudications, and the WTO's limited resources for providing expertise in regulatory matters, suggests that the DSP is an inappropriate forum to resolve complex disputes regarding the permissibility of a member's regulatory measures under the GATS. Moreover, the institutional perspective of the WTO will likely militate in favor of a member's liberalization commitments and obligations at the expense of its regulatory objectives. This could weaken domestic regulatory regimes for financial services and thereby increase financial fragility in many financial systems.

Moreover, dispute panels could use various tests and standards of review that would make it difficult to uphold the validity of a regulatory measure that may derogate from a member's commitments. These standards of review might possibly rely on a necessity test (or similar test) that would make it difficult for a member to demonstrate that its departure from a WTO obligation or commitment was justified on prudential grounds. For instance, a member might be require to show that the prudential measure in question was the least restrictive measure possible to accomplish the regulatory objective. This would substantially restrict domestic autonomy, especially in a sensitive area like banking regulation. Moreover, when evaluating the validity of substantive standards of banking regulation, a panel might possibly resort to the international standards adopted by various supervisory bodies (e.g., Basel Committee) as a benchmark for determining the legality of a regulatory measure. This would be objectionable on policy grounds precisely because the standards these bodies approve are determined primarily by the rich industrial states and therefore should not be universally applicable to all countries that are subject to WTO dispute proceedings. The use of the DSP to determine the limits of prudential regulatory standards may undermine the sovereignty and regulatory discretion necessary for WTO members to apply efficient standards of financial regulation.

Because the DSP is an inappropriate forum to decide disputes regarding the scope and substance of a member's prudential regulation, it is important to reach some consensus over the types of legitimate regulatory standards and practices that could have the effect of restricting trade in financial services but that may be necessary to reduce systemic risk and to protect consumers and investors. These international norms of prudential supervision are not found in binding treaties or in customary international law, nor should they be found in the standards adopted by IFIs, such as the Basel Committee, on the grounds of accountability and legitimacy. Alternative international regulatory structures therefore should be considered as a way of building more efficient international standards of prudential supervision and for determining what types of controls to place on cross-border capital flows. These standards should be adopted through an effective decision-making process that is accountable to those countries that are subject to their application. Furthermore, these countries must have the opportunity to exercise some type of meaningful influence over the development of such international standards.

The overall objective of WTO members regarding financial sector issues will be to negotiate liberalization commitments on a national-treatment and market-access basis but to maintain their regulatory discretion to impose prudential controls that may have the effect of restricting cross-border trade in financial services, possibly in derogation of their specific commitments. The substantive content and scope of a WTO member's prudential controls may not be within the purview of the GATS and WTO dispute settlement process. The GATS does not divest domestic regulators of legal authority to adopt substantive requirements of financial regulation. For many countries, however, there are market pressures and official incentives from international organizations to adhere to the prudential regulatory standards of international financial institutions (IFIs).

IEOs—Accountability and Legitimacy The issue of accountability has been addressed differently by different international economic organizations. The hierarchical structure of the World Bank and the IMF and the vertical flow of their legal rights and obligations mean that the issue of accountability must be addressed by asking *who makes decisions* that affect the rights and obligations of members and *to whom* the decision makers are accountable. The Fund and the World Bank both have their own Boards of Governors, which exercise general oversight authority. The Executive Boards of both organizations exercise operational oversight. The IMF Executive Board delegates and oversees the day-to-day management functions of the Fund to a managing director and staff. The IMF Executive Board is composed of twenty-four directors elected by various geographical groupings of states, while the eight states with the largest Special Drawing Rights (SDRs) subscriptions and capital contributions are entitled to elect their own executive directors. The vote of each executive director is weighted according to the percentage subscription or capital contribution that its constituency makes to each organization. For instance, the United States holds approximately 17.14 percent of the IMF SDR subscription and is therefore entitled to a weighted vote of 17.14 percent on the Executive Board. Because most major IMF decisions must be based on a supermajority vote of 85 percent, the United States holds an effective veto over many IMF proposals. Of course, this works the other way. For the United States to succeed in getting the Executive Board to approve one of its own proposals, it must also get a supermajority of 85 percent of the votes on the board.

A country's quota also determines its access to the Fund's financial resources and, conversely, determines the Fund's ability to draw against the quotas of members with strong balance of payments in order to provide the financing. Critics maintain, however, that the Fund's formula for allocating quotas and voting rights has not kept pace with the changes in relative economic influence of certain countries. For instance, based on purchasing power parity, Mexico has more than three times the share of world GDP and nearly ten times the population of Belgium, yet the value of its quota is about 55 percent of that of Belgium. Similarly, China has over twelve times the population of the United Kingdom and its economy is twice as large; yet the value of its quota is only 59 percent of the UK quota, and the UK has a permanent chair on the Executive Board, whereas China does not. The IMF's future effectiveness in discharging its mandate will suffer unless it addresses these economic and demographic disparities by reforming its formula for allocating member quotas.

In addition, the Executive Boards of the Fund and the World Bank have been criticized on accountability and legitimacy grounds for failing to allocate quotas to their members on the basis of one member, one vote and for failing to design their economic restructuring and financial assistance programs in ways that support the economic interests of the recipient countries (Stiglitz, 2002). On the other hand, an argument can be made that the weighted voting system supports the *realist* view of international politics—that international organizations can be effective only if they have the support of the world's leading economic and political states. In other words, the effectiveness of economic policy making at the Fund and the World Bank will depend on whether the states with the most economic and financial influence have an incentive and are willing to utilize their resources to ensure that international policy objectives are met. This suggests that the voting structure of these organizations should reflect the global economic power distribution among states, which presently is based on a country's allocated subscriptions and contributions to the operations of these organizations.

By contrast, if the decisions of international economic organizations are based on other criteria in addition to capital contributions and subscriptions, such as, for example, population, then the influence of countries such as Brazil, China, and India would be much greater and possibly would rival the influence of wealthier developed countries, such as the United States and Japan. In this scenario, wealthier developed countries would have less incentive to contribute resources and expertise to international organizations in which they could not exercise controlling influence. This problem would become especially acute during a financial crisis, when the international organization itself does not have the resources to stabilize the crisis and therefore must rely on the resources of wealthier countries to do so. This was illustrated in the Mexican peso crisis in December 1994. At the height of the crisis, with several major Mexican banks on the verge of collapse, the IMF lacked the resources to stabilize the Mexican banking system. It was therefore incumbent on the United States, which had significant economic exposure to the crisis, to assist the IMF in adopting a rescue program, which was based primarily on the provision by the United States of a subsidized loan of more than $60 billion from an emergency Treasury fund to cover the debts of Mexican banks to creditors in the United States, Europe, and Japan. Although the economic virtue of the U.S. emergency loan was criticized as a bailout for Wall Street, which later contributed to the moral hazard that precipitated the Asian crisis in 1997 (Stiglitz, 2002), it provided the necessary liquidity to stop Mexico from spiraling further into economic collapse. Indeed, without the support of its most economically influential member, the IMF could not have managed the crisis.

Indeed, the voting weights in the IMF and the World Bank are allocated by and large on the basis of a member's financial contribution to the Fund's operations. The support of the world's most economically influential countries—the United States, Germany, Japan, Britain, Saudi Arabia, and China—is crucial because they have the most votes individually on the Executive Board and are in a position to block certain programs and loans for recipient countries. The disproportionate influence exercised by these countries because of the voting allocation has been criticized as undermining the accountability and legitimacy of the decisions taken because many IMF members that are subject to the various conditions and requirements of economic restructuring and financial assistance programs play little, or no, role in the decision-making process that often decides their economic fate. Another important weakness with the existing voting system is that it allocates votes according to a formula that can be revised only with the approval of a supermajority vote of 85 percent. This means that a country like Britain, which is becoming relatively less influential in the world economy compared to a country like China, has the ability to forge a coalition with another similarly situated country like France to block any reallocation of voting weights that favors China at their expense.

In contrast, the WTO appears to meet many of the criticisms leveled against the Fund/World Bank because of its horizontal decision-making structure, which is based on one member, one vote and because all members have more or less equal procedural opportunity to influence WTO decision making. WTO members each have one vote, and in theory, each member has an equal right to initiate proposals and to participate in deliberations in the WTO committee system. In practice, however, the WTO General Council makes most decisions on the basis of consensus, and any disputes or objections are usually worked out in committee meetings before the proposal is passed up for Council consideration. The consensus principle may be set aside only in certain situations where members fail to reach consensus on a particular issue, in which case the Ministerial Conference and the General Council can render interpretative decisions with the approval of a three-quarter-majority vote of the WTO membership.

The consensus principle, however, usually determines whether a specific proposal is successful. Consensus is usually decided on the basis of any number of meetings of committees and small groups of representatives that convene, sometimes informally, on a more or less ad hoc basis to address particular issues of concern. The large, economically dominant members are usually best equipped to influence such negotiations to their advantage—often at the expense of poorer, developing countries—because they usually have better access to information, expertise, and resources. Moreover, it is generally understood that for any proposal to be approved based on consensus there must be support from the four major economic powers—Canada, the European Community, Japan, and the United States—before the proposal can be formally submitted to the relevant Trade Council and then on to the General Council.

The operations of the WTO committee system have been criticized for being opaque and the selection process irregular regarding which members are invited to participate in particular committees. Although each member has one vote, in practice the strongest economic powers exercise the most influence in the operations of the organization. Moreover, the consensus principle does not work effectively because most issues are decided in advance in the relevant committees where, it is argued, some countries are not invited to participate, and then later, during plenary meetings of the General Council, members that are politically less influential are pressured by more powerful states to go along with what was decided. It is argued that the opaque structure and the lack of consistent procedures for determining which members will participate in which committees undermines the accountability of the WTO to its members and subjects the poorer, weaker states to the interest of the more powerful states (Footer, 2004).

Another mechanism of WTO accountability is the dispute settlement process that allows members to enforce rights and obligations under the WTO Agreements. Unlike the IMF or the World Bank, which can withdraw benefits to members (e.g., by restricting access to financing facilities), the WTO as an organization cannot impose sanctions or withhold benefits (with few exceptions) to members that are violating their commitments and obligations under the Agreements. The only way to hold members accountable for their obligations is through dispute settlement. The DSP is regarded as an accountability mechanism because it allows members to vindicate their rights and to hold other members accountable for breaching their obligations. This accountability mechanism has particular relevance in the financial regulation context because it allows members to challenge other members' regulatory measures if they violate the GATS. Specifically, members may use the DSP to institute proceedings against a country for maintaining domestic regulatory standards that are not transparent or for maintaining measures that may not be least restrictive in terms of their impact on international trade to accomplish a valid regulatory objective.

The DSP, however, has been criticized on a number of grounds, as discussed earlier, particularly with respect to accountability because its ad hoc approach addresses only the issues raised in a particular dispute. This process is haphazard and will not produce efficient or adequate international standards of financial regulation. Moreover, it will have a particularly pernicious impact on the economic growth prospects of poorer countries and may favor developed countries because, if dispute panels rely on standards adopted by the Basel Committee and other IFIs, it will undermine the development of efficient economic and financial regulation for many countries.

Another concern raised by the legitimacy issue is whether the policies and programs adopted by IMF/Bank are actually improving economic growth and development in recipient countries. Stiglitz (2002) has observed that during the late 1990s the IMF imposed a neoclassical orthodoxy on many countries that received IMF assistance. The IBRD followed a similar approach in promoting privatization and antiregulatory competition laws for many developing countries as part of the Bank's economic restructuring programs (Newburg, 2000). Since the late 1990s, the IMF and World Bank have tempered somewhat their enthusiasm for advising countries to follow a strict regimen of budget cuts and wholesale privatizations of key industries. In the end, the legitimacy of IMF/Bank programs will be measured not only in terms of economic growth and development but also by the degree that institutions of civil society and social justice are promoted.

The GATS domestic regulation disciplines may also undermine the legitimacy of regulatory standard setting because they disproportionately impact developing and poorer countries that have not traditionally been as efficient or knowledgeable in devising regulatory standards as have developed countries. For instance, the requirements for regulatory transparency in Article VI may adversely affect developing countries compared to developed countries, which have experience in administering complex regulatory states and are better able to generate information on regulatory standards, putting them in a better position to comply with Article VI. Also, the WTO negotiation process for liberalization commitments on market access and national treatment generally benefits richer countries, which have the expertise and the negotiating skills to agree to commitments that favor their own political and economic needs, often at the expense of developing countries. It should be added that the DSP itself is used much more by developed countries than by developing or emerging-market members because it is expensive to institute DSP proceedings and requires specialized advice and assistance that only developed countries and some developing countries can afford. Thus, very few claims are brought by developing countries, especially against developed countries.[55]

Although the GATS contains no provisions similar to the GATT that expressly recognize special and differential treatment for developing countries, Article XIX of GATS requires members to undertake future negotiations to reduce barriers to trade in services and also allows developing countries in the negotiations to offer fewer commitments than developed countries. Moreover, Article IV(3) of GATS recognizes the principle of special and differential treatment for the WTO's least developed members (which may not include many developing countries), but nevertheless establishes the principle that liberalization can have differential effects and produce disproportionate benefits and costs for countries with different economic structures. To this end, WTO members have embarked on a new trade round, the Doha Development Agenda, which emphasizes special and differential treatment for developing countries. The Doha trade round covers the so-called Singapore issues, which include financial services, and provides the opportunity for countries to negotiate a liberalization framework that respects good regulatory practices and provides autonomy for countries to experiment with different regulatory approaches in dealing with the challenges of global financial markets.

International Cooperation with Other IFIs The efficient regulation of global financial markets requires that international organizations and standard-setting bodies operate within a coherent institutional framework that is designed to promote cooperation and coordination of standard setting, implementation, and enforcement. This requires that international, regional, and national authorities work together and share jurisdictional authority over the supervision and regulation of the financial system as it relates to systemic risk. The existing institutional structure of international financial regulation fails to achieve these objectives, in part because there exist few formal institutional linkages that can facilitate the work of the global standard-setting bodies with the implementation and enforcement efforts of regional and national authorities. Despite the lack of progress in this area, international economic organizations have taken some steps toward improving cooperation and coordination among themselves in addressing issues that affect financial stability and regulation. These efforts, discussed here, can provide a basis for further institutional reform at the international level.

For example, under both the GATT and the GATS, the WTO has a general obligation to consult and accept certain IMF factual "findings of statistical and other facts . . . relating to foreign exchange, monetary reserves and balance of payments" (Article XII: 5(e)).[56] This means that if the WTO is considering the application of a member to impose import restrictions in derogation of its existing commitments because of a balance-of-payments problem, the WTO must consult the IMF about the member's balance of payments and external financial situation.[57] The WTO, however, is not required to accept the IMF's interpretations or views regarding whether a country's financial condition justifies its non-compliance with WTO obligations. Rather, the WTO shall accept all statistical findings and other related facts on a member's balance of payments and monetary reserves and any legal determinations by the Fund regarding the consistency of a member's exchange arrangements with the IMF Agreement (GATT, Article XV:2). As one expert noted, the Fund's role is to provide its expertise on balance-of-payments assessments, not to decide whether the WTO balance-of-payments exceptions apply (Siegel, 2002).

The WTO balance-of-payments exceptions provide some flexibility for countries seeking to maintain financial stability during the liberalization process. The GATT's experience with the balance-of-payments exception helped many developing countries stabilize their economies during times of crisis or when there was a clear threat to financial stability. The more lenient standard available for developing countries under the GATT and the GATS for restricting imports recognizes the special economic pressures they face. This mechanism promotes legitimacy of standards because it allows countries to engage international organizations in negotiations regarding the need for special trade restrictions as they make the transition to liberalized economies.

Despite these limited efforts, much work remains to be done to improve the coherence of the institutional structure of international financial regulation. Before considering the relevant reform issues, it is necessary to survey the efforts of regional institutions in developing frameworks of financial regulation and to consider whether these are appropriate models for global governance reform.

THE EUROPEAN UNION

The European Community exercises significant legislative and regulatory authority over financial regulation in European Union (EU) member states. This authority derives from several treaties, including the Treaties of Rome (1958), Maastricht (1993), and Amsterdam (1997), which provide a legal basis for the regulation of banking and financial services, including a fundamental right to provide financial services under conditions of competitive equality.[58] Although banking supervision has been left to the member states, the Maastricht Treaty made extensive amendments to the Treaty of Rome to create a European Central Bank that has authority over monetary policy and certain regulatory issues that govern the operations of banks and credit institutions in the 25 EU member states.

The Structure of EU Financial Markets

The wholesale banking markets in Europe have experienced a significant degree of integration primarily because of the euro; however, other areas of financial services, such as investment services and securities, insurance, and most areas of banking remain extremely fragmented (Adam et al., 2002). Although interest rate differentials have substantially converged in the interbank markets, the capital markets remain essentially segmented within national jurisdictions, while very little cross-border activity takes place in corporate loans and in banking services. The composition of most investment funds is substantially biased toward home markets (European Central Bank, 2002; Cabral et al., 2002). Although some of the fragmentation may be attributed to regulatory obstacles and legal barriers, the major causes have more to do with macroeconomic, social, and cultural factors. For instance, differences in the risk appetite of investors across jurisdictions affect the types of investment products offered, while market imperfections often result in major obstacles to the efficient flow of capital throughout the EU. EU institutions have sought to reduce these barriers through legal and regulatory reform, but these policy instruments form only part of the solution to achieving integrated EU financial markets. Increased integration in EU financial markets will occur primarily because of increased convergence in macroeconomic policymaking and harmonization in social and cultural factors that influence investors attitudes toward risk. Any final conclusions regarding the extent of integration in EU financial markets must remain preliminary until further research has been undertaken to measure, in a more precise manner, the actual degree of financial integration in the European Union.

The Legal and Institutional Framework

The Treaty of Rome of 1957 established the European Economic Community, which was renamed the European Community (EC) by the 1992 Treaty of Maastricht.[59] The EC has legal personality and therefore can enter into negotiations with other states and international organizations regarding issues within its exclusive and shared areas of competence.[60] For instance, the EC is a member of the World Trade Organization and conducts negotiations with other WTO member states on behalf of EC member states that are parties to the WTO Agreements. In contrast, the European Union does not have international legal personality and therefore cannot conduct negotiations or act on behalf of EU member states. The proposed Constitution for Europe (Treaty Establishing a Constitution for Europe) would provide the EU with international legal personality and further centralize its institutional authority to regulate various areas of the economy and financial markets.

EU legislation provides a comprehensive set of rules and principles to govern the regulatory practices of EU member states.[61] The original source of these powers lies with the European Community Treaty (Treaty of Rome), articles 67–73, which requires member states to "progressively abolish between themselves all restrictions on the movement of capital belonging to persons resident in the Member States and any discrimination based on the nationality or on the place of residence of the parties or on the place where such capital is invested."

The supervisory framework for banking and financial services within the European Union's internal market has relied primarily on the principles of home-country control and minimum harmonization. According to the principle of home-country control, regulatory authority over banks that conduct activities through their branches in other member "countries" lies with the competent authorities in the state where the institution's head office is located. According to the principle of minimum harmonization, member states are required to harmonize what are considered the essential areas of banking regulation while being free to surpass the minimum standards of equivalence and to maintain national regulation in areas not harmonized (Caixa-Bank, ECJ case, 2004). The minimum standards to be incorporated in national regulation by all member states were established in directives issued by the EC Council.[62]

EC regulation does not prescribe the type of banks or banking system a member country must have. Each country continues to develop its traditional banking system under the growing impact of EC legislation and increasing competition in the European market. EC Banking Directives adopt a functionalist approach to financial regulation by requiring the same type of activity to be subject to the same regulatory rules, even though the activity may be performed by different types of institutions (e.g., universal bank or investment bank).[63] Also, EC directives do not require member states to adopt a particular institutional structure of banking supervision. For instance, states may use a single regulator for prudential supervision or divide those responsibilities between two or more bodies. Before accession to the EU, a state must comply with EC banking directives and regulations, which may result in considerable adjustment to its banking laws and regulations.[64]

The principle of home-country control is premised on the notion of common objectives and trust in one another's standards (Peter Paul and others, ECJ case, 2004). The advantage of mutual recognition is that it generates a competitive process of regulation that leads eventually (in theory) to convergence of regulatory standards. Mutual recognition based on home-country rules reaches a common standard more quickly than regulation based on host-country rules. For this approach to succeed in establishing efficient standards of regulation across states, it is not necessary to create an international organization or body with regulatory authority. However, it might be necessary to establish a transnational body to operate a system of surveillance and to facilitate implementation and enforcement. Thus far, the EU legislative framework of home-country control and minimum harmonization has accomplished a great deal in promoting the objectives of the EU internal market and has been suggested as a model for reforming the international financial architecture (Giovanoli, 2000). Nevertheless, host-country authorities can still create obstacles to cross-border trade within the EU in the form of legislation or regulation that protects consumers and investors—the so-called general good exception. Recent efforts at institutional consolidation at the EU level in banking, insurance, and securities regulation and creation of the European Central Bank and the euro have significantly changed the regulation of financial markets in Europe.

The European System of Central Banks

The Maastricht Treaty of 1993, otherwise known as the Treaty on European Union (TEU), established the European Central Bank (ECB) and the European System of Central Banks (ESCB), both of which became operational on 1 June 1998.[65] This was a historic event, not only because of the creation of the euro but also because it established a single monetary policy for countries within the eurozone *and* provided the ECB with authority to regulate the institutional and operational aspects of payment systems throughout the ESCB.[66] It should be recalled that the ECB presides over the Eurosystem, which is composed of the ECB and the 12 EU member states that have adopted the euro, and has responsibility for certain regulatory issues within the ESCB, which covers all 25 member states of the European Union. The ESCB regulatory framework has been accompanied by a number of legal acts and regulatory standards that address institutional and operational issues for the conduct of monetary policy within the Eurosystem and the regulation of payments systems throughout the European Union. The creation of the ESCB/ECB framework and the adoption of the euro have created a new monetary and financial law for Europe. This legal and regulatory framework is dynamic and develops over time to take account of the changing structure of EU banking and financial markets.

The ESCB regulatory framework has emerged as an important arena for the regulation of systemic risk in both the Eurosystem and across the EU. It consists of a number of legal acts, regulations, nonbinding guidance notes, and opinions that provide the governance framework for monetary policy and payments systems regulation. The legal basis for the ESCB regulatory framework can be found in Part III and Title VII of the Treaty that established the European Community, along with the Protocol on the Statute of the European System of Central Banks and European Central Bank (the Treaty and ESCB Statute). The ECB is required to implement the regulatory tasks of the ESCB in a decentralized manner by having "recourse to the national central banks to carry out operations which form part of the tasks of the ESCB."[67] The decentralized approach to executing and implementing ESCB regulatory objectives suggests that many ESCB regulatory tasks are carried out by member-state central banks and national banking regulators under the laws of their national jurisdictions. This means that member-state laws will govern the contractual, regulatory, and other legal issues that arise regarding the national central banks relationships with market participants and the infrastructure of clearing and settlement.

Within the ESCB regulatory framework, the ECB's primary tasks are to conduct monetary policy,[68] oversee foreign exchange operations, manage the official reserves of the member states, and promote the smooth operation of the payments systems.[69] Article 105 (5) of the Treaty states that "the ESCB shall contribute to the smooth conduct of policies pursued by the competent authorities relating to the prudential supervision of credit institutions and the stability of the financial system."[70] Article 25.1 of the ESCB Statute authorizes the ECB to "offer advice to and be consulted by the Council, the Commission and the competent authorities of the Member States on [all relevant legislation]." The ECB's advisory role in supervising credit institutions, however, can only be extended into a more direct prudential function if it satisfies the requirements of Article 105 (6) of the Treaty that state, in relevant part, "the Council may, acting unanimously on a proposal from the Commission and after consulting the ECB and after receiving the assent of the European parliament, confer upon the ECB specific tasks concerning policies relating to the prudential supervision of credit institutions." The EU Council of Ministers would therefore need to agree unanimously to confer prudential supervisory and regulatory powers upon the ECB. This would require strong political support—which presently does not exist—within the Commission and Parliament to vest the ECB with prudential supervisory powers.

Although at present the ECB exercises no direct authority in influencing the prudential regulation of banks in any EU state, its broad mandate to promote the smooth functioning of the payments systems throughout the EU may imply that it has the power to issue regulations or opinions in interpreting the treaty or ESCB statute that would allow it to set standards to be implemented by member-state regulators in some areas of prudential supervision. This interpretation reflects the general view that the ESCB framework is not static but rather dynamic and has the capacity to evolve and to expand its powers, if necessary, in order to meet the regulatory challenges of evolving financial markets.

In addition, the ECB's overall management of the ESCB involves it in two important areas: payments systems regulation[71] and the provision of settlement systems in member-state economies, and the oversight of clearing systems and other money transfer systems operated by commercial banks and large market participants, such as securities custodians. The Governing Council of the ECB can issue common oversight policies that may have implications for the conduct of monetary policy, systemic stability, the promotion of harmonized regulatory structures across the EU, and the regulation of cross-border payments within the EU and between the EU and non-EU countries. These common oversight policies are administered on a decentralized basis in which the national central banks provide the necessary facilities and oversight of payment systems within their national jurisdictions. The ECB has primary responsibility for overseeing cross-border payment systems in euros and between euros and other currencies, as well as cross-border payment systems throughout the EU.

In the area of settlement systems, the ECB and member-state central banks are authorized to accept payments and financial collateral in the form of electronically recorded interests in dematerialized securities from certain institutions that include large money center banks, public entities, central securities depositories, and regulated custodians of financial assets.[72] In addition, the ECB has an important power—that it has not yet exercised—that allows it to adopt regulations to ensure the efficiency and soundness of EU clearing and settlement systems within and among EU member states and also between the EU and non-EU countries.[73]

The ESCB and Accountability Unlike the IFIs, the accountability and independence of the ESCB are provided for in treaty and statute. For instance, the European Central Bank is accountable to EU finance ministers and to the Parliament. At first glance, the principles of accountability and independence may seem contradictory and, when implemented into a financial regulatory regime, can result in a clash of regulatory policy objectives. Although the EU treaty and the accompanying legislative framework provided for the institutional independence of the ECB and an independent regulatory policy for the ESCB,[74] it nonetheless incorporates the legal requirements of accountability for the ECB with respect to other EU institutions. For instance, the ECB must issue reports on a regular basis to the European Parliament that provide financial information and statistics regarding the operations of the ESCB banking system. Moreover, the ECB president is required to appear before the Parliament to report regularly on monetary policy and on regulatory and technical matters under ECB control. Moreover, the ECB's acts and policies in managing the ESCB are subject to judicial review by the European Court of First Instance and the European Court of Justice, while the delegated acts of national central banks and regulators in exercising authority related to the operation of the ESCB are subject to review by national courts. Another form of accountability obliges member-state central banks and regulators to be accountable to the ECB and to be subject to enforcement actions by the ECB if they fail to comply with the requirements of the ECB/ESCB regulatory framework.[75]

The ESCB provides a flexible regulatory framework that is supported by EU law, not in a rigid or prescriptive manner but rather in a decentralized structure that allows the ECB to delegate implementation details to member-state central banks. The ECB's broad authority to issue regulations and guidance to govern important aspects of the payments systems, which may impact the prudential supervision of financial institutions, creates a transnational regulatory framework that now covers 25 European countries. It should be emphasized that the ECB's regulatory authority over the payments system can provide it with much leverage in enforcing international standards of financial regulation, especially with respect to the banking industry, which could possibly serve as a mechanism for implementing international financial standards and principles of global governance.

EU Financial Services Action Plan The Financial Services Action Plan (FSAP)[76] constitutes an important step for establishing a harmonized legislative and regulatory framework for achieving a common European market in financial services. The FSAP proposes priorities and time frames for legislative and other regulatory measures to address three strategic objectives: (1) a single market for wholesale financial services, (2) open and secure retail markets, and (3) modernized prudential rules and supervision of intermediaries and securities firms. In particular, the last objective impacts most directly on financial stability and seeks to keep EU regulatory standards of prudential supervision up-to-date in order to contain systemic or institutional risk (e.g., capital adequacy, solvency margins for insurance). Moreover, the FSAP is coupled with the newly adopted institutional structure known as the Lamfalussy process, which attempts to expedite the adoption and implementation of EU regulatory rules to take account of rapid developments in Europe's financial markets.

The FSAP seeks to address prudential supervision by taking the following measures: incorporating latest regulatory practices of international bodies (e.g., Basel Committee, IOSCO) by adopting proposed directives on the winding up and liquidation of banks and insurance companies and on electronic money, as well as proposals to amend the capital adequacy standards of banks and investment firms and to amend the solvency margins for insurance companies. Moreover, it seeks to create a unified framework to assess the prudential supervision of financial conglomerates. It also establishes arrangements to increase cross-sectoral cooperation and coordination among national regulatory authorities, especially with respect to banking supervision and insurance and securities regulation.

The FSAP also emphasizes the need to enhance market integrity by controlling the growing problem of market abuse. The Market Abuse Directive requires member states to "[s]et common disciplines for trading floors to enhance investor confidence in an embryonic single securities market" and requires member states to create a civil offense of market abuse and manipulation and to establish a single enforcement agency in each member state. Moreover, the EU Parliament and Council adopted a Prospectus Directive in 2003 that provides a uniform standard of disclosure for EU companies that seek to list their securities on an exchange. For instance, this allows a company that has qualified under Italian law to list its securities on the Rome stock exchange to list those same securities on the London stock exchange with only minor changes to the prospectus document. Similarly, the EU has made the reporting requirements of the International Accounting Standards mandatory in 2005 for all publicly traded companies.

A major premise of the EU FSAP is that there is a necessary relationship between the degree of liberalization and regulatory harmonization in financial markets *and* the degree of integration of those markets. The EU FSAP presumes that the reduction or elimination of regulatory and legal barriers to cross-border trade in financial services will lead to financial market integration. The FSAP approach, however, fails to make the important distinction between the creation of a liberalized framework of financial regulation and the creation of truly integrated financial markets. Similarly, those advocates of a single EU securities regulator have failed to address this problem of distinguishing between integration and liberalization and the implication of this for the success of EU regulatory integration programs.

Institutional Consolidation in Europe The role of EU institutions in regulating the investment services and insurance sectors is undergoing significant change, as institutional consolidation occurs rapidly. In investment services and securities regulation, the Lamfalussy Committee's recommendations for a consolidated four-level institutional structure for European securities regulation has been adopted.[77] Level 1 refers to EU framework legislation and essential measures, which will be adopted by the standard co-decision procedure by the Council and the Parliament. These two bodies will also agree on the nature and extent of the implementing measures to be decided at Level 2 on the basis of Commission proposals. Level 2 refers to EU implementation and the nonessential measures, which will be defined, proposed, and adopted by the Commission and the ESC, while the Committee of European Securities Regulators (CESR) will act in an advisory capacity. Level 3 refers to strengthened cooperation between regulators to improve implementation, which will be designed to improve consistency of day-to-day transposition and implementation of legislation adopted at Levels 1 and 2. This stage involves the Member States and the CESR. Finally, Level 4 refers to enforcement and involves the adoption by the Commission and the member states of strategies to ensure uniform and effective enforcement.

The ESC and CESR have begun acting in a regulatory capacity and have been initially successful in expediting the regulatory standard-setting process by making it more flexible and efficient. The Lamfalussy program is essentially a regulatory process that relies on existing comitology procedures as set forth in Article 202 of the Treaty of Rome to develop EU securities legislation based on proposals from national finance ministers and regulators and in consultation with industry. The EU FSAP has recognized the Lamfalussy program as an essential element in achieving the EU Treaty objectives of an internal market for capital movement and trade in financial services.[78]

The institutional structure of the Lamfalussy program has been criticized as being too slow and as subject to protectionist influences from national authorities.[79] It is argued that these weaknesses are obstacles to achieving the objectives of the FSAP and thereby justify the creation of a single EU securities regulator. However, advocates of increased centralization of EU securities regulation have not given adequate thought to the question of whether EU economies (including accession-country economies) have achieved sufficient levels of convergence and integration in their financial market structures and practices to justify increased centralization and consolidation of securities regulation at the EU level. Indeed, the lack of integration between EU financial markets, especially in equities and retail financial services, suggests that the European Union (including the accession countries) may not be an optimal economic area for a single securities regulator. This is premised on the notion that the institutional design and scope of a financial regulator should depend, in part, on the extent of integration in the financial market over which it regulates. In other words, the *domain of the regulator* should be the same as the *domain of the market*. The domain of a financial market can be determined, in part, by its degree of integration.

Although the Lamfalussy program speeds up and consolidates regulatory decision making through enhanced comitology powers, it is essentially a regulatory process that does not necessarily involve substantive harmonization of EU securities legislation and therefore is not a significant departure from traditional notions of intergovernmental coordination in EU policymaking. Although the early stages of implementation of the Lamfalussy program have ignited much controversy concerning the scope of legislative authority for Community institutions, Lamfalussy streamlines decision making and requires consultation and transparency and does not undermine the vital role that national regulators and market participants play in regulating securities markets. The Council of Ministers and Parliament have recognized the early success of the Lamfalussy program and have approved its adoption for Europe's other financial sectors—banking, insurance, and financial conglomerates. In particular, in January 2004, the Council approved the recommendation of experts to establish an identical four-level institutional structure for the prudential supervision of banks that operate in EU member states. Similar institutional structures were approved in 2004 for the regulation of insurance firms and financial conglomerates.

Notwithstanding the lack of integration in EU financial markets, the objectives of the EU treaties to create a seamless internal market for goods, services, and capital will require a certain degree of EU regulatory authority in terms of both institutional design and harmonized standards and principles. Indeed, the institutional design of financial regulation should be flexible and always responsive to developments in financial markets. At the present stage of EU financial development, EU regulatory authorities should promote a twofold financial policy that links the institutional design and scope of EU financial regulation to the degree of integration in EU financial markets. This means that broad principles devised at the EU level should be implemented by national authorities, which would adopt national rules that respect the economic, institutional, and legal differences among EU countries. Indeed, further efforts that go beyond the Lamfalussy framework that do not take account of further integration in EU financial markets might undermine financial development and reduce the overall efficiency of EU capital markets.

THE NORTH AMERICAN FREE TRADE AGREEMENT

The North American Free Trade Agreement (NAFTA) constitutes a regional treaty that promotes a free trade area for Canada, Mexico, and the United States.[80] It creates an institutional framework of rules and principles for the regulation of trade, including trade in financial services, among the three member states. NAFTA's objectives include the elimination of barriers to trade in goods and services, the promotion of conditions of fair competition, and an increase in the amount of cross-border investment. Its member states are subject to legally binding dispute resolution that can be initiated by signatory states or by private parties (including corporations) of the signatory states. Although NAFTA does not establish a formal international organization, it has a secretariat that administers its dispute resolution function. NAFTA's institutional governance is administered primarily by the various regulatory agencies of the signatory states through their ongoing negotiations for increased market access and coordination of prudential regulatory practices.

NAFTA'S Legal Framework

Chapter 14 of NAFTA contains the provisions regulating cross-border trade in financial services and investment in financial institutions. The main principles to be applied to the regulatory practices of signatory states are national treatment, most-favored-nation status, and market access. The scope of these principles is broad, applying to all measures taken by a signatory state to regulate financial institutions in its territory that are owned or controlled by investors of other NAFTA states. They also apply to all treatment of investors who own or seek to own those institutions and to all cross-border trade in financial services between persons in different NAFTA states.[81]

Article 1403 promotes market access by requiring NAFTA states to permit investors of one state party to establish a financial institution in the territory of another party.[82] This means that financial service providers and firms of NAFTA states can establish banking, insurance, securities, and other financial operations in other NAFTA states. NAFTA states, however, have discretion to require banks or financial firms of other NAFTA states to incorporate as a subsidiary in the host jurisdiction as a condition for establishing operations.[83] This allows host states to impose the full array of their regulatory powers in the areas of capital adequacy, payment system regulation, insolvency, and corporate governance on the local operations of financial firms based in other NAFTA states. Furthermore, each state must allow its residents to purchase financial services from providers located in the territory of other state parties (Article 1404(2)). This obligation, however, does not require states to allow those service providers to do business or solicit in the territory of the host state without adequate regulation and registration.

The national treatment and most-favored-nation principles mean that NAFTA signatories are required to provide market access on a nondiscriminatory basis to the financial service providers and investors of other NAFTA states.[84] The national treatment principle means that NAFTA states must provide regulatory treatment of financial firms that is "no less favorable" than the treatment it provides to domestic firms under like circumstances (Article 1405). The "like circumstances" test can be met with either different or identical regulatory treatment of domestic and foreign financial firms if such treatment affords equally competitive opportunities (Article 1405(5)). A state affords equally competitive opportunities if its treatment of financial institutions and cross-border financial service providers of another NAFTA state does not disadvantage their ability to provide financial services as compared with the ability of domestic financial firms under like circumstances (Article 1405(6)). In determining whether there has been a denial of equal competitive opportunities, a dispute panel may consider economic factors, such as market share, profitability, or firm size (Article 1405(7)).[85]

The NAFTA most-favored-nation principle requires a state party to provide the financial firms of other NAFTA states treatment that is "no less favorable" than the treatment it provides to financial firms of any other country (including non-NAFTA countries) under like circumstances (Article 1406). State parties, however, may depart from this principle by providing more favorable regulatory treatment to firms based in countries (NAFTA or non-NAFTA) whose prudential regulatory standards have been recognized by agreement or arrangement with the host state as being of a high standard or as having achieved a harmonized standard (Article 1406(2)). It is not clear whether this means a harmonized international standard (i.e., Basel Accord) or an acceptable harmonized standard negotiated on a bilateral or regional basis. Where a state party does recognize the prudential standards of another NAFTA or non-NAFTA state and thereby affords financial firms of that state more favorable treatment as compared to firms of other NAFTA states, the state affording such beneficial treatment must provide an adequate opportunity for other NAFTA states to demonstrate that they too have achieved, or will achieve, equivalent regulation and oversight and implementation of regulation (Article 1406(3)). Moreover, in the case where a NAFTA state has recognized the prudential measures of any other state as part of an international agreement or arrangement, the state party must allow other NAFTA parties an adequate opportunity to negotiate accession to the relevant agreement or arrangement (Article 1406(4)).

This should be compared to paragraph 3(c) of the GATS Annex on Financial Services, which requires WTO members that have afforded beneficial treatment to firms of member states that have entered international agreements or arrangements on prudential regulation to provide an "opportunity" for other WTO members to negotiate accession. In addition, the NAFTA MFN requirements will probably not invalidate the requirements of the Basel Committee's principles on consolidated supervision that allow Basel Committee members to allow more lenient regulatory treatment of foreign banks' global operations that are based in jurisdictions that are compliant with the Capital Accord.

NAFTA also provides minimum requirements for the composition of corporate boards and senior management. For instance, no state party may require financial institutions of another party to employ or engage individuals of a particular nationality in senior management positions or other key positions (Article 1408(1)). By contrast, states are permitted to require financial institutions to have only a simple majority of its board of directors consist of nationals of the host state, or persons who reside in the territory of the host state (Article 1408(2)).

Article 1410 contains a broad prudential exception similar to the GATS prudential carve-out that allows states to exercise prudential regulatory controls that may result in a departure from their NAFTA obligations.[86] States are allowed to take reasonable prudential regulatory measures to protect investors, depositors, financial market participants, policy holders and policy claimants, or persons to whom a fiduciary duty is owed by a financial institution or cross-border financial service provider (Article 1410(1)(a)). It also allows states to take whatever measures are necessary to protect the safety, soundness, and integrity of financial institutions or cross-border financial service providers (Article 1410(1)(b)), and it authorizes states to take necessary measures to protect the integrity and stability of the financial system (Article 1410(1)(c)).[87] A state party may also limit financial transfers by a foreign bank or cross-border financial services provider of another NAFTA state through the use of regulatory controls applied on a nondiscriminatory and good-faith basis if such measures are intended to promote the safety, soundness, and integrity of domestic financial institutions or financial service providers. The broad language of the NAFTA prudential carve-out provides state parties with wide discretion to take a number of regulatory measures that may substantially restrict cross-border trade in financial services and relax certain obligations under the treaty. For instance, U.S. bank regulators, acting on authority under the U.S. Patriot Act, can impose special measures against Mexican banks that utilize the U.S. correspondent banking system if the US. secretary of the Treasury designates Mexico as having taken inadequate regulatory measures to curb money laundering and terrorist financing (Alexander, 2002).

In addition, NAFTA provides a negotiating framework for its signatory states to agree to periods of phased implementation and to schedules of liberalization commitments for various financial services sectors. NAFTA allows state parties to list specific exemptions and limitations of their obligations for specific financial sectors. But it is important to note that if the state does not specifically list an exemption or a limitation of an obligation to a specific financial services sector, it is required to comply fully with the treaty's requirements for that sector. This requirement to provide a positive list of exemptions and limitations in order to depart from obligations under the treaty is the opposite of the approach in the GATS where states are required to liberalize their financial sectors on a national treatment or market access basis only if they have expressly committed to do so in their schedules of commitments. This negative obligation approach under the GATS leads to a more gradual implementation of liberalization commitments and allows states to retain more control over when they will implement their national treatment and market access commitments. In contrast, under NAFTA, full liberalization is presumed to have taken place unless a state negotiates a specific exemption or limitation to such commitments. Such a negotiating framework favors states with a high level of expertise and understanding regarding their trade policy objectives and militates against states with incomplete understanding of the implications of their liberalization commitments.

The NAFTA negotiating framework has allowed Mexico to move at a slower pace regarding its liberalization commitments than have Canada and the United States. Although Mexico has agreed to allow Canadian and U.S. financial institutions to establish wholly owned Mexican subsidiaries in banking, securities, and insurance, it has maintained certain safeguard provisions that include aggregate market share limits and individual market share caps. For example, the aggregate market share limit for both Canadian and U.S. banks is 15 percent of the total capital in the Mexican banking industry. Similarly, in the securities industry, the aggregate market share limit for individual Canadian or U.S. firms is 20 percent of the total capital in the Mexican securities industry. Regarding bank acquisitions, Mexico has listed a limitation on the acquisition of Mexican banks by Canadian or U.S. financial service providers if the acquisition results in the Canadian or U.S. firm owning one or more Mexican commercial banks with authorized capital in excess of 4 percent of the total capital of all commercial banks in Mexico. This limitation has the effect of protecting the four largest Mexican banks from being taken over by Canadian or U.S. firms. In the insurance sector, aggregate and individual market share limits have been virtually phased out.

Although NAFTA has allowed Mexico to follow a more gradual path toward trade liberalization in financial services, it has essentially been driven by the expansionist tendencies of U.S. financial conglomerates and their desire to tap the growing Mexican market. NAFTA's free-trade principles and its emphasis on host-state regulatory control will lead to further liberalization of cross-border financial trade in the NAFTA area. The need for Canadian and Mexican banks to operate in the U.S. dollar market will mean that further financial liberalization will inevitably lead to further domination by U.S. financial institutions and firms of NAFTA financial markets. U.S. banks, securities firms, and insurance companies will by and large have a competitive advantage that will allow them to make further gains in global financial markets. Moreover, the heightened concern with financial crime and increased risk sensitivity of capital standards will lead to more complex bank regulatory standards and compliance controls that will put Mexican banks at a cost disadvantage vis-à-vis their U.S. and Canadian counterparts.

Regulatory Impact and the Host-State Principle In contrast to the home-country control principle in the European Union, NAFTA relies on the host-country principle, which places great emphasis on the dominance of national regulatory standards in the local jurisdiction where the financial institution operates. As discussed, although chapter 14 of NAFTA creates certain obligations for signatory states to liberalize their financial service markets, host-country regulatory principles will be controlling for the local operations of a financial firm from another NAFTA state. The host-country control principle is highlighted even more with the prudential exception of article 1410, which allows states to depart from their NAFTA obligations in the pursuit of prudential regulatory measures or policies. The broad discretion afforded to the local regulator under prudential exception reinforces the regulatory autonomy of the host state and makes it extremely difficult for another state or private party in a NAFTA state to challenge the adoption of prudential regulatory measures. This will reinforce the power and dominance of U.S. regulators to require Canadian and Mexican financial firms to comply with a number of U.S. requirements taken ostensibly as prudential measures but that have the ultimate effect of making it more difficult for Canadian and Mexican firms to penetrate the U.S. market. Examples of this already exist with respect to compliance with the 1999 U.S. Financial Services Modernization Act.

Each federal state party of NAFTA must ensure that states or provinces do not violate the national treatment or most-favored-nation standards. This means that each party cannot treat another NAFTA party less favorably than it treats a third party (either a NAFTA or non-NAFTA country).[88] There are two aspects to national treatment: (1) verification of whether the practice of national treatment in fact matches the principle; and (2) the relationship between national treatment and reciprocal treatment that involves national treatment given by country A to banks of country B and whether such treatment is economically equivalent to the national treatment accorded by country B to banks of country A. This second point is significant because U.S. banking and securities regulation is far more stringent than corresponding regulations in Canada, Mexico, and the European Union. As a result, national treatment granted by the United States is not comparable to reciprocal treatment granted by other states. The United States's leading position in international financial markets and the reserve currency status of the U.S. dollar enhance the bargaining power of U.S. regulators to insist on higher standards of regulation that are applied through the national treatment principle.

It is important therefore to note that national treatment and MFN status do not mean reciprocal treatment. The discrepancy between national treatment and reciprocal treatment was directly addressed by the Second Banking Directive, which directs the EC Commission to make proposals to the Council of Ministers to obtain in other countries "effective access comparable to that granted by the Commission to credit institutions from that third country."[89] The negotiating leverage that the United States exerts because of its large financial market and the role of the U.S. dollar has enabled it to prevail in most situations in rejecting EU demands for reciprocal treatment.

One of the weaknesses of the national treatment principle is that financial service providers may undertake regulatory arbitrage. For example, all things being equal, financial service providers tend to migrate from high- to low-regulation areas. On the other hand, the search for areas with less regulation is constrained by the customers' desire to purchase products from stable financial institutions. Reputable banks often can pay lower interest rates on deposits than banks with weaker reputations. A bank can build reputation not only by maintaining a higher ratio of reserves to deposits but also by choosing a jurisdiction that offers a credible deposit insurance system and where strict prudential supervision is applied. For example, the competitive threat to the U.S. banking system that is posed by offshore financial centres in the U.S. dollar deposit market is limited by reputational considerations (Herring and Litan, 1995: 81). On the other hand, the growth of the Eurodollar market in the early stages was only marginally constrained by reputational considerations. The highest interest rates on dollar deposits available in London and Luxembourg were the result not of higher expected default risk of the financial institutions but of U.S. regulations that imposed ceilings on deposit interest rates for U.S. financial institutions in U.S. territory.

A crucial distinction should be made therefore between regulation that enhances reputation from regulation that is outright anticompetitive. Differences in regulatory burden due to differences in deposit insurance and quality of supervision enhance the reputation of the banking system and need not lead to regulatory arbitrage, whereas interest rate ceilings do. This is important to understand because high-regulation countries that adopt the host-country principle fear a race to the lowest standard and seek international coordination of regulation to minimize the effects of regulatory arbitrage.

CONCLUSION

The increasing integration of global banking systems and the further consolidation of payments systems around a few key currencies suggest the
need for a more concerted global governance structure for financial regulation. In this regard, the present international legal framework of financial regulation does not cover most of the relevant activities involving the
regulation of systemic risk. The International Monetary Fund provides
short-term liquidity for members experiencing payment imbalances and
can provide rescue packages for qualifying members in financial crises.
The IMF and the World Bank use their conditionality programs as leverage to induce borrowing members to adopt financial reforms that affect
systemic stability. Although the IMF and the Bank perform surveillance
over their member states, they do not have any authority to set standards
for prudential supervision or to require their membership to adopt such
standards except as part of a conditionality program. Moreover, the Fund
has no jurisdiction to regulate cross-border flows of capital, unless the
capital flow is necessary to secure a transfer for current international transactions.

The World Trade Organization plays a more peripheral role in the regulatory debate. The GATS requires WTO members to open their markets
according to national schedules of commitments. It has jurisdiction over
capital movements only when they are ancillary to cross-border services
transactions. Members may depart from their liberalization commitments
for prudential reasons. The WTO has not defined the term "prudential
reasons," but it may look for guidance from other international supervisory bodies, such as the Basel Committee. This should raise a number of
concerns for most WTO members on the grounds of accountability and
legitimacy because they played little, or no, role in creating the Capital
Accord or the core principles of banking supervision.

Despite the existing gaps in the international regulatory system, the
international and regional organizations and institutions discussed in this
chapter have made significant progress in allowing states to coordinate
their regulatory actions and policies to improve their management of systemic risk. Effective and efficient international financial regulation necessitates close cooperation and coordination among states within a broad
multilateral institutional framework. International economic organizations provide an important component of this framework, but the existing
framework lacks coherence, accountability, and legitimacy and thus merits restructuring in order to achieve the objectives of efficient regulation.
Indeed, reforming the governance structure of the IFIs would redefine the
limits and possibilities of their activities in the area of financial regulation.
By establishing more effective, accountable, and legitimate decision-
making structures, they will enhance international financial standards and
thereby improve the overall efficiency of financial regulation. Now that

the international legal framework of financial regulation has been analyzed with respect to its legal scope and governance structure, we turn to possible theoretical explanations as to how international norms and standards emerge in state regulation and whether it is necessary to have a binding international legal framework to regulate systemic risk.

4

International Soft Law and the Formation of Binding International Financial Regulation

Most international standards and rules for banking regulation and supervision have evolved from a purely nonbinding and voluntary role to an increasingly precise and obligatory status backed by both official and market incentives and sanctions. This has been demonstrated by the purportedly voluntary international financial standard-setting process in Basel, which was originally intended to apply only to the G10 countries but has now been extended by the IMF and the World Bank to most of their member countries through surveillance and conditionality programs. The haphazard development of these international standards and their uneven application to developed and developing countries has produced a vast, but loosely coordinated, international financial regulatory regime that is ill equipped to deal with the threats posed by today's globalized financial markets.

As discussed in chapter 3, binding international legal rules govern only limited areas of the international financial system. Most of the international rules, guidelines, standards, and other arrangements that govern financial regulation are not of a legally binding nature and are therefore generally referred to as "international soft law." This chapter examines the theoretical framework of international soft law and how it embraces both *legally nonbinding* and *binding* rules and standards of international financial regulation. The theoretical framework adopted extends the analysis beyond traditional sources and principles of public international law to identify other relevant sources of state economic conduct that influence the development of international norms and standards of banking regulation.

The chapter analyzes international soft law and the formation of binding international norms of financial regulation. As discussed in earlier chapters, international financial regulation may include a wide range of normative and institutional arrangements, from binding "hard" law (i.e., WTO treaty obligations) to various forms of nonbinding soft law rules (Basel Accord), to arrangements that share some characteristics of hard and soft law but are not legally binding (IMF Agreement). This spectrum of arrangements has occurred in other areas of international economic regulation, such as the efforts of the Organization for Economic Cooperation and Development to devise multinational standards of corporate governance and antibribery and corruption standards. This chapter suggests that international soft law has served as a flexible mechanism to develop international norms and standards of banking regulation, but increasing integration in global financial markets requires more concerted efforts to ensure that international standards apply to all countries and financial systems and that the process of standard setting is accountable and legitimate. We examine the role of international soft law in banking regulation and in particular its application under the Basel Accord and the Financial Action Task Force's antimoney-laundering standards. We argue that the particular form of international soft law that has emerged for banking regulation violates principles of global governance because the standard setting is controlled by the G10 and OECD countries and that other countries are subject to those standards through a variety of official and market incentives that undermine efficiency and legitimacy.

Although soft law once served as a useful instrument for developing international standards of banking regulation, globalized financial markets require a more coherent international legal framework that more effectively manages the use of official incentives by international economic organizations and channels the pressures of global financial markets to induce more efficient financial regulation. This will require greater institutional linkages between the IFIs and international economic organizations so that a greater number of countries can participate in international standard setting. Discriminatory trade barriers imposed by G10 countries to restrict market access to banks from jurisdictions that do not follow G10 regulatory standards should be reconsidered in light of different approaches to prudential regulation. Moreover, more empirical data are needed to analyze the extent to which certain prudential regulatory regimes attract foreign investment and foreign entry into the financial sector. As proposed in chapter 5, a multilateral treaty framework may be necessary to ensure that most states that regulate the major financial systems adhere to accepted principles of capital adequacy, payment system regulation, and antimoney-laundering requirements. This would promote a level playing field among competitors and enhance market confidence and regulatory compliance. Moreover, it would improve the pricing of financial risk and lead to more efficient and stable financial markets.

SOFT LAW AND THE INADEQUACIES OF PUBLIC INTERNATIONAL LAW

An analysis of the concept of international soft law must be done within the context of an examination of the sources of public international law. There is a growing recognition of the inadequacy of the traditional sources of public international law, as enumerated in Article 38 (1)(a)–(d) of the Statute of the International Court of Justice,[1] to explain and describe the normative development of many areas of interstate relations (Wellens and Borchardt, 1989). The traditional sources of international law are classified as follows: (a) treaties that establish rights and obligations expressly recognized by states; (b) international custom as evidence of a general practice of states and accepted by states as law; (c) general legal principles of the world's leading legal systems; and (d) subsidiary sources, including judicial and arbitral decisions (ICJ Statute). The two most cited sources are treaties and international custom (customary international law) (Oppenheim's, 1996).[2] Treaties create legally binding rights and obligations between states and can take the form of multilateral, regional, or bilateral agreements. Many treaties (though not all) contain procedures for enforcement or dispute resolution that allow state responsibility to be invoked under a treaty for breach of obligation that may result in liability and/or reparation.

International custom takes the form of customary rules or principles that must be evidenced by (1) a general or uniform state practice with respect to the particular rule or obligation, and (2) accepted by states as a legal obligation (*opinio juris*) (Ibid.: 26–27).[3] State practice forms the basis of customary international law. It consists of patterns of state behavior or conduct that contain both material and subjective elements that are necessary for a state (or states) to form or maintain legally binding customary rules (Mendelson, 1995: 177). The material element takes the form of actual deeds (e.g., administrative decisions and the adoption of regulatory rules) that are observable and manifest, while the subjective element consists of a state's attitude or intent, which may present itself in certain acts or behavior, such as official statements by heads of state or governments, diplomatic correspondence, or votes at international organizations, that provide evidence of a state agreeing to or believing it has a legal obligation.[4] The actual practice of states is the material element of state practice, while the subjective element consists in the state's consent or belief that its performance or omission, or that of other states, is required by international law. To be legally effective, it is not sufficient for the state's belief to be evidenced by passive acceptance or acquiescence; there must be evidence of an active and deliberate effort to reaffirm or develop a rule of international law.

The absence of a binding international legal commitment to implement the Basel Accord and other international financial standards has taken these standards outside the scope of customary international law and treaties. Nevertheless, more than 100 countries claim to have implemented the 1988 Capital Accord and are undertaking transition arrangements to implement Basel II. It should not be forgotten that the European Community has incorporated the Capital Accord into EU law and has committed itself to implement Basel II, as well. The growing consistency of state practice with the Basel Accord and other international financial standards suggests that it is possible to have a uniform practice of states without *opinio juris*, that is, a general practice of states which does not have as its motive the formation of customary rules of international law.[5] In this sense, the subjective element of state practice does not contain the belief that it has a legal obligation. The absence of a legal obligation provides regulators and standard setters with the necessary flexibility to respond rapidly to developments in financial markets and to implement nonbinding standards in a particular manner that suits the needs of their jurisdictions. This is why international soft law will remain viable as an instrument for reforming international financial regulation.

Other sources of international law include general principles of law whose validity derives from the world's leading legal systems and from subsidiary sources such as judicial decisions and the works of leading publicists. General principles of law have derived mainly from private law principles, such as estoppel, reparation, and jurisdiction (Harris, 1991). The growing importance of public administrative law, however, in most jurisdictions means that commonly accepted principles of public law can potentially qualify as general principles of law and thereby become sources of international law. This appears to be taking place in a number of countries where there is growing convergence in public law principles with respect to banking and financial regulation that has been influenced substantially by international soft law principles. In fact, the standards of the Basel Committee and the Core Principles of banking supervision have directly influenced and shaped the development of national banking law principles, including liability rules for senior officers and directors and even the rules that define tier 1 and 2 capital. This dramatic convergence of domestic banking law principles could arguably constitute a future source of international law.[6]

As a general matter, however, the sources of public international law are increasingly viewed as unsatisfactory for explaining the variety of international obligations and commitments undertaken by states in many areas of international relations. This is especially true in finance, the environment, telecommunications and technology, and the regulation of multinational corporate groups where legally nonbinding international standards and codes play a prominent role in governing state conduct. The enormous expansion of activities by international organizations and standard-setting bodies and the increasing use by states of informal, legally nonbinding agreements and instruments to mediate and regulate their foreign relations have marked a dramatic shift away from formal international lawmaking and toward informal soft law techniques of standard setting and implementation. As a result, state behavior and conduct have become increasingly influenced in a "permissive, prescriptive and prohibitive way" by an unprecedented number of international nonconventional or nontreaty agreements, which have been adopted by states acting through a variety of international organizations and bodies.

INTERNATIONAL SOFT LAW AND THE FORMATION OF BINDING PRINCIPLES AND NORMS

International soft law refers to legal norms, principles, codes of conduct, and transactional rules of state practice that are recognized in either formal or informal multilateral agreements (Wellens and Borchardt, 1989). Soft law generally presumes consent to basic standards and norms of state practice, but without the *opinio juris* necessary to form binding obligations under customary international law. On the basis of these characteristics, soft law may be defined as an international rule created by a group of specially affected states that have a common intent to voluntarily observe the content of such rule with a view of potentially adopting it into national law or regulation. Another important characteristic of soft law is that political bargaining controls the ongoing interpretation and application of rules to state parties and their nationals.

International soft law generally provides flexibility for states in taking measures to regulate complex and sensitive areas of international relations. Soft law permits arrangements whereby states can voluntarily implement standards and practices that are generated on the international level through informal consultations and negotiations among states and international organizations. The soft law process in the formation of international norms of state behavior can be crucial in finding the right mix between hard and soft standards by which to regulate particular issue areas. This is particularly important in determining what role, if any, soft law plays in facilitating the development of international standards of banking supervision. These nonbinding international norms shape and constrain the regulatory practices of major states and may eventually be implemented into national law in a manner that, at least in theory, respects states' sovereignty and independence.

The existence of international rules and obligations outside traditionally recognized legal sources (i.e., treaty or uniform customary state practice) has proved controversial among international economic lawyers. But their importance in influencing state regulatory practice has been recognized by leading international financial lawyers (Gold, 1982). Indeed, while evaluating whether certain IMF currency regulations constituted soft law, Gold defined soft law as:

> [T]he essential ingredient of soft law is an expectation that the states accepting these instruments will take their contents seriously and will give them some measure of respect. Certain other elements are postulated. First, a common intent is implicit in the soft law as formulated, and it is this

common intent, when elucidated, that is to be respected. Second, the legitimacy of the soft law as promulgated is not challenged. Third, soft law is not deprived of its quality as law because failure to observe it is not in itself a breach of obligation. Fourth, conduct that respects soft law cannot be deemed invalid. (Gold, 1982: 156)

On the basis of this definition, the essential elements of international soft law are: (1) whether there is in fact a common intent among the parties that certain principles be implemented and observed, and (2) whether it is desirable to transform these principles into hard law. In order to accomplish the second element, one must take into account the various interconnections between soft law norms and national and regional processes by which they may be implemented as "hard" law.

Gold's definition of soft law has been applied to international banking regulation to hold that a particular instrument or report may become soft law if it has at least a quasi-legitimacy to it derived from the collective intent of those involved in the preparation of that instrument or report, and if the standards and principles advocated therein ought to be observed (Norton, 1995: 216). According to this definition, the normative content of the standard or principle in question depends on its legitimacy, which derives from the collective intent of those parties who adopted it. One can infer that the collective intent of the parties that adopted the standard must be based on their consent to be subject to that standard. It would be illegitimate, therefore, for a state to be expected to comply with a standard if its consent was not obtained beforehand. A state's consent can be based on proactive conduct or passive acquiescence. In either case, it should be voluntary and not obtained through duress or coercion. The emphasis on consent as evidence of the intent of states to recognize international soft law obligation is analogous to voluntarist notions of international law that emphasize the importance of state consent for determining the validity of international legal obligations.

The concept of soft law has been analyzed from a number of perspectives and disciplines, which reveal its complexity as a social science concept. International lawyers have invoked legal doctrine to analyze international soft law principles by focusing on the main elements of a legal system, which are *precision* of rules, degree of *obligation*, *delegation* of authority for adjudicating compliance, and *sanctions* and enforcement (Wellens and Borchardt, 1989; Abbott et al., 2000).[7] These elements are not static but evolve and develop according to interstate relations and state practice. These elements are often used to evaluate the legal scope and effect of a state's international obligations and commitments.

Precision of rules or standards is important for determining the content and scope of a state's legal rights and obligations. For instance, the level of precision in rules or standards can limit a state's discretion in determining how it should comply with a particular obligation or commitment. Soft law rules that are more precise and specific tend to be more obliging for the addressee of the obligation, even though there may be no international legal obligation to comply, because the expectations are more clearly defined in the rule. In contrast, vagueness and ambiguity in a rule increase the ability of a state to interpret its entitlements and obligations in a biased manner that may depart from the original intent of the parties to the agreement. The lack of precision in soft law rules therefore can permit states to avoid their commitments more easily and potentially undermine the carrying out of the agreement by all parties. In politically sensitive areas, such as arms control or banking regulation, states may deliberately pursue vague agreements for the purpose of maintaining ultimate discretion regarding the interpretation and performance of their commitments. The lack of precision of a rule may also result from the rule's immaturity and from the state's inexperience in using the rule in practice. For contentious issues, however, the optimal precision of the rule may require a sufficient degree of ambiguity that respects political disagreements but which can form the basis for future negotiation. Too much precision in rule type may be inappropriate, especially where states are uncertain regarding how their obligations will be interpreted in the future. A sufficient level of ambiguity in the rule allows states to learn by doing and to extend the level of precision once they are aware of the implications of their obligations.

The second element concerns the degree of *obligation*, which can extend from legally binding obligations of a precise and specific nature to vague, hortatory norms of a divergent nature "which do not create enforceable rights and obligations" but nevertheless create commitments and expectations in softer form.[8] A form of soft obligation can arise from legally nonbinding commitments that provide an indirect form of pressure on states that may restrict their freedom of action but nevertheless create no binding international legal obligations in a strict sense. In contrast, a legally binding obligation under international law can be created only by state parties or international organizations that have the competence to do so, and the subjects that are bound by such obligation must acknowledge the source of these obligations as authoritative (Schachter, 1977). Most international norms and principles do not fall under international law and therefore create a softer form of obligation or commitment that shapes and influences state behavior. Although it can be argued that the content of soft law lacks any type of obligation, the better view holds that various dimensions of soft law contain different degrees of obligation or "loose commitments" (Wellens and Borchardt, 1989). The degree of obligation often depends on the level of precision of the rule or principle, and therefore the elements of precision and obligation can be mutually dependent in certain cases.

The third element is *delegation*, which involves the extent to which states accept third-party resolution of their claims or disputes. This may also involve rule interpretation, rule making, and related fact-finding tasks. The extent of delegation to third parties to adjudicate claims or to determine rights and obligations may vary according to institutional structures. In public international law, rights and obligations are usually recognized by arbitral tribunals and judicial bodies as the legal basis for their decisions. In contrast, international soft law instruments often provide that disputes and claims will be resolved by negotiations between the parties and not adjudicated by independent third parties (Aust, 2000). In the absence of third-party dispute resolution, states and the relevant international organizations are primarily responsible for assessing compliance with both hard and soft international norms and for holding other states accountable for complying with their commitments. A higher level of delegation to independent bodies to resolve disputes suggests a more legalized international regime, while lesser delegation suggests a softer, less legal framework that relies more on political negotiations and compromise to resolve disputes.

The fourth element involves *sanctions*, both direct and indirect, which can be defined as the withholding of a benefit or the imposition of a penalty on a state or its nationals for certain conduct that may not comply with international soft law norms. It should be recalled that sanctions that arise from the enforcement of rights and obligations under international law are not applicable in the soft law context, and therefore state responsibility does not arise in a formal sense. International soft law, however, provides various degrees of *soft liability* that may involve procedural requirements, such as reporting and consultation and mandatory negotiations to provide good-faith interpretations of soft law norms and rules (Seidl-Hohenveldern, 1979). As discussed later, international financial soft law provides a particular type of *soft liability* in the form of official and market incentives and indirect sanctions that play a significant role in influencing state economic conduct. The intensity and scope of these sanctions varies according to a number of factors that apply differently to different states. There is a lack of uniformity across states in the application of sanctions for the same type of breach of a particular norm.

On the basis of this descriptive framework, we find that there is no sharp division between hard and soft law; rather, a fluid spectrum exists through which the elements of *precision, obligation, delegation,* and *sanctions* can evolve at different degrees and sometimes independent of each other. International soft law norms provide a system of rules and principles in which these elements are either fully developed or undeveloped to various degrees. For instance, states may deliberately pursue policies and reach agreements that are initially nonbinding in nature but that may later develop into binding obligations that reflect increased trust and coordination between states in particular issue areas. But, as the collapse of the Bretton Woods par value system demonstrates, this process can switch into reverse and lead to a softening and even a dissolution of international legal obligations if states so decide.

The process of forming binding international standards of banking regulation involves testing various combinations of these elements to determine the extent and scope of soft law. International soft law can provide a flexible mechanism for determining the proper mix of soft and hard law to regulate a particular issue area. As a conceptual matter, the process of devising international norms and rules for banking regulation has involved a particular form of international soft law that has precise, non-binding norms that are generated through consultations and negotiations among the major state regulators. This particular form of international soft law has provided the necessary political flexibility for states to adopt international rules and standards into their national legal systems in a manner that accommodates the sovereign authority of the nation-state.

The conceptual framework discussed here suggests that, in devising international economic norms and institutions, states should adopt flexible combinations of hard and soft law to address particular issues areas of international concern. For example, states should define the specific threat to the international system and then develop a political consensus on what measures should be adopted at the national level. It is important to agree on the degree of precision and obligation of the standards adopted and equally important to avoid an inflexibly uniform implementation approach that relies excessively on a uniform framework that does not recognize diverse economic and legal structures.

Moreover, it should be mentioned that international soft law can have particular legal effects and consequences in national and regional legal systems. International soft law may serve as a basis for ongoing negotiations and consultations between states within existing institutional structures. Soft law that is promulgated in written agreements may contain such hortatory language as "all states shall endeavor to cooperate," which can have the effect of removing a state's discretion not to cooperate from its domestic jurisdiction. Further, soft law rules and principles can be used to interpret treaty provisions or customary international law and can serve to shape and constrain the development of legally relevant state practice. International soft law has taken on a particular form in banking regulation, where the leading developed countries have promulgated voluntary international agreements and instruments that do not constitute traditional sources of international law but that aim to commit all states to adopt and implement these standards into their own regulatory systems. For instance, the Basel Capital Accord and the Core Principles on banking supervision have taken on a particular international status that serves as a normative basis for the adoption of national legislation to implement these standards into regulatory practice. Most states commit themselves to implement the Accord and the Core Principles into national law. The European Community has committed itself to implement the Capital Accord into EU law through directives.

Although international soft law has been criticized as a contradiction in terms and as a backdoor attempt to render legal certain areas of international relations that should remain political, it provides states with a flexible mechanism to develop norms and standards in complex and politically sensitive issue areas where the benefits of cooperation and of devising standards to regulate state behavior are significant and can reduce the transaction costs for states in pursuing their objectives. Soft law provides states with incentives to negotiate and exchange information, which can lead to a more informed understanding of state interests and provide the basis for more effective and efficient cooperative frameworks. States can use particular combinations of "hard" and "soft" law to regulate their behavior and to promote international norm building. Indeed, international soft law can arise from agreements that would otherwise not be possible in a treaty or other enforceable agreement because of the existence of fundamental differences among states and their reluctance to be bound by specific legal obligations in technical areas of law that significantly impact their national interests.

THE FORMATION OF BINDING INTERNATIONAL SOFT LAW NORMS: THE CASE OF THE BASEL COMMITTEE AND THE FINANCIAL ACTION TASK FORCE

In the area of international banking supervision, the formation of international standards of financial regulation has involved various types of "soft law" principles and rules that have been adopted by the national banking regulators of the G10 countries under the aegis of the Basel Committee. These soft law agreements have the overriding objective of reducing systemic risk in the international banking system and of promoting competitive equality among banking institutions. They do this by exhorting their members and other countries where international banks operate to cooperate in the exchange of information and to coordinate regulatory activities such as setting capital adequacy standards for all internationally active banks.

Although the Basel rules and standards are not enforceable under international law, they are sustained by a number of official and market measures that make the standards sanctionable without losing their soft law status (Giovanoli, 2002). For example, the International Monetary Fund uses the Basel principles as a benchmark of good banking regulation against which IMF members are evaluated under Article IV surveillance programs. The IMF also has discretion to make compliance with the Capital Accord and other international banking standards a condition for receiving financial aid. Similarly, the World Bank uses the Basel Accord as a benchmark in its lending programs, and has stated that "the international community is likely to expect all countries to adopt and implement the Basel Committee's recommendations" (2001). Moreover, market forces may impose a sanction in the form of a higher risk premium on capital investment for countries that fail to demonstrate adherence to Basel standards. It is not surprising, therefore, that more than one hundred countries claim to have adopted the Basel Accord into their national banking regulations (Hawkins and Turner, 2000), even though most countries exercise little or no influence in its promulgation. The use of sanctions by international organizations and of capital cost penalties by financial markets undermines the so-called voluntary nature of the Basel framework. Moreover, the extent to which official and market sanctions are used to pressure states (especially in developing and emerging market economies) to comply with so-called voluntary international agreements raises the important issue of the nature of a state's obligation to implement and comply with international financial standards.

Most countries are exposed to certain disciplines and pressures to adhere to the Basel Accord. The most important of these are official sector discipline, market discipline, market access requirements, reputation, international spillovers, and economies of scale (Ward, 2002; Giovanoli, 2002). Alexander and Ward (2004) have examined how these factors influence the development of international banking norms.

Official Sector Discipline

Official sector discipline can take the form of IMF/World Bank financial assistance programs that require or induce the recipient countries to make economic and regulatory adjustments as a condition for receiving aid. IMF conditionality programs often take the form of standby arrangements whereby the Fund permits a member country to make purchases (drawings) from the IMF General Resources Account up to a specified amount and over a period of time in return for the member's promise to observe the terms of the arrangement (IMF, 2004b). The terms of the arrangement may require the recipient country to adopt and implement international "best practices" of banking supervision as a condition for making drawings. The World Bank also negotiates conditions in its Financial Sector Adjustment Loans that may include the recipient country promising to adhere to best international standards, such as the Core Principles for Effective Banking Supervision (BCBS, 1997). The Basel Committee's Core Principles Liaison Group (CPLG) adopted the Core Principles in 1997 as international benchmarks for bank regulators. The IMF and World Bank often conduct Core Principles Assessments (CPAs) for members undergoing Article IV surveillance programs and for determining whether a member qualifies for further drawings under standby arrangements or other financial assistance programs (IMF, 2000b).[9]

The Core Principles are stated broadly with a view to giving states flexibility in implementation and interpretation. For instance, core principle 8 states:

> Banking supervisors must be satisfied that banks establish and adhere to adequate policies, practices, and procedures for evaluating the quality of assets and the adequacy of loan loss reserves.

In contrast, Core Principle 6 provides a more prescriptive rule that encourages states to set minimum capital adequacy standards for "internationally active banks" that "must not be less than those established in the

Basel Capital Accord." For example, an emergency IMF recapitalization program for a member's banking sector would likely involve a CPA to ensure that the country's regulatory regime required banks to adhere to the Capital Accord (IMF, 2004c). Basel II, however, will create ambiguity regarding implementation of the Accord because of the discretion it grants regulators under pillars 1 and 2. Indeed, it is not clear how much discretion the IMF and World Bank will give to countries subject to a CPA, and whether this may lead to significant differences in implementation between countries depending on the terms of their IFI financial assistance program. Although the generality of the core principles can probably be reconciled with the regulatory discretion granted under Basel II, there exists potential for conflict between, on the one hand, implementation of the core principles and Basel II, and, on the other hand, adherence to official sector programs.

Although the World Bank continues to use financial sector adjustment loans to influence state regulatory policy, it began in the 1990s to utilize conditionality programs less for prudential regulation and more for bank privatization and recapitalization programs (Cull, 1997). This research shows that 63 percent of the adjustment loans before 1990 had conditions related to banking supervision, while 88 percent had conditions related to prudential regulation. In contrast, between 1990 and 1997, 79 percent of the loans had conditions related to banking supervision, while 71 percent had conditions related to prudential regulation. The percentage of loans listing conditions for banking supervision and prudential regulation was less than the percentage of loans listing privatization and recapitalization, the latter two both exceeding 90 percent. Moreover, since the debate over Basel II began, the World Bank has expressed a concern that developing countries may not have the proper incentives to adopt and implement Basel II (Ward, 2002) and that this could serve as a focal point for future Bank conditionality programs. The significant role played by the World Bank in overseeing implementation of so-called voluntary international banking norms calls into question the legitimacy of the standard setting process and raises important issues regarding the desirability of exporting international financial standards that are devised by the rich countries for the most sophisticated financial markets to developing countries.

Market Discipline

The objective of market discipline would be to show that compliance with international financial standards would lower funding costs for the sovereign and its financial institutions. But Kenen (2001) has criticized the use of market discipline on the basis of two reports by the Financial Stability Forum (2000a, 2000b) that suggest that market participants and ratings agencies would likely be concerned with absolute compliance with international standards and less concerned with a country's progress toward implementation. The FSF reports state that official incentives are required because there is no guarantee that market participants will always base their decisions on the need to comply with international standards. Moreover, market participants will always have an incentive to focus on the upside of risk because of principal-agent problems and may be unconcerned with aggregate losses. This may lead them to avoid focusing on a country's compliance or progress in implementation and may lead many weak financial systems to ignore the need to upgrade their regulatory standards and to improve implementation, which may lead to significant negative externalities for international financial markets (Kenen, 2001).[10] Market discipline will at best encourage countries to state that they have implemented international standards, even if they have not in fact implemented them.

Restricting Market Access

A national authority's decision to restrict market access is likely to influence more countries to adopt international standards. For example, the Basel Concordat provides that host countries review the supervisory and regulatory regimes of home countries with a view to determining whether the home country regime is adequate. The Core Principles and the Capital Accord have defined "adequate" as being in compliance with the Basel Committee framework and other relevant international standards. In the European Economic Area (EEA), the Second Banking Coordination Directive allows member states to restrict access to third-country banks (i.e., branches or agencies) outside the EEA whose home country regimes do not meet EU standards, but in no case can they treat non-EEA banks more favorably than banks based in EEA states.

To this end, the U.S. Financial Services Modernization Act of 1999 and the Foreign Bank Supervision Enhancement Act of 1991 grant the Federal Reserve authority to issue banking licenses to foreign banks only if they are "subject to comprehensive supervision or regulation on a consolidated basis by the appropriate authorities in its home country" and if they are "well-capitalized and well-managed" on a global basis. U.S. regulators have discretion to relax the requirement to permit authorization of banks not subject to comprehensive regulation where "the appropriate authorities in the home country of the foreign bank are actively working to establish arrangements for the consolidated supervision" of the bank.[11] U.S. regulators can withdraw the license if they determine that the home country regulator has failed to make "demonstrable progress" in establishing comprehensive supervision or regulation of the foreign bank. Moreover, under the Financial Services Modernization Act of 1999, the Federal Reserve has authority to evaluate the quality of the home country supervisor, including an assessment of whether it applies and enforces international standards such as the Capital Accord, before it decides whether to permit a bank incorporated or based in that jurisdiction to conduct universal banking activities in the United States as a financial holding company.

The EU Financial Conglomerates Directive requires U.K. authorities to judge the equivalence of the supervisory regime of a third country (non-EU) state. If the third country regime fails the equivalence test, the U.K. authorities are required to apply its regime to the global operations of the third country financial firm as a condition for the issuance of a license permitting the firm to operate in the U.K. market.

U.S., U.K., and EU regulatory practice in this area has been supported by the FSF report (2000b) that states:

> National authorities should be encouraged to give greater consideration to a foreign jurisdiction's observance of relevant standards as one of the factors in making market access decisions.

This means that the supervisory regimes of developing countries and other non-G10 states will be judged adequate if they adopt a regime that is at least as strict as, but not necessarily identical to, the Basel framework and other relevant international standards. As a practical regulatory policy, the best way to gain access is for them to adopt the international benchmark. In addition, banks in non-G10 countries may have an incentive to lobby their governments to seek adoption of the Basel framework because such a comprehensive regulatory regime may limit entry, and thus reduce, competition in the banking market. The type of banks that would seek the adoption of Basel regulations would normally be larger, more sophisticated banks with the resources to comply with the requirements. They would be in a strong market position to limit competition and foreign access to their markets.[12]

The other option for a bank based in a non-G10 jurisdiction that seeks to gain access to the G10 markets is for it to establish a subsidiary in the host state. Indeed, the U.K. FSA requires the banks from countries whose regulatory regimes are judged inadequate by the U.K. authorities to incorporate locally (Ward, 2002a). If the foreign bank already has a branch operation but its home country regulator is later judged inadequate, it will have to convert to a subsidiary or exit the market.

Market Signaling

Many countries will perceive adherence to the Basel standards as a mark of good regulatory practice that will enhance their reputation with market participants and help them to obtain lower-cost funding from banks and the capital markets. Banks and other financial firms that operate outside the G10 will adopt Basel II and other international standards, not necessarily because there will be capital savings or because it may be more convenient for risk management purposes but because they will want to signal to the world that they have moved to the latest, most sophisticated models and have received the approval of the G10 regulators.

Moreover, regulators will want to be viewed as sophisticated, as well and, even if they are reluctant to implement the Basel framework because of its high costs, they may be induced to do so for signaling reasons. If we assume that here are two types of states, one for which the adoption of the Capital Accord will be much more costly because its regulatory and financial system is at a lower level of sophistication and another for which adoption of the Accord will require relatively lower compliance costs because of the sophisticated nature of its economy, then both types of countries will be able to signal that they are sophisticated by implementing the model. There are obvious inefficiencies in such an approach, which does not allow the less sophisticated jurisdiction to adopt a framework that more adequately suits its stage of economic and financial development.

One solution could be to allow non-G10 regulators, for signaling purposes, to implement "a simpler and harsher version" of the Basel framework (Ward, 2002), one that would not require, for instance, that non-G10 banks implement some of the more complex and technical requirements of pillar 1 of Basel II. In the area of financial crime, banks would be allowed to adopt less onerous disclosure and transparency standards under the FATF Forty Recommendations that would reflect the degree of development and sophistication of their economies. They would therefore be able to signal to the world that they operate adequate antimoney-laundering controls.

Cross-Border Externalities

The spillover of negative externalities from one jurisdiction to another may arise from the implementation of a regime that has more relaxed standards than the G10 regimes and thus may lead banks to arbitrage between regimes. Regimes with perceived lower standards will then collect underpriced financial assets. This is a type of adverse selection.

Moreover, regarding Basel II, if banks on the IRB approach in pillar 1 are able to lower their regulatory capital charges for an asset that would be priced higher by a bank that uses the standardized approach, regulators will be pressured to adopt sophisticated internal ratings models along the lines proposed by Basel II but that may not be beneficial for banks and financial markets of less-developed countries.

Regulatory Costs

The design of a regulatory regime incurs high fixed costs because a high level of expertise is required for regulators and staff to design regulatory policy. This can be especially expensive for developing-country regulators, who have often fewer skilled staff and whose regulatory regimes suffer from relatively high design costs. A global regime therefore may be viewed as a lower-cost option, because it can be taken off the shelf. Nevertheless, implementation and enforcement costs can be prohibitive for many countries.

Enforcement also requires skills and other institutional costs. An international regime may be cheaper to enforce if it involves coordination and collaboration with other authorities. An international regime of precise rules requires less skill and resources to enforce than a regime of standards, whose more general and vague nature requires greater skills in interpretation and implementation. Precise rules are easier to copy and involve less interpretation and discretion in implementation than do more broadly stated standards. It may be more efficient for a state to adopt an international regime than to devise its own, especially if that regime is based on a prescriptive set of rules that lends itself to adoption in different jurisdictions, but the introduction of external or international rules always leads to higher costs of implementation and possibly enforcement.

Most national regulators outside the G10 regard the Basel Accord and other international standards as soft law. The official and market incentives outlined earlier create pressures that may exercise undue influence over their national policies. The real incentives and sanctions are determined by the IFIs in their assessments and funding choices and by the G10 countries in determining market access. IMF and World Bank conditionality is likely to take account of a country's progress, rather than its actual compliance with international standards at any one point in time. By contrast, Core Principles Assessments do take account of actual compliance. U.S. and U.K. regulatory standards look to the foreign regime's equivalence with either U.S./U.K. standards or international standards. Although the IMF/World Bank may allow states to implement standards at a phased pace, market access rules in the EU and in the United States encourage foreign regulators to move quickly in implementing standards in a way that may threaten to undermine financial stability.

This discussion argues that the adoption of IFI standards, especially the Basel Accord, may not lead to the most efficient development of financial markets in the non-G10 countries. This international soft law framework also raises issues of accountability and legitimacy. Indeed, the adoption of standards and rules in the Basel framework may create a governance gap. The Committee has attempted to address this, at least in the Core Principles, by creating a Core Principles Liaison Group (CPLG) that creates a forum for discussion of these issues with non-G10 regulators. Although this allows some non-G10 countries to influence the development of the Core Principles, the G10 retains sole authority over developing the Capital Accord. Although non-G10 countries can make comments to the Basel Committee, the Committee has no obligation to recognize them. The standard-setting process remains dominated by the G10, even though, as demonstrated earlier, these standards are increasingly being applied on a global basis.

The factors discussed suggest that international financial soft law can influence state behavior in a number of ways, including the creation of official incentives by international economic organizations and of market incentives that penalize countries whose international equity and bond markets carry higher costs of capital. These official and market incentives assume varying degrees of intensity depending on the type of conduct and the state involved. These incentives and indirect sanctions, however, suffer from a lack of uniformity in application and often work against the interests of small and developing countries, in contrast to countries with more political and economic influence, which often have the capability of minimizing and withstanding the costs of noncompliance with soft law norms.

The Financial Action Task Force

The development of international antimoney-laundering standards by the Financial Action Task Force has been a more inclusive process than the development of standards in international banking generally. Regulators have involved more countries and have provided a peer review process that involves consultation and mutual assessment of regulations and laws with a view to adopting standards that reflect a broad view of economic and legal structures.

The Financial Action Task Force has been in existence only since 1990, but it has had an extraordinary impact on the development of international norms to combat financial crime and money laundering. Despite its rather limited membership and informal legal status, FATF has seized the agenda in setting international standards and rules that must be adopted not only by its membership but by all other states under threat of sanctions. Although the FATF Recommendations do not reflect a common practice of all states with *opinio juris* and therefore cannot be considered customary international law as such, they have had a significant impact in shaping the policies and laws of many of the world's leading economic powers and emerging economies and in fostering recognition that money laundering is a threat to the systemic stability and integrity of financial systems. Moreover, FATF's compliance review process and designation of noncooperative countries, which carries the threat of sanctions, has created a limited international legal regime that has the potential to be transformed into a more comprehensive international legal framework for the control of financial crime. FATF has become the single most important international body in terms of formulating antimoney-laundering policy and developing international standards for disclosure and transparency for financial institutions.[13]

FATF's efforts to establish and enforce standards and rules impose a higher level of obligation than the Basel Committee framework because of the institutional willingness to impose sanctions. The so-called FATF Forty Recommendations have been extended beyond merely nonbinding voluntary standards and are considered binding principles backed by the threat of sanctions. As discussed in chapter 2, FATF's threat to impose sanctions in June 2000 against fifteen designated jurisdictions led most of them to adopt and implement the necessary changes in their legal systems to become compliant with FATF requirements. The designated jurisdictions that failed to comply with the FATF requirements were blacklisted by FATF and subject to further sanctions that prohibit OECD-based firms from doing business in these targeted jurisdictions. In October 2001, FATF adopted antiterrorist financing recommendations that require all OECD states to adopt strict controls to prevent third-party intermediaries and professionals from facilitating transactions with designated terrorists. The FATF antiterrorist financing sanctions are also backed by United Nations Security Council Resolution 1373.

Although the FATF approach owes much to the Basel Committee approach, it has evolved into a more ambitious undertaking because its member states can agree to impose sanctions against noncomplying countries or territories. FATF took the work of the Basel Committee a step further by stressing the importance of requiring its member states to implements its standards. In 1991, FATF issued a statement indicating that its members had agreed to a process of mutual assessment to ensure that the Forty Recommendations were being put into practice (FATF, 1996b). The members also agreed to expand the membership of the task force and to influence nonmember jurisdictions to follow the forty points (FATF, 2003). Significant components of FATF's work thus have been devoted to promoting compliance with the Forty Recommendations and to cultivating antimoney-laundering efforts in nonmember nations or regions. As part of its agenda, therefore, FATF conducts on-site peer evaluations of member adherence to the Forty Recommendations. An evaluation team composed of legal, regulatory, and law enforcement experts from the comember states visits the subject country and conducts a thorough review of its antimoney-laundering infrastructure. The results of this evaluation are published in a report that is reviewed internally by the FATF membership.

In addition, multilateral treaty frameworks may indirectly influence the formation of binding international financial norms. Treaties addressing corruption, financial crime, and terrorism often contain language that is deliberately left ambiguous because state parties prefer not to incur specific and precise obligations that may impinge on sensitive areas of state policy. Although the Forty Recommendations are generally viewed as voluntary soft law standards where states have discretion regarding implementation, some multilateral treaties dealing with corruption and money laundering make reference to international soft law standards in order to clarify the meaning of vaguely drafted treaty provisions. For example, the United Nations Convention against Transnational and Organized Crime (2000) (the Palermo Convention) is the most significant multilateral treaty addressing organized and financial crime. Article 7 addresses a state's obligation to implement measures to combat money laundering, and Article 7(3) provides that, "[i]n establishing a domestic regulatory and supervisory regime," states "are called upon to use as a guideline the relevant initiatives of regional, interregional and multilateral organizations against money laundering." The treaty's interpretative notes make clear that the relevant multilateral and regional initiatives include the FATF Forty Recommendations and the various standards adopted by FATF regional bodies. Subsequent implementation programs cross-reference the FATF standards to add clarity to the obligations under the Convention (Gilmore, 2003). Similarly, the United Nations Convention against

Corruption (2003) contains identical language in Article 14 (4) and (5) and makes reference to the FATF Forty Recommendations and regional agreements in the interpretative notes.

The Palermo Convention and the FATF Forty Recommendations mark an important development in the formation of binding international financial norms in which ostensibly voluntary FATF standards are used as benchmarks for defining legally binding obligations under a multilateral treaty. In one way, it could be called international law through the backdoor, but for the global governance debate, it raises important issues regarding the legal relevance of international financial standard setting and the need to ensure that the decision-making process is accountable and legitimate.

One may argue that FATF's efforts, with the institutional support of the OECD, have been instrumental in developing and formalizing international antimoney-laundering norms and standards and in shifting such standards from voluntary recommendations to an increasingly binding international regime. Moreover, the increasing legal relevance of the regime is indicated in part by its high degree of precision and obligation, although the requirements are denoted as recommendations. The existence of a peer-review compliance assessment exhibits a degree of delegation, although one that is not as forceful or as independent as an independent tribunal or arbitrator (e.g., the WTO dispute settlement body). Moreover, peer review undertaken by the same countries that promulgate the standards provides a higher level of legitimacy than the Basel framework and also offers a more direct form of accountability.

FATF's use of various procedures and compliance evaluations that allow all assessed jurisdictions to offer input on the development of standards and programs for their respective systems enhances the legitimacy and accountability of the standard setting and implementation process.[14] Nevertheless, the FATF regime suffers from serious weaknesses, discussed in chapter 2. Although the regional inspection panels engage local officials in a dialogue regarding their needs and capabilities, the standards that are applied are essentially determined by the OECD member countries. Despite significant improvements in transparency and accountability, FATF standard setting lacks legitimacy because of the threat of countermeasures that can be imposed against any jurisdiction that fails to comply. The weaknesses in governance of both the Basel Committee and FATF suggest the need for further reforms in international standard setting.

The substantive content and scope of international financial regulation has been influenced chiefly by the regulators of the world's major financial systems, and the standards and rules they have produced do not find their origins in traditional sources of public international law but rather are a result of bargaining and softer techniques of implementation that seek to utilize indirect forms of pressure on states to adopt these standards. These indirect forms of pressure include a variety of official and market incentives that play a crucial role in shaping the development of state regulatory practice. It is important to note that the present international financial regulatory regime derives primarily from these sources and should be viewed with concern because most countries that are subject to these standards have not played a role in their promulgation and have not consented to their adoption. As evidenced by the aftermath of the Asian financial crisis, these standards often result in poor regulatory and economic policy for many countries and thereby undermine economic growth and development (Stiglitz, 2001). Reform efforts should focus on devising decision-making and institutional structures that are more accountable and legitimate and on developing a regulatory framework that relies less on the role of official and market incentives.

Moreover, increased integration and interdependence in international banking markets suggests that the existing international soft law framework is no longer a second-best arrangement for generating efficient standards of banking regulation. Indeed, increasing integration and cross-border activity may require further institutional and legal consolidation at the international level to promote more effective and accountable international regulation. This would require states to move forward through the soft law process by building on the collective intent of most states to develop binding international rules of banking regulation. States could potentially delegate the adjudication of violations to an international financial authority, but states would retain ultimate enforcement authority, including sanctions.

CONCLUSION

The development of a substantial body of international regulatory norms for banking and financial regulation has raised important normative issues for international economic lawyers regarding the sources of state regulatory practice and the role of traditional sources of public international law in explaining state conduct in these areas. International soft law may be defined as an international rule created by a group of specially affected states in a particular issue area that have a common intent to observe voluntarily the content of such a rule with the intention of possibly incorporating it into the national law or administrative regulations. The chapter suggests that, although international soft law has provided a flexible framework for developing standards of international financial regulation, the efficient regulation of financial systems requires "harder" legal standards that create more stable expectations for market participants in their cross-border activities. The existing framework of using official and market incentives and sanctions to promote adherence to international standards is haphazard and is unevenly applied to developed and developing countries, undermining principles of accountability and legitimacy. Therefore, the instrument of international soft law should be modified to incorporate some legally binding standards of banking regulation that can be applied flexibly within and across different economic systems.

In addition, the effect of official and market incentives has been to create a type of obligation that is relevant in a normative sense and influences the development of state practice in the areas of bank regulation and antimoney-laundering controls. However, an optimal set of international regulatory standards has been difficult to develop because uniform international standards can have widely diverging effects in different economic systems. This is why the existing Basel framework and FATF Recommendations may be inappropriate for many countries on economic grounds. Moreover, the process through which these standards have been promulgated, applied, and implemented under IMF/World Bank supervision raises issues of political legitimacy and accountability. The particular type of international soft law that has fostered the widespread application of these standards outside the small circle of countries that devised them raises important issues of global governance and whether the legalization process through which these international standards assume a more binding character is an efficient legal framework for the effective regulation of systemic risk.

5

Strengthening the Global Financial System through Institutional and Legal Reform

This chapter argues that effective international financial regulation requires a treaty regime that combines legally binding principles of effective regulation (i.e., capital adequacy and consolidated supervision and allocating LOLR function) and a mechanism for developing nonbinding soft law codes (capital adequacy formulas and coordination of enforcement) derived from the binding principles. The implementation of such binding and nonbinding standards and rules requires an international institution to facilitate the development of such norms and to oversee their implementation. This international institution could delegate the process of devising soft law international codes and formulas to existing international bodies, such as the BIS committees, IOSCO, IAIS, and FATF. The treaty framework establishing such an international authority must contain procedures to ensure the political accountability and legitimacy of the institution to its signatory states.

The central dilemma in analyzing international soft law and determining the appropriate model or approach to regulate international economic relations is deciding what combination of soft and hard law should be used to govern particular areas of state conduct under different circumstances. Soft law provides states with a flexible instrument to pursue their policy objectives by entering into agreements that establish norms and standards of practice but that allow states freedom of action to alter their practices when they view it necessary to do so in the pursuit of their national interests. As discussed in chapter 4, although soft law is legally nonbinding, it nevertheless plays an important normative role in shaping and constraining state conduct and often has considerable legal effect in influencing the development of international legal norms and national law and regulation. Moreover, the use of soft law as an instrument of foreign economic policy can be adequately analyzed through the lens of rational institutional or neoliberal institutional theories of international relations. According to these theories, states are unitary actors in an anarchical international political system that seek to overcome the high transaction costs of unilaterally pursuing their policy objectives by entering into agreements with other states that produce collective action benefits. Ideally, these collective action benefits exceed the sovereignty costs that states incur by entering into such agreements, which may restrict their autonomy or freedom of action. The importance of soft law is that it lowers a state's sovereignty costs by allowing states the unilateral freedom to exit or modify their commitments or obligations if those commitments produce fewer benefits or higher costs than originally anticipated when the agreement took effect. Soft law provides states with a mechanism for ongoing negotiations and learning by doing in international politics.

Before we discuss our proposals for reform of the institutional framework and functions of international financial regulation, we analyze transaction costs and sovereignty costs in international relations and how they affect state calculations to pool their sovereignty in establishing formal and informal institutional structures. We then consider institutional reform for regulating international financial markets. We suggest that it will be necessary to provide a particular form of soft law within a broad, binding treaty framework that allows the necessary political flexibility for states to implement international standards and rules into their national legal systems. States could then move forward through this institutional structure in a manner that builds on the collective intent of most states to find the proper mix between binding and nonbinding standards and rules for the international regulation of financial markets. States could delegate the interpretation of standards and adjudication of violations to international financial organizations, but states would retain ultimate authority regarding implementation and enforcement.

OVERCOMING THE OBSTACLES: SOME THEORETICAL PERSPECTIVES

In a liberal international financial system, each nation faces risks that may emanate from behavior entirely outside its jurisdiction. Even economically and politically powerful states may face risks that derive from financial crises in poor countries. The desire to manage risks may lead to two polar reactions: (1) the attempt by the rich and strong to manage the poor and weak and to protect the rich from external threat, or (2) cooperation between all countries to manage risk internationally. All procedures for international regulation fall somewhere on a scale between these two extremes. Other than in the polar first case, international regulation involves some pooling of sovereignty, even if only at the level of initiating proposals or in facilitating intergovernmental negotiations.

Treaties designed to establish international economic authority and procedures generally fall into two categories: (1) agreements that create supranational organizations that exercise powers of norm generation and sanctions over their members and (2) intergovernmental organizations in which the main powers are exercised by member states while the organization itself plays only an administrative and facilitative role. The first type of organization represents a deeper pooling of sovereignty at the international level, while the second provides its member states with ultimate responsibility for agreeing to standards and imposing sanctions. For instance, the International Monetary Fund represents a pooling of sovereignty at the supranational level to promote monetary stability and economic growth. The IMF Articles of Agreement creates a supranational organization that possesses legally cognizable powers and obligations that extend vertically to its member states. In contrast, the World Trade Organization Agreements create rights and obligations that are essentially horizontal or intergovernmental and therefore provide states with ultimate authority for negotiating and creating standards and for imposing sanctions through self-help remedies, which exist in the WTO dispute-settlement understanding.

Most multilateral economic treaties serve a vital function in regularizing state behavior and contain procedures to ensure some form of accountability to member states. Treaties, however, present a number of difficulties, especially regarding the regulation of complex areas of international relations, because they often involve the pursuit of international goals that have high transaction costs. Moreover, their hard-law status can lock states into restrictive commitments and obligations whose consequences cannot be foretold with a reasonable degree of accuracy because of inadequate information and uncertainty regarding future circumstances and events.

TRANSACTION COSTS

International norm building involves various forms or levels of legally non-binding soft law standards as rational responses to the uncertainty that surrounds the negotiations of agreements between states that do not want to bind their freedom of action in the face of unforeseen circumstances. Indeed, in domestic law, parties confront similar problems as they negotiate a contract, which often makes legally nonbinding arrangements preferable. Transaction costs arise because of a number of factors, including the complexity of the subject matter, technical aspects of negotiations and drafting, and coordination problems among the parties (Caporaso, 1993: 61). These factors and others make it difficult for private parties—as they would for governments—to agree on legally binding and prescriptive obligations. Rather, legally nonbinding agreements may reduce transaction costs because they are often associated with rules that are less prescriptive and because they allow for flexibility in interpretation and do not unduly bind a state's future conduct, especially in light of unforeseen circumstances. Moreover, the lower level of commitment in soft-law agreements may improve coordination benefits among the parties, which may improve the likelihood of final agreement and may serve as a basis for ongoing negotiations to build on existing agreements.

Moreover, the international anarchy in which states exist creates uncertainty for states as they pursue their national interests. States are rational egotists that seek power and wealth and that enter legally binding and nonbinding agreements to improve their relative position vis-à-vis other states. States suffer from asymmetries of information, however, that limit their ability to foresee all or most contingencies that may arise under any agreement. Asymmetries of information also prevent governments from knowing the most rational or efficient approach for pursuing their national interests. States also lack complete information about whether other states are abiding by their commitments or what policies they may be following in pursuit of similar interests. The role of international institutions is to facilitate state negotiations and to serve as points of engagement for states to derive the information necessary to reduce information imbalances and to enhance their overall knowledge of the relevant environment. International law, however, has provided a weak edifice for states in regulating their international economic relations. Unlike domestic legal systems, international law contains many gaps and uncertainties regarding the expectations of states, especially in the economic realm. For instance, the transaction costs for most countries of operating national regulatory systems in the absence of coordination by an international authority may become so great that states may decide to delegate certain powers and responsibilities to international financial organizations that can perform the necessary functions of rule generation and surveillance of institutions and markets.

The uncertainty surrounding a state's future compliance with international commitments or obligations may lead states to develop institutional structures that oversee compliance within a framework of ongoing political negotiations. This may prove to be an optimal approach, especially in areas of sensitive state policy and regulation, because it involves delegation of compliance to institutional bodies composed of states, rather than to judicial tribunals, and thereby forces states to internalize the high costs of unforeseen commitments within the political bargaining process. International financial bodies, as shown in chapter 2, have played an effective role in this regard through oversight and surveillance, as well as in generating information that can assist in further negotiations and in producing technical rules and mediating disputes. The high transaction costs of uncertainty may also be addressed by adopting less precise rules and standards that at least represent a consensus on general standards but that allow states to have flexibility in interpretation and implementation and to use the general guidelines as a basis for future negotiations in which more precise rules can be worked out over time. Other approaches might involve the adoption of precise but nonbinding rules that create a prescriptive framework of commitments that can be applied in a number of different circumstances. In this way, states can learn through experience while retaining ultimate discretion regarding actual compliance. These approaches permit states to structure their agreements carefully through political bargaining so as to gain the benefits of coordination and the further institutionalization of obligations, while limiting transaction costs and reducing uncertainty regarding future circumstances.

Because treaties must overcome these difficulties, they are typically a compromise, and inevitably inflexible. Moreover, because they necessarily embody some degree of accountability to their signatories, they tend to be slow moving. These are rather unattractive characteristics in the field of international financial regulation. It is therefore not surprising that developments have taken a different route, with the major role in developing international soft law standards being played by international bodies of national regulators, such as the Basel Committee, IOSCO, IAIS, and FATF.

SOVEREIGNTY COSTS

"Sovereignty costs" pose a major obstacle to the negotiation of binding international agreements because the obligations undertaken can result in reduced national autonomy and freedom of action (Martin, 1993). These costs can be significant, especially where a supranational organization assumes authority over essential areas of economic policy or regulation. Concern about sovereignty costs can lead states to opt for agreements that contain softer forms of obligation and less precise rules. Indeed, international soft law provides states with a variety of institutional mechanisms to reduce or limit sovereignty costs. For instance, by limiting delegation to third-party judicial bodies or tribunals, states can still benefit from the increased expectations of compliance by other states, while maintaining the psychological benefit of knowing that any alleged breach on their part will have to be resolved within a framework of political bargaining and negotiation.

The analysis and concept of sovereignty costs has been addressed from a variety of perspectives (Keohane, 1984; Abbott and Snidal, 1998: 10–12). Sovereignty costs may vary across issue areas. For example, Abbott and Snidal argue that sovereignty costs are particularly high in issue areas that touch upon national security but are not as high in areas of economics or the environment. We contend, however, that, because banking regulation is an integral component to the economic health and systemic stability of a financial system, the sovereignty costs in allocating regulatory authority to a supranational institution are extremely high.

Sovereignty costs can also vary across states depending on their size, wealth, and political power. The sovereignty costs to large or hegemonic states that enter binding treaties may be much higher than those for smaller, less influential states because powerful states usually have more

autonomy and capacity for pursuing their policy objectives, which could
be significantly eroded if they undertake certain international obligations.
In contrast, smaller states may have lower sovereignty costs because they
generally have less autonomy and freedom of action when compared to
large states and therefore would lose far less autonomy by incurring obligations in international agreements or by participating in international
organizations. Although sovereignty costs erode national autonomy and
freedom of action, states may derive significant collective action benefits
from international cooperation and coordination in certain issue areas by
entering agreements (hard or soft law) that make it easier for states to
coordinate their pursuit of national objectives. International agreements
and instruments may therefore produce benefits (e.g., reduced transaction
costs) for states in excess of the costs of lost sovereignty or freedom of
action that the states incur by entering agreements or interacting in certain
institutional structures. Although large states may incur higher sovereignty costs by entering certain agreements, they may derive higher benefits from their participation in certain institutions or international organizations because they are able to utilize these structures to achieve their
objectives more efficiently than if they pursued them unilaterally. The soft-
law process allows strong and weak states to cooperate in developing, for
instance, a particular model of international norms and rules that is binding and relatively precise but that delegates oversight for compliance to
national political institutions. This allows weak states to be protected by
the expectations of certain types of behavior, while strong states maintain
a high degree of influence over compliance and future negotiations.

Regarding international financial regulation, the Basel framework contains norms that are relatively precise but nonbinding, and delegates authority to national political institutions to ensure implementation and enforcement. In this way, sovereignty costs are minimized. The Basel
framework permits states to regularize their behavior and to comply with
international soft law rules by adopting national regulation. As more
countries adopt these rules, they assume an obligatory status that may
eventually result in binding customary international law. This type of international norm building provides the necessary political and legal basis
at the national level that may ultimately recognize the benefits of delegation to an international authority to ensure compliance. This is where
an international supervisory authority can play a role in monitoring compliance, proposing rules of conduct, and orchestrating enforcement at the
national level.

The Basel framework and other informal international standard-setting
bodies have significantly influenced the process of devising international
norms and rules to regulate international financial markets. Indeed, the
Basel Accord and the post–September 11 antimoney-laundering recommendations of the Financial Action Task Force involve a form of international soft law that has precise, nonbinding norms that are generated
through consultations and negotiations among the major state regulators.

This particular form of international soft law provides the political flexibility necessary for states to adopt international rules and standards into their national legal systems in a manner that accommodates the sovereign authority of the nation state. Through multilateral negotiations and the steady accumulation of nonbinding obligations, states go through a process of learning by doing that builds on their collective intent to accomplish generally agreed-upon international objectives. As trust and expectations converge, states can eventually delegate adjudication of violations to an independent third party, which can seek objectively to uphold international standards. State sovereignty is respected because states are allowed to retain ultimate enforcement authority, including sanctions.

The problem here is, of course, the predominant role of the major states. An effective soft law regime works by consensus, and a grudging consensus imposed by the major states upon others is likely to be less effective than a consensus in which all participate. While the existence of a legal structure does offer some protection to weaker countries, whose sovereignty is compromised by the very fact of being economically (and perhaps politically) dominated by the developed countries, the fact that structure is determined by the G10 raises the obvious question of whose interests are being protected.

The "obvious" solution of increasing the representation on the Basel committees runs the risk of overloading the decision-making mechanisms and reducing their flexibility. The partial solution adopted at the Financial Stability Forum, to involve a wider range of countries in consultation committees, is attractive, but these committees have no policy or standard-setting function. They produce reports that identify weaknesses and problems with regulation and policy in the financial sector but offer few meaningful proposals for reform.[1] The FSF has essentially become a "talk shop" that meets semiannually with no agenda for meaningful reform. A more consolidated institutional structure is required to devise effective regulatory standards to control systemic risk.

Ultimately, those who face the choice between a soft law and a formal treaty regime may come to the conclusion that both have their place. The treaty lays down a method for developing general principles that should guide the regulators and a mechanism for developing codes derived from those principles. The task of developing the codes can then be entrusted to a less formal body, akin to the current BIS Committees.

GLOBAL GOVERNANCE: THE INSTITUTIONAL AND LEGAL STRUCTURE

It should be recalled that the original purposes and institutional structures of the Bretton Woods institutions were complementary and intended to facilitate efficient and accountable international economic policymaking. The objective of the aborted International Trade Organization was to eliminate barriers to trade in goods, services, and intellectual property by taking jurisdiction over the underlying transaction of goods or services, whereas the IMF Articles of Agreement addressed primarily the issue of exchange rate stability and balance of payment support. The World Bank had an overarching role of promoting long-term economic growth and development by providing loans to support infrastructure projects in war-ravaged member countries. Since their inception, all three international organizations have expanded into multiple and often overlapping areas that, combined with their inadequate accountability in decision making and legitimacy regarding member ownership of programs, have undermined their effectiveness. Accordingly, new institutional structures should be devised to more closely coordinate the work of these organizations not only with each other but also with other international standard-setting bodies. This has particular relevance for reforming the institutional structure of international financial regulation by focusing on realigning the work of the various IFIs and IEOs in a more coherent fashion than presently exists in order to promote the objective of efficient international financial regulation.

The establishment of effective, accountable, and legitimate institutional structures of international financial regulation can build on existing structures of international economic governance to develop a normative and institutional framework to promote efficient financial regulation. To achieve this, we propose a multilateral framework treaty that is based on binding high-level principles and universal membership. The treaty would establish an international organization that would be led by a Global Financial Governance Council composed of the representatives of member states. The treaty would require member countries to agree to principles of good financial regulation, such as capital adequacy, consolidated supervision, and adequate corporate governance structures for banking institutions. The promulgation of detailed and specific regulatory rules and formulas would be delegated to expert bodies that would be composed of national regulators from both developed and developing countries. These expert bodies would be similar to existing international standard-setting bodies, but their memberships would be open to all countries, with regulators from systemically relevant economies serving permanently and regulators from smaller, less-developed financial systems serving on a rolling-term basis. The treaty would also establish an institutional structure headed by the Governance Council that would be composed of representatives at the deputy ministerial level and that would meet every few months but no fewer than four times a year to oversee the standard-setting activities of the expert bodies (see figure 5.1). The Council would be responsible for approving standards set by the expert committees. However, an important principle of the treaty would permit any state to decide not to adhere to a particular set of standards if the state determined that compliance would severely undermine its economy or financial stability. Although states would exercise ultimate authority in making such a determination, they would be encouraged to consult other states in making such decisions. This would lower sover-

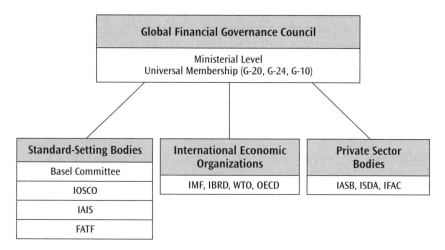

Figure 5.1 The institutional structure of international financial regulation.

eignty costs by allowing states to exercise ultimate control over implementation of international standards and would protect states from being subject to standards that might be inappropriate for their economic and financial systems.

The Global Financial Governance Council with representatives from all states would be authorized by treaty to delegate the authority to develop international standards and rules for financial regulation to existing international supervisory bodies. It would also delegate surveillance and enforcement mechanisms to international organizations with broad-based membership (i.e., the International Monetary Fund or the World Trade Organization), leaving ultimate implementation authority with national authorities. The traditional responsibilities of international organizations, such as the IMF's role to intervene in certain financial crises, would be maintained and perhaps more specifically defined as set forth by proposals of international commissions. For example, the Meltzer Report (commissioned by the U.S. Congress) proposed that the IMF move away from broader responsibilities of enhancing financial stability and revert to its original mission of providing short-term liquidity for members experiencing temporary payments problems. The World Trade Organization would monitor its members' schedules of commitments to liberalize cross-border trade in financial services and would adopt generally accepted principles of prudential supervision as defined by expert international bodies to ensure that members do not impose disguised trade barriers to restrict trade in financial services. The World Bank would continue with long-term loans for development assistance that would also provide infrastructure assistance and training for regulators in emerging economies to ensure that high standards of financial regulation are implemented.

International supervisory bodies, such as the Basel Committee, would continue their expert work in developing technical rules and standards for issues such as capital adequacy and consolidated supervision. IOSCO would focus on precise and market-driven rules for accounting and auditor integrity and independence. FATF would assume a more high-profile role, addressing issues of money laundering and the role of third-party intermediaries in providing financial assistance to terrorists groups. The international bodies, because of their more flexible structure, are capable of promulgating standards and rules in an expert environment of consensus with an overall objective of applying such standards not only to the G10 developed countries but also to all countries whose economies participate in the international financial system. Although these bodies of expert regulators would remain somewhat autonomous in their institutional structure and standard-setting procedures, they would have a formal treaty objective of establishing norms and rules that would apply to all members of the international community.

The multilateral treaty adopting this institutional structure of international financial regulation would have the objective of making all countries, regional economic areas, and the relevant international organizations signatories. The treaty would encompass general principles of prudential supervision and market conduct but would leave the detailed formulation of these principles to the expert international bodies. International bodies would have broader membership that represented large and small countries from the developing world and emerging market economies. The dominance of the G10 and OECD over standard setting would end. The detailed rules and standards promulgated by these bodies would be on offer for implementation by the national authorities of all member states under the supervision of the relevant international organization and/or standard-setting body. Each state would exercise the ultimate decision whether to implement the standards into its national regulatory regime. This would reduce sovereignty costs and maintain autonomy for national regulators to adopt standards beneficial for their financial systems. The type of official incentives and sanctions used by the IMF and the World Bank to induce states to comply with G10 norms would be prohibited by international organizations and other states. If a state decided to implement particular standards, it would do so under the supervision of the relevant international organization and/or standard-setting body to which it belonged.

An equally important function of the Global Governance Council and its related international organizations and bodies would be to recognize and promote the various international standards it promulgates and to engage in an ongoing dialogue and consultation with national authorities. Essentially, the Council and its related institutions should be involved in facilitating and developing international standards for the four main areas of financial regulatory policy that are deemed essential for efficient financial regulation (Eatwell and Taylor, 2000). These areas are *authorization and guidance, information and surveillance, cooperation and coordination, and enforcement and policy.* These areas are discussed below.

Since multinational banks now operate in what are becoming seamless financial markets, the effective management and control of systemic risk on a global level requires a standard-setting process that is global in scope and effective for and accountable and legitimate to the economies subject to its jurisdiction.[2] Indeed, this would apply whether the domain of the market were defined in terms of institutions, products, currencies, or even geographic areas. Moreover, international standards must establish effective mechanisms to allocate jurisdictional authority between national regulators in order to supervise more effectively the transnational operations of banks and bank holding companies. This should ensure that the holding company's subsidiaries keep adequate capital and do not maintain excessive gearing within the group structure.

Authorization and Guidance

The authorization of firms to operate in financial markets must be controlled by a licensing system in which firms and individuals are licensed to operate only after demonstrating that they are fit and proper, that they have adopted effective control and risk management procedures, and that they satisfy capital adequacy and other prudential standards. Regulatory authorities must have discretion to refuse, or rescind, a license when firms or individuals fail to comply with required standards.

In addition, authorities should provide guidance through frequent communication with the firms they regulate. The regulator should foster a good relationship with supervised firms by providing advice concerning a firm's internal operations. In this way, firms can be encouraged to provide a continuous flow of information. This type of cooperative relationship is far more efficient than adversarial inspections.

The international financial institutions (IFIs) should take the lead in setting standards that national authorities can use when considering whether to authorize or provide a license to multinational financial institutions so that they can operate on a transnational basis. The authorization process may be conducted under the type of home/host country arrangements that have been adopted by countries that adhere to the Basel Committee's principle of consolidated supervision. The IFIs would have the responsibility for ensuring that common authorization procedures are followed and that information is fully shared between regulators. To reduce arbitrage, the IFIs should establish minimum standards for authorizing financial institutions, senior managers, and directors. Countries would be allowed to adopt stricter authorization standards for both institutions and individuals, thus creating the potential for competition between jurisdictions above the minimum standard.

Information and Surveillance

The information disclosure system is an aspect of the broader task of surveillance. Effective surveillance is required to ensure that firms adhere to regulatory standards and rules. Some observers note that surveillance should be considered essentially as an intelligence operation (Eatwell and Taylor, 2000: 191). The accurate assessment of the changing structure of financial markets and of the level of risk to which markets are exposed necessitates that regulators utilize effective surveillance techniques. Moreover, regulators should be better informed than the market participants that they regulate. Accordingly, regulators should have access to confidential information that is relevant for performing their surveillance function. Traditional legal privileges that protect such confidential information from being disclosed should not apply to financial regulators. Indeed, the role of regulators would be greatly enhanced and more legitimate if it were known that they had broader and more accurate information about markets.

Information and surveillance are crucial components for effective international regulation. The Bank for International Settlements and the Basel Committee have provided a wealth of information on the development and performance of international financial markets and of suggested accounting standards for banking institutions.[3] The IFIs and the BIS can assist in the surveillance function by providing high standards of information disclosure so that market actors and national regulators can have access to the most recent and accurate information concerning international investment, short-term capital flows and liquidity, and interest rates. It would be necessary to harmonize national legal standards related to the confidentiality of information held by financial firms and eventually to adopt one international standard for the disclosure of proprietary information related to financial markets.

The question of the disclosure of information raises a second issue— what type of accounting standards or system should be used to disclose relevant financial information. The disclosure of accurate and relevant information to the public, investors, creditors, and regulators is the very foundation of an efficient market and effective regulatory system. The International Accounting Standards Board (IASB)[4] and the International Organization of Securities Commissions (IOSCO) have made significant progress in reforming international accounting standards following the corporate governance scandals of the late 1990s and early 2000s. In December 2003, the IASB issued revisions for standards that govern the valuation of financial instruments. These standards are known as IAS 32 and IAS 39 and regulate disclosure issues for securities and other financial assets. IAS 32 creates rules for determining whether financial instruments should be classified as debt or equity and requires that the nature and extent of the financial risks and the business purpose of the instruments be disclosed. IAS 39 covers the measurement and recognition of the value of financial instruments and determines when they should be included in financial statements and how they should be valued. For example, it requires that derivatives be reported at fair or market value, as opposed to their historic costs. Although some issues remain outstanding regarding the valuation of macro-hedging for portfolios of interest rate risk, IAS 39 makes significant improvements in requiring the reporting of the true scope and the extent of risk in financial instruments.

IAS 32 and IAS 39 are major steps in achieving international convergence because both standards closely approximate their counterpart provisions under the U.S. Generally Accepted Accounting Practices (GAAP).[5] These international accounting standards will form a key component of the newly established international regulatory regime and will improve early-warning systems intended to avert the types of financial crises that have occurred in recent years. International standards that are consistently applied across jurisdictions will help ensure market discipline and deter accounting arbitrage.

Under a consolidated global regime, the IFIs with responsibility for setting accounting standards—the Basel Committee, IOSCO, IASB, and IFAC—should continue their work, but with more input from developing and emerging-market countries. Regarding actual surveillance, the International Monetary Fund has extensive experience, through its Article IV surveillance programs, in monitoring compliance by its member states with various international financial standards. The IMF would continue its surveillance under the proposed regime, but it would no longer have the authority to withhold credit and to deny access to other types of financing to countries deemed not to be in compliance with international standards if the countries in question had specifically opted not to comply with specific standards. The IFIs, working with the IMF, would be involved in reviewing and assessing the regulatory performance of states that had expressed their willingness to abide by international standards. This would involve assessing the surveillance systems of individual countries and providing advice to those states regarding compliance with international standards. Such a surveillance system has not been adopted in the current international financial system and would be difficult to achieve because it would require high standards of disclosure that are not yet accepted by national authorities.

Cooperation and Coordination

As a preliminary matter, it should be recognized that international economic treaties already contain strong principles that require international economic organizations to cooperate and assist one another in the exercise of their functions. For instance, the WTO Charter states in relevant part:

> With a view to achieving greater coherence in global economic policymaking, the WTO shall cooperate, as appropriate, with the International Mon-

etary Fund and with the International Bank for Reconstruction and Development and its affiliated agencies.[6]

Moreover, the 1996 Declaration on the Contribution of the World Trade Organization to Achieving Greater Coherence in Global Economic Policymaking provides:

> The interlinkages between the different aspects of economic policy require that the international institutions with responsibilities in each of these areas follow consistent and mutually supportive policies. The World Trade Organization should therefore pursue and develop cooperation with the international organizations responsible for monetary and financial matters, while respecting the mandate, the confidentiality requirements and the necessary autonomy in decision-making procedures of each institution, and avoiding the imposition on governments of cross-conditionality or additional conditions.[7]

The IMF treaty contains hortatory provisions that envision Fund cooperation with other international organizations and bodies.[8] In contrast, the WTO Agreements expressly provide for cooperation in its external relations with other international organizations. Specifically, Article III: 5 of the WTO Charter and several provisions of the GATT and the GATS contain mandatory provisions for cooperation with the IMF.

The executive officials of all international standard-setting bodies and organizations should be encouraged to review the implications of cooperation among different organizations regarding issues of global financial policymaking. This cooperation may necessitate the adoption of binding multilateral or bilateral agreements similar to the 1996 IMF/WTO cooperation agreement that implemented the obligation of cooperation between the two organizations.[9]

These existing international linkages provide a framework for further cooperation and coordination in international financial regulation. Indeed, many goals of an efficient international financial policy can be achieved by effective coordination of the activities of national authorities. This has been demonstrated by the work of the Basel Committee in exchanging vital information on capital markets and in coordinating the regulatory supervision of financial institutions that operate on an international basis. This type of cooperation and coordination has also been achieved bilaterally through such agreements as the EU-U.S. 1999 Statement of Cooperation on the Exchange of Information for the Purposes of Consolidated Supervision.[10] Such close cooperation is necessary for the comprehensive consolidated supervision of banks that have multijurisdictional establishments.

Under the proposed international regime, the IFIs should have the authority both to reach agreement with national supervisors and to facilitate agreements among supervisors on a common framework for information sharing that can be used as a basis for reciprocal bilateral cooperation among supervisors and with banking institutions that have material operations in foreign jurisdictions. This type of surveillance role could build on current bilateral agreements, such as the EU-U.S. agreement, to promote further exchange of information in investigations and enforcement.

Regarding confidential information, international regulation should require national authorities to ensure that any information obtained through bilateral or multilateral avenues is used only for lawful supervisory purposes, without prejudice to defendant rights in criminal cases. To the extent permitted by national law, supervisory authorities and their agents should keep confidential all information obtained pursuant to such authorized exchanges. It is contemplated that, in certain circumstances, information provided by one supervisor to supervisors in other countries might be disclosed to third parties if such an action served a lawful supervisory purpose. Specifically, when a supervisor received a request for information from a third party, the supervisor who received the request would consult with the supervisor who had provided the information in order to solicit that supervisor's views on the propriety of releasing such information. Prior consent would be obtained from the supervisor who originated the information if consent was required by the laws or regulations of the originating supervisor's country.

In the event that a supervisor was required to disclose information according to the rules of any interstate agreement, it would be understood that that supervisor would cooperate in seeking to preserve the confidentiality of the information to the extent permitted by law. In all cases of disclosure to third parties, to the extent required by national law, the supervisor who disclosed the information would notify the supervisor who originated the information of the disclosure.

In addition, the advent of global banking has made it possible for a network of depository institutions to be linked by sophisticated telecommunications and computer systems. The IFIs could take the lead in creating such a network by assisting national authorities to adopt the necessary technology and standards for an efficient payment and clearing system. National authorities could agree to require their banks to participate in a single network of international payments and deposits that would be a closed system to which banks from participating jurisdictions would belong and for which a common, transnational regulatory framework could be devised. Such an international payments system could facilitate cross-border transfers and reduce the risk of contagion if a bank defaulted on its counterparty obligations.

Enforcement and Policy

An effective international financial regulatory regime depends on the enforcement and implementation of international standards. The transnational nature of financial risk necessitates uniform principles concerning procedures for enforcement of financial regulation that take account of the growing number of multijurisdictional cases. For this kind of financial regulation to be effective, adhering states must enact appropriate legislation that imposes jurisdiction not only on violations or offenses that occur solely in the enforcing jurisdiction but also on acts or omissions that occur in other territorial jurisdictions but that affect the financial markets of the sanctioning state. National authorities should also have competence to prosecute regulatory breaches or offenses in which elements of the violation have occurred in foreign jurisdictions, as well as in the territory of the prosecuting state. These expansive concepts of extraterritorial jurisdiction should be used to regulate electronic trading systems and to prosecute market abuse offenses that utilize the Internet to manipulate and threaten the integrity of financial markets.

To fulfill the enforcement function, it will not be necessary to enforce international standards directly, but it will be necessary to provide information and evidence and to apply political pressure to national authorities to ensure that they enforce international standards. Moreover, enforcement cases that concern the transnational operations of financial conglomerates involve many difficult legal issues, including whether to pierce the corporate veil in cases that involve corporate breach, whether to attribute liability to controlling third persons or to those who are knowingly concerned,[11] and issues of double and multiple jeopardy in criminal cases.

Another of the most important regulatory functions is the policy function. The Basel Committee, IOSCO, and other IFIs have already undertaken this function by adopting international standards and rules of prudential practice. The consensual approach has been important in providing legitimacy to the development of such standards and in gaining broader support for their implementation. But the voluntary approach means that the initiative lies with national authorities to adopt international standards. By contrast, a more effective global regime would need to adopt a proactive policy function in which it would develop and adopt standards and rules of regulatory practice that national authorities would then be bound to implement. The policy function should also continuously adapt the scope and content of regulation to the changing structure of international markets and to the changing character of firms. The consolidation of the existing financial regime would raise numerous political and legal issues regarding the type of powers to delegate to international bodies and the role that states would play in influencing the development of international standards and rules of financial regulation. Political reality demands that the IFIs coordinate their functions with national regulatory authorities. The IFIs' primary role would be to facilitate harmonization of standards and procedures, develop a global scope and relevance for decision making, and, when appropriate, exercise regulatory authority on a global scale.

The treaty framework should also address what role, if any, central banks should play in winding up or bailing out a bank that has operations in multiple jurisdictions. Indeed, the *ex post* side of international banking regulation requires rules of action that determine which central bank has authority to intervene and rescue a failing bank *and* what standards, if any, to determine if a bank is eligible for a rescue. Because there is no international lender of last resort, the treaty could create a committee of central bankers that would make decisions regarding the *who*, *when* and *how* of the lender of last resort (LOLR). Initially, it might be preferable to restrict the jurisdiction of the committee to banks that operate in two or more monetary jurisdictions, yet this might not adequately address the systemic threat posed by banks that operate only in one monetary jurisdiction, but have substantial cross-border operations and exposures. The composition of the committee could include a cross-section of the world's leading central bankers, but also provide representation to many central banks (perhaps on a rotating basis) from developing and emerging market economies. The committee would coordinate its activities with the other regulatory committees that deal with *ex ante* issues and would be accountable to the Governance Council. However, it would have discretion to act in times of crisis without specific approval of the Governance Council in order to prevent contagion. The committee would need to adopt rules (similar to consolidated supervision) to allocate jurisdictional authority to one or more central banks depending on the nature and extent of the banking crisis. Moreover, specific rules would need to be devised for financial holding companies to determine which central bank would be primarily responsible for organizing a bailout or a windup of a bank conglomerate with subsidiaries in multiple jurisdictions.

The efforts of the Basel Committee and other IFIs demonstrate that national financial supervisors are capable of performing some of the functions of global regulation, such as exchanging information and establishing voluntary international standards to reduce systemic risk. The effectiveness of this informal and voluntary approach to cooperation and standard setting worked well for developed countries in the immediate aftermath of the Bretton Woods system. Today, however, the changing structure of international financial markets and the increased risk of systemic failure require a more formalized structure of binding international standards and effective supervision and enforcement. The international activities of banks are subject to overlapping and disjointed national regulatory structures that must be coordinated and subject to harmonized standards if the risks to financial markets are to be minimized.

CONCLUSION

A major weakness in the existing international regime is that IFI standard setting is dominated by a few rich or large countries that exercise regulatory control over the major financial institutions. The existing standard-setting process has proved effective in some ways because the standard setters are few in number and can operate outside the glare of public attention, but the increasing global reach of these international standards necessitates a more accountable and legitimate process that can be influenced by countries that have hitherto played a small role in setting international financial norms. This chapter suggests that effective control of systemic risk in global financial markets requires further consolidation of the existing institutional framework of international financial regulation. To accomplish this, a Global Financial Governance Council should be established by multilateral treaty. Its responsibilities would include the adopting of binding international principles and rules of regulatory practice primarily for the banking sector. The Governance Council would set broad principles of regulatory governance and delegate the rule-making and standard-setting responsibilities to specialized supervisory bodies, such as the Basel Committee and IOSCO. The IFIs would adopt standards of prudential supervision, which would then be reviewed and approved by the Governance Council and thereby made binding on all member states. Member states, however, would have the option of exempting themselves from particular standards or rules that they can show undermine economic development or financial stability.

Although the delegation of standard setting and supervisory authority to the IFIs would entail sovereignty costs, it would lead to a significant reduction in transaction costs through improved coordination and surveillance. This would produce efficiency gains for regulators and market participants that exceed the costs associated with losing national authority.

According to this approach, international regulation would become more efficient because it would be promulgated by expert regulators working in the IFIs and more accountable and legitimate because the Governance Council with universal membership would have to provide ultimate approval. The Governance Council would take decisions based on a consensus of senior ministers representing all the states concerned. They would act on the proposals of the IFIs (whose membership would also be open to universal representation). IFI regulatory policy would be focused on global financial markets, and not solely on national markets.

Since financial stability is a public good, the scope of international regulation should be global. Previous proposals for a World Financial Authority (Eatwell and Taylor, 2000) deliberately did not address the institutional and political constraints of designing such a global regime. Global institutions, especially those as powerful as a World Financial Authority, would require an unprecedented pooling of national sovereignty at the international level. This would be very difficult to accomplish, even in the European Union, where banking regulation remains nationally based. It is therefore crucial that the success of international regulation must depend on nation states, especially in the area of coordination, implementation, and enforcement. Our current proposal seeks to address some of the political and institutional constraints by allowing states to reduce transaction costs in regulatory policymaking by using the existing IFIs as points of engagement for standard setting and surveillance. The problem of sovereignty costs is addressed by allowing all states to be involved in the standard-setting process and to exercise ultimate decision-making authority regarding national implementation. This approach attempts to strike a balance between the needs of effective regulatory policymaking and economic sovereignty. In the absence of a more effective international approach than currently exists, the scope and the severity of financial crises are likely to increase in the future.

6

Incentives versus Rules

Alternative Approaches to International Financial Regulation

The analysis for this part of the book has been motivated mainly by the interests of financial regulators and the institutions that they regulate; however, regulators are not the only ones in government who worry about incentives. Much of government activity involves the motivation of private interests to further the public good. For example, when government imposes taxes, it weighs the public good from tax revenues against the incentive effects of the tax. In many cases, the purpose of the tax is its incentive effect, rather than the revenue generated. Similarly, when government seeks to limit the level of systemic risk within the financial environment, many of its actions affect the incentives of private financial institutions. This problem has been evident in various aspects of international financial regulation, which the following chapters consider in detail. This chapter begins by discussing more generally whether there is even a role for incentive-based regulation to reduce systemic risk. Chapters 7–10 then analyze these very problems by examining the nature of systemic risk in different cases. A common theme that runs throughout this volume and is highlighted in the following chapters is the importance of setting appropriate standards in order to gain the most from an incentive-based approach toward financial regulation. Chapter 7 begins by considering the current debate over settlement systems and the need for minimum standards in national payment systems to foster greater harmonization at an international level. The efficacy of capital adequacy requirements in the recent Asian financial crisis is the focus of chapter 8. Clearly, one of the important lessons from this crisis was the establishment of clear analytical links between microeconomic risk taking and macroeconomic outcomes. The discussion in chapter 9 turns to an analysis of some of the suggested solutions as recommended by the Basel Committee and others international bodies, namely the use of internal ratings and private agency credit assessments in the recently released Basel II proposals, as well as the use of subordinated debt as a tool to enhance market discipline. Finally, in chapter 10, we discuss the idea that national financial markets may vary according to their legal system, institutional structures, business customs, and practices. Uniform international financial regulatory standards may not have the same impact on a particular financial system that it has on others, which may result in different types of systemic risk. Although financial markets are becoming seamless, their structures are not homogenous. Thus, chapter 10 sets out a list of specific standards of corporate governance as advocated by various international bodies and their specific relevance to financial institutions.

In regulating the market risk exposure of financial institutions, the approach taken to date has most often been a rule-based regime that sets a relationship between exposure and capital requirements exogenously. The recent efforts to reform the 1988 Basel Accord in the direction suggested by the Basel II Consultative Paper have increasingly emphasized an incentive-based stance toward financial regulation, whether through market discipline or increased transparency. This approach has some appeal not only because it is endogenously determined, so market participants can use their own information to determine regulatory standards, but also because of its greater sensitivity to changes in risk profiles. Similarly, it is claimed that rule-based regulation makes inefficient use of managerial expertise, whereas an incentive-based approach uses the insights of managers to gain an informational advantage in setting regulatory standards. However, as theoretical and empirical evidence has long indicated, there is a tradeoff between fostering an efficient allocation of resources and ensuring the safety and soundness of financial institutions. The use of a well-functioning safety net is one example of an important tradeoff in this regard that, if appropriately designed, can prevent systemic complications but can also give rise to moral hazard issues.

This chapter considers the role of market discipline and whether it is effective enough to be relied upon as the only tool of financial regulation. We argue from the outset that if the former is true, there needs to be at the minimum an incentive-compatible framework in place a priori. For example, the suggestion in the recent Basel II proposals that financial institutions be allowed to use publicly available assessments of private credit rating agencies, as well as their own internal credit ratings, to determine capital standards is an example of an incentive mechanism that has been used to promote the idea of market discipline. An appropriate incentive framework, as outlined in the proposal, should also include a regulatory and supervisory framework, accounting rules and practices, and disclosure requirements. However, better information disclosure alone will not suffice as long as the incentives for excessive risk taking remain. That is, without an appropriate design for enforcement, albeit through market disciplinary measures, the use of internal ratings models and external assessments could be subject to strong incentives for manipulation through excessive risk taking. This chapter begins by briefly considering the "incentive problem" in regulation using a principal-agent framework. The following section considers the design of an incentive-compatible regulatory system that encourages prudent behavior and efficient financial intermediation. The discussion continues by assessing the nature of the tradeoff between incentive- and rule-based regulation by analyzing the interaction between regulatory and agency incentives. The chapter concludes by considering the challenges in designing appropriate incentive mechanisms to regulate financial markets through market discipline.

DO INCENTIVES WORK?

The main characteristics of the regulator's problem are the opportunity that exists for firms to improve their economic payoffs by engaging in unobserved, socially costly behavior or "abuse" and the inferior information set of the regulator relative to the firm. These characteristics are related, since abuse would not be unobserved if the regulator had complete information. The basic idea that the firm has an information advantage and that this gives the firm the opportunity to take self-interested actions is the standard *principal-agent* and *moral hazard* argument. The more interesting issue is how this information asymmetry and the resulting inefficiencies are played out in a regulatory setting. Does the firm have better information? Perhaps the best evidence that regulators possess information inferior to the firm's lies in the fact that they employ incentive mechanisms, rather than relying completely on explicit directives. For example, governments have tried to promote financial safety and risk avoidance by reducing abusive practices in different environments not only through direct quantitative limits but also through bonus schemes; for example, they promote energy conservation by offering bonus schemes (i.e., tax breaks) for firms that invest in energy conservation. Regulators believe that the firm has better information about the costs and benefits of conservation and the technology for achieving it and that a better result can be obtained by providing incentives rather than directives. An analogy could be made to efforts to contain systemic risk in capital markets through incentive-based financial regulation.

Systemic risk is to financial markets what dirty smoke is to the environment. In calculating the cost of production, the factory owner rarely accounts for the costs that the smoking chimney imposes on society. The dirty smoke is an externality. Its production has an impact on the welfare of society, but that impact is external, and it is not priced through the market. The factory owner does not pay for the extra costs of laundry or for the medical bills the smoke precipitates. This failure introduces a fundamental shortcoming into the workings of the market, in that the costs to the factory do not reflect the costs of the pollution to society as a whole. The result is pollution. The factory produces more smoke than would be the case if all society's costs were accounted for in the factory's balance sheet. Similarly, financial firms do not always price the costs that their losses might impose on society as a whole into their accounts. Taking risks is a crucial activity for financial institutions, but markets, in reflecting only the private calculation of risk, underprice the risk faced by society. Consequently, like factory owners, investors in free markets may participate in excessive risk taking (Eatwell and Taylor, 2000).

Similarly, an argument can be made for containing systemic risk in capital markets through the introduction of mandatory subordinated debt (SD). As with environmental pollution, financial regulators could choose to limit the financial activities of firms through direct controls. However, like firms that invest in energy conservation, financial firms have better information about the costs of their activities than the regulator and are probably more knowledgeable about the risks they face. Moreover, given the highly dynamic and innovative nature of today's financial markets, with their various instruments, regulators might be at even a greater disadvantage than their counterparts who regulate the natural environment. Thus, given the greater information asymmetries in this setting, incentive mechanisms such as an SD requirement might be significantly more effective than using explicit directives on their own.

The aforementioned conditions exist to some extent because of the inferior quality and quantity of the information received by regulators about the circumstances of any regulated firm compared to the firm's own information resources. This is true because the firm is the source of virtually all the regulator's information, and the firm can effectively filter much of that information. The firm's managers are likely to have better information, despite the best efforts of regulators to stay informed, and the asymmetry is deliberately exacerbated by the choice of a judicial-type process for making regulatory decisions. It is not that regulators are unaware of what it is they regulate, especially as they collect much information about firms over time. Although regulators are better informed than depositors or investors, their information is always inferior to the information that the firm itself possesses.

AN INCENTIVE STRUCTURE FOR FINANCIAL REGULATION

The main question, and the focus of much of this chapter, is what the government can do to ensure that owners, supervisors, and the market itself exert sufficient pressure on managers to avoid excessive risk taking. In more developed financial markets, authorities use several measures, including erecting entry barriers, enforcing modest capital requirements at or above the minimum 8 percent Basel Committee capital-to-risk-weighted-assets ratio, and scrutiny by one or more of the supervisory agencies. The problems encountered by supervisory authorities in emerging markets are even greater, in part because of the small and often more concentrated nature of their economies, where shocks often are larger and more volatile and where everyone's ability to monitor banks is hampered by poorer information. Thus, in both industrialized and developing markets, governments need to enhance the incentive mechanisms to encourage each of the potential monitoring groups—supervisors, owners, creditors, and market participants—to curb excessive risk-taking activities by financial institutions.

We now turn to the role of incentives for each of these groups to provide a better regulatory environment. Today, most regulatory authorities have moved to engage in prudential supervision to ensure solvency as their main task. In the early years, bank supervision mostly involved ensuring compliance with government directives on credit allocation and other issues. There is still a need to provide the appropriate incentives for supervisors both to monitor market participants and to take actions based on their observations. To begin, supervisors need receive sufficient compensation so that qualified personnel are not lured into the private sector. Moreover, if regulators' salaries are low, individuals may be tempted to accept lower pay now in exchange for a lucrative salary later, introducing the possibility of corruption. The disincentive for effective supervision can be reduced only by raising supervisory pay at least close to private-sector levels. Similar efforts have been made to create "bonded regulators"; some portion of a supervisor's compensation is deferred and held as a bond from which deductions can be taken depending on the outcome in the financial sector.[1] Another measure might be to bar supervisors from switching to the private sector for a certain period following their employment with the supervisory agency; in the United States, bank supervisors cannot take a job with a commercial bank that they have supervised until after a period of twelve months or more. Recommendations have also been made to commit supervisors in advance to a certain course of action, such as "prompt corrective actions" or "structured early intervention and resolution." Such quasi-automatic responses include mandatory rebuilding of capital; structured and prespecified publicly announced responses by regulators triggered by decreases in a bank's performance below established criteria; mandatory resolution, for example, by sale, recapitalization, or liquidation, of a capital-depleted bank at a prespecified point when capital still exists; and market value accounting and reporting of capital. A continuing problem with the establishment of such prefixed rules is that governments may be tempted to rewrite them during difficult times, even in highly industrialized countries, such as happened in Japan in 1997–1998 (when scheduled deregulation was deferred) and in the United States in the 1980s (when the GAAP for S&Ls was replaced by less stringent accounting standards).

Investors or owners who own equity in a bank in principle have both the ability and the incentive to monitor the actions of their bank. They tend to provide effective self-regulation when they have much at risk, in the form of either capital or future expected profits. Moreover, well-capitalized banks are usually well monitored by their shareholders. On the other hand, small shareholders might tend to free-ride, so it is important that government make sure that there are large stakeholders or strategic investors who can bear greater responsibilities for monitoring the bank's activities. Inside and outside investors need to face the loss of their investment, and they and their managers need to realize that there exists the very real possibility of bank failure or exit from the industry if they are to discourage excessive risk-taking activities.

In this light, some emerging markets have raised their minimum capital ratios above that for many industrialized countries to compensate for the riskier environments in which they operate. For example, in Argentina, the minimum capital adequacy ratio is 11.5 percent, with even higher requirements for banks engaging in riskier activities and with weaker risk management capacity. Moreover, banks in most countries with 8 percent capital adequacy requirements usually have capital ratios in excess of the minimum criteria; the United States has an average capital ratio of almost 12 percent. Even then, capital adequacy ratios are by nature backward-looking accounting indicators of the solvency of financial institutions. The demise of banks with high measured capital ratios has not been an uncommon occurrence (Dhumale, 2000). The increased incentives to engage in excessive risk taking when the capital adequacy position is weakened makes it even more important not to rely on capital adequacy alone. As Table 6.1 indicates, countries have relied on various measures, from limiting entry to enhancing the liability of directors and shareholders to the issuance of subordinated debt (SD). These are discussed in the following sections. While some of these methods may be relatively blunt, the costs of not using them can be quite high. Owners of financial institutions will behave more prudently, that is, will be more risk averse, if they have more to lose in the form of capital, future expected revenue, profits, and so on. Similarly, supervisors need to have the appropriate incentives both to monitor and to enforce the correction of any discrepancies they reveal through their evaluations. Finally, deposit holders tend to provide better market discipline if they are not always fully (100 percent) covered by implicit or explicit deposit insurance schemes.

Given appropriate incentives and the abilities, market participants who enter into creditor relationships with banks could serve as monitors. Their ability to monitor would depend on the quality and quantity of information they receive, which, in turn, would depend on the quality of the bank's accounting standards and practices. To solve the information requirements, some countries have recently enacted extensive disclosure requirements, supported by increased liabilities, mandatory ratings by at least two private ratings agencies, and online credit reporting system (New Zealand, Chile, and Argentina, respectively). In addition to information, creditors need the appropriate incentives to monitor market prac-

Table 6.1. Regulatory Framework for Selected Countries

Country	Minimum Capital Adequacy Ratio (Tier 1 + Tier 2)		Loan Classification Requirements (no. of days before loan is NPL)	Limit on Risk Exposure (% of FOREX assets to be held)	Single Exposure Limit (% of capital)
	Tier 1	Tier 2			
G-10					
Japan	4%	4%	At bank's discretion	Part of mkt. risk	20% of tier 1
United Kingdom	4%	4%	At bank's discretion	No limit	25% of tier 1
United States	4%	4%	90	Not relevant given $US	15% of capital, 10% for secure assts
Latin America					
Argentina	11.5%	<tier 1	90,> 180 nonrecover	Closely monitored	25% of tier 1
Mexico	Subject to authority		90 for cmrcl; 180 for mortgages	15% in US$ + 2% in all others	10% single; 30% corporate
Chile	5.75%	2.25%	90	<20% of capital	5%–25%
Asia & Pacific					
Hong Kong	4%	4%	90	Monitored by HKMA	25% of tot. capital
India	None	<tier 1	210	Not allowed	Corp: 25%; grp: 50%
Indonesia	4%	4%	90	<20% of capital; <25% exposure for single currency	85%
Korea	None	≤ tier	180	20% of capital	45%
Malaysia	8%	0%	180	No restrictions	None
Thailand	4.25%	4.25%	90	Net long 20% tier 1; net short 15% tier 1	25% of tier 1

Source: World Bank data

tices, such as the possibility that they will be allowed to suffer losses. Although small depositors are unlikely to be good monitors of banks, large debt holders are better equipped to fulfil this role. One example of using such incentives has been the mandatory issuance of SD by banks so that if the current owners of a bank fail to ensure a safe and sound bank, the subordinated holders can take over the bank. A more detailed discussion of this type of proposal follows in the next sections.

THE PROS AND CONS OF INCENTIVE- VERSUS
RULE-BASED REGULATION

As mentioned before, rule-based regulation makes inefficient use of managerial expertise, whereas an incentive-based approach uses the insights of managers and market participants to gain an informational advantage in setting regulatory standards. But, incentive-based regulation is not without its problems, especially the large number of issues arising from the strategic interactions among the different decision-making agents within financial institutions. In general, incentive-based regulation promotes a more "hands-off" regulation and gives financial institutions greater freedom to choose the amount and level of risk they wish to accept.

The flexibility of an incentive-based approach derives from the fact that it is not directly prescriptive but creates incentives through other means, such as penalties. In more general terms, an incentive-based system tries to solve what is known as a "mechanism design" problem by specifying a framework, for example, a penalty device, that financial institutions take into account when choosing risk and committing regulatory capital. Ideally, the design of this mechanism makes it incentive-compatible for financial institutions to choose the socially desirable risk profile. The success of such a program depends on how well the regulator anticipates the strategic opportunities that such a mechanism might create. In short, while an incentive-based system is less intrusive, it creates a host of strategic issues.

Furthermore, even more serious are the problems that arise as a result of a conflict of interest within the financial institutions. As at other large institutions, an integral feature of modern banks is the separation of owners from day-to-day decision making. The ownership is diffuse, and there are numerous small shareholders who have little impact on most decisions. In the end, in many cases it is the incentives of the traders at the bank, for example, that determine what specific strategies the bank might adopt on a particular day. Therefore, the extent to which the owners or managers can control the actions of their agents, their traders in this case, becomes very important. However, as most rule-based regulation takes the form of exogenous specification for capital for a given level of risk, as well as some form of inspection, the effects of such agency problems on the success of regulatory mechanisms have often been ignored. Indeed, this agency problem, which a rule-based system cannot handle, is the central issue in determining the success of an incentive-based regulatory system.

Herein lies the tradeoff between the inefficiencies that occur in setting the appropriate regulatory incentives in a rule-based system and the agency problems that exist in a managerial-based incentive system. Although a rule-based system avoids the agency distortions, it does not take into account the diversification benefits of holding different types of risks. As a result, banks often feel that they are forced unnecessarily to retain regulatory capital in excess of the risks they are undertaking. However, under a managerial-based incentive system, the owners and shareholders need to be assured that their interests are aligned with those who actually make the strategic decisions, that is, managers or traders, lest they over-expose themselves; moreover, the costs of such overexposure can have systemic implications. Therefore, to understand the effectiveness of an incentive-based regulatory system, it is important not to consider the bank as a single entity whose actions are directly influenced by the regulatory incentives alone. Rather, to evaluate such a scheme, there needs to be a full understanding of the effect of regulation on the incentives of all the various relevant agents within the bank.

THE ROAD AHEAD

The analysis in this chapter has tried to address most of the issues from the perspective of both regulators and the institutions they regulate. However, regulators are not the only ones in government who worry about incentives. Much of government activity involves efforts to influence private interests in a way that benefits the public. Governments may impose taxes, for example, less for the revenue they generate than to influence behavior; for example, the U.S. government has imposed significant taxes on tobacco products that are intended less to generate funds than to discourage the use of tobacco. Similarly, when government seeks to limit the level of systemic risk within the financial environment, many of its actions affect the incentives of private financial institutions. This problem has been evident in the recent proposals by the Basel Committee, which faces difficult challenges in the future. The Committee has recognized the possible effect, through distorted incentives, of some of its original requirements, the increased competition in the financial services industry, and the notable effects of market risk on bank portfolios. In finding solutions, it not only has to address each of the former issues but must account for the differences among its potential clients. Clearly, a need exists for a risk assessment framework that not only avoids the problems of potentially cosmetic adjustments to capital ratios but also is easily adaptable to different macroeconomic, institutional, and financial conditions. For example, by allowing financial institutions to play a greater role in setting their own capital requirements, the Basel II proposals have recognized the information advantages of the banks themselves and the potential value of rating agencies. However, before these reforms can be put into practice, they require at least the setting of appropriate incentives for private agents and some standards for internal ratings mechanisms, in addition to better coordination of international regulatory standards.

The aforementioned conditions exist to some extent because of the inferior quality and quantity of information received by regulators about the circumstances of any regulated firm when compared to the firm's own information resources. This is true because the firms, which provide virtually all the regulator's information, can effectively control what information they release. Managers are likely to have better information, despite the best efforts of regulators to stay informed, and often the imbalance is worsened by the choice of process for making regulatory decisions. Information provided by active and liquid markets can complement existing accounting-based capital rules and provide a public trigger during difficult times. By issuing such signals, the market not only gives regulators more time to react but also increases the accountability of future actions by both the bank and policymakers.

The issues addressed in this chapter suggest that before designing any incentive based regulatory mechanism, the tradeoff between regulatory and agency incentives must be recognized and addressed. A better understanding of these various costs and benefits should result in a more resilient regulatory structure for the future. Regulation itself is an incentive mechanism. The regulator and the firm are engaged in a strategic game in which each party tries to maximize the benefits of its reactions relative to the other party's actions. Every aspect of regulation, including accounting rules and management standards, has an effect on the incentives of the firm. In many ways, it is not that regulators are given a choice of whether to use incentives; rather, their focus must remain on how to best utilize these incentives to promote systemic stability.

7

The Economics of Systemic Risk in International Settlements

Chapter 6 described some of the underlying reasons for choosing an incentive-based regulatory framework to minimize systemic risk. The present chapter attempts to highlight the implications of not using such incentives by considering one particular case in which the lack thereof could in fact increase overall risk to the economy as a whole. The chapter sets out some of the important issues regarding the recent growth in the movement of global funds that have raised concerns about the potential for increased systemic risk in the payments system.[1] The payments system is the channel through which funds are transferred between financial institutions in the form of electronic debit and credit-book entries. Given the sheer growth in the number and the large volume of transactions currently processed through such payment systems, participating financial institutions incur serious intraday credit exposure. Such exposure can give rise to settlement failures and, consequently, systemic risk. To prevent such settlement failures from turning into a systemic crisis, central banks and regulatory authorities need to play a balancing act; while filling the potential liquidity gap as implicit guarantors of the settlement system, they must catalyze risk-reduction policies to reduce the externality problem, that is, to reduce systemic risk.

This chapter examines the extent to which different settlement systems affect the nature of systemic risks and the potential vulnerability of the financial system to such problems. An important consideration throughout the analysis is whether externalities can be reduced if individual institutions fully internalize the costs of their actions specifically by creating private submanagement systems as low-cost alternatives. The proposed standards for payments and risk control features, including the length of time during which participants are exposed to credit and liquidity risks, are addressed (BIS, 1994). Moreover, given the international nature of present-day payment settlements, the role of various regulatory and legal structures needs to be considered. The chapter discusses the role of public intervention through prudent regulation in the payments system by considering the cost, risk, and efficiency arguments for reducing systemic risk through various systems. Economic theory suggests that government action can be justified if there is an externality. Systemic crises can cause the economy to suffer from suboptimal economic performance, which can affect society as a whole. The ultimate effects of a "chain reaction" failure of financial institutions can exact economywide losses that were not accounted for in the original costs. Clearly, the risk that precedes such systemic crises implies lost economic efficiency and therefore calls for appropriate preemptive regulatory responses. Insofar as payment systems generate externalities, their prices need to reflect the appropriate incentive schemes for financial institutions. There has already been some debate among countries on the appropriate design of payment systems; this debate has reflected the countries' individual approaches to regulation. While the EU has been leaning toward systems with collateralized overdrafts, the United States prefers a noncollateralized system with a fee for overdrafts.

Reducing payments-related credit risk through increased collateralization and charges on overdrafts can have serious systemic costs if market participants decide to participate in private subpayments systems. Consequently, the very reason—better risk management—for which collateralized methods are replacing other systems is undermined. The ultimate goal for regulators is to find methods to internalize the costs of such activities, and the creation of intermediate private netting markets might serve only to introduce further credit risk into the system. Thus, if the ultimate responsibility is to lie with the lenders of last resort, it might be easier for central banks to avoid agency problems by actively managing such risk themselves and discouraging such private submanagement systems. With any system, the systemic nature inherent in a single settlement failure requires the establishment of minimum regulatory standards, whether in terms of interest charges, collateralization requirements, or loss-sharing agreements. The chapter concludes by discussing the establishment of such standards and the associated tradeoffs between their costs and their ability to reduce risk.

BACKGROUND

The debate on payments settlement systems has concentrated on the appropriate pricing of credit exposure to account for negative externalities caused by settlement failures. Such failures could be the result of time delays, institutional shortcomings, or liquidity gaps. Each of these issues could lead to serious systemic crises, and therefore the role of guarantor becomes crucial for the success of the entire financial system. At the same time, it is also important that the guarantor establish appropriate incentives to reduce moral hazard behavior. While the central banks act as the ultimate guarantor, they also need to foster a greater sense of responsibility among market participants through appropriate regulation. Herein lies the critical tradeoff between payments systems—the need for liquidity versus the need to reduce unnecessary credit exposure.

There are two types of payments systems: real-time gross settlement (RTGS) and multilateral netting system. The most important feature of an RTGS system is that it provides instant settlement with finality as soon as a payment order arrives, provided that sufficient funds are available in the account of the sending bank. Settlement refers to the actual transfer of funds from a sending to a receiving bank. Finality means that the settlement is unconditional and irrevocable. In an RTGS system, real time implies that payment orders are continuously executed, while gross settlement means that for each payment order, the total gross amount of funds is transferred. Settlements in netting systems do not occur immediately upon receipt of payment orders. The system immediately informs the receiver whether the order meets some minimum criterion, but the actual settlement does not occur until the end of the day. At this point, the system calculates the net payments or settlement obligations for all participants, and then the settlements are completed.

A crucial difference between RTGS and netting systems is that netting systems have only contingent finality. Although most netting systems disallow any retraction of the orders and in this sense the orders are final, the finality is conditional upon the probability of settlement failure. That is, if a failure occurs because one or more participants in the system has insufficient funds, the netting system has to allow that participant to rescind its order. Therefore, the finality is highly dependent on the daily success of settlement. Netting systems are also different in that they do not need to be operated by a single settlement agent, since the system has two separate operations: clearing and settling. The clearinghouse receives and records all payment orders and checks whether the minimum criteria are fulfilled before calculating the net settlement obligations of each participant. The settlement agent then completes the actual transfer of funds. Thus, the clearinghouse can be managed by any private or public bank or nonbank organization. The settlement agent, however, needs to have the endowment of a guarantor, and therefore central banks seem to be the natural choice. Consequently, separating roles is not possible in an RTGS system. Table 7.1 lists the various RTGS and netting systems presently in operation and planned in selected countries.

Recent debates and research on interbank settlement systems have concentrated on the pricing of daylight overdrafts to control their use. Faulhaber, Philips, and Santomero (1990) and Humphrey (1989) have examined the role and the optimal design of a pricing mechanism with the

Table 7.1. Funds Transfers Systems in Selected Countries

Country	Name of RTGS System	Type	Year of Implementation
Belgium	ELLIPS	RTGS	1996
	CH	Net	NA
Canada	IIPS	Net	1976
	LVTS	Net	1997
France	SAGITTAIRE	Net	1984
	TBF	RTGS	1997
	SNP	Net	1997
Germany	EIL-ZV	RTGS	1987
	EAF2	Net	1996
Italy	BISS	RTGS	1989
	BI-REAL	RTGS	1997
	ME	Net	1989
	SIPS	Net	1989
Japan	BOJ-NET	Net+RTGS	1988
	FEYCS	Net	1989
	Zengin	Net	1973
Netherlands	FA	RTGS+Net	1985
	TOP	RTGS	1997
	8007 SWIFT	Net	1982
Sweden	RIX	RTGS	1986
Switzerland	SIC	RTGS	1987
United Kingdom	CHAPS	RTGS	1984
	Euro version of CHAPS	RTGS	1999
United States	CHIPS	Net	1970
	Fedwire	RTGS	1918
Cross Border	ECU	RTGS	1983

Source: Bank for International Settlements (1998)

Federal Reserve in the United States. The result has been the introduction, in 1994, by the Federal Reserve of a fee for daylight overdrafts. Alternatively, European central banks have decided to collateralize rather than price overdrafts. This choice fits the long-term desire of European countries to progressively move toward settlement systems with little intraday credit exposure, as evident in their desire to meet the Lamfalussy Standards, whether through RTGS or net settlement systems. These standards specify that European Union countries must have RTGS systems in place before they can be linked under an all-encompassing system within the Union, that is, Target.[2] There has already been progress toward this goal in most EU countries, including the United Kingdom, which has not even joined the EMU. There are larger private opportunity costs to collateralizing overdrafts, because financial institutions must deposit their loanable funds as noninterest-bearing reserves with the central bank; however, the total benefits of these reserves, which include benefits to society as a whole, outweigh their costs if they minimize systemic risk associated with settlements.

Settlement Risk

Settlement risk is at the heart of the various risks associated with payment systems. It is the risk that one or more participants will be unable to settle, which may or may not lead to financial losses, depending on the magnitude and risk-reducing measures in place. Settlement risk is present in different forms in different payment systems, usually as credit, liquidity, or unwinding risk; however, the interrelationship of these risks can make it difficult to differentiate among them.

Credit risk arises when the purchaser of an asset defaults by failing to settle any or all of its obligations. Credit risk is a function of the potential loss exposure when a buyer initiates a transaction by ordering its bank to transfer funds but then cannot make payment without requiring an overdraft. Credit risk arises when the two sides of a transaction do not pay simultaneously. In payments systems, credit risk can be separated into "first-payer risk" and "receiver risk." First-payer risk refers to the risk faced by the party that pays first that the corresponding payment will not be received from the counterparty. Receiver risk arises when a receiver assumes that a received payment is final before it actually is and pays its obligation. Receiver risk also exists in RTGS systems when financial institutions are indirect users, that is, when they are not members of the payments system but use a bank that is a member. An indirect user is exposed to receiver risk because of the lag between the time its bank receives payment and the time it notifies its customer. Credit risk can be easily overlooked in payment systems, since the extension of such credit is not intentional but the result of routine payment operations; furthermore, such extensions usually last for less than one day. However, given the large size of such exposure, the risk can be real and significant to indirect users.

Credit risk is especially acute in foreign exchange transactions because of the involvement of payments systems from different countries. The main risk in the settlement of forex transactions is that one party will settle its part and the other party will fail to do so. This is often referred to as Herstatt risk.[3] Such cross-currency settlement risk occurs because the payment systems operate during nonoverlapping hours as a result of the different time zones in which the major central banks are located. Although credit risk is present in both RTGS and netting systems, it is smaller in the latter, especially if there is lots of "traffic" with other users in the system. Heavy traffic means that the netted amount of payment due or owed are small, resulting in little credit exposure. Thus, a bank with few or no dealings with other banks benefits less from the netting system's ability to limit credit risk. Since the Herstatt episode, various international efforts, including the *BIS Report on Foreign Exchange Settle-*

ment Risk and Continuous Linked Settlement Systems (CLS), a central bank–induced private-sector initiative, have tried to provide solutions to prevent potential "traffic jams."[4]

Unwinding Risk

Unwinding risk can occur when receivers are not able to settle transactions because some instructions have been revoked, or unwound. Unwinding occurs when there is settlement failure in netting systems and the daily payment orders need to be revoked. Unwinding causes serious losses to netting users, for these users may have already used the amounts to make payments in other systems, which will now be defaulted. These costs only increase in light of the international nature of payment systems in present-day transactions. Moreover, after unwinding occurs, users need to renegotiate their positions, which can lead to further financial losses. The management of unwinding risk is even more difficult than credit risk management, since the creditworthiness of all parties in the netting system, rather than only that of the counterparties in the transaction, needs to be verified to prevent settlement default. Clearly, there are high information requirements for the successful management of such risk, since unwinding risk exposes every user to every other user's risk. Unwinding risk is a systemic risk because of its ability to affect more than one user. The chain reaction caused by the settlement failure of one transaction can be widespread. Some netting systems allow for the day's transactions to be unwound to limit the damage, but, given the size of present-day payments, the amount involved can exceed $1 trillion. Thus, unwinding can raise doubts and concerns for investors regarding the stability of the entire system, creating a systemic crisis from a local individual settlement problem.

Liquidity Risk

Liquidity risk exists when payment orders cannot be settled because of a lack of liquidity, even though all parties are financially healthy. Although liquidity risk exists in both RTGS and netting systems, its presence is more pronounced in RTGS systems, since gross settlements require greater liquidity to settle each participant's exposure to every other participant's liquidity risk. Unlike other transactions, immediate liquidity at settlement time is crucial, and even a temporary liquidity shortfall can create severe problems. Liquidity risk can be reduced if all parties in the payment system retain sufficient liquidity, that is, cash or reserve balances, which can be used for clearing purposes. However, maintaining liquidity has serious opportunity costs to participants, since cash or reserve balances held by financial institutions do not earn interest income. Consequently, a tradeoff exists between the value of reducing liquidity risk and the costs of maintaining sufficient liquidity in the system. Liquidity risk is a systemic risk, since a liquidity shortfall for one participant can lead to liquidity shortfalls for other counterparties resulting in a chain reaction of systemic liquidity shortfall. As mentioned before, RTGS systems are more likely than netting systems to suffer from liquidity risk, since a shortage at any time brings the entire system to a halt.

Credit risk remains prevalent in all systems, whereas unwinding and liquidity risk are more peculiar to specific systems. The degrees of unwinding and liquidity risk depend on the type of system in practice. Unwinding risk exists exclusively in netting systems, whereas liquidity risk is present mainly in RTGS systems. If any one participant suffers from any of these risks, it exposes all other participants, as well; herein lies the systemic nature of the problem.

RISK MANAGEMENT IN RTGS AND NET SETTLEMENT SYSTEMS

Recent reforms in net settlement systems in different countries have concentrated on reducing systemic risk, as well as on the interventionist role of the central bank in case of a systemic failure. For RTGS systems, efforts have centered on reducing the growing credit exposure of central banks. The objective of these reforms and regulations has been to improve the safety features of payment systems by forcing private participants to internalize the social costs of third-party risk (Passacantando, 1991). Banks' exposure to such payment risks ceases when settlements are finalized through payments received from the central bank. Thus, at a very basic level, settlement risk can be lowered by reducing the size of a bank's exposure, as well as by preventing unnecessary payment delays. Furthermore, it has been widely accepted that systemic risk in payment systems can be better controlled in RTGS systems than in net settlement systems.

RISK MANAGEMENT IN RTGS

Central banks provide RTGS systems to commercial banks and other selected institutions such as government agencies and, in some countries, clearinghouses for securities and derivatives exchanges (BIS, 1998). The design issues related to RTGS systems vary by countries, but two areas related to risk management that are commonly discussed are central banks' policies regarding the granting of intraday credit and the establishment of queuing systems. Intraday credit is useful in an RTGS system, since it is able to reduce payment blockages that may arise when receiving banks do not execute their transactions before checking that the sending banks are "covered." In an RTGS system, the "cover principle" ensures that the sending bank has sufficient reserves, or cover, in its reserve account at the central bank before payment is executed. An important systemic risk concern in the RTGS system is the risk of a liquidity shortage. This risk can be reduced by increasing the liquidity held by the member banks. As mentioned before, the opportunity costs of retaining liquidity can be high. Consequently, individual banks do not want to bear the entire cost of potential chain reactions caused by liquidity shortages and choose a level of liquidity that is lower than the social optimum; this is yet another example of how private banks do not internalize the costs of their activities that can have negative externalities on society as a whole.

Central banks often provide minimum intraday liquidity to payments systems for the smooth running of the RTGS system. Although unlimited central bank intraday credit could reduce ensuing delays caused by the "cover principle," it might create a moral hazard problem so that banks would begin to manage their intraday liquidity less efficiently while assuming that the central bank would bail them out of a liquidity crisis. Reserves held at the central bank under minimum reserve requirements, collateralized intraday loans/overdrafts, and noncollateralized loans and overdrafts are extended to member banks under intraday liquidity programs. Essentially, the central banks face a tradeoff whereby they reduce liquidity risk in the payments system but simultaneously increase their own credit risk. However, as central banks, they realize that the social costs and systemic impact of a liquidity shortage far outweigh the higher potential credit risk they face. Clearly, central banks face less credit risk if they make only collateralized loans. Although collateralized loans from central banks are cheaper for private banks than clearing their balances, liquidity risk still exists. Collateralized loans are still relatively costly to banks, since the banks could invest the same collateral in assets that offer higher interest. Consequently, the opportunity cost still exists, motivating private banks to hold less liquidity than is required to eliminate liquidity risk from the entire system.

Although RTGS systems are supposed to operate continuously, some payment orders are not always executed. In the standard case, for instance, when a sending bank has insufficient funds, the payment order is rejected unconditionally by the central bank and returned to the sender. The sending bank may then prioritize this particular payment order and resubmit it to the RTGS system when sufficient funds are available to cover the transaction. However, the rejected payment order of the sending bank can lead to settlement delays for other banks, which may have already included this payment in their daily liquidity management. A buildup of such delays can cause gridlock in the entire payment system. The systemic costs of such delays can be large and need to be accounted for. A bank is forced to delay its payment when it has insufficient liquid reserves or has already exceeded its permitted overdraft or credit limits with the central bank. As discussed above, one solution is to provide temporary liquidity in the payments systems through intraday credit. Similarly, banks can learn to manage their payment traffic with lower levels of liquidity. This option has high costs for private banks, since they need to employ better liquidity management systems, such as input sequencing and the splitting of payment orders. Each of these measures entails high costs, including extra equipment and staffing. Moreover, such measures to increase liquidity benefit all participants in the payments system. Thus, if the decision is left to the private banks alone, they may not take on such

costly responsibilities for fear that "free riders" might take advantage of
the banks that do incur the costs.

At a very basic level, the following definitions might help to elucidate
the problem. Humphrey defines payment reserves or overdraft limits of
private banks as

$$\bar{L} = \sum_i \bar{l}i \tag{1}$$

The $\bar{l}i$ represents the limits for each bank, while the $\bar{L}$ is the aggregate limit
for all of the banks in the entire system. Settlements occur at a rate r times
the number of permitted overdrafts:

$$S = \bar{L}r \tag{2}$$

Thus, in order to prevent settlement delays, when overdraft limits ($\bar{L}$) are
reduced, the rate at which the settlement payments are made (r) needs to
increase, and vice versa. As mentioned before, some central banks are
granting intraday credit to increase ($\bar{L}$). Increasing (r) is a solution, but it
imposes high costs on private banks and raises their suspicions about the
free-rider problem. Central bank intervention is justified, since the social
costs of settlement delays and gridlock can be large and systemic.
Therefore, central banks need to consider subsidizing the costs of increasing (r) and preventing gridlock. The probability (p) of gridlock and its
social costs can be defined:

$$p(G) = p(I - S) \tag{3}$$

$$p(G) = p(I - Lr) \tag{4}$$

$$SC = PC + p(G) \tag{5}$$

$$SC = PC + p(1 - Lr) \tag{6}$$

where

$0 \leqslant p \leqslant 1$
$G = Gridlock$
$PC = Private\ costs$
$SC = Social\ costs$

The key to preventing settlement delays becoming a systemic problem is
the probability (p) of gridlock; ideally, private banks should be solely responsible for any delays they might cause, and for the subsequent costs.

Since gridlock is the result of settlements that are not executed or (1-S), the central bank can try to subsidize the costs of increasing (r) through "optimization" (BIS, 1998). In this case, increasing (r) might be considered a public good. As an alternative to returning the payment order to the sender, optimization requires that unexecuted payment orders remain in centrally located and managed queuing system. In this case, the central bank retains all payment orders that require cover in a centrally located queue, which releases them as soon as sufficient funds are available. Such a system might provide a more orderly flow of payments, since the system can more efficiently manage payment requests that will offset and provide cover to each other to some extent. Of course, a moral hazard problem might arise if banks rely too heavily on this queuing system to manage intraday liquidity. It may also increase interdependence and settlement risk if banks begin to anticipate and direct final payments ahead of the queue. Nonetheless, it is at least one way to prevent a temporary payment gridlock from developing into a systemwide problem. Table 7.2 describes the differences between queuing systems in some countries.

Delivery-versus-Payment Systems

Another common method for reducing a specific type of credit risk called principal risk in various securities transactions in RTGS systems has been the use of delivery-versus-payment (DVP).[5] DVP eliminates the credit risk inherent in a transaction because it requires all payments to occur with finality at the same time. Such settlement procedure requires that a link exist between a real-time security clearing system and a monetary clearing system before a securities transaction can be completed. The United States and Switzerland use such DVP systems to ensure that securities are transferred from the seller to the buyer if and only if funds are transferred from the buyer to the seller. Since this requires real-time payment finality in every transaction, DVP works only in an RTGS payments scheme. DVP can also be used in foreign exchange transactions to eliminate the cross-

Table 7.2. Intraday Credit Policies and Centrally Located Queues in RTGS Systems

Countries Whose RTGS Systems Provide:	Centrally Located Queue	No Centrally Located Queue
Central bank intraday credit	Belgium France Germany Italy Netherlands Sweden	United Kingdom United States
No central bank intraday credit	Switzerland	Japan

Source: Bank for International Settlements, 1997–1998

currency settlement risk; in this case, it is called payment-versus-payment (PVP). PVP requires that both systems have RTGS systems and over-lapping operation times, and the payment orders must be sent during these overlapping times. While such synchronization of operating hours may be easily arranged within Europe, it requires longer hours of oper-ation in other places. In response, the U.S. Federal Reserve extended its operations to eighteen hours per day, but other financial centers have not indicated any changes so far. Moreover, although all EU countries have established RTGS systems and Japan is considering moving the bulk of its payments to RTGS, it is interesting to note that even today the dollar side of settling forex transactions continues to be conducted through CHIPS (Clearing House Inter-Bank Payments System), a net settlement system.

Although DVP systems eliminate credit risk, their costs can prohibit their immediate adoption. There are vast technical and coordination re-quirements that would require the absorption of greater information for each RTGS system in every country. Another potential cost of DVP sys-tems is their effect on increasing systemic risk. The linking of RTGS sys-tems for simultaneous settlement of each part of forex or other securities transaction might reduce cross-currency settlement risk, but it can lead to further settlement delays. If the settlement of one part of the payment order is conditional upon settlement of another, a delay in one system will cause settlement delays in others. These delays could be the result of li-quidity or more mundane technical problems, but, in any event, domestic RTGS systems will essentially be importing problems of foreign RTGS systems because of the links between them. Therefore, although DVP sys-tems eliminate some types of credit risk (e.g., cross-currency settlement, Herstatt), they can be interrupted themselves for no fault of their own. This situation is exacerbated by their potential to create systemic prob-lems, especially if liquidity problems occur as exchange rates and secu-rities prices change rapidly (BIS, 1995a).

RISK MANAGEMENT IN NET SETTLEMENT SYSTEMS: CENTRALIZED VERSUS DECENTRALIZED

Although credit risk exists in netting systems, the main concern in these systems is unwinding risk. Unwinding risk is most prevalent when a net-ting system fails to settle. Thus, reforms and efforts to reduce unwinding risk focus on reducing the probability of settlement failures. BIS and other authorities have recently been encouraging members of netting systems to improve and pay greater attention to their risk management efforts. Central banks distinguish between "secured" netting systems and all oth-ers. In a secured system, credit exposures due to intraday overdrafts can be controlled *ex ante* through caps and *ex post* through loss-sharing agree-ments. A secured system is one that is able to settle all of its net obligations at the end of a clearing cycle even when the largest net-debit position is unable to settle. Banks can establish a settlement guarantee by, for example, posting collateral in advance, depositing capital at the clearing-house, forming joint backup settlement agreements with other members, or agreeing to a government guarantee.

If the settlement failure is the result of temporary liquidity problem, it is reasonable to assume that the central bank can play an important role. However, if the failure is related to a solvency problem, any assistance from the central banks will only exacerbate the situation in the long run. Therefore, it is crucial that the authorities be able to decipher the source of the failure. In cases where settlement failure stems from a liquidity crunch and the allotted collateral in the system is insufficient, the central bank could offer assistance. The situation could be described more aptly using definitions like those used earlier; however, in this case it is the total aggregate shortfall, $\bar{F}$, rather than the aggregate net overdraft limits, $\bar{L}$, of the banks that are of importance.

$$\bar{F} = \sum_i \bar{f}i \qquad (7)$$

It is also assumed that under a net settlement system, in accordance with the Lamfalussy standards, a temporary shortfall is appropriated to the other banks according to an *ex post* loss-sharing rule supported by their joint collateral, $\bar{C}$. If $F - C \leq 0$, where the total shortfall $\bar{F}$ is less than the amount of available collateral put forth by the private banks, the private banks have successfully internalized the social costs of their activities. However, the critical situation arises when $F - C > 0$, where the total shortfall is greater than the available collateral. In this case, if in fact it is a problem of illiquidity and not insolvency, the central bank might step in to compensate for the temporary shortfall in the private banks' collateral to prevent a systemic crisis. That is, the central bank could add additional liquidity, A, to the existing pool of collateral, C, so that $A + C = F$. By providing the additional liquidity A, the central bank provides a public good that would otherwise not be available if it were left to the private market alone. Of course, such provisions have social benefits and avoid possible settlement failures and their ensuing problems. Again, the significant factor that needs to be considered before providing the A is whether the problem is only one of temporary illiquidity and therefore not related to insolvency issues; in some cases, illiquidity can turn into insolvency absent central bank intervention.

Other settlement risk management efforts in netting systems that have been encouraged by central banks include direct monitoring by banks of other banks. The financial exposure created by one bank for another in this system provides a strong incentive for creditor banks to monitor debtor banks. Moreover, private financial institutions may have better access to information on other banks than is available to central banks or other banking supervisors. However, a natural shortcoming in such decentralized bilateral monitoring arrangements in netting systems is the free-rider problem. Banks realize that any excess losses created by a member of the netting system will be shared among all of the remaining members. This cost-spreading feature reduces the incentive for banks to monitor other banks as closely as they should. One solution has been to increase the costs specifically for the bank that has failed as an effective monitor by making it pay greater amounts in collateral relative to the other members. Such is the basic idea in Calomiris's recent scheme, which suggests that banks police themselves by requiring every bank to finance a small proportion of its assets by selling subordinated debt to other institutions—that is, to foreign banks—with the stipulation that the yield on this debt cannot be more than 50 basis points higher than the rate on corresponding riskless instruments (Calomiris, 1999).[6] The yield cap would guarantee that banks cannot compensate these debt holders with large spreads when they participate in high-risk activities. As the essence of Calomiris's recommendation is to reduce these very risks, investors would buy subordinated debt only when they were sure that the bank's activities were low risk. If in fact a bank were unable to convince other banks of its aversion to risk, it would not be allowed to function. In this way, Calomiris would exploit the access to greater and better information that bankers are believed to have. His solution aligns the incentives of private banks and regulators alike by mandating that the social costs of high-risk activities not be borne by the government alone.

However, even a larger burden were mandated in case of a failure, decentralized monitoring within a netting system might not promote sufficiently effective and intensive monitoring. The problem will be exacerbated as more participants enter the system. In this case, not only will there be a greater burden because of the need to monitor additional banks, but banks will realize that their potential losses will be further reduced as they are shared between even more participants. Centralized monitoring has been considered as an alternative. In this case, moral hazard problems may arise, given that participants are not under the constant scrutiny of other members. Further complications may arise when such a central authority makes choices regarding the use of common resources to bail out temporary liquidity crises. In any case, net settlement systems seem more naturally attuned to private rather than centralized risk management methods, given the information advantages participants have, compared to regulators. However, without appropriate incentives, such private monitoring can be inefficient and can exacerbate the large social costs it intends to mitigate.

IS COEXISTENCE AN ALTERNATIVE?

If one considers netting systems with decentralized risk control mechanisms and gross settlement systems with centralized risk controls such as collateralized overdrafts, neither one seems clearly superior to the other.

Ideally, central banks try to minimize their credit risk exposure and prefer RTGS, which are settled without the use of central bank intraday credit. Although secured net settlement systems are preferred by private banks, they leave the central banks far more exposed. Optimization through queuing and central bank intraday liquidity provisions might promote RTGS, but the costs of maintaining noninterest-bearing reserves or pledging collateral remain high for private banks. One market-based solution has been to offer more incentives, such as paying interest on end-of-day reserves. It has even been suggested that an active market for intraday credit might emerge as a result of such incentives. In this way, not only are the costs for private banks minimized, but also the probability of gridlock is simultaneously reduced through market-based incentives.

Another solution has been to consider the benefits of each system and examine whether they can coexist while promoting risk control measures. It is possible for more than one payment system to serve an economy, as is the case in the United States and Japan (Summers, 1994).[7] However, research suggests that the existence of two systems may encourage private banks to choose the lower-cost rather than the lower-risk alternative. While netting systems are less costly for private banks in terms of liquidity management, they give rise to unwinding risk in cases of a settlement failure. Research has shown that the cost of holding extra liquidity in an RTGS system exceeds the benefits of the reduction in systemic and settlement risk (Garber and Weisbrod, 1992). In Garber's analysis, the opportunity cost of holding securities as collateral is estimated to be 25 basis points. The expected cost of settlement failure in netting systems is the actual loss on the liquidity advances from the central bank, A, to make up the total shortfall, $F - C$. The actual loss is calculated as the probability of repayment (i.e., if it is a bank failure, repayment $= 0$), multiplied by its net debit position. The results of this analysis indicate that the aggregate cost of settlement failure in a netting system is only half the cost of retaining liquidity in an RTGS system, suggesting that a netting system is the lowest-cost alternative. An important caveat is the assumption that central banks are assumed to be risk neutral, rather than risk averse, in this exercise—an assumption that could substantially increase the expected costs of settlement failure in netting systems (Folkerts-Landau and Garber, 1992.)

The present evolution of payments systems indicates that the European RTGS systems, with collateralized, interest-free overdrafts, and the U.S. RTGS systems, with uncollateralized overdrafts with interest charges, will both continue to exist. The lack of a common design of wholesale payments systems for the major international currencies suggests that there might be a preference for one system over another. For instance, it has been suggested that at planned levels of interest charges and collateralization, the interest-free, collateralized system in Europe could cost more than the interest charge–based, uncollateralized overdraft system in the United States. Because of the lower total costs, banks would prefer to conduct all financial transaction in U.S. dollar terms (see Chakravorti, 1996, and Folkerts-Landau and Garber, 1996). Given the relative liquidity of the U.S. money and foreign exchange markets, the U.S. market could become the preferred environment for financial transactions to a point where it could isolate and render other markets ineffective. Therefore, in assessing the coexistence of systems across markets, it is important to consider not only the liquidity arguments of each system but also the relative level of interest charges and collateralization requirements so as not to violate certain minimum standards by exacerbating distortions between different markets.

POLICY CONSIDERATIONS: THE SHIFT TOWARD COLLATERALIZED RTGS SYSTEMS

The phenomenal growth in payments increases not only the risk of settlement failure but also the systemic impact of such failures. An appropriately designed payment system is crucial for financial stability and efficient operation, especially during periods of financial distress. Many countries have undertaken reforms to reduce the credit risk associated with the growth of intraday credit exposures in net settlement systems and in RTGS systems with central bank provisions for overdrafts. To internalize some costs of the externalities in netting systems—to prevent systemic crises—central banks have encouraged caps and/or charges on overdrafts and the use of loss-sharing agreements. Using such market-based incentives, the liquidity benefits of a netting system are preserved as participants are required to contribute a limited amount of collateral to a pool (equal to the largest net debit position in the pool), rather than fully collateralize their own net debit positions. However, by and large, especially in Europe, recent efforts have sought to reduce intraday payments–related credit in netting systems by restructuring them into RTGS systems with collateralized overdrafts. Despite the apparent liquidity advantages of netting arrangements, there are several reasons for this gradual shift. First, systems, markets, and financial instruments are evolving at much faster rates than the political bodies that find it difficult to keep updating the rules to prevent abuse. Second, the immense task of coordinating legal rules inherent in nonsynchronized settlement systems across international boundaries (i.e., Herstatt risk, forex transactions) can be complex even in a cooperative and legal environment. Finally, central banks continue to be forced into the role of lenders of last resort and can limit their exposure better through collateralized RTGS than netting systems.

As mentioned before, the replacement of netting with RTGS systems with collateralized overdrafts might encourage an active market for intraday credit; payments made during periods of low liquidity could qualify for discounts, whereas other payments would offer different premiums depending on the liquidity in the market at that particular time. Again, the risk of insufficient liquidity within an RTGS system raises concerns about settlement delays and, ultimately, gridlock. Some suggested solutions to this problem are for central banks to pay interest on bank reserves to encourage holdings of settlement liquidity or to "optimize" payments through efficient queuing mechanisms and to create a link between RTGS systems and securities settlement systems to complete delivery-versus-payment.

Another cost of reductions in payments-related credit in both RTGS and netting systems through the imposition of charges on overdrafts and collateralization is the pressure to create private subnetting systems as low-cost alternatives to RTGS systems with collateralized or interest-bearing overdrafts (Folkerts-Landau and Garber, 1992). For some private financial institutions, the liquidity argument would be a strong reason to participate in such private subnetting arrangements. Consequently, the very reason—better risk management—for which collateralized RTGS systems are replacing netting systems would be undermined. In this case, central banks would hope to regulate these private netting systems but even then would increase the overall risk in the system by possibly distorting payment patterns and adding further to the externalities of the overall payments systems. As regulators, their ultimate goal is to find methods to internalize the costs of such activities, and the creation of intermediate private netting markets might serve only to reduce the central bank's direct exposure to credit risk by allowing them to assume some of their burden on only a temporary basis. However, in the end, as lenders of last resort, the central banks bear the ultimate responsibility for risk management, and to avoid agency problems it might be easier to actively manage such risk on their own.

CONCLUSION

The buildup of systemic risk in netting systems is essentially the result of the collection of credit extensions issued by banks to one another. These "orders" are netted against one another and settled in cash or by delivery of the appropriate securities or foreign exchangeat the end of the clearing cycle. If any of the participants in this system defaults by exceeding its net debit position, it may be necessary to unwind the entire set of transactions. Another type of settlement risk in netting systems is caused by the lag in payments, leading one participant who is owed a payment to prematurely consider the transaction final. That is, one party may assume that payment is final even though, in the settlement lag, the payee may receive additional information from elsewhere in the system that might affect the status of the final payment. Clearly, there are advantages to accessing such information, especially for private banks that can minimize the costs of maintaining liquidity for payment purposes, but, in cases of settlement failures, the potential for systemic disruptions is large. RTGS systems try to eliminate such systemic risk by posting early-warning indicators in payments and settlement systems. They require financial institutions that are attempting to make a payment or to effect a settlement to post "cash in advance" (or collateral or securities). RTGS systems do not allow the insolvency of a single financial institution to be transmitted to others through the payments system, since settlements are never conditional on the solvency of the paying institution.

Most EC countries have indicated their strong preference for adopting RTGS systems in the very near future. Some of these countries reason that removing interbank credit altogether from the payments systems will reduce the "inherently uncontrollable" nature of interbank credit in netting systems (Bank of England, 1998). Others in the EC have questioned the legal standing of netting systems, particularly the lack of a common approach to insolvency and the effect of this on multinational participation that has the potential to cause the entire system to unwind. The use of RTGS systems has only recently become more widespread. This delay is in some part a result of the significant liquidity costs discussed earlier. These costs can be lessened if central banks are willing to pay interest on reserve balances, which would encourage financial institutions to hold clearing balances in excess of the legal minimum. These balances, coupled with collateralized overdrafts, would provide greater liquidity for RTGS systems, and the collateral could also support delivery-versus-payment securities transactions. One way by which collateralization internalizes the costs of the risks in payments systems is by reducing the threat of gridlock. In a sense, such collateralization is a way of privatizing the clearing and payments systems. It not only reduces the need for central banks to monitor and control risk taking by financial institutions but also limits the extent of the financial safety net.

One way of resolving the apparent conflict between different approaches toward establishing payment systems is to recognize that there is a tradeoff between the efficiency of the financial system and the amount of risk assumed by the public sector. To the extent that regulatory differences between countries exist at any point in time, they reflect national preferences and judgments regarding risk and efficiency and national preferences on the risk-efficiency spectrum at that particular time. On the other hand, given the large value and the international nature of present-day wholesale payments, the effects of any disruptions that arise could present a global systemic threat. Consequently, while it is important that each country decide on its degree of regulatory action, the systemic nature inherent in a single settlement failure requires the establishment of at least minimum standards, whether in terms of interest charges, collateralization requirements, or loss-sharing agreements.

8

A Microeconomic Examination of Financial Fragility

A Test of Capital Adequacy Standards

As mentioned in chapter 6, in order for an incentive-based approach toward financial regulation to be most effective, appropriate standards must be in place; this clearly presents a challenge for standard setters throughout the world. On the one hand, standards need to be set high enough so that they abide by certain well-defined economic norms that minimize overall costs to both the individual and society. However, these standards involve a tradeoff, and it is equally important that they not become unreasonably prohibitive by nature or regulators risk creating incentives for microeconomic agents to find short cuts. Herein lies the focus of this chapter—the need for capital adequacy standards that are not subject to cosmetic or "window dressing" adjustments. Recent banking crises in Asia have highlighted the importance of having in place a sound domestic financial system, especially a prudential regulatory, supervisory, and accounting framework, before a nation undertakes financial-sector liberalization. The Asian crises have highlighted the link between liberalization and ensuing financial fragility and the tradeoff between the benefits of liberalization and the costs of increasing financial fragility in developing markets. These costs have been drastic enough to force some to question the benefits of moving away from a financially repressive system before an economy's market institutions are ready to do so. Moreover, the speed at which the recent Asian crisis spread attracted even greater attention to the systemic nature of the aforementioned costs inherent in present-day markets. Consequently, the efficacy of standardized regulations that extend beyond national boundaries has been questioned, given that countries risk attracting systemic threats even during crises in other parts of the world. This chapter examines the responses of banks in three Asian countries—Thailand, Indonesia, and South Korea—to one such universal standard, capital adequacy, and that standard's effect on the probability that such crises will occur.

During financial liberalization, banks encounter greater competition and expose themselves to greater risks. The timely implementation of prudential supervision becomes essential to the maintenance of the systemic health of the financial industry, including the sound management of individual financial institutions. Prudential policies can limit the risk exposure of the financial industry by ensuring that individual institutions are managed properly. Controlling credit risk through the implementation of a minimum capital adequacy standard has been a key prudential supervisory measure. In this light, many countries have started or already adopted the capital adequacy standards set by the Basel Committee of the Bank for International Settlements (BIS) in 1988 to strengthen domestic regulation. An analysis of whether banks have responded to risk-based capital adequacy requirements by making cosmetic adjustments rather than effective changes is crucial to determining future supervisory policies. If banks are able to rely heavily on cosmetic responses to capital requirements, the efficacy of the BIS guidelines will be limited, especially in some developing countries where macroeconomic conditions can be especially volatile in the absence of prudential accounting standards.

The object of the chapter is to explicate the link between the relative level of an individual bank's adequacy and the fragility of the banking system. Specifically, the probability of a banking crisis is modeled, using one characteristic of individual banks—their capital adequacy ratios. Banks in the three countries studied are first separated on the basis of these characteristics and then tested categorically against various macroeconomic, institutional, and financial factors. Although there has been much evidence of the link between financial development and economic growth, evidence of the connection between financial liberalization and financial fragility at a microeconomic level has been rare. This chapter not only attempts to fill this gap but also highlights the importance of microprudential regulations during the financial liberalization process. It is hypothesized that after liberalization, banks are pressured due to greater competition within the financial sector from home and abroad. As a result, capital adequacy regulations need to be improved to preclude overexposure to different types of risk and to reduce the probability of a systemwide crisis. Although in many cases these improvements might imply more stringent quantitative standards, greater attention must also be paid to the quality of the capital banks hold in their portfolios. While it is generally agreed that there were some obvious regulatory failures during the Asian crisis, this chapter examines the precise nature of the possible sources of failure in the capital adequacy requirement, including its lack of transparency, ineffective accounting standards, and a weak institutional framework. The next section includes a closer examination of the link between financial liberalization and financial fragility and a review of capital adequacy regulation. In the succeeding sections, the methodology and the actual model are tested. The final sections discuss the importance of distinguishing between cosmetic and effective changes to capital adequacy ratios to avoid the systemic threats that can grow out of microeconomic weaknesses in domestic banking systems, as we have witnessed in Asia.

BACKGROUND
Financial Liberalization

The positive effects of financial liberalization on capital accumulation, advocated by McKinnon and Shaw, as well as the increase in future growth rates, suggested by King and Levine, have been overshadowed by recent increases in financial fragility (McKinnon, 1973; Shaw, 1973; King and Levine, 1993). Banking sectors in many parts of the world have suffered from numerous problems, many of which turned into systemic crises, as indicated in recent studies (Lindgren, Garcia, and Saal, 1996). In many of these countries, banking-sector problems became evident immediately after financial sector deregulation. These episodes suggest that the benefits of financial liberalization need to be weighed against the costs of increased financial fragility. In fact, a basic premise that emerges from some of these crises suggests that some degree of financial regulation might be preferred to premature liberalization in developing countries (Stiglitz, 1994).

In many countries, the pursuit of accelerated liberalization policies for greater efficiency in financial markets further emphasizes the need for certain regulatory standards. These standards need to balance the productive benefits of increased liberalization within the financial sector with the increased probability of a banking crisis. Prudential regulation aims to protect the stability of the financial system, as well as all depositors. Although prudential macroeconomic regulation is often acknowledged as essential for systemic stability, it is the microeconomic regulatory standards that many liberalization programs have increasingly dismantled in some countries (Long and Vittas, 1992). For example, many countries began to remove controls on international capital flows as part of their liberalization programs. At a macroeconomic level, this allowance opened the way for local financial intermediaries to gain access to a greater volume of funds, which was often required by local borrowers. However, it also exposed them to foreign exchange risk, which prudential foreign currency exposure limits tried to curtail. Unfortunately, these limits were circumvented by local banks, which continued to lend, except that now they did so in foreign currency to unhedged domestic borrowers. In this way, they met the foreign currency exposure limit by transferring their foreign exchange risk to credit risk. Consequently, it was no surprise that currency crises almost always preceded or accompanied banking crises (Kaminsky and Reinhart, 1998).

Financial liberalization provided banks greater freedom and the opportunity to increase their exposure to risk. Although such measures might increase the productivity of funds, they can lead to a point where the level of risk might be greater than what is socially optimal. This condition is further complicated in the presence of perverse incentives, including moral hazard, by state-backed insurance schemes. Effective prudential regulation and supervision are needed to control such behavior and to realign appropriate incentives at both the macroeconomic and the microeconomic levels. Given that the probability of a systemic banking crisis may be greater in financially liberalized systems, the chapter examines whether there is a link between an individual bank's behavior and the fragility of the banking system.

POSTLIBERALIZATION BANKING BEHAVIOR

The change in the postliberalization behavior of banks usually increases banking risks and affects banking soundness, especially in the absence of a proper supervisory framework. Following liberalization, banking systems in many countries have experienced significant problems with large capital inflows in the absence of adequate internal controls and prudential oversight to contain the increased risk of new and expanded activities.[1] The recent experience of many banks in East Asia proved the importance of having these regulatory measures in place prior to liberalization; in their absence, banks risk systemic failure, which can develop into an economywide crisis.

In the 1990s, East Asian countries pursued a variety of liberalization policies within the financial sector; steps included removing many barriers to entry, increasing the scope of bank activities, allowing foreign banking, and loosening foreign exchange controls. Thailand introduced the Bangkok International Banking Facility, which attracted foreign borrowers by offering preferred interest rates. These lower rates not only increased competition among Thai banks and financial institutions (FIs) but also squeezed the profit margins of other domestic banks, forcing them to enter into riskier activities. Indonesian liberalization allowed the number of banks to increase from 64 in 1987 to almost 239 in 1997 (IMF, 1998). Korean policy allowed finance companies to become merchant banks so that they could begin lending and borrowing in foreign currency, an area in which they had little experience. The number of Korean banks increased from six in 1993 to thirty in 1996 (Jae-Kwon, 1998). With an increase in the number of banks and FIs, there was a subsequent expansion in lending to the private sector at an ever-increasing rate (Table 8.1). Between 1990 and 1997, bank lending in real terms grew at 18 percent in Indonesia and Thailand and 12 percent in Korea (BIS, 1998).

This sudden and rapid growth in bank lending in itself implies that even borrowers with marginally viable projects were granted credit. Moreover, it stretched the capacities of banks to appraise and monitor

Table 8.1. Credit Growth in East Asian Countries 1990–1996 (%)

Country	Annual Growth of Loans	Loan Growth/ GDP Growth	Net Domestic 1990	Credit/GDP 1996
Indonesia	20	122	45	56
Korea	14	123	68	79
Malaysia	13	134	80	136
Thailand	14	176	84	130

Source: World Bank (1998)

borrowers, causing their portfolios to decline in asset quality. Other factors specific to the Asian banks included a buildup of nonperforming loans to industries targeted and supported by government policy. Government intervention in the internal management of banks suggested that officials had less regard for the interests of bank depositors than they did for ensuring the continuance of prescribed government lending policies to specific sectors, even if they were nonprofitable. For example, the average profit margins of *chaebols*[2] fell to negligible level in the mid-1990s, and some even went bankrupt; government pressure forced banks to extend preferential loans to small and medium-scale businesses in Indonesia, agricultural and rural industries in Thailand, and the Bumiputera community in Malaysia (Miller and Luangaram, 1998; Rahman, 1998). Furthermore, when these governance problems within the banks' corporate management eventually became known to depositors, the belief that financial institutions were protected by the government raised moral hazard issues. Consequently, market discipline failed to exert effective control, since depositors had little incentive to monitor the management of financial institutions. It is now accepted that the timely implementation of prudential policies is essential to avoid further economic instability during the financial liberalization process. Among such policies, some involve the implementation of better risk-management measures at the microeconomic level, including those that monitor foreign exchange exposure, restrict insider trading, and limit credit and exchange rate risk.

Capital Adequacy

In 1988, the Basel Committee of the BIS, in an effort to prevent banks from increasing their credit risk, agreed to require that banks actively engaged in international transactions hold capital equal to at least 8 percent of their risk-weighted assets. Since January 2001, the Basel Committee has been proposing a more "fine-tuned" approach to calculating capital adequacy in several drafts of its Basel II Consultative Papers, which are discussed in more detail in the following chapters. In drawing up capital standards, ratios are calculated on a consolidated basis. Capital includes both core capital (tier 1) and supplementary capital (tier 2); assets are weighted item by item to reflect credit risk. Off-balance sheet engagements are also included in risk-weighted assets after conversion using credit conversion factors. Supplementary capital can be made up of revaluation reserves, gains on securities valuation, and general provisions for loan losses within the limits set in the Basel framework and subordinated term debts. Gains on securities valuation may be included up to a maximum of 45 percent, and general provisions for loan losses are limited to a maximum of 1.25 percent of risk-weighted assets. Total supplementary capital may not exceed total core capital. Risk weightings are largely determined by the asset transaction counterpart and are set at 0 percent for government and central banks, 10 percent for domestic public sector institutions, and 20 percent for banks. A 50 percent weight is assigned to loans secured by mortgages on residential property; the weight is 100 percent for other claims. The Accord allows national supervisory authorities a certain degree of freedom in fixing the extent of supplementary capital, setting the magnitude for risk weights for assets, and dealing with other issues of risk assessment. For example, in 1996, the European Union updated its the Capital Adequacy Directive (CAD) in conjunction with the BIS proposal for market-risk calculation. The latest version introduced by the Basel Committee incorporates market risk in response to the increased volatility of the exchange rate and interest rates as restrictions on capital flows are removed. The Basel Committee permits two measures of market risk: a standardized method proposed by the Committee and banks' own internal risk management models.

CAUSES OF BANKING-SECTOR CRISES

The literature cites several mechanisms as the causes of banking-sector problems. Banks are financial intermediaries whose main liabilities are mainly short-term deposits and whose assets are a mixture of both short- and longer-term loans. When the value of these assets falls short of the value of the liabilities, a bank becomes insolvent. The value of bank assets is reduced when borrowers are unable to service their debt. Banks attempt to reduce some of this credit risk through diversification, efficient screening processes, and the use of collateral. However, there are costs involved with each of these, and, therefore, there is a limit to the amount of risk a bank can reduce through such means. Banks further complement their diversification efforts by holding a certain level of equity and compulsory reserves to protect themselves against the aforementioned risk. Economic shocks that negatively affect the economic well-being of bank borrowers and whose effects cannot be offset through any of the previously mentioned risk-reducing measures produce systemic threats to banks and to the banking sector at large. Theory suggests that banking systems that are less capitalized are more vulnerable to these shocks—declines in asset prices, cyclical downturns, periods of trade deterioration (Kaminsky and

Reinhart, 1998; Gorton, 1988). One of the goals of this chapter is to test whether this was the case in the banking crises that occurred in the three countries under consideration—that is, whether banks with relatively higher capital reserves reacted more effectively than their counterparts with lower capital reserves to changes in macroeconomic, financial, and institutional conditions.

Financial Factors

Financial liberalization can lead to high short-term interest rates as interest rate control measures are removed (Pill and Pradhan, 1995). Similarly, contractionary monetary policy, fiscal tightening, or even a general increase in international interest rates can raise short-term interest rates. Most banking crises in the United States were preceded by an increase in short-term interest rates (Mishkin, 1996). Although bank balance sheets certainly deteriorate when there is an increase in the number of nonperforming loans, their value can also drop when the rate of return they receive on assets is less than the rate they pay on liabilities. When short-term rates increase, banks need to pay higher interest rates on their liabilities, that is, to their depositors. Since bank assets consist mainly of loans of longer maturity at fixed interest rates, they do not necessarily receive the corresponding higher rates of return. The time needed for banks to readjust the assets in their portfolio can cut into bank profitability and even lead to possible losses. These losses are compounded when there is an increase in real interest rates. Some borrowers are not able to sustain the new rates and are to some extent forced to surrender their loans, further damaging the asset side of the balance sheet. Banks anticipate limited exposure to interest rate risk since the business of financial intermediation in itself typically involves products with different maturities. However, a sudden increase beyond rational expectations can cause severe damage to bank balance sheets and can seriously threaten the whole banking system.

Financial liberalization has also been known to cause an illiquidity crisis in domestic banks. Chang and Velasco (1998) have found that such illiquidity is almost always rooted in a previous bout of financial liberalization measures that accentuated the maturity mismatch between international assets and foreign liabilities. In addition, capital flows from abroad caused by an opening of the capital account and/or falls in world interest rates magnify the problem by making available large amounts of resources that can be intermediated by domestic banks. These problems are only worsened when these foreign loans are short in maturity, as they were in the late stages of the Asian crisis. Any increase in the number of these foreign loans only exacerbates the vulnerability of domestic banks so that a creditor's panic, that is, a creditor's refusal to roll over these short-term loans, can lead to a bank run. In countries with fixed exchange rates, such banking problems may arise by speculative attacks against the currency. If a devaluation is expected, depositors suddenly withdraw their domestic currency deposits and convert them into foreign currency deposits abroad, leaving domestic banks illiquid.

Macroeconomic Factors

Previous research has demonstrated that a weak macroeconomic environment is often associated with emerging banking crises (Gorton, 1988). Low GDP growth, high inflation, depreciation of the exchange rate, and high interest rates have been known to significantly increase the probability of systemic problems within the banking sector. Although these macroeconomic conditions play an important role, structural characteristics of the economy are also significant. These characteristics are especially meaningful since the three countries being considered had only recently undertaken financial liberalization programs before the onset of their banking crises. Under these conditions, the vulnerability of the system to sudden capital outflows is an important indicator of financial sector fragility (Calvo and Reinhart, 1994). The high real interest rates is a good proxy by which to examine the extent to which financial liberalization has progressed in certain countries (Galbis, 1993). Banking-sector problems may be the result of a country's success in balancing other aspects of the economy (e.g., taming high levels of chronic inflation). An inflationary environment has been known to foster an overblown financial sector, since banks are able to profit from the different spreads and float on payments. When countries are able to control these levels, bank revenues subside, causing serious problems within the entire sector (English, 1996).

The effect of macroeconomic instability on bank balance sheets is also a major source of systemic risk to the banking sector. An increase in the number of nonperforming loans is devastating and can be precipitated by a number of factors, including an increase in short-term interest rates, an increase in real interest rates, and a sudden devaluation in the presence of a mismatch in foreign currency borrowing (liabilities) and local currency lending (assets). An unforeseen domestic currency depreciation reduces the value of the loans owed to banks, threatening their profitability. Some countries have tried to limit banks' level of exposure to such foreign exchange risk, but many banks circumvent the regulations by lending directly in foreign currency. Although such transfer of foreign exchange risk to the borrower might postpone the inevitable losses, the currency depreciation still threatens the banks' balance sheets when borrowers are unable to repay, thus increasing the banks' nonperforming loans.

Institutional Factors

A key goal of financial liberalization programs is a reduction in government intervention in lending and borrowing activities. Although, when tight government control exists, many potentially productive loans are deemed too risky by the authorities and are therefore rejected, control does offer some advantages, including fewer moral hazard problems.

Given the heavy influence of government interventions in bank operations, it is almost assumed that the government will support and insure bank deposits if necessary. However, after financial liberalization, if deposits are not insured, the slightest deterioration in the quality of a bank's assets can trigger a panic as depositors begin to withdraw their deposits before the bank declares bankruptcy. Such panic runs create illiquidity and accelerate the onset of bank insolvency. In a situation of incomplete information, it is not long before depositors at other banks suspect that they may face similar risks and begin withdrawing their funds, leading to a systemic panic. Deposit insurance plays an important role in allaying such fears and preventing contagion among the banking sector.

There is a common belief that as soon as private banks are released from tight government control, they pursue unnecessarily risky projects ex ante with the knowledge that insurance schemes will prevent them from failing; furthermore, they assume that, should they fail, the insurance agent will compensate depositors for their losses. However, in most cases, liberalization implies that banks must purchase their own insurance policies, with the government acting as an implicit guarantor. If the insurance premiums paid by the banks do not fully reflect the level of risk banks undertake in their portfolios, moral hazard problems arise. In some ways, the government creates serious incentives for taking on excessive risk and even subsidizes such behavior through implicit guarantees. Consequently, a well-designed and effective system of prudential regulation and supervision must accompany financial liberalization. Otherwise, banks will partake in excessive risks, and banking crises will occur as a result of the moral hazard problem.

RESEARCH METHODOLOGY AND DATA

Choice of Variables

In our review of the banking crises in Thailand, Indonesia, and Korea, the choice of macroeconomic, financial, and institutional explanatory variables is based on the theory that underlies previous explanations, as well as data availability. For the financial effects we used the ratio of M2 to foreign exchange reserves, the ratio of bank cash and reserves to bank assets, and lagged variations of credit to GDP ratios. The M2/FOREX variable tests the sensitivity of the probability of banking crises to sudden capital outflows caused by sudden exchange rate variations. This ratio is known as a good predictor of a country's vulnerability to balance of payment crises (Calvo, 1996). The CASH/ASSETS variable is a liquidity measure, and the $CRED_{t-n}$ variable measures the extent to which financial liberalization has progressed in each country. From the previous explanation, it seems that in a liberalized environment, growth in credit to the private sector might be financing excessively risky loans.[3] For macroeconomic effects, the rate of growth of real GDP (GRO), the real interest rate (RINT), the rate of inflation (INF), and the rate of change of the exchange rate

(DEP) are included, for reasons mentioned before. Although each of these macroeconomic variables indicates the extent of the liberalization process, this analysis concentrates on their effects on bank balance sheets. Finally, the institutional effects are measured by using a dummy variable to indicate the existence of a deposit insurance scheme (INS); to examine the extent to which prudential supervisory measures exist within appropriate regulatory institutions in each country, GDP per capita is used as a control variable. It has been suggested that higher GDP per capita ratios indicate more effective governance and fewer moral hazard problems. Again, rather than simply considering the individual effects of each of the variables by themselves, in this analysis we examine whether there are different reactions between banks of high capital adequacy and those of low capital adequacy within varying financial, macroeconomic, and institutional environments during the crisis.

The banking crisis dependent dummy variable was constructed by using definitions suggested in several studies (Caprio and Klingebiel, 1996; Kaminsky and Reinhart, 1998; Demirguc-Kunt and Detragiache, 1997). These studies played an important role in differentiating between periods of financial distress and those that could be classified as crises. It was important to distinguish between different episodes of banking-sector fragility in each of the countries to properly account for the behavior of the individual banks during a crisis.[4] According to the definitions developed in these studies, several banks in each of the three countries suffered from severe crises in 1997. Korea, Thailand, and Indonesia all witnessed a substantial deterioration in the quality of their bank portfolios. Estimates of nonperforming bank loans were between 30 and 35 percent of outstanding loans in Indonesia and between 25 and 30 percent in Korea and Thailand (World Bank, 1998). The Indonesian authorities initially closed down sixteen banks in 1997 and a further ten in 1998 after the establishment of the Indonesian Bank Restructuring Agency. Korea was forced to close sixteen out of thirty merchant banks and supported the operations of others through large capital injections and voluntary agreements for recapitalization. Thailand closed fifty-six finance companies in 1997 and sustained the survival of others by converting central bank loans into equity.

Statistical Model

In this study, the logit regression technique is used to analyze the choice probabilities. Lo (1987) has already indicated the advantages in applying this type of model to multiple discriminant analysis. The logit model has the form:

$$P_i = \cfrac{1}{\left(1 + \cfrac{1}{e^{(B_0 + B_1 x_{i1} + B_2 x_{i2} + \ldots B_n x_{in})}}\right)}$$

P_i = probability of banking crisis in the ith country
X_{ij} = jth variable of the ith country

$$\text{Odds Ratio} = \frac{P_i}{1 - P_i} = e^{(B_0 + B_1 x_{i1})} = e^{B_0}(e^{B_1})^{x_{i1}}$$

The logit model is a nonlinear model. Estimation of B can be carried out by the method of nonlinear maximum likelihood methods. This model is used because it possesses a number of advantages over the linear regression model. First, it is well known that the linear regression model, if applied to a dichotomous dependent variable, suffers from heteroscedasticity, whereas the logit model does not. Second, extrapolation of the linear function yields probabilities outside the (0,1) range. However, the logistic curve is bounded by the values 0 and 1. Third, the logit model is consistent with random utility maximization as shown by Mcfadden et al. (1973). On both statistical and theoretical grounds, the logit model is preferred here. Another feature of the logit model is the *odds ratio*, which is a ratio of the probability that an event will occur (i.e., a banking crisis) to the probability that it will not occur. This exponential relationship provides an interpretation for β: the odds increase multiplicatively by e^β for every single unit increase in x. Therefore, to summarize, the coefficients give the change in the log of the odds ratio of a banking crisis per unit increase in the respective macroeconomic, institutional, and financial variables. Taking the antilog of this coefficient provides the percentage change in the odds per unit increase. However, to calculate the probability of a banking crisis itself per unit change in any single variable, the following equation is used:[5]

$$\frac{\partial P_i}{\partial x_i} = B_i P_i (1 - P_i)$$

Greater use of the odds ratio will be made later as it will help to show the marginal increases in the probability of bankruptcy as the different variables increase and decrease.

Data

The banks included in this sample are from Thailand, South Korea, and Indonesia. The period under examination is 1996–1997, and data sources included *International Financial Statistics* (IFS), BIS Annual Reports, and various central banks reports. We studied eighteen Indonesian banks, thirty Korean banks, and seventy-five banks and finance companies in Thailand. As a general rule for the following analysis, there needs to be some system that can determine bank quality. Both capital adequacy ratios and the ratio of nonperforming loans to total loans have been used to reflect portfolio quality; this study relies primarily on capital adequacy. Relatively higher-quality portfolios were defined as those with greater than mean capital adequacy ratios in each country. Table 8.2 shows the average capital adequacy (CA) ratio for all banks used in each country sample, as well as the distribution of these banks according to their CA ratios. Employing this division shows whether or not banks with low capital adequacy (Low CA) and high capital adequacy ratios (High CA) were susceptible to their expected weaknesses. Thirty-five percent, 48 percent, and 67 percent of the banks were classified as Low CA in Thailand, Korea, and Indonesia, respectively. The hypothesis for the present model suggests that banks with higher capital adequacy ratios are less vulnerable to negative macroeconomic, financial, and institutional shocks. Their lower-ratio counterparts should be more likely to suffer from the negative effects of these variables, thus contributing to the faster rate at which these banks reach a crisis level.

It is also important for comparative purposes to account for country fixed effects, since each country's banking sector has unique attributes, to avoid overestimating or underestimating the magnitude of certain sovereign characteristics. Such effects are often included to allow for the possibility that the dependent variable may change cross-country independent of the explanatory variables included in the logistic regression. However, in logit estimations, including country fixed effects would require the exclusion of any banks that did not suffer a crisis. In this particular sample, this would require the omission of a considerable amount of already limited information; to avoid such sample biases, the entire sample is examined, albeit without fixed effects.

Results

The final model included nine variables as described earlier: GRO (rate of GDP growth), the real interest rate (RINT), the rate of inflation (INF), the rate of change of the exchange rate (DEP), the ratio of M2 to foreign exchange reserves (M2/FOREX), the ratio of bank cash and reserves to bank assets (CASH/ASSETS), lagged variations of credit to GDP ratios $(CRED_{t-n})$, a dummy variable to indicate the existence of a deposit insur-

Table 8.2. Capital Adequacy Distribution of Banks in Thailand, Korea, and Indonesia (in percent)

Country	Average CA Ratio	Low CA	High CA
Thailand	9.3	35	65
Korea	9.5	48	52
Indonesia	11.9	67	33

Source: Goldstein (1997).

ance scheme (INS), and GDP per capita as a control variable (GDP/CAP). The coefficients and *t*-statistics are shown in Table 8.3. Tables 8.4, 8.5, and 8.6 show the results for the specific countries under consideration. Banks that suffered a banking crisis were assigned a 1, and others were assigned a 0. Therefore, a negative coefficient suggested that an increase in any of the variables would reduce the probability of a crisis, whereas a positive coefficient suggested that there was a direct relationship between the probability of a banking crisis and an increase in the variable.

Table 8.3 shows results for the entire sample from all the countries divided into three main categories: All, High Capital Adequacy (CA), and Low CA. In each of the three cases, the probability of a banking crisis decreased with an increase in GDP growth, confirming the positive effects of a strong economy for avoiding systemic crises. The other significant macroeconomic variables include the real interest rate and inflation (RINT,

Table 8.3. Entire Sample

	All		High CA		Low CA	
	Estimated β (t-statistic)	Exp (β) (% Odds Change)	Estimated β (t-statistic)	Exp (β) (% Odds Change)	Estimated β (t-statistic)	Exp (β) (% Odds Change)
Macroeconomic						
GRO	−0.213***	0.808	−0.178**	0.837	−0.256***	.774
	(1.83)	(−19.2)	(1.692)	(−16.3)	(2.32)	(−22.6)
DEP	0.003	1.02	0.012	1.01	−0.032	0.969
	(0.023)	(2.0)	(0.263)	(1.2)	(0.312)	(−3.1)
RINT	−0.043*	1.04	0.023*	1.02	0.107*	1.11
	(0.792)	(4.4)	(0.862)	(2.3)	(0.732)	(11.3)
INF	0.032**	1.03	0.038**	1.04	0.027***	1.03
	(1.351)	(3.3)	(1.418)	(3.9)	(1.772)	(2.7)
Financial						
M2/FOREX	0.036**	1.04	0.041	1.04	0.022*	1.02
	(1.02)	(3.7)	(0.634)	(4.2)	(0.923)	(2.2)
CASH/ASSETS	−0.021	0.979	−0.008	0.992	−0.013	0.99
	(0.581)	(2.1)	(0.432)	(−0.8)	(0.192)	(−1.3)
$CRED_{(t-2)}$	0.032**	1.3	0.161**	1.17	0.204***	1.23
	(1.263)	(3.3)	(1.382)	(17.4)	(2.091)	(2.3)
Institutional						
INS	0.462**	1.59	0.612	1.84	0.531*	1.7
	(1.81)	(58.7)	(0.719)	(84.4)	(0.821)	(70)
GDP/CAP	−0.082***	0.921	−0.053***	0.95	−0.071**	0.931
	(2.13)	(−7.9)	(2.32)	(−5.2)	(1.938)	(−6.7)

***significance at .01 level, **significance at .05 level, *significance at .10 level

INF), also confirming the negative effects of increases in nominal and real interest rates on both the quality of bank portfolios and the sector as a whole. In further examining the differences between high-CA and low-CA banks, we find some unexpected results within the macroeconomic variables. The positive effects of higher GDP growth in preventing a crisis is greater for low-CA banks than for their high-CA counterparts by almost 6.3 percentage points (22.6% vs. 16.3%). Similarly, the negative effects of inflation are greater on high-CA banks than on low-CA banks by 1.2 percentage points. The earlier hypothesis suggested not only that high-CA banks ought to be more resistant to negative macroeconomic shocks but that they should also gain more from improvements in macroeconomic conditions than their low-CA counterparts; in fact, these results suggest quite the opposite.

As predicted for the financial variables, external vulnerability measured by the M2/FOREX ratio significantly increases the probability of a crisis in all three categories, suggesting the high sensitivity of this probability to sudden capital outflows. Similarly, growth in credit (CRED$_{(t-2)}$), which proxies for the degree of financial liberalization in each economy, significantly increases the likelihood of a crisis, suggesting that a boom in private credit certainly precedes banking crises. For financial variables, the only significant coefficient that did not follow the hypothesis was the M2/FOREX value. The negative effects of a high M2/FOREX ratio, which increases the probability of a crisis, are greater for high-CA banks than for low-CA banks by 2 percentage points.

Finally, for institutional variables, the deposit insurance variable (INS) has significant positive values in all three categories. Therefore, it appears that the existence of an explicit deposit insurance scheme plays a significant role in promoting a crisis, possibly through moral hazard. Similarly, negative coefficients of the GDP/CAP variable, which proxied as a control variable for effective governance measures, suggest that an environment in which effective supervision can be carried out is less likely to suffer from a crisis than one that lacks such supervision. Although the GDP/CAP variable confirmed one part of the hypothesis with its negative coefficient, it is surprisingly lower for low CA than for high-CA banks, which ought to gain the most from an effectively regulated financial environment. In each of these cases, if high-CA banks were intended to be better prepared to resist negative capital outflow shocks and increases in nominal and real interest rates while making more effective use of a positive macroeconomic and supervisory environment, these results suggest otherwise. Although such anomalous results are not the case for each variable in the aggregated sample, the result certainly suggests that a closer examination of each country sample is warranted.

Table 8.4 shows the results from Thailand. To begin, the average capital adequacy ratio for the sample was 9.3—almost 1.3 percentage points higher than the required 8 percent. Banks with ratios greater than 9.3 were classified as high CA, and the remaining were classified as low CA.

Table 8.4. Thailand

	High CA		Low CA	
	Estimated β (t-statistic)	Exp (β) (% Odds Change)	Estimated β (t-statistic)	Exp (β) (% Odds Change)
Macroeconomic				
GRO	−0.293	0.746	−0.036	0.965
	(0.182)	(−25.4)	(0.132)	(−3.53)
DEP	0.426***	1.53	0.017***	1.02
	(2.263)	(53.1)	(2.189)	(1.7)
RINT	0.216**	1.24	1.34**	1.14
	(1.532)	(24.1)	(2.012)	(14.3)
INF	0.336	1.39	0.621	1.86
	(1.032)	(39.9)	(0.361)	(86.08)
Financial				
M2/FOREX	0.073***	1.07	0.238*	1.27
	(2.031)	(7.6)	(1.633)	(26.8)
CASH/ASSETS	−0.216	0.805	−0.186	0.831
	(0.289)	(−19.4)	(1.232)	(−16.9)
CRED$_{(t-2)}$	0.146**	1.16	0.431	1.54
	(0.732)	(15.7)	(0.893)	(53.8)
Institutional				
INS	0.712**	2.04	0.911***	0.042
	(1.621)	(103)	(2.02)	(−59.8)
GDP/CAP	−0.026	97.4	−0.012	0.989
	(0.762)	(−2.56)	(0.281)	(−1.2)

***significance at .01 level, **significance at .05 level, *significance at .10 level

Among the macroeconomic variables, RINT is an important determinant, as indicated by the positive and significant coefficients for both types of banks. In some ways, the reasons for the significance of these real interest rates can be traced to liberalization policies undertaken by the Thai government during the early 1990s. During this period, in their effort to attract foreign capital, they abolished interest rate ceilings, relaxed foreign exchange controls, eased rules for finance companies, and expanded the scope of permissible capital market activities. The entry of foreign banks with the establishment of the Bangkok International Banking Facility (BIBF) increased competition for major clients, including MNCs that were attracted by the lower cost of funds on the BIBF. Such increased competition reduced the profit margin of the domestic banks, forcing them to enter into even riskier activities; subsequently, the rise in RINT further squeezed their already marginally profitable portfolios. The exchange rate

(DEP) is also significant and positive for both high- and low-CA banks. Financial institutions in Thailand had borrowed heavily abroad in foreign currencies and had lent to domestic borrowers in local currency, leaving themselves exposed to exchange rate losses soon after the Thai currency depreciated. Seventeen percent of domestic credit in Thailand was made up of loans that had been funded by foreign currency borrowing by banks operating on the BIBF (Bank of Thailand, 1997). The total foreign currency liabilities of Thai banks and finance companies were 775 percent of their foreign currency assets in 1996 and amounted to nearly 35 percent of M2. However, again it appears that the negative effect of the exchange rate and the real interest rate on the probability of a crisis is surprisingly greater, by 51.4 percentage points and 9.8 percentage points, respectively, for high-CA banks.

The M2/FOREX coefficient is the only significant and positive financial variable for both high- and low-CA banks in Thailand. This is especially noteworthy given that the proportion of foreign bank lending intermediated by the domestic banking sector was falling in Thailand during this period. However, this decline in the share of the domestic banking sector in foreign borrowing was more than compensated for by the increasing importance of finance companies that were "not licensed to accept deposits from the public yet they issued promissory notes at terms comparable to time deposits at commercial banks" (IMF, 1997b). Finally, for institutional variables, insurance (INS) is significant. The INS coefficient is significant and negative for low-CA banks and positive for high-CA banks. Again, this ought not to be the case, since it implies that those banks that hold higher-than-average CA ratios not only do not gain any advantage but also may be penalized for doing so. As perverse as these results seem, Thailand's treatment of recently troubled finance companies during the 1980s might be revealing. More than half of these potentially insolvent financial institutions in Thailand were rescued by the Financial Institutions Development Fund. The Thai government also simultaneously established the Property Loan Management Organization to purchase and restructure nonperforming property loans from banks. Furthermore, any international bank that arranged a syndicated loan for a finance company was assured that the Central Bank would support the company in case of future problems (Bank of Thailand, 1997). These rescues may have sent the wrong signals to financial institutions by suggesting that, as a bank's condition worsened, its rescue package would improve. Such experiences may have led financial institutions to lower their CA ratios, since the opportunity cost of holding capital becomes even greater given the high expectation of government rescues.

Table 8.5 shows the results from Korea, where the average capital adequacy ratio was 9.5, more than 1.5 percentage points higher than the required 8 percent. Using this average to distinguish between low- and high-CA banks, the following results were calculated. For the macroeconomic variables, the significant and negative coefficients for GRO indicate

Table 8.5. Korea

	High CA		Low CA	
	Estimated β (t-statistic)	Exp (β) (% Odds Change)	Estimated β (t-statistic)	Exp (β) (% Odds Change
Macroeconomic				
GRO	−0.426**	0.653	−0.237***	0.789
	(1.26)	(−34.7)	(2.01)	(−21.1)
DEP	0.173	1.19	0.436	1.54
	(0.832)	(18.9)	(1.07)	(54.7)
RINT	0.233***	1.26	0.382**	1.46
	(2.31)	(26.2)	(1.77)	(46.5)
INF	0.621	1.86	0.823	2.28
	(0.776)	(86.1)	(0.592)	(127)
Financial				
M2/FOREX	0.393	1.48	0.792	(2.21)
	(1.32)	(48.1)	(0.362)	(120)
CASH/ASSETS	−0.223	0.801	−0.638**	0.53
	(1.43)*	(−19.9)	(1.96)	(−47.2)
CRED$_{(t-2)}$	0.332	1.39	0.426	1.53
	(1.27)	(39.4)	(0.89)	(53.1)
Institutional				
INS	0.322	1.37	0.583	1.79
	(1.23)	(37.9)	(2.17)	(79.1)
GDP/CAP	−0.094***	0.91	−0.183***	0.833
	(2.36)	(−8.9)	(1.921)	(−16.7)

***significance at .01 level, **significance at .05 level, *significance at .10 level

that the probability of a crisis decreased with an increase in GDP growth for both low- and high-CA banks. In fact, the large predicted rate of growth of GDP may have even worked as an offsetting factor against the probability of a crisis, giving the coefficient its negative sign. The other significant macroeconomic variable is RINT, whose positive coefficient indicates that it increases the probability of a crisis. As in other countries, the important role of real interest rates for Korea can be traced to parts of its liberalization program. Korea undertook deregulation of its financial sector in 1993 and eliminated many interest rate controls, removed restrictions on corporate debt financing, and allowed increased competition in financial services (World Bank, 1998). Such liberalization allowed many Korean finance companies to convert to merchant banks and to engage in foreign lending and borrowing activities in which they had very little experience.[6] This lack of expertise was evident in the rather risky lending decisions of these newly formed banks, a problem whose effects were felt only after real interest rates were forced to rise and many borrowers were unable to service their loans, reducing the quality of many loan portfolios.

For the financial variables, the CASH/ASSETS coefficient was significant and negative, indicating that a lack of liquidity led to a higher probability of a crisis. Its significance is no small part a result of overinvestment in both the corporate and the real estate sectors, after which returns to investment fell. In addition, lenders continued to make loans to projects that were unreasonable from the outset; for example, *chaebols'* profit margins fell to minute levels in the mid-1990s, forcing several into bankruptcy (Miller and Luangaram, 1998). The lack of liquidity was the direct result of lending that had been collateralized by a highly inflated and unsustainable real estate market, as well as by speculative activity on a similarly bloated stock market. As soon as equity and property prices fell, the ensuing liquidity crunch contributed greatly to the crisis. Also, the mismatch between many Korean banks' short-term liabilities and their longer-term assets helped incite the liquidity crisis. The ratios of short-term debt to reserves were substantially over 1 at the end of 1996, suggesting a financially fragile situation because reserves were insufficient should foreign banks be unwilling to roll over the debt owed to them. Furthermore, the detrimental effect of low CASH/ASSETS, that is, low liquidity, was worse for high-CA than for low-CA banks, suggesting that banks with high CA ratios may have felt justified in using assets that, although they were acceptable under CA accounting standards, were in fact not very liquid at all.

Finally, both institutional variables for high- and low-CA banks were significant. The INS coefficient was positive and significant for both high- and low-CA banks, possibly suggesting a moral hazard problem. Historically, many Korean loans had been refinanced at preferential rates by the Central Bank or by special government funding schemes that reduced the incentive for the lending bank to evaluate the creditworthiness of the borrower and monitor the performance of the loan (Folkerts-Landau and Takatoshi, 1995). Similarly, the GDP/CAP was significant and negative for both high- and low-CA banks. However, it was lower for the low-CA than for the high-CA banks, suggesting that low-CA banks gained more from an ineffective regulatory environment. This may have in many ways been the result of not only weak legislation but also weak enforcement and compliance measures (Reisen, 1998). The insider lending restrictions appear to have been difficult to supervise and enforce because of a lack of transparency in accounts and political pressure on regulators (Folkerts-Landau and Takatoshi, 1995). This same political pressure was also applied to banks in Korea to induce them to lend to specific corporate borrowers, even after the borrowers had run into difficulties (International Monetary Fund, 1997a). Finally, when these banks suffered financial distress themselves, supervisors exercised regulatory forbearance instead of insisting on remedial measures; for example, the Central Bank in Korea relaxed the provisioning rules in 1996 in response to losses suffered by the banks due to falls in equity prices (International Monetary Fund, 1997a).

Table 8.6 indicates the results for Indonesia. The average capital adequacy was 11.9, the highest of all three countries. For the macroeconomic variables, the exchange rate (DEP) was significant and positive, suggesting that a rapidly depreciating exchange rate increased the likelihood of a crisis. Of the three countries considered here, Indonesia was most attractive to foreign investors not only because of its liberalization of the capital account in the 1970s but also because of its use of a managed unitary exchange rate system associated with subsidies (Nasution, 1997). Later steps, including the lifting of restrictions on foreign investments and large privatization programs, encouraged large capital flows in the early 1990s. These were arranged mainly through foreign loans to the banking

Table 8.6 Indonesia

	High CA		Low CA	
	Estimated β (t-statistic)	Exp (β) (% Odds Change)	Estimated β (t-statistic)	Exp (β) (% Odds Change)
Macroeconomic				
GRO	−0.232	0.792	−0.019	0.981
	(0.872)	(−20.7)	(0.739)	(−1.8)
DEP	0.207	1.23	0.732	2.07
	(1.96)	(22.9)	(1.78)	(108)
RINT	0.423	1.52	0.718	2.05
	(1.21)	(52.6)	(1.32)	(105)
INF	0.196	1.22	0.673	1.96
	(0.932)	(21.6)	(0.851)	(96.01)
Financial				
M2/FOREX	0.531***	1.7	0.026**	1.03
	(2.02)	(70.1)	(1.82)	(2.6)
CASH/ASSETS	−0.003	0.997	−0.182	0.833
	(1.33)	(−0.31)	(0.892)	(−16.6)
CRED$_{(t-2)}$	0.173	1.18	0.521	1.68
	(1.261)	(18.9)	(0.342)	(68.4)
Institutional				
INS	−0.073*	0.929	−0.416***	0.659
	(0.821)	(−7.04)	(2.31)	(−34.1)
GDP/CAP	−0.182*	0.833	−0.261***	0.77
	(1.03)	(−16.7)	(1.93)	(−22.9)

***significance at .01 level, **significance at .05 level, *significance at .10 level

sector, which became even larger in the mid-1990s in light of the high interest rates and highly profitable equity market. After the speculative attacks on its currency in 1997, Indonesia decided to move from a managed float to a free-float exchange rate, which eventually required even more adjustments because of the extreme pressure on the exchange rate. Therefore, the exchange rate played a crucial role in increasing the probability of a crisis.

The M2/FOREX variable is significant and positive, indicating that a higher value increases the probability of a crisis for both types of banks. The high level of domestic M2 money deposits compared to international reserves prior to the crisis in Indonesia seems consistent with the predicted significance in the model. At the end of 1996, the M2/FOREX ratio was almost 7 in Indonesia. This evidence, which proxies the trends and levels of the short-term asset/liability positions of domestic depositors in the Indonesian financial system, also suggests that there may have been a problem of reserve illiquidity in Indonesia. Before the crisis in Indonesia, the magnitude of foreign currency reserves were clearly not sufficient to honor the outstanding stock of deposits at even the existing exchange rate, much less after the drastic devaluation that occurred. The M2/FOREX variable was also higher for high-CA banks than their low-CA counterparts, suggesting that a lack of foreign reserves was more detrimental to the former.

The INS and the GDP/CAP variables were significant for the low-CA banks in both cases. The INS had a negative coefficient for low-CA banks, indicating that there may have been a serious moral hazard problem, especially for low-CA banks. In the early 1990s, for example, of six banks that were facing distress, five had been recapitalized under the authority of the Indonesian government. Such high levels of insurance coverage for low-quality banks seems to have reduced the probability of a crisis much more for them than for their high-CA counterparts. Finally, GDP/CAP is negative and significant for low-CA banks, suggesting that lower-quality banks thrived more under a lax and unsupervised regulatory environment. Although Indonesia had the Basel CA requirements in place, it lacked the loan loss provisioning rules and the foreign exchange exposure limits (Folkerts-Landau and Takatoshi, 1995). Formal closure mechanisms for insolvent banks were not explicitly set out in the banking laws. But the results suggests an even more serious situation: not only may low-CA banks have escaped regulatory scrutiny, but they may have also benefited from too much supervisory protection. Although CA ratios were readily observable, these failures may have been the result of intangible aspects, including the laxity with which regulations were enforced and the inadequacy of bank supervision. Any examination of such qualities is inherently subjective and imprecise, but some attempts have been made (see Table 8.7). Indonesia is ranked weak in both categories, which may help to explain the reported results.

Table 8.7. Indicators of Strength and Quality of Bank Regulations in Selected East Asian Countries

Country	Enforcement of Regulations	Quality of Bank Supervision
Indonesia	Weak	Weak
Korea	Weak	Fair
Thailand	Fair	Weak

Source: For quality of bank supervision, Claessens and Glaessner (1998); enforcement of regulations, Reisen (1998)

Discussion

During the past few decades, systemic financial crises have plagued countries throughout the world, and it has become increasingly important to understand the links between weaknesses within the financial sector and the economy as a whole. The object of the present exercise has been to provide at least one connection between the relative level of an individual bank's capital adequacy and the effects of this factor on the fragility of the banking system. To this end, banks from three Asian countries plagued by the crisis were selected, separated according to their capital adequacy ratios, and then tested categorically against various macroeconomic, financial, and institutional variables.

This study suggests that the role of the macroeconomic environment cannot be overstated. Low GDP growth is associated with increased risk to the banking sector for both high- and low-CA banks. As described earlier, some of the results contradict the original hypothesis that high-CA banks ought to gain more from improvements in GDP growth than their low-CA counterparts; in fact, the results suggest otherwise. Similarly, evidence shows that high rates of inflation (INF) and high real interest rates (RINT) increase banking-sector problems. Again, the original hypothesis posited that high-CA banks should be more resistant to inflationary pressures than their low-CA counterparts, but the results suggest the opposite. To further illustrate this point, it might be worthwhile to plot high- and low-CA banks for the entire sample against the logit function (Figure 8.1). The inflation rate is used as the horizontal axis, and the other variables are set at their mean values.

The first point is that the high CA logit function rises much faster than the low CA function in the domain beyond 0. Furthermore, the high CA bank function reaches the 0.5 probability level—the last assumed feasible point at which a crisis is avoidable—when inflation is less than 0 (-0.55), whereas with low-CA banks the function approaches the 0.5 level at a positive inflation rate (0.38). This confirms that for high-CA banks to avoid

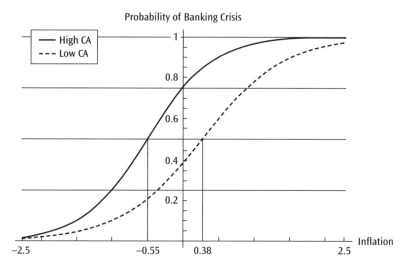

Figure 8.1 Plot of estimated probabilities as functions of INF by using low and high CA banks.

the onslaught of a crisis (the 0.5 probability level), the inflation rate needs to be negative. Of course, this is rather unlikely in a recently liberalized environment, but it reemphasizes the importance for high-CA banks of government policies aimed at keeping inflation low, even though high-CA banks were assumed to be better equipped to handle the situation. Clearly, high-CA banks have not lived up to expectations, performing in this case worse than their low-CA counterparts.

If we consider the other variables that did not react as had been hypothesised, we find that the presence of an insurance scheme increases the probability of a crisis. This suggests that problems of moral hazard behavior exist to some degree. Furthermore, in an extreme case (i.e., Thailand), the results indicate that low-CA banks face a lower probability of a crisis under such insurance schemes when all other variables are held constant. Figure 8.2 shows these results using a logit function.

As in Figure 8.1, the high-CA banks reach the 0.5 probability level of facing a crisis when insurance is less than 0 (−7.5), whereas the low-CA banks approach the 0.5 level at a positive insurance level (1.5). It is difficult to interpret the level of insurance coverage with pinpoint accuracy, but what is important here is the relative effect of each scheme on each type of bank for the probability of a crisis. For low-CA banks, the curve shows that at the 0.5 probability level, the insurance schemes can rise to 1.5 and not precipitate a crisis. Similarly, at the INS = 0 level, a high-CA bank has a 0.84 probability of facing a crisis, while a low-CA bank has a 0.43 probability. Clearly, these findings and those illustrated in Figure 8.1 negate the original hypothesis that high-CA banks are more resistant to macro-

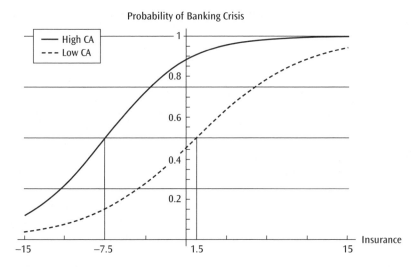

Figure 8.2 **Plot of estimated probabilities as functions of INS by using low and high CA banks.**

economic shocks, as well as more capable in an effectively regulated environment. The increase in the slopes of each function in Figures 8.1 and 8.2 after they pass the critical level of 0.5 is also noteworthy. The slope of the high-CA banks in both figures approaches $P = 1$ asymptotically at a much faster rate than the slopes of the low-CA banks. Again, this suggests that if high-CA banks were exposed to higher inflation and greater insurance after they passed the 0.5 level, they would face a crisis much sooner than their low-CA counterparts. As mentioned, these functions also demonstrate the invalidity of the hypothesis regarding the benefits of maintaining high capital adequacy ratios in this setting. However, before condemning the use of the ratio itself, it might be important to consider the ways in which different countries may have applied—or misapplied—them to their portfolios.

Cosmetic versus Effective Adjustments

The results suggest that the responses of many bank portfolios to the Basel capital adequacy requirements have by no means been standard. In a study by Wall and Peterson, the researchers divided country responses to this requirement into two distinct categories—cosmetic and effective (Wall and Peterson, 1996); banks that manage to increase their capital ratio with little or no effect on the probability of failure have implemented "cosmetic" changes, while those that do reduce this probability execute "effective" changes in their capital ratios.

Cosmetic changes in bank ratios are possible because of the rather imprecise nature of both capital and risk measures as proxies for the financial health of banks. That is, in many cases, banks with high capital ratios are able to compensate themselves by increasing their risk exposure, since managers have private information that is inaccessible to regulators. This situation arises when capital requirements do not adequately take into account the relative riskiness of assets. In fact, empirical evidence suggests that higher capital requirements lead to an increase in risk. Kahane (1977), Koehn and Santomero (1980), and Kim and Santomero (1980) have indicated that a higher required capital ratio increases asset risk, which can lead to a higher probability of failure; conversely, banks with minimally adequate capital reduce their risk exposure. In extreme cases, however, Calem and Rob (1996) have shown, severely undercapitalized banks may take more risk in an attempt to meet capital requirements. Moreover, studies have also indicated that banks' credit responses to such capital requirements generally take longer at smaller banks, which may require up to a few years to fully adjust their portfolios to meet the higher capital requirements.

Another way of making cosmetic changes is to exploit the difference between capital as measured for regulatory purposes and the banks' true economic capital. Regulatory accounting generally records assets at historical costs, rather than at their current market value. Thus, capital as recorded for regulatory purposesmay differ substantially from the economic capital needed for the bank's long-term solvency. A bank can exploit these differences to increase its capital as measured by regulatory accounting criteria. The Basel Committee has recognized such differences and tried to address them in its 1999 proposals:

> The current risk weighting of assets results, at best, in a crude measure of economic risk, primarily because degrees of credit risk exposure are not sufficiently calibrated as to adequately differentiate between borrowers' differing default risks. Another related and increasing problem with the existing Accord is the ability of banks to arbitrage their regulatory capital and exploit differences between true economic risk and risk measured under the Accord.

As a result, at least one inexpensive way for banks to maintain or even increase their capital ratios is to avoid recognizing losses on depreciated assets and to accelerate recognition of gains on any assets that may have appreciated in value. Some evidence in this particularly study suggests that banks may have increased their regulatory capital by selling their appreciated assets, while simultaneously delaying their recognition of losses. Moreover, as institutions that specialize in financial assets, banks can use gains and losses in securities to adjust their capital ratios. However, the market is aware of such cosmetic attempts, and banks do not always resort to this method. Empirical studies have shown that gains in trading are more often done to boost or smooth earnings fluctuations rather than to increase their capital ratios.[7] In some cases where such earnings have been used to increase capital ratios, the market has been aware of the accounting tricks and has interpreted them as a signal of weakness in the bank's future earnings, causing a reduction in the value of the bank.

Effective means by which banks can raise their capital ratios include reducing the volume of loan assets, increasing their retained earnings, issuing new securities, and shifting the focus of their portfolios to less risky assets. Analyses of reduction in the volume of credit during the 1980s and 1990s in most studies are inconclusive. Although there does appear to have been a slowdown in credit growth during this period in many countries, it is not certain that it was the new regulation, that is, the introduction of the Basel standards in 1988, that constrained the volume of credit. Again, it is difficult to ascertain whether the slowdown was the result of more stringent capital requirements or ofgeneral macroeconomic conditions. Banks can also improve their capital accounts by reducing their credit risk and reallocating their portfolios from more to less risky assets. Such changes often involve moving away from lending to private borrowers and increasing the lending of more securitized products that carry smaller capital charges. Finally, a rather costly but effective way to increase capital adequacy is to issue new securities. However, as with most public share offerings, the rate of return that banks must pay is higher than that for alternative products, such as bonds and deposits, and therefore most banks try to avoid this option at any cost. However, for banks that are heavily undercapitalized, equity infusions are the primary mechanism by which they can recapitalize themselves quickly.

CONCLUSION

Inadequate preparation for financial liberalization can contribute greatly to macroeconomic, institutional, and financial weaknesses in developing countries. Timely implementation of prudential supervision is essential to maintain the systemic health of the financial sector and the sound management of its institutions. The implementation of minimum capital adequacy standards has been an important initiative in this right. Changes in the composition and size of banks' portfolios to meet risk-based capital requirements are crucial for formulating appropriate regulatory policies. In this context, and given the possible sources of failures in the capital adequacy requirements during the recent Asian financial crisis, this chapter considered specific weaknesses within the financial sector in three Asian countries, especially the lack of transparency, ineffective accounting standards, and inadequate institutional framework.

The data suggested that some banks in these countries may have utilized cosmetic adjustments to increased capital ratios. Some banks may have increased their risky assets, utilized off-balance-sheet activities, or resorted to using capital gains from the sale of capital assets, including real estate and securities, to boost their ratios. Some may have also revalued their reserves during stock market booms to make the most of the huge capital inflows that followed the liberalization of their country's capital accounts. Although regulators cannot prevent all cosmetic changes to capital ratios, they should at least be able to adjust regulatory requirements to prevent banks from gaining benefits through cosmetic changes. Cosmetic changes to equity can be partially eliminated by requiring mark-to-market accounting for securities. Similarly, loan loss provisions created for credits of doubtful or estimated losses should be excluded from supplementary capital if they reflect an identified deterioration in asset values, and loan loss provisions should reflect declines in the economic value of banks' assets. Strengthening prudential supervision by preventing cosmetic changes and enhancing effective ways of increasing capital ratios seems to be essential for the sound management of banks and financial systems; additionally, similar efforts should be made to impose leverage restrictions.

When institutions in recently liberalized countries have not been allowed sufficient time to develop, financial institutions in these settings are more easily able to make cosmetic adjustments because accounting principles, loan classification standards, and disclosure requirements are not well developed. This has been the case particularly for the countries examined in this study, where banks that carried assets of questionable quality did not make sufficient provisions. Some of these banks then tried to reduce the amounts the should have been diverted to loan loss reserves by restructuring loans or usingother devices. In fact, if these capital ratios had been adjusted, taking into account the underprovisioning, the ratios would have been much lower than they appeared. The setting and monitoring of international banking standards helps to reduce such opportunities for cosmetic adjustments in capital ratios. New international banking standards need to set out clearly the criteria and rules for key adequacy ratios and to establish rules for the classification of loans, requirements regarding provisions for loan losses, and a ban on the use of illegal accounting devices. Finally, it is important to remember that supervision and regulation are neither infallible nor likely to prove sufficient to meet all the intended goals. The Basel standards, as effective as they can be, cannot substitute for a bank's own internal scrutiny of the market participants and the market's scrutiny of the banks. Therefore, every attempt ought to be made to increase such information, in both quantity and quality, from the regulated banks themselves. Again, the recently released Basel II Consultative Paper has made much progress in addressing many of these issues as it tries to "fine-tune" and align the true risks that banks face with the level of capital they are required to hold. Chapter 9 turns to these and other related issues.

9

Reforming the Basel Accord and the Use of Subordinated Debt

Making Markets Work for the Regulator

As noted in the previous chapter, recent discussions by the Basel Committee and by other national and international authorities have yielded several proposals to increase the effectiveness of market discipline by using an incentive-based stance toward financial regulation. This approach has some appeal not only because it is endogenously determined, so that market participants can use their own information to determine regulatory standards, but also because of its greater sensitivity to changes in risk profiles. Another popular suggestion for increasing market discipline has been the proposal that banks be required to hold subordinated debt (SD) that is unsecured, uninsured, and junior to deposits. The issuance of such debt would increase market discipline not only by providing better and more timely information but also by creating a financially sophisticated class of creditors with better incentives for monitoring financial institutions.

Although both of these proposals are not without their technical shortcomings and may not be the ultimate solution, this chapter argues that the implementation of subordinated debt and of Basel II could be significant steps toward the stated goal of enhancing the effectiveness of market discipline. Both proposals are able to do so by pricing risk more accurately, by increasing transparency by making more information readily available, and by making risk takers more accountable for their activities. Basel II represents a major push forward in banks' efforts to align and "fine-tune" their true economic risks with the level of capital they are required to hold. The 1988 standards are dated and are now looked upon as blunt measures for determining capital allocations that often tended to skew lending priorities. One of the main advantages of subordinated debt is that it, along with other similarly designed mechanisms, can provide government regulators with earlier warning signals, affording them more time to react. Moreover, since this information is directly linked to the market's assessment of an institution's risk profile, market transparency should minimize issuing banks' ability to manipulate their yields. Thus, subordinated debt should improve the incentive mechanism as these debt holders feel an even greater need to become better monitors lest they face the possibility of suffering major losses in the event of a bank failure because of the subordinated position of their claims. This chapter begins by looking at the more recent Basel II and subordinated debt proposals. The following sections turn to some of the difficulties that have been raised with their implementation, especially on a technical level. The chapter concludes by discussing some of the competitive and coordination issues that underlie many incentive-based approaches to financial regulation.

BASEL II: BACKGROUND

An important measure for controlling credit risk in recent years has been the widespread implementation of minimum capital adequacy standards. In 1988, the Basel Committee of the BIS (Bank for International Settlements) agreed to require banks actively engaged in international transactions to hold capital equal to at least 8 percent of risk-weighted assets in an effort to prevent banks from increasing credit risk through greater leverage. However, many supervisors have since complained that the credit risk component of the 1988 Basel Capital Accord was too narrow to deal with the market, liquidity, and operational risks that increased with the growth of banks' trading and derivative books. The original intention of the Basel Accord had been to prevent a slide in international capital ratios as a result of aggressive competition for market share by the leading banks during the mid-1980s. The Accord had hoped to harmonize the different levels and approaches to capital among the G10 countries. Since its inception, the introduction of a risk-based structure for calculating capital ratios that assigns different capital weights to fewer asset classes (both on- and off-balance-sheet) has been one of the Committee's greatest contributions. Its method not only marks a significant improvement from the previously used gearing ratio method used by national regulators but also creates less incentive for off-balance-sheet activities. Moreover, the Accord was designed with the intention that it would be updated periodically. In 1996, an amendment introduced capital requirements in respect of market risk and allowed banks to use VaR (Value at risk) and other models.

Most countries incorporated the Basel standards into their regulatory framework, at least to strengthen the soundness of their commercial banks, to raise their credit ratings in international financial markets, and to achieve a universally recognized international standard. These countries understood that convergence with the Basel Accord was necessary to ensure capital adequacy, as well as to stand on equal footing with international banks in global financial markets. These standards were applied to commercial banks, including local and foreign bank branches. Local banks were included, since further liberalization meant that they were expected to become more active in international business. The Basel Committee has continued to update its rules since 1988 by recognizing other weaknesses, especially in the original credit risk approach, which could distort incentives in bank risk taking, for example, the securitization of wholesale credit. It also witnessed increasing competition in the financial services industry on both a geographic and an industrial level to include banks, finance companies, and insurance agencies. This meant that capital requirements needed to go beyond the G10 banks and to include emerging markets in developing countries. The Accord's original methodology has occasionally proved inadequate for some of these markets, and the 8 percent minimum capital ratio has been criticized as being too low for certain economic conditions. The Basel Committee continued to reemphasize that the 8 percent should be regarded as only a minimum and that it should not be seen as a sufficient measure for all markets. The Basel Committee has faced difficult challenges since the inception of the 1988 Accord. As a regulator, it has recognized the possible distorted incentives inherent in some of its original mandates, the increased complexity of the financial services industry, and the notable effects of operational as well as credit risk on bank portfolios. In finding solutions, it not only needed to address each of these issues but also had to account for the differences among its potential clients. Clearly, a need existed for a risk assessment framework that would align the true economic risks banks face with the level of capital they are required to hold.

BASEL II CONSULTATIVE PAPERS

As mentioned earlier, the Basel Committee has been releasing revised drafts of its New Capital Accord over a period of several years. The First Consultative Paper was released in June 1999, the Second Consultative Paper in January 2001, the Third Consultative Paper in April 2002. The 1988 Accord provided essentially only one option for measuring the appropriate capital of internationally active banks. The best way to measure, manage, and mitigate risks, however, differs from bank to bank. An Amendment was introduced in 1996 that focused on trading risks and that allowed some banks for the first time to use their own systems to measure their market risks. The new framework, known as Basel II, provides a spectrum of approaches, from simple to advanced methodologies, for the measurement of both credit risk and operational risk in determining capital levels. It provides a flexible structure in which banks, subject to supervisory review, can adopt the approach that best fits their level of sophistication and their risk profile. The framework also deliberately builds in rewards for stronger and more accurate risk measurement.

The new framework intends to provide approaches that are both more comprehensive and more sensitive to risks than the 1988 Accord, while maintaining the overall level of regulatory capital. The new framework is less prescriptive than the original Accord. At its simplest, the framework is somewhat more complex than the old, but it offers a range of approaches for banks capable of using more risk-sensitive analytical methodologies. The Basel Committee believes that the benefits of a regime in which capital is aligned more closely to risk significantly exceed the costs, resulting in a safer, sounder, and more efficient banking system. The new Accord consists of three mutually reinforcing pillars, which together contribute to safety and soundness in the financial system. The need for rigorous application of all three pillars is emphasized in the Second Consultative Package.

Pillar 1: Minimum capital requirements
Pillar 2: Supervisory review
Pillar 3: Market discipline

The Committee is working to modernize the current system of risk weightings that is contained in the 1988 Basel Capital Accord. Pillar 1 develops the theme of a two-strand approach to calculating capital requirements that uses either a set of standardized ratings-based risk weightings or the bank's assessment of the exposure's default risk, as outlined in the first set of proposals. The new capital standards being developed by international financial institution regulators could potentially have a big impact on the efficiency and the competitiveness of the overall banking industry. Such changes could create a huge edge for banks that are to receive favorable treatment under the new rules. Although the new Basel Capital Accord will not be implemented until the end of 2006, finalization is expected by the end of 2004.

The 1988 regulations have been widely criticized as simplistic, lacking in risk-recognition accuracy, and too broad. These criticisms have some merit, though people might simultaneously argue that the 1988 rules can be quite complicated in areas such as multiuse credit facilities, syndications, and risk participations. The old rules were easier to learn and easier to regulate and had a "one-size-fits-all" framework. The new rules are complex and designed to be more accurate and will present many regulatory challenges, including the need for substantial continuing training for regulators and examiners. Moreover, all banks are currently bound by the same rules. Under the new regulations, a bank that qualifies under the more advanced provisions might have a competitive advantage over nonqualifying banks, at least in some types of business activities. The reason is that capital requirements will be lower under the Accord's more advanced approaches than under the Accord's default rules for some specific portfolios. The more capital a bank is required to hold, the more costly its activities will be.

Some may view the Accord as unfair and burdensome. It might appear that it forces banks down yet another unnecessarily complicated compliance path. A closer look, however, reveals that it will encourage banks to create more accurate models of risk recognition and required capital determination. It will also allow for more effective capital determination and product pricing. This will encourage more efficient credit allocation industrywide and will produce a healthier banking system.

Minimum Capital

As discussed earlier, the Basel Accord contemplates giving banks a choice in capital determination: the standardized approach or one based on a bank's own internal ratings. The latter requires validation of the bank's internal models and procedures by bank regulators. The standardized approach, for example, imposes a 20 percent credit conversion factor on loan commitments of less than a year's duration. The current rules have no such provision. Risk weightings also would change. Instead of carrying a 0 percent risk weight, agency ratings would be considered in determining the risk weight for OECD (Organization for Economic Cooperation and Development) sovereign exposures. An AAA rating would carry a 0 percent risk weighting, but a B-minus rating would carry a 150 percent risk weighting. This complexity is magnified further in the treatment of bank counterparty risk. Each nation's bank regulators may select either of two options. All banks in a given country would get a risk weighting either one category lower than the country's sovereign rating or one based on its own credit rating. In theory, this rating could be higher than the sovereign rating of the country in which the bank is located, but the bank's risk weighting could not be lower than 20 percent. Similarly, corporate counterparty risk would be driven by credit ratings. Instead of 100 percent risk weighting, as under the current rules, claims on corporations and other business entities would be 20 percent, 50 percent, 100 percent, or 150 percent, depending on the entity's credit rating. Unrated entities would carry a 100 percent risk weighting, though regulators would have the right to increase the weighting in the case of default or credit quality concerns.

Under the IRB approach, a bank estimates each borrower's creditworthiness, and the results are translated into estimates of a potential future loss amount. These form the basis of minimum capital requirements. The framework allows for the use of either a foundation method or, for corporate, sovereign, and bank exposures, more advanced methodologies. In the foundation methodology, banks estimate the probability of default associated with each borrower, and the supervisors supply the other inputs. In the advanced methodology, a bank with a sufficiently developed internal capital allocation process will be permitted to supply other necessary inputs, as well. Under both the foundation and the advanced IRB approaches, the range of risk weights will be far more diverse than in the standardized approach, resulting in greater risk sensitivity.

Banks that wish to qualify under the more favorable capital treatment, the Advanced Internal Ratings-Based Approach, have much to consider. There are four main risk components under the new system: probability of default, loss given default, exposure at default, and maturity. Regulators will require reliable data to support internally generated estimates for these components; since a key factor in reliability is the amount of time over which the data are collected, bank systems should begin capturing such information sooner rather than later. The foundation IRB approach mandates predetermined values for PD, LGD, and EAD, while the advanced approach allows banks the flexibility to use their own internally validated values. The new framework also introduces more risk-sensitive approaches to the treatment of collateral, guarantees, credit derivatives, netting, and securitization under both the standardized approach and the IRB approach. These discounting measures all fall under credit risk mitigation techniques as classified under the Second Paper.

Operational Risk

Although the 1988 Accord set a capital requirement simply in terms of credit risk, the overall capital requirement (i.e., the 8 percent minimum ratio) was intended to cover other risks, as well. In the attempt to introduce greater credit risk sensitivity, Basel II has done much to develop a suitable capital charge for operational risk. The work on operational risk is in a developmental stage, but three different approaches of increasing sophistication (basic indicator, standardized, and internal measurement) have been identified. The basic indicator approach utilizes one indicator of operational risk for a bank's total activity. The standardized approach specifies different indicators for different business lines. The internal measurement approach requires banks to utilize their internal loss data in the estimation of required capital.

BASEL II—SOME CRITICISMS

Private Credit Rating Agencies—An Incentive Problem

One of the main issues that Basel II addresses in its proposal is the construction of new risk weights by using the assessments of private credit rating agencies. Unfortunately, the use of outside agencies raises a serious problem, namely the need to provide these agencies with appropriate incentives to consider the full implications of their ratings on overall systemic risk. Otherwise, there exists the possibility that these private agents may act either in their own interests or in that of the borrower in hopes of maximizing their own gains by issuing favorable ratings. There is also the question of the quality of each rating agency, as well as of the standards they apply. Consequently, there needs to be some mechanism to reduce incentive effects for both private credit agencies and their client banks so that they are unable to ignore the costs of increasing systemic risk when seeking to maximize their short-run profits—in economic terms, the public good problem.

Internal Ratings Model—An International Coordination Problem

The other concern regarding Basel II is its use of an internal ratings model in the absence of any documented consensus on capital accounting standards at an international level. If the internal ratings method is adopted, it needs to be scrutinized and to incorporate standards that are acceptable in all jurisdictions. Differences in financial innovations and technological advances in recent years could play a role in encouraging market participants to engage in regulatory arbitrage through various means, including cosmetic adjustments. If financial regulation is too restrictive in one jurisdiction, both providers and users of financial services can simply move to a less restrictive and less costly jurisdiction. Competitive pressures could cause financial centeres to become engaged in competitive deregulation. This could lead to a bare-essential approach to financial regulation as authorities compete to have firms locate within their jurisdictions, resulting in a less than socially optimal level of regulation overall. If financial institutions engage in regulatory arbitrage, it is important for different national authorities to coordinate theor regulatory policies in order to avoid not just the risks inherent in competitive deregulation but also the dangers that lax rules in one country will have an adverse effect on the ability of other countries to enforce their financial regulations. Furthermore, to the extent that regulatory laxity represents a higher level of risk, the possibility of systemic spillover effects on more conservatively regulated jurisdictions needs to be considered. Therefore, it is to be expected that different regulations will to some extent exacerbate distortions between markets by providing certain advantages and disadvantages to different participants, they should all uphold at least certain minimum standards.

Other Criticisms

Although there have been some specific criticisms regarding Basel II since its First Consultative Paper was released in January 2001,[1] by and large most banks and market participants and the supervisory community believe the new proposal shows a genuine willingness on the part of the Basel Committee to establish a flexible and risk-sensitive capital adequacy framework. However, as a proposal with overriding regulatory impact, it was bound to have some critics. Topics that have elicited criticisms have included "level-playing field" concerns, double counting, and noninclusion. At a very general level, there has been much concern about the lack of attention given to issues of liquidity. Recent crises have indicated that one of the primary sources of international systemic risk is the potential for a sudden drying up of liquidity, or a funding crisis. Critics believe that the Committee could at least begin to address this problem by considering it, even on a broad level.

Operational risk has been the source of much discontent among industry observers. Criticisms have ranged from the arbitrariness of ythe inclusion in the total regulatory capital charge to the proposed methods for calculating its value. The idea of basing the capital charge on the size of the firm has been severely criticized, especially since larger firms are bound to be overcharged relative to their levels of risk. Another issue that received much attention but that has been removed was the introduction of a charge—the w factor—for residual risk in the use of credit risk mitigation instruments. Critics contended that legal risk, which the residual risk is meant to cover, fell within the definition of operational risk and hence was already specifically charged for under the proposed framework. Such "double counting" could potentially impose high transaction costs on derivatives and other credit protection instruments. These same critics from the derivatives industry were also concerned that the w factor imposed a disparate charge in treatment between bank guarantees (w = 0) and credit derivatives (w = 0.15). This difference in charges could have had significant consequences on the derivatives industry as protection buyers sought to restructure their transactions as guarantees, rather than as credit default swaps.

Other, more general concerns have included the importance given to pillar 2, the supervisory review process. With banking supervision varying from country to country, and the Basel rules interpreted more strictly in some jurisdictions than in others, banks based in countries where supervision is traditionally strong will face disadvantages. Similarly, in some countries, including the United States, where the Basel rules would apply to parent holding companies as well as to banks, there are other level-playing-field concerns. In order for the Basel rules to be effective in preventing systemic risk, all essential players—leading investment banks as well as other nonbank financial institutions—would need to be included. It is not at all clear at this point whether these rules would be applied universally in all countries.

SUBORDINATED DEBT: BACKGROUND

Proponents of mandatory subordinated debt (SD) hope to create an entire class of financially sophisticated creditors who realize that they will not be bailed out by the government should the banking organization fail. Among bank liabilities, subordinated debt is uninsured and would be among the first to lose value in the event of a bank failure. Moreover, with the knowledge that in case a bank becomes insolvent, the holders of SD are unlikely to be protected by implicit government guarantees, holders of SD become an especially strong instrument of direct market discipline. However, it is important to note in order for market discipline to have its full effects, SD must be unsecured and uninsured so that its value is un-equivocally threatened when an institution increases its level of risk. Pro-ponents also argue that higher levels of SD can increase market discipline indirectly by making the bank's costs more sensitive to risk. In the end, it is the market's view of a particular institution's risk profile that will affect the SD's yield and provide better and more timely signals to both the market and the regulator.

Advantages of Subordinated Debt

Although more risk-based capital standards and risk-based deposit in-surance premiums are slowly becoming standard devices for regulators, they are still no substitute for the discerning ability of the market to assess and price risk. Added to this already formidable task is the ever-increasing need to keep pace with institutions whose technical competence becomes more sophisticated and complex on a daily basis. Most banks dedicate a huge amount of resources to the task of pricing risk, and it is only logical, from a regulatory perspective, that supervisors should have similar ca-pabilities. Therefore, by encouraging market participants to play a greater role in monitoring and controlling bank risk through SD obligations, reg-ulatory authorities arm themselves with similar if not equal capabilities to sustain systemic stability. It is this very ability of the market to react to even the slightest changes in risk profiles that regulatory discipline by itself does not possess. Most regulatory authorities are able to react only to blatant violations of certain standards or rules; they are not able to—and often choose not to, in order to retain some objectivity—detect banks that take on marginal increases in their risk profiles and penalize them. Most regulatory discipline, even under risk-based capital and insurance premium standards, occurs across broad classifications of risk and is un-able to adjust to minor, albeit crucial, changes in a bank's risk profile.

As mentioned before, the recent regulatory shift toward risk-based rules has been accompanied by a commitment in advance from supervi-sors to certain courses of action, such as "prompt corrective actions" and "structured early intervention approaches." Such interventions include imposition of higher capital requirements; structured and prespecified publicly announced responses by regulators, triggered by decreases in a bank's performance below established criteria; mandatory resolution of a capital-depleted bank at a prespecified point when capital still exists; and requirements for market-value accounting and reporting of capital. One of the problems with the establishment of such prefixed rules is that gov-ernments may be tempted to rewrite them during difficult times; this has happened even in highly industrialized countries, such as Japan in 1997–1998 (deferral of scheduled deregulation) and the United States in the 1980s (replacement of the GAAP for S&Ls with less stringent accounting standards). It is hoped that the SD requirement will supplement these earlier corrective efforts by providing better incentives for regulators to take actions sooner and to avoid regulatory forbearance.

That certain policymakers have delayed the recognition of bank failures or have financed economically unwise bailouts for politically or socially desirable reasons rather than follow the dictates of economic prudence is not a surprise. Such regulatory forbearance has only exacerbated the incentive problem by allowing banks with low or even negative net value to continue their operations. The best policy for supervisors who wish to avoid such intervention often requires that rules be established *ex ante*, which reduces the ability of policymakers to influence decisions about the closing of financial institutions. Reducing regulatory forbearance and occurrences of government bailouts is one goal of SD requirements. Proposals to link regulatory action to signals from the SD market, rather than other types of uninsured deposits, is one effort in this direction. For one thing, uninsured deposits provide significantly less information to regulators so that a "silent run" by depositors may pass unnoticed, whereas a comparable amount of SD dumped on the SD market would most certainly affect its price and alert regulators.

Technicalities

Various technical issues still confound even the most arduous proponents of the SD proposal. Proposals concerning the maturity, the issue frequency, the required level of SD, the size of banks required to undertake an SD mandate are varied and numerous. For example, most proposals call for an SD requirement of between 2 and 5 percent of total assets. If this amount is required in addition to and not instead of a bank's current capital requirements, it might have other, negative effects. It is of course important to set a requirement large enough to make the discipline matter, but it is equally important to realize that an excessively large capital requirement could place an unnecessarily heavy burden on some well-capitalized banks, causing them to reduce their lending and inhibiting economic growth. Similarly, the differences between the SD of "large" and "small" banks need to be considered closely. To begin, the transaction costs of issuing SD could be too heavy for small banks and might impair their overall financial health; furthermore, it is likely that the secondary market for small banks' SD would be less liquid, if liquid at all, than that for the SD of their larger counterparts. Consequently, there would be very little information contained in the spreads of any but the largest banks. The maturity and the issue frequency of the SD are also important issues and need to be considered closely. If banks are required to issue SD frequently, it might be too costly for them and give investors less incentive to monitor bank performance, since they are assured that their SD will mature before the occurrence of any bad events. Similarly, if the maturity is too long, banks could escape market discipline by going for years without issuing any further SD.

Finally, the issue of participation in this SD market remains an important matter. Recognizing that one of the main goals of the SD requirement is to create a financially sophisticated class of creditors with better incentives for monitoring, perhaps it is worth considering allowing only member banks to become holders of the SD. The financial exposure created by one bank for another in this system would provide strong incentives for banks to monitor one another. One natural advantage of such decentralized monitoring arrangements is the mitigation of the free-rider problem. Holders of the SD would recognize that any losses they create will have direct repercussions on their own portfolios, by increasing the costs not only for the defaulted bank but also for the bank that failed as an effective monitor (through higher yields in the SD market). Such is the basic idea in Calomiris's recent scheme that calls for banks to police themselves. He would require every bank to finance a small proportion of its assets by selling SD to foreign banks with the stipulation that the yield on this debt cannot be more than 50 basis points higher than the rate on corresponding riskless instruments. The yield cap would guarantee that banks could not compensate these debtholders with large spreads when they participated in high-risk activities.[1] As the essence of Calomiris's recommendation is to reduce these very risks, investors, that is, other banks, would buy SD only when they were sure that the bank's activities were low risk. If in fact a bank were unable to convince other banks of its aversion to risk, it would not be allowed to function. In this way, Calomiris exploits the access to greater and better information that other bankers, and not bank supervisors, are believed to have. Such direct debt holding by member banks might align the incentives of private banks and regulators by mandating that the social costs of high-risk activities not be borne only by the public at large.

CONCLUSION

Although there are several technical issues that still require further work, there are clearly some positive indications that both Basel II and an SD requirement can allow banking regulators to take greater advantage of the signals provided by the market they govern. Each proposal has the potential to capitalize on market discipline to provide better and more timely information, prevent regulatory forbearance, and avoid costly bailouts by national insurance schemes. The increased reliance on market participants in both of these proposals is to some extent a result of the inferior quality and quantity of information received by regulators about the circumstances of any regulated firm compared to the firm's own information resources, since the firm can effectively decide what information it will provide to regulators. The information provided by an active and liquid SD market can complement existing accounting-based capital rules and provide a public trigger during difficult times. By issuing this type of signal, the market not only gives regulators more time to react but also increases the accountability of future actions by both the bank and policymakers. Similarly, by insisting on the subordinated position of such debt, the SD requirement provides greater incentives for a class of financially sophisticated investors to become even better monitors.

Similarly, if capital requirements are to be based on internal models, as suggested in Basel II, there need to be at least minimum standards. In order for these standards to be effective, regulatory policies must be coordinated at an international level. In this regard, national authorities will have to find a balance between national autonomy and coordination with other authorities. Since the economic case for international policy coordination in capital requirements is based on the presence of cross-border transactions and spillover effects, these could be used as points of reference in determining the boundaries of coordination efforts on regulation. This raises questions of whether the regulatory framework should be focused on the organization of markets, rather than institutions. Systemic stability regulations tend to be institutionally focused; this follows directly from the nature of systemic risk, which is assumed to be triggered by institutional insolvency. However, one of the features of financial markets today is the increasing blurring of distortions between different types of financial institutions and other related agencies. The evolving nature of their various roles means that regulations that are too narrowly focused will be rendered obsolete very quickly. Thus, in the context of developing a comprehensive incentive-based regulatory framework, the importance of an institutional focus within an international context cannot be emphasized enough. The proposed implementation of Basel II and/or SD only reinforces the notion that regulators are rarely offered the decision whether to use incentives; they can decide only how to use incentives more efficiently to promote public goods, or, in this case, systemic stability.

10

Enhancing Corporate Governance for Financial Institutions

The Role of International Standards

One of the main points discussed in chapter 9 was the varying interpretations of similar rules across different countries, whether in the context of Basel II or of subordinated debt. Global governance of financial systems must take account of the idea that national financial markets may vary according to their legal system, institutional structures, business customs, and practices. Uniform international financial regulatory standards may not have the same impact on one financial system that it has on others, which may result in different types of systemic risk. Although financial markets are seamless, their structures are not homogenous. This chapter argues that the application of global governance to financial regulation must take account of certain standards and principles of corporate governance, some of which are advocated by international financial bodies, that address the internal operation and management of financial institutions.

Global financial systems have undergone marked structural changes during the past few decades as a result of various forces, including deregulation, technological change, and financial innovation. These factors have changed the environment within which financial firms operate and the ways in which activities have been undertaken. Given the central role of financial institutions and markets in society as a whole, the conduct of such financial intermediaries and the environment in which they operate remains particularly important. In this light, it has been argued that the forces of financial reform and structural adjustment have generally paid inadequate attention to governance issues for financial institutions. This chapter hopes to fill this gap by discussing standards of governance for and within financial institutions. The analysis in this chapter recognizes that there are significant differences in the legislative and regulatory frameworks across countries with respect to the functions of corporate boards and senior management. For example, in some legal systems, the company board is known as a supervisory board. This means that the board has no executive functions. By contrast, in other legal systems, the board exercises broad powers and has the authority to establish the general framework for management of the company. Because of these differences, the notions of boards of directors and senior management are used not to identify legal constructs but rather to describe and explain two types of decision-making functions within a bank. These different types of functions, which are known as corporate governance structures, are discussed, as are sound practice strategies that underscore the need for banks to adopt strategies for their operations and to establish accountability for implementing these strategies.

This chapter also discusses the major principles of corporate governance for financial institutions as set forth by the Basel Committee and the International Organisation of Securities Commissioners (IOSCO). The influence exercised by these bodies in setting standards of financial regulation for advanced economies suggests that they also will have a significant impact in establishing standards of corporate governance for financial institutions. These standards of corporate governance are likely to become international in scope and will likely be integrated into the regulatory practices of the leading industrial states. The globalization of financial markets necessitates minimum international standards of corporate governance for financial institutions that can be integrated into financial systems in a way that will reduce systemic risk and enhance the integrity of financial markets. It should be noted, however, that international standards of corporate governance may result in different types and levels of systemic risk for different jurisdictions because of differences in business customs and practices and the institutional and legal structures of national markets. We argue, therefore, that the adoption of international standards and principles of corporate governance should be accompanied by domestic regulations that prescribe specific rules and procedures for the governance of financial institutions that address national differences in political, economic, and legal systems.

The chapter begins by briefly considering "governance" within this context, using a *principal-agent* framework. It then discusses the general principles of corporate governance for financial institutions that the Basel Committee has adopted for all banking institutions operating in the G10 industrialized countries. We then discuss principles of corporate governance for securities firms as set forth by IOSCO. The overriding theme is the belief that transparency of information is integrally related to accountability in that transparency can provide government supervisors, bank owners, creditors, and other market participants sufficient information and incentive to assess the management of a bank. The chapter concludes by considering these and other issues related to the governance role of financial institutions in the overall economy.

BACKGROUND

Corporate governance for all institutions, including financial intermediaries, has become an important issue in various national and international forums. In 1997, the Organization for Economic Cooperation and Development (OECD) issued a set of corporate governance standards and guidelines to assist governments in their efforts to evaluate and improve the legal, institutional, and regulatory frameworks for corporate governance in their countries. The OECD guidelines also provide standards and suggestions for stock exchanges, investors, corporations, and other parties that "have a role in the process of developing good corporate governance."[1] Such corporate governance standards and structures are especially important for banking institutions that operate on a global basis. To this extent, the OECD principles may serve as a model to be applied to the governance structure of multinational financial institutions.

The OECD report goes as far to suggest that sound corporate governance of financial institutions needs to be in place in order for banking and financial supervision to operate effectively. Consequently, banking supervisors have a strong interest in ensuring that there is effective corporate governance at every banking organization. Supervisory experience underscores the necessity of having appropriate levels of accountability and managerial competence within each bank, especially multifunctional banks that operate on a transnational basis. A sound governance system can contribute to a collaborative working relationship between bank supervisors and bank management.

Even the Basel Committee has recognized that the primary responsibility for good corporate governance rests with boards of directors and senior management of banks. But the Basel Committee's 1999 Report on Corporate Governance also suggests that there are other ways that corporate governance can be promoted, including:

- for governments, through laws and regulations;
- for securities regulators and stock exchanges, through disclosure and listing requirements;
- for accounting professionals, through audit standards on communications to boards of director and senior management and through publication of sound practices;
- for banking industry associations, through initiatives related to voluntary industry principles and agreement on publication of sound practices (BCBS, 1999b)

In this respect, legal issues crucially affect improvements in the corporate governance of financial institutions—for example, in creating enforceable contracts, including those with service providers; clarifying governance roles of supervisors and senior management; ensuring that corporations operate in an environment that is free from corruption and bribery; and in seeing that laws, regulations, and other measures align the interests of managers, employees, and shareholders. All of these can help promote a strong business and legal environment that supports corporate governance and related supervisory activities.

THE UNIQUENESS OF BANKING REGULATION

The role of banks is integral to any economy. They provide financing for commercial enterprises, access to payment systems, and a variety of retail financial services for the economy at large. Some banks have a broader impact on the macro sector of the economy by facilitating the transmission of monetary policy by making credit and liquidity available in difficult market conditions (Turner, 2002). The integral role that banks play in the national economy is demonstrated by the almost universal practice of states of regulating the banking industry and providing, in many cases, a government safety net to compensate depositors when banks fail. Financial regulation is necessary because of the multiplier effect that banking activities have on the rest of the economy. The large number of stakeholders (e.g., employees, customers, suppliers) whose economic well-being depends on the health of the banking industry rely on appropriate regulatory practices and supervision. Indeed, in a healthy banking system, the supervisors and regulators themselves are stakeholders acting on behalf of the society at large. Their primary function is to develop substantive standards and other risk management procedures for financial institutions in which regulatory risk measures correspond to the overall economic and operational risk faced by a bank. Accordingly, it is imperative that financial regulators ensure that banking and other financial institutions have strong governance structures, especially in light of the pervasive changes in the nature and structure of both the banking industry and the regulation that governs that industry's activities.

GOVERNANCE: THE PRINCIPAL-AGENT PROBLEM

The main characteristics of any governance problem are that the opportunity exists for some managers to improve their economic payoffs by engaging in unobserved, socially costly behavior or "abuse" and that outside monitors have only inferior information compared to managers inside the firm (Shleifer and Vishny, 1997: 741). These characteristics are related, since abuse would not be unobserved if the monitor had complete information. The basic idea that managers have an information advantage and that this gives them the opportunity to take self-interested actions is the standard *principal-agent* argument. The more interesting issue is how this information asymmetry and the resulting inefficiencies affect governance within financial institutions. Does the manager have better information? Perhaps the best evidence that monitors possess inferior information relative to managers lies in the fact that monitors often employ incentive mechanisms, rather than relying on explicit directives alone.[2]

The preceding illustrates the wide range of potential agency problems in financial institutions that involve several major stakeholder groups, including but not limited to shareholders, creditors/owners, depositors, management, and supervisory bodies. Agency problems arise because responsibility for decision making is directly or indirectly delegated from one stakeholder group to another in situations where stakeholder groups have different objectives and where complete information that would allow the first group to exert control over the decision maker is not readily available. Among the most studied agency problems in the case of financial institutions are those that involve depositors and shareholders or supervisors and shareholders. While that perspective underpins the major features of the design of regulatory structures (e.g., capital adequacy requirements, deposit insurance), problems of incentive conflict between management and owners have become a focus of recent attention.[3]

The resulting view that financial markets can be subject to inherent instability induces governments to intervene to provide depositor protection in some form or other. Explicit deposit insurance is one approach, while explicit or implicit deposit guarantees of deposits are another. In either case, general prudential supervision also occurs to limit the risk incurred by insurers or guarantors. To control the incentives of bank owners who rely too heavily on government-funded deposit insurance, governments typically enforce some control over bank owners. Controls can involve placing limits on the range of activities; linking deposit insurance premiums to risk; and aligning capital adequacy requirements to business risk.[4] While such controls may overcome the agency problem between government and bank owners, it must be asked how significant this problem is in reality. A cursory review of recent banking crises suggests that many concerns relate to decisions that reflect agency problems involving management. Management may have risk preferences different from those of other stakeholders, including the government, owners, and creditors, or limited competence in assessing the risks involved in its decisions and yet have significant freedom of action because of the absence of control systems that are able to resolve agency problems.

Adequate corporate governance structures for banking institutions require internal control systems within banks to address the inherent asymmetries of information and the potential market failure that may result. This form of market failure suggests a role for government intervention. If a central authority could know all agents' private information and engage in lump-sum transfers between agents, it could achieve a Pareto improvement. However, because a government cannot in practice observe agents' private information, it can achieve only a constrained or second-best Pareto optimum. Reducing the costs associated with the principal-agent problem and thereby achieving a second-best solution depends to a large extent on the corporate governance structures of financial firms and institutions and the way information is disseminated in the capital markets.[5]

The problem of asymmetries of information is also linked to differences in financial risk appetite between managers and owners. Because of the incentive structure of firms and the legal principle of limited liability, managers and owners of financial firms may have an incentive to underprice financial risk and thereby create too much risk for the broader economy. This can result in large social costs and increased financial fragility. A major concern of the financial regulator is to ensure that the bank or financial firm incurs the total costs of the financial risk it creates. One way to do this is to address the corporate governance problems of asymmetries of information and the different risk preferences of managers and owners and other stakeholder groups, such as creditors and employees. For example, the manager of the bank's asset sheet may have an incentive to assume too many risky assets in the banking book because, for instance, risky assets pay higher commissions. The costs incurred should these assets default may not be fully borne by the manager(s) who assumed them for the bank. In the case of a bank default or run, these costs could easily become social costs for the broader economy. The primary goal of financial regulation is therefore to reduce the social cost of financial risk taking. One way to do this is by aligning the incentives of market participants with the costs they create in financial risk taking.

In pursuing this task, the financial regulator is acting on behalf of the broader public interest, that is, it is representing the stakeholder interests of society at large by seeking to adopt a regulatory framework that incentivizes market participants to price financial risk in an efficient manner in order to minimize its social costs for the broader economy. The growing reality of global banking markets has made it necessary to develop international standards of corporate governance for banks and financial institutions that will promote more efficient pricing of financial risk. Significant efforts by the Basel Committee and by the International Organization of Securities Commissions are discussed in the following sections.

THE BASEL COMMITTEE AND CORPORATE GOVERNANCE STANDARDS

The Basel Committee has in recent years issued several articles that address specific topics related to corporate governance of financial institutions. The most important of these reports are "Principles for the Management of Interest Rate Risk," "Framework for Internal Control Systems in Banking Organizations," "Enhancing Bank Transparency," and "Principles for the Management of Credit Risk" (all available at www.bis.org). These reports highlight the essential strategies and techniques for sound corporate governance of financial institutions. The corporate governance practices espoused by these reports can be summarized as follows:

1. Establishing strategic objectives and a set of corporate values that are communicated throughout the banking organization
2. Setting and enforcing clear lines of responsibility and accountability throughout the organization
3. Ensuring that board members are qualified for their positions, have a clear understanding of their role in corporate governance and are not subject to undue influence from management or outside concerns
4. Ensuring that there is appropriate oversight by senior management
5. Effectively utilizing the work conducted by internal and external auditors, in recognition of the important control function they provide
6. Ensuring that compensation approaches are consistent with the bank's ethical values, objectives, strategy, and control environment
7. Conducting corporate governance in a transparent manner.

The Basel standards recognize that senior management is an integral component of the corporate governance process, while the board of directors provides checks and balances to senior managers, and that senior managers should assume the oversight role with respect to line managers in specific business areas and activities. The effectiveness of the audit process can be enhanced by recognizing the importance and independence of the auditors and by requiring timely correction by management of problems identified by auditors. The organizational structure of the board and management should be transparent, with clearly identifiable lines of communication and responsibility for decision making and business areas. Moreover, the nature and extent of transactions with affiliates and related parties should be itemized.[6]

BASEL II

The Basel Committee has developed principles to address many of the corporate governance challenges that face multinational banking groups. Basel II, however, contains the first detailed framework of rules and standards that supervisors can apply to the practices of senior management and the board for banking groups. Bank supervisors will now have the discretion to approve a variety of corporate governance and risk management activities for internal processes and decision making, as well as substantive requirements for estimating capital adequacy and a disclosure framework for investors. For example, under pillar 1, the board and senior management have responsibility for overseeing and approving the capital rating and estimation processes.[7] Senior management is expected to have a thorough understanding of the design and operation of the bank's capital rating system and its evaluation of credit, market, and operational risks. It will be expected to oversee any testing processes that evaluate the bank's compliance with capital adequacy requirements and its overall control environment. Senior management and executive members of the board should be in a position to justify any material differences between established procedures set by regulation and actual practice.[8] Moreover, reports provided to senior management should include a detailed account of the bank's internal-ratings-based approach for determining capital adequacy.

Pillar 1 has been criticized as allowing large, sophisticated banks to use their own internal ratings methodologies for assessing credit and market risk to calculate their capital requirements. This approach relies primarily on historical data that may be subject to sophisticated applications that may not accurately reflect the bank's true risk exposure, and it may also fail to take account of outlier events that could not be foreseen by past data. Moreover, the narrow focus on historical data does not address the incentive compatibility question of whether the bank's risk-taking behavior is optimal for the broader economy (Ward, 2002b).

Pillar 2 seeks to address some of these problems by providing for both internal and external monitoring of the bank's corporate governance and risk management practices. Banks are required to monitor their assessments of financial risks and to apply capital charges in a way that most closely approximates the bank's business risk exposure. Significantly, the supervisor is now expected to play a proactive role in this process by reviewing and assessing the bank's ability to monitor and comply with regulatory capital requirements. The supervisors and bank management are expected to engage in an ongoing dialogue regarding the most appropriate internal control processes and risk assessments systems, which may vary among banks depending on their organizational structure, business practices, and domestic regulatory framework.

Moreover, it will be necessary that Basel II corporate governance practices interact with local regulations that create different corporate governance and accounting requirements. For instance, EU member states will be required to adopt the International Accounting Standards by 2005. Banks that have operations in the United States or that are listed on a U.S. exchange will be required to disclose accounts and to have them verified under oath by senior management and third-party advisers. A major weakness of the Basel II regime is that it does not sufficiently take account of the implementation problems regulators may have in respect of reconciling Basel II corporate governance framework with local regulatory requirements.

Pillar 3 also addresses corporate governance concerns by focusing on transparency and market discipline mechanisms to improve the flow of information between bank management and investors. The goal is to align regulatory objectives with the bank's incentives to make profits for its shareholders. It seeks to do this by improving reporting requirements for bank capital adequacy. This covers both quantitative and qualitative disclosure requirements for both overall capital adequacy and capital allocation, which are based on credit risk, market risk, operational risk, and interest rate risks.

Pillar 3 sets forth important proposals to improve transparency by linking regulatory capital levels to the quality of disclosure. This means that banks will have incentives to improve their internal controls, systems operations, and overall risk management practices if they improve the quality of the information regarding the bank's risk exposure and management practices. Under this approach, shareholders will have more and better information with which to make decisions about well-managed and poorly managed banks. The downside of this approach is that in countries with undeveloped accounting and corporate governance frameworks, the disclosure of such information might lead to volatilities that might undermine financial stability by causing a bank run or failure that would not have occurred had the information been disclosed in a more sensitive manner. Pillar 3 has not yet provided a useful framework for regulators and bank management to coordinate their efforts in the release of information that might create a volatile response in the market.

Pillar 3 attempts to address some of these problems by allowing regulators to rely on national legal principles of confidentiality to preclude the home regulator, in certain circumstances, from disclosing to a foreign regulator or other party the bank's proprietary information or other information that might unjustifiably undermine confidence in the financial system.

IOSCO'S RESPONSE TO THE PRINCIPAL-AGENT PROBLEM

The principal-agent problem as outlined poses a systemic threat to financial systems when the incentives that drive management decisions at a banking or securities firm are not aligned with those of the owners of the firm. This may result in management's having risk preferences that are different from those of the firm's owners, as well as those of other stakeholders, including creditors, employees and the public. The financial regulator represents the public's interest in seeing that banks and securities firms are regulated efficiently so as to reduce systemic risk. IOSCO recognizes the threat that market intermediaries and some investment firms pose to the systemic stability of financial systems. In its report entitled "Objectives and Principles of Securities Regulation" (www.iosco.org/docs-public/1998-objectives-documents03.html),[9] IOSCO adopts internal corporate governance standards for investment firms so that they can conduct themselves in a manner that protects their clients and the integrity and stability of financial markets. IOSCO places primary responsibility for the management and operation of securities firms on senior management.

The responsibility for the overall governance of an investment firm should lie with management, which should have responsibility for compliance with appropriate standards of conduct and adherence to proper procedures. This includes the proper management of all risks associated with the operation of the firm. Regulation, however, should not be responsible for removing risk from the marketplace, as risk is inherent to the enterprise system; rather, it should be responsible for reducing risk that arises from the activities of the firm and that may have a systemic character. Proper management of risk may affect stakeholders at large, such as the public and creditors, that is not related to the risk inherent in the market itself. To do this, there must be periodic evaluation of risk management processes within a regulated entity, and this evaluation must involve regulators and external auditors.

IOSCO recognizes the problem of operational risk and defines it as "the risk of loss through a failure of systems or deliberate or negligent conduct of staff."[10] High levels of operational risk may have systemic implications when they involve large investment firms with global operations. This was clearly the case in the Barings and the Daiwa collapses, which resulted from the failure of senior management to implement adequate internal control procedures for staff; broader issues of ensuring that various subsidiaries of the financial group were complying adequately with home and host state regulatory standards were also implicated. What is clear from the Barings and the Daiwa fiascos is that home and host country regulators must communicate more and must coordinate their investigations along the lines of the Basel-IOSCO-IAIS standards for supervising multinational conglomerates. They must adhere to the generally accepted standards of consolidated supervision based on home country control.

In addition, operational risk must be managed by internal procedures designed to prevent misconduct or negligence. Because the regulator cannot practically expend the resources to ensure that such internal procedures are adhered to on a day-to-day basis, senior management must take this responsibility. Senior management must make itself aware of the nature of the firm's business, such as its internal control procedures and its policies regarding allocation of risk for particular activities. It must also ensure that it can capably discharge its responsibilities. It must clearly set forth lines of responsibility in the management command structure and provide adequate access of communication for those involved at all levels of the firm's operations. All relevant information concerning the firm's risk must be made available to management in a timely manner. This information should be made available to the regulator upon request.

The specific structure of the firm's internal organization should be determined by the firm's size, the nature of its business, and the risks and activities it undertakes. Despite firms' differences along these dimensions, the regulation of market intermediaries and investment firms should adhere to the following standards: (1) high standards of fair dealing with customers to ensure market integrity; (2) clear terms of engagement in contracts with customers; (3) procurement of all relevant information on customers' backgrounds; (4) adequate disclosure to customers to allow them to make a balanced and informed investment decision and high levels of staff training in the sale of products; (5) proper protection for customer assets; and (6) compliance with any relevant laws, codes, or standards as they apply to the firm, as well as with all internal policies and procedures; and avoidance of any conflict of interest to ensure fair treatment of customers and public.

Moreover, IOSCO emphasizes that senior management must be directly responsible for all firm policies that involve proprietary trading. The firm should make available to the regulator information regarding the firm's own proprietary trading and should determine that the firm's net capital is sufficient in relation to its risk exposure. This information should provide an understanding of the firm's overall business and risk profile, including that of its subsidiaries and affiliates. Management should also have personal liability for overseeing the firm's compliance with regulations regarding margin trading and the detection of conflicts of interest or manipulative practices.

CONCLUSION

Many observers agree that the banking and financial industry is one sector that has been greatly affected by major structural changes, in part because of the pressures of increased globalization. The consequences of such changes include but are not limited to increased competition, squeezed profit margins, and intense pressure to cut prices and quickly develop and market new products with shorter life cycles—all within significantly shorter turnaround times. In addition, the banking industry has been subjected to the competitive forces of deregulation in both its activities and its prices. The internationalization of financial markets necessitates the establishment of universal standards for corporate governance for financial institutions. These standards include but by no means are limited to (1) enhanced monitoring; (2) improved disclosure and accounting practices; (3) better enforcement of corporate governance rules and the corporate governance framework; and (4) the strengthening of institutions through market discipline.

This chapter acknowledges that different structural approaches to corporate governance exist across countries and encourages practices that can strengthen corporate governance under diverse structures. To improve the framework within which such institutions must strive to operate effectively, an important task for supervisors and regulators is to ensure that incentives exist to encourage senior bank management to adopt good regulatory practices that approximate the economic risk exposure of the financial institution. Because different national markets have different types of economic risk to protect against, there is no universally correct answer that can work in every financial market, and laws need not be uniform from country to country. Global governance of financial markets should therefore include a concept of corporate governance that may take different forms in different countries but that nevertheless addresses the threat to global systemic stability posed by the internal operations and management strategies of financial institutions. Recognizing this, banking regulators can put in place sound governance practices that take different forms according to the economic and legal structure of a particular jurisdiction. Nevertheless, the organizational structure of any bank or securities firm should include four forms of oversight: (1) oversight by the board of directors or supervisory board; (2) oversight by nonexecutive individuals who are not involved in the day-to-day managing of the business; (3) direct line supervision of different business areas; and (4) independent risk management and audit functions. Regulators should also utilize approximate criteria to ensure that key personnel meet fit and proper standards. These principles should also apply to government-owned banks, but with the recognition that government ownership often implies different bank strategies and objectives.

11

Summing Up and Conclusion

The New International Financial Architecture—Promise or Threat?

Since the mid 1990s, creating a "new international financial architecture" has been the subject of an active debate among academics and policy-makers in national treasuries, central banks, and international financial institutions (IFIs), such as the IMF and World Bank. By "architecture" we mean the structure of financial rules and procedures that define the scope and operation of international financial markets. In this book, we argue that this architecture has evolved haphazardly in response to a series of financial crises over the last thirty years that has resulted in an international regime that generates inefficient rules for the regulation of systemic risk in global financial markets. We suggest that the efficient regulation of systemic risk in global financial markets requires that IFI standard setting and decision making be effective, accountable, and legitimate for the countries and jurisdictions subject to IFI standards. *Effectiveness* can be measured by the efficiency of the standards and rules to regulate and control systemic risk. Controlling systemic risk means the reduction of the externality of financial risk taking. *Accountability* requires the institutional structure to be transparent and contain clear lines of authority and establish consistent procedures for how countries participate in the decision-making process. *Legitimacy* means that all countries and jurisdictions subject to the standards have played a meaningful role in their promulgation—either directly or indirectly—and that the standards take account of their economic interests. These principles form the key elements of an efficient global governance regime for financial markets. However, they are not mutually exclusive in the sense that the design of an effective standard-setting process that leads to efficient regulatory rules also implies improved accountability measures, such as clearer procedures for country participation and enhanced responsibilities of the IFIs to their accountee countries. Similarly, improved regulation of systemic risk also implicates the legitimacy of the standards adopted because of the impact of efficient regulation on a country's economic growth and development. Essentially, these principles of global governance are linked by the overriding objective of controlling and managing systemic risk.

We argue that the institutional structure of international financial regulation fails these three principles because it does not efficiently regulate systemic risk in the global financial system. These institutional failings contribute to lower long-term economic growth rates for developed and developing countries, but especially for developing and emerging market economies. In this chapter, we argue why international financial regulation is not efficient. We propose an analytical approach that confronts both the growing homogeneity of investor behavior and the macromanifestation of systemic risk. This approach suggests that international financial standard setting does not adequately address the externality of bank risk taking and its cross-border dimension. We then discuss other areas of regulatory concern, such as the growing systemic threat posed by large financial conglomerates and multinational banking groups, and future avenues of research for the regulation of systemic risk in global financial markets.

As was made clear in preceding chapters, one of the most important themes in the debate is the management of systemic risk, that is, the risk that the financial decisions of individuals and firms pose for the viability of the economic system as a whole. Sadly, from this perspective, some of the proposals and institutional approaches to reform that are currently in favor are likely to do more harm than good; they are more threat than promise.

EXTERNALITIES

Chapter 1 discussed how financial risk taking creates externalities and therefore is a concern of public policy. By externalities, we mean that the costs and benefits that accrue to society are external to the calculations of the individual risk-taking investor and thus are not accounted for in the marketplace. The externality equals the difference between private loss and social loss. Investors do not take account of externalities because of market failures that can arise in the financial sector due to asymmetries of information between lenders and borrowers *and* investors and issuers.[1]

The case of environmental externalities provides an analogy where the factory owner does not take into account the costs imposed on society at large by the dirty smoke billowing from his chimney. The result is socially inefficient because the factory owner does not take into account the full social costs of production when considering how much to produce. Similarly, in financial markets, the failure of a major financial institution may impose costs on society at large that exceed the losses incurred by investors. The classic example is a bank failure, which can create a panic among depositors that can spread from bank to bank, ruining both the solvent and insolvent. In calculating the expected return of its investment, the first bank did not take account of the potential social costs that could be created by its investment losses. The first bank's failure to internalize the social costs of its risk-taking activity would lead it rationally to take on greater risks than what would have been rational had it taken the social costs into account.

In markets where significant externalities exist, competitive markets will be socially inefficient because risk is mispriced. The objective of public policy is to devise a regulatory framework that reduces these inefficiencies by incentivizing market participants to price risk efficiently.

The analogy of environmental externalities, however, can be misleading, because the externalities that are generated in financial markets can be transmitted *macroeconomically* and therefore have a much broader systemic effect.

Financial markets are markets for stocks of assets, the value of which depends on the expectation of their future value. When expectations among investors are shared, any factor that leads to a shift in expected future values (e.g., a bank run panic) will have an immediate effect on the value of financial assets, and on the major macrofinancial variables, such as the interest rate and exchange rate.

So the failure of a single firm can, by influencing expectations, have an influence not only on its immediate counterparties, or even just on firms that deal in similar products, but also, through its impact on expectations, on financial markets as a whole and then, via the interest rate or the exchange rate, on the real economy at home and abroad.

Yet, despite all the discussion of externalities, contagion, and panics, a peculiarity of market expectations is that they seem to be remarkably stable (or tranquil) for substantial periods of time, even when underlying real circumstances might be decidedly unpropitious. In consequence, the financial markets can resemble the cartoon character who, having run off the edge of the cliff, remains suspended for some time in midair, with no visible (or rational) means of support, before suddenly plunging into the abyss. Periods of tranquillity defined by stable expectations and stable market confidence may sustain the illusion that financial markets are truly reflecting a strong real economy. The shattering of that illusion can be catastrophic. One of the tasks of financial regulation is to keep markets away from the cliff edge and, when they rush over, to ensure that the damage to the economy as a whole is minimized.

INTERNATIONAL REGULATION

As discussed in chapter 1, following the Second World War, the IMF Articles of Agreement permitted national authorities to impose and maintain severe controls on domestic financial systems. Most G10 countries maintained regulations that kept domestic financial markets segmented with strict rules governing the scale and content of borrowing and lending. For instance, U.S. authorities fixed the rate of interest that banks could pay on savings accounts (Regulation Q). Other countries utilized exchange controls that severely limited cross-border capital flows and buttressed an international system of fixed exchange rates.

The lynchpin of the IMF fixed exchange rate regime was the U.S. dollar, which was convertible into gold at $35 an ounce and convertible into other reserve currencies at predetermined par values. This ended on August 15, 1971, when President Nixon ordered his treasury secretary, John Connolly, to close the gold window. The major reserve currencies were all floated by 1973. A new era of fluctuating exchange rates had begun.

Under the fixed exchange rate system, the private sector was more or less freed from foreign exchange risk because of governmental controls that kept currencies at their par values. In contrast, the post-Bretton Woods system confronted the private sector with a brave new world of fluctuating exchange rates. Because forex risk had been privatized, there was a pressing need to hedge against the costs imposed by floating exchange rates. Banks and financial firms needed to be able to diversify their portfolios at will by changing the mix of currencies and financial assets in line with the changing perception of foreign exchange risk. It was necessary to create new financial instruments, such as futures contracts and derivatives, which demanded the removal of many of the regulatory barriers that had limited the possibilities for managing financial risk.

Gradually, restrictions on foreign exchange trading were abolished and domestic restrictions on cross-market access for financial institutions were lifted. Also, quantitative restrictions on the provision of credit were eliminated in most developed countries. A global market of monetary and financial instruments was thus created.

As restrictions on domestic and cross-border banking and capital flows were lifted, the ability of regulators to effectively regulate their financial systems was challenged by increasingly irrelevant national jurisdictional boundaries. So, in response, the modern era of international financial regulation was born in January 1975 with the formation of the Committee on Banking Supervision and Regulatory Practices by the Group of Ten central bankers. The so-called Basel Committee (based at the Bank for International settlements) was formed in response to the first appearance of a new form of internationally propagated instability when the Bankhaus Herstatt collapsed in 1974 because of huge exposures in forex dealings that left several major U.S. banks dangerously exposed to settlement risk. An international financial crisis was averted only after the German Bundesbank intervened to guarantee Herstatt's liabilities.[2] At the time, neither German nor U.S. regulators were properly equipped to deal with the cross-border repercussions of a bank default in the forex market. The Basel Committee's task was to coordinate the activities of national regulators within the new international financial marketplace. As discussed in chapter 2, the Committee has developed minimum capital standards for banks and a detailed catalogue of principles and codes of good practice for bank regulators.[3]

The Committee began promulgating in 1999 a substantial revision to the 1988 Capital Accord known as Basel II, which after much revision was finally approved in 2004 and has become the subject of much academic and practitioner interest. Basel II addresses the problem of systemic risk in the banking sector by proposing to make the assets and capital calculations of banks more sensitive to the economic risks that banks actually face. A major criticism of Basel II is that it disproportionately focuses on the particular economic risks that banks create for themselves and not on the aggregate risk that banks create for the entire financial system.

A PROPOSED ANALYTICAL FRAMEWORK

Future work to rebuild the international financial architecture along the lines we propose should adopt an analytical framework that recognizes that the externality of systemic risk is in large part manifest through what Keynes called a "beauty contest." In Keynes's contest, beauty was not in the eye of the beholder. Rather, the game is won by those who can most accurately assess what others think is beautiful. In financial markets, knowing what others believe to be true is the key to knowing how markets will behave. The markets are driven by what market participants believe average opinion believes average opinion believes, and so on, ad infinitum (Keynes, 1936: chapter 12).

For such markets to be liquid and reasonably stable, it is not enough that markets should be large, but rather it is fundamental that they should be characterized by a wide range of participants with heterogeneous objectives *and* with confident expectations that markets will be stable (Persaud, 2000, 2001).

Liquidity in financial markets occurs when buyers and sellers are broadly balanced. Markets become illiquid when the objectives of investors become homogeneous. For instance, liquidity vanishes when everyone believes everyone will sell. Markets can fall over the cliff when average opinion believes that average opinion has lost confidence in financial assets.

So what contributes to heterogeneity? First, individual investors and traders must have different financial objectives. Traditional economics described this as the difference between those who were seeking income certainty and those who were seeking wealth certainty, with their different patterns of risk aversion, different investment time horizons, and so on (Robinson, 1951).

Second, different access to information can lead investors to behave differently, even if their goals are the same.

Third, stability becomes a convention when average opinion believes that average opinion believes that markets are stable. Convention (meaning a belief in stability) is vital for financial markets, because convention creates and sustains heterogeneity. For example, if it is believed that the exchange rate of the dollar to the pound sterling oscillates between $1.40 and $1.45, then once the rate rises above $1.45, buyers will enter the market to support the dollar. Similarly, if the rate falls below $1.40, then investors will sell dollars. This power of stable expectations should not be underestimated. By defining the *expected* range of movements in asset prices, it fixes the *actual* range of fluctuations in current asset prices. But, of course, once convention is breached, then the flood will follow.[4]

Fourth, government regulation may create heterogeneity by forcing investors into segmented markets. For example, the U.K. mortgage market used to be legally separated from other investment markets, and mortgages were allocated mainly by quantity controls and less by price. Similarly, the Glass-Steagall Act segmented U.S. financial markets, and most countries adhered to the IMF fixed exchange rate regime that had the effect of segmenting national financial markets.

Indeed, the liberalization of financial markets that has occurred over the last three decades has inevitably reduced the heterogeneity in financial markets. By definition, liberalization has reduced segmentation, and cross-market correlations have arisen sharply.

Moreover, liberalization has been accompanied by a growing professionalization of financial management (BIS, 1998: chapter 5) and extensive consolidation of financial institutions (Group of Ten, 2001). Because most investments are now managed by mutual funds, pension funds, and insurance companies, they are increasingly subject to uniform investment management practices in which the funds are locked into sophisticated wholesale money markets where securitization and repackaging results in a more homogeneous fund flow from previously segmented markets (Kurz, 1987). This professionalization of investment management has reduced the heterogeneity of investor preferences as expressed in the marketplace. The continuous pressure to maximize short-term returns leads the professional investor to prefer a myopic (i.e., short-time horizon) investment as an optimal investment strategy. As professional investment becomes more uniform, so does professional information services—both in source and in processing—again making for a more homogeneous market. Also, consolidation of financial institutions is clearly becoming a major homogenizing force as well.

Financial liberalization has also probably weakened the power of convention to keep markets stable. After all, in the immediate postwar era, much of market convention was imposed by government regulation— fixed exchange rates, for example. All that has gone. However, the growing homogeneity of traders with common beliefs and common information may well reinforce conventional stability, making the loss of that convention dependent on the beliefs of private investors, with potential catastrophic consequences for the economy.

MACROECONOMIC AND MICROECONOMIC ASPECTS OF
INTERNATIONAL REGULATION

Public policy also needs to take into account that beliefs about average opinion transmit externalities through macroeconomic variables (e.g., the interest rate, exchange rate, or the general level of stock prices). So effective regulation of firms should be conceived in conjunction with macroeconomic policy. This is particularly true for international financial markets, where a major focus of systemic risk is the exchange rate.

In policy terms, macroeconomic action may be a far more efficient means of reducing systemic risk than traditional microeconomic regulation. An excellent example of this was the macroeconomic focus of regulatory policy in the aftermath of the Asian financial crisis of 1997–1998. It is clear that an important component of the crisis was the excess foreign exchange exposure of financial and other institutions in many of the Asian markets. As a result, the IMF urged the authorities in those economies to tighten regulation of short-term forex exposure. The tightening is supposed to take place microeconomically by means of regulations that impact on the actions of individual firms. This is a complex task that requires a significant input of a scarce resource—trained regulators. Moreover, the quantitative measures proposed are likely to have an uneven effect, limiting the forex exposure of financial institutions but missing many holdings outside the financial sector.

The same goal could be attained macroeconomically by adopting measures that raise the cost of short-term borrowing abroad, such as "Chilean-style" short-term capital controls, which would encourage all firms (financial and otherwise) to reduce their exposure (Agosin, 1998). The higher cost of short-term forex borrowing "prices in" the risk externality and hence increases economic efficiency. This macro approach would also have the advantage of economizing on scarce talent.[5]

The IMF has justified its move into financial regulation by reference to its powers of macroeconomic surveillance embodied in Article IV of its Articles of Agreement. It might therefore be hoped that the macroeconomic dimension of systemic risk would be at the fore both of its analysis and of its regulatory proposals.

Indeed, the IMF has proposed the construction of "macroprudential indicators" (MPIs) to assess the "health and stability of the financial system." As currently constructed, MPIs "comprise both aggregated microprudential indicators of the health of individual financial institutions and macroeconomic variables associated with financial system soundness" (Hilbers, Krueger, and Moretti, 2000; see also Evans, Lane, Gill, and Hilbers, 2000).

This attempt to link microrisk to the performance of the macroeconomy is laudable and is exactly where the debate on effective international regulation should be going. However, there is a flaw in MPIs as currently conceived: there has been no attempt to link the microeconomic risk taking to the risk created by the interactions of firms, in other words, by the beauty contest.[6] Just adding up micro-data won't do. The whole is not just greater than but behaves very differently from the sum of the parts.

A further manifestation of the relationship between microeconomic risk and macroeconomic performance that is apparently neglected in the IMF's current approach derives from the links among risk management, financial contagion, and the trade cycle. Strict regulatory requirements on risk exposures will cause firms to reduce lending as a result of a downturn in the economy, thus exacerbating the downturn. In an upturn, the perceived diminution of risk and the availability of regulatory capital will tend to increase banks' ability to lend, stoking the boom (see Jackson, 1999; BIS, 2001b).

This procyclicality of regulation is further amplified by the contagion-inducing techniques of risk management. During the Asian crisis, for example, financial institutions followed the instructions of their risk models by reducing their exposure to emerging markets throughout the world. These cutbacks help spread the crisis, as reduced lending and reduced confidence fed the financial downturn. The key to the problem, once again, is the link between microeconomic actions and macroeconomic consequences. Rational risk management by individual firms precipitates a macroeconomic reaction that, in a downturn, can place those firms and other firms in jeopardy, indeed, can overwhelm the firms' defenses entirely.

Yet, because the links between regulation and macroeconomic policy are so little understood, there is no coherent policy response to this perverse consequence. Under pressure, regulators have adopted pragmatic solutions. At the onset of the Latin American debt crisis in the early 1980s, many major U.S. banks were technically bankrupt, since Latin American assets held on their books had lost most of their value. Nonetheless, U.S. regulators allowed those assets to be revaluated in the banks' balance sheets at their maturity value, hence boosting the banks' notional capital and preventing a sudden collapse in lending and liquidity.[7] In the autumn of 1998, many assets held on the balance sheets of financial institutions in London and New York were, if marked to market, worth nothing. Again, the regulators did not insist on an immediate (potentially catastrophic) write-down.

For all countries, there is the further difficulty that even if some sort of macroeconomic response were available to offset the procyclicality of regulation, macroeconomic policy is essentially national, while the problem may well be international in origin and scope.

National Approach

And it is the international dimension that is notable, and oddly missing, in the IMF's new approach. The FSAPs are appraisals of national financial systems. Yet many of the risks faced by a given national economy may well, in a seamless international financial system, emanate from outside the territorial boundaries of the nation state. It is precisely the national focus of regulators that has been persistently exposed as inadequate in recurrent crises in the past twenty years. It seems quite unsatisfactory to conduct an appraisal of the financial health of Colombia, for example, when many of the risks to which that country is exposed are external. And it is equally unsatisfactory to conduct an FSAP of the United Kingdom, when Britain is so obviously an integral part of the European Union and of a worldwide financial system. At the very least the IMF should be conducting FSAPs on major collectivities of states, say the G7 or the East Asian economies taken together.

SUMMING UP

To summarize: effective international regulation requires a new approach. This new approach must confront both the growing homogeneity of investor behavior and the macromanifestation of systemic risk. Sadly, neither of these issues is prominent in current reform proposals.

CURRENT POLICY AND LEGAL DEVELOPMENTS

The financial events of 1998 stimulated today's interest in international regulation. They represented the first post-World War II crisis in which events in emerging market economies seriously threatened the financial stability of the West *and* where the origins of the crisis were clearly to be found in the workings of liberalized markets and private sector institutions.[8]

But the center of the conflagration was the near-failure of the hedge fund Long Term Capital Management. More than any of the other problems in the fall of 1998, the threat posed by LTCM's difficulties to international financial stability illustrated beyond all reasonable doubt that the international financial system had entered a new era.[9] This was not a problem of sovereign debt or macroeconomic imbalance, or even a foreign exchange crisis. Rather, it was the manifestation of the market propagation of systemic risk created by the market-driven decisions of a private firm.

In response, the G7 established the Financial Stability Forum, bringing together national regulators, central banks, treasury departments, and international financial institutions to tackle international financial problems on a coordinated international basis. As discussed in chapter 4, the IMF and the World Bank set up new financial sector assessment programs (FSAPs). The FSAPs involve the Bank and the IMF in detailed microeconomic appraisals of the financial markets and regulatory institutions of selected countries. This level of interest in private sector structures represents a significant departure in IMF/Bank surveillance of a nation's economic affairs and in particular marks a turning point in the Fund's surveillance activities.[10]

The IMF's task is of considerable sensitivity, as it could be drawn into the position of "grading" national financial systems, with any downward revision of grades having the potential to produce dramatic financial consequences (IMF, 2000b). Nonetheless, the IMF, despite its institutional flaws, exercises its surveillance function with some degree of legitimacy that is recognized by treaty. To this end, the IMF now encourages and in some cases requires countries that seek its assistance to conform to international regulatory codes and standards. In other words, the Fund has the ability to use financial penalties (withdrawal of offers of assistance) to *enforce* conformity to those standards. As discussed in chapter 3, however, one must doubt the ability of the IMF to enforce regulatory codes upon the more powerful countries that do not seek its financial assistance.

The Principles—Basel II and Beyond

What are the principles guiding the new IMF-World Bank initiative? For instance, FSAP surveillance concentrates on a country adhering to international standards and rules of good regulatory practice as developed by the Basel Committee, the International Organization of Securities Commissions, the International Association of Insurance Supervisors (IAIS), and the Financial Action Task Force (FATF).[11] But it is the principles underlying Basel II that are the most important intellectual foundations of the new international financial architecture.[12]

As discussed in earlier chapters, Basel II is a response to the growing obsolescence of the 1988 capital adequacy rules and the ease by which banks could circumvent their requirements. It is a typical feature of dynamic financial markets that regulatory rules will become outdated. Basel II seeks to address this by providing capital rules that are far more flexible and bolstered by an extension of supervision—qualitative assessment of and management of risk by public officials—and by market forces. These are the so-called three pillars of Basel II. Pillar 1 contains a determination of regulatory capital, now heavily weighted toward use of banks' internal risk weighting models, as well as the views of ratings agencies. Pillar 2 provides the framework of supervisory review, and pillar 3 is market discipline, enforced by greater disclosure of banks' financial status, as well as by their internal risk management procedures.

A particularly important aspect of Basel II is its emphasis on the role of firms' own risk management procedures and on market discipline. One might think that this is a rather odd approach to confront systemic risk, which is by definition an externality that internal procedures do not encompass and that is not accounted for in the marketplace. But perhaps of even greater importance is the powerful tendency of the pillar 1 and pillar 3 proposals to increase the homogeneity of financial markets.

First, the emphasis on the use of a firm's internal risk management systems may increase homogeneity in financial markets, because these systems are by definition market sensitive. While firms' models may differ in detail, they are constructed on similar analytical principles, estimated on similar historical data, and sensitive to the same market information.

Generally, good risk management involves firms holding a portfolio of assets that are not volatile and the prices of which are not highly correlated—not correlated in normal times, that is. If, however, the volatility of a given asset rises sharply, the models of most firms will tell them to sell. As all try to sell, liquidity will dry up. As liquidity vanishes, volatility will spread from one asset to another. Previously, uncorrelated assets will now be correlated in the general sell-off, enhanced by the model-driven behavior of other institutions caught up in the contagion. In conventional times, these models may encompass a wide range of behavior; in extreme circumstances the models will encourage firms to act as a herd, charging toward the cliff edge together (Persaud, 2000).

Second, the emphasis on full disclosure with uniform requirements across jurisdictions may reduce the divergences in information that have in the past created diversity of views. Today, information is ever more readily available, and disclosure of price-sensitive information is legally required in many jurisdictions. Insider dealing on private information is, rightly, a criminal offence and is a form of market abuse. But the attainment of equal information is bought at a cost—increased homogeneity and, hence, potentially reduced liquidity.

Because pillars 1 and 3 promote greater homogeneity, considerable weight is placed on pillar 2 (enhanced supervision) to inhibit the behavior that generates systemic risk. Unfortunately, pillar 2's broad scope of regulatory discretion will likely lead to an essentially subjective, personal interaction between bureaucrat and risk taker that may result in inconsistent or ineffective standards, and potentially to regulatory capture (Ward, 2002a, 2002b).

The drive toward homogeneity is not confined to the Basel II banking proposals. As financial markets become seamless, spanning banks, securities firms, insurance companies, pension funds, and so on, regulators are increasingly adopting functional approaches that disregard which type of institution is generating the risk, and instead apply the same regulatory rules to the same types of financial risk. For instance, in considering the relationship between banking and insurance, then Chairman of the U.K. Financial Services Authority, Sir Howard Davies, stated that "[o]ur general view is that the capital treatment should in principle be the same, where the risks are the same." So the competitive pressures for homogenization throughout financial markets are being reinforced by regulators.

Consolidated Supervision and Basel II

Chapter 2 discussed the Basel Committee's principles of consolidated supervision and how they apply choice of jurisdiction rules to allocate regulatory authority over the transnational operations of banks and banking groups. These principles have evolved in response to the lessons learned from major banking collapses (e.g., BCCI) and to the demands of increased consolidation and conglomeration in global banking markets. The consolidated supervision rules provide that the regulator of the jurisdiction where the bank or banking group has its principal office should have ultimate supervisory responsibility for the banking group's global compliance with capital adequacy and other prudential standards. The home state regulator should cooperate and coordinate with the host state regulators to ensure that the bank's branch, subsidiary, and agency operations comply with home and host state regulatory standards. This may involve exchange of proprietary information regarding the bank's operation and risk management practices as well as coordinating national enforcement actions and the bank's adherence to international standards. The home state regulator should take the lead with respect to principles of prudential supervision (i.e., capital adequacy), while the host state regulator takes the lead in overseeing compliance with liquidity requirements and payment system regulation. Under the post-BCCI amendments to the Revised Concordat, however, the host state authority can reject a foreign banking group's application for a branch or subsidiary if the host state authority believes the home state authority provides inadequate supervision or regulatory standards to its bank's global operations.

Consolidated supervision in the case of Basel II presents a number of difficult issues for home and host state authorities and bank management. For instance, consolidated supervision would allow the home state regulator to exercise overall authority for ensuring that the global operations of the banking group adhere to capital adequacy standards as set forth in the standardized, foundation, or internal-ratings–based approach. Host state regulators, however, would still have ultimate authority to reject the application, or to terminate the license, of a foreign bank or banking group if the foreign bank were seeking to operate under Basel II in the host jurisdiction and the host authorities had not approved Basel II. Also, even if the foreign bank has agreed to abide by the host state's capital requirements for its operations in the host jurisdiction, the host regulator may still have the authority, under its domestic law, to deny a license to the foreign bank if the host regulator believes the foreign bank's (or banking group's) global capital allocation to be inadequate and to pose a threat to the safety and soundness of the local banking sector. This could result in a direct conflict between jurisdictions, because a foreign banking group may be required to implement Basel II in its home jurisdiction and in other foreign jurisdictions that have approved Basel II, while other host regulators may restrict or prohibit a license to a foreign bank because it adheres to Basel II in its global operations.

The Basel Committee believes that home and host state regulators should agree on a single approach for implementing Basel II to a bank's international operations and has adopted a statement of principles (2003) to achieve this. The principles on home-host state coordination in implementing Basel II seek to eliminate conflicting and duplicative regulatory requirements between home and host regulators by encouraging host authorities to defer to home authorities regarding implementation of Basel

II to the global operations of the home state bank. For instance, the principles encourage regulators to adopt a single approach for determining capital requirements for a banking group's global operations. This would involve agreement on a single capital measurement approach (standardized, foundation, or advanced) and for consistent validation methods and techniques to measure capital for the bank's international operations. The principles also seek consistent approaches across jurisdictions for assessing compliance with pillar 2 supervisory review and pillar 3 market discipline requirements. Although the Committee recognizes that host state regulators have not relinquished their domestic legal powers to regulate foreign banks, they strongly encourage host state regulators to assist home regulators that have adopted Basel II in applying it to the foreign operations of their home state banks.

Because most developed countries will adopt Basel II in some form, developing countries and emerging economies are likely to come under tremendous pressure from the G10 and the IFIs to permit foreign banks to operate under Basel II in their markets. This could increase systemic risk in these jurisdictions because the presence of large foreign banks on Basel II may have a disproportionate impact on the composition of credit risk in the local banking sector and potentially undermine financial stability. This presents a number of regulatory policy concerns for host country regulators who have not adopted Basel II or have adopted modified versions of it. For instance, it may create competitive distortions between foreign banks and local banks because the foreign banks on Basel II could potentially benefit from less stringent capital rules than local banks. Indeed, by utilizing the advanced capital approaches of Basel II, foreign banks can qualify for lower levels of capital and depending on their size in the local banking markets this could result in a significant undercapitalization of the local banking sector, thereby threatening banking sector stability. The potential systemic risk could be greater for developing countries whose banking systems are relatively small in comparison with developed countries and whose macroeconomic frameworks are typically more fragile and subject to increased volatility. Indeed, a major criticism of Basel II has been its potential for procyclicality and how this might have an adverse effect on economic development in developing countries.

International standard setters therefore must clarify the jurisdictional competence of host state regulators to determine the capital requirements of foreign banks seeking to operate in host state territory. As discussed in chapter 5, host state authorities must have the discretion to opt out of international standards if these standards are perceived as undermining national economic objectives and financial stability. International committees under the aegis of the proposed Global Financial Governance Council would engage in intense negotiations in order to reach consensus over divisive issues, such as Basel II and FATF antimoney-laundering controls. It is envisaged that most negotiations will lead to consensus agreements that take account of the economic needs of both developed and developing countries, rather than the existing system whereby international standards are devised by the world's richest countries and imposed through the IFIs on other countries. The principles of accountability and legitimacy require greater involvement by developing and emerging market countries in international financial decision making. Similarly, the principle of effectiveness requires a decision-making structure that is institutionally and procedurally coherent, yet allows a large number of countries to participate on expert standard setting committees, whose decisions would ultimately be approved by senior ministers of all member countries.

The Case of Bank Insolvency and Financial Conglomerates The Basel Committee's consolidated supervision principles do not apply to bank insolvency. Although the European Community has adopted a Directive for allocating regulatory and insolvency law jurisdiction for bank insolvency, there are no treaties or customary international law principles that apply in this area. Both home and host state regulators have jealously guarded their authority to institute insolvency proceedings against banks with operations in their jurisdictions. The legal systems of many states have attempted to address this by adopting what is known as the "universal approach" for the winding up and administering of a bank's global assets. The universal approach provides that the home state regulator can assert jurisdiction over the banks global assets and, after consultation with local regulators, prioritize creditor claims according to the law of the home state (or by other agreement of the home-host regulators).[13] In the case of an individual bank, this can be relatively straightforward, but when the bank operates in a complex network of affiliates and subsidiaries in multiple jurisdictions a number of difficult issues arise regarding the division of regulatory authority over the conglomerate's operations and which legal system's insolvency law should determine the priority and validity of various creditor claims in different jurisdictions.

Although many jurisdictions recognize the universal approach as a general principle, most national insolvency laws allow the regulator to depart from this approach in order to protect local creditors and to maintain financial stability. For instance, if a number of systemically important local banks and firms have claims on assets that are located within the host jurisdiction, the host regulator might be reluctant to permit those assets to be liquidated by the home regulator to pay off other creditors whose claims have priority under the home country's law, especially if doing so might threaten financial stability. As a result, some of the most complex questions in international financial regulation arise during the insolvency of a banking group or financial conglomerate with a multitude of branches and subsidiaries in different jurisdictions. The authority to administer the local assets of a conglomerate will be mainly a matter of local law and domestic jurisdiction.

This unilateral power of state regulatory authority is conditioned by the national interest in protecting local creditors and investors and insulating the local banking sector from systemic risk. It pays less regard to the interests of foreign regulators and their efforts to protect their financial sector from the systemic risk emanating from the insolvency of a foreign bank that has branches, subsidiaries, or affiliates operating within its jurisdiction. The lack of cooperation and coordination in resolving the insolvency of a financial conglomerate with cross-border operations and the absence of international agreement in this area provide an inefficient model for regulating systemic risk. The potential systemic risk posed by the insolvency of a bank(s) within a financial conglomerate is enormous because of the cross-border exposures and counterparty relationships it has with other banks and financial firms within the group structure. As most international banking is conducted by banks that operate within multinational group structures, the failure of one bank in the group can set off a chain reaction that reverberates throughout the group and across jurisdictions and could also potentially undermine the viability of financial firms outside the group and the broader economy.

A major challenge not addressed in this book but awaiting future research concerns how to devise an effective global regime for instituting and managing the insolvency of multinational banks or financial conglomerates. This would involve determining priority rules for creditors of individual banks within the group and for creditors of several banks across the group. Important issues will need to be addressed, including whether deposit insurance schemes should be given mutual recognition or whether netting and close-out arrangements in different jurisdictions should be recognized after the bank becomes insolvent. Moreover, how should the insolvency of an individual bank in one jurisdiction affect the functioning of other banks in the same group but which operate in different jurisdictions? Perhaps an international priority rule should be adopted for creditors of failed banks that would apply across jurisdictions. Policymakers have also addressed the possibility of stripping out the conglomerate's systemic functions and operating this separately from the failed banking group, thus allowing the conglomerate to be wound up with little systemic risk. This policy would have an *ex ante* effect of reducing the moral hazard of the too-big-to-fail syndrome that afflicts many large banks and financial conglomerates (Hupkes, 2004). To accomplish this, it will be necessary to ascertain precise criteria for determining which functions of the conglomerate are systemic and how they can be insulated from the other functions of the financial group. Moreover, it will be necessary to recognize these criteria and to devise mechanisms to separate the systemic component of a financial group's operations by international agreement—either binding or soft law.

The regulatory challenges posed by multinational bank holding companies and financial conglomerates will continue to raise important economic and legal issues regarding the efficient regulation of systemic risk. Future research in this area should address the very nature of the principal-agent problem within these large, complex financial institutions and how it affects systemic risk.

Other Legal Approaches Most of the legal analysis in this book has addressed public law approaches to regulating systemic risk. In contrast, several private law approaches have emerged to reduce credit and legal risk in securities markets. The two most important of these are the master agreement derivatives contracts and the adoption of uniform choice of law rules for determining ownership interests in securities that are traded by electronic bookkeeping entry and held in indirect holding systems. The International Swaps and Derivatives Association, Inc. (ISDA) and other financial trade associations publish standard master agreements that contain effective enforcement provisions for derivatives contracts that permit contractual termination and close-out netting for nondefaulting parties in the event of a counterparty default or insolvency. Similarly, the Hague Conference on Private International Law has approved the Hague Convention on Indirectly Held Securities in 2003 that requires signatory countries to implement into their domestic law a uniform choice of law rule for the taking of property interests in securities held in indirect holding systems. These approaches attempt to reduce legal uncertainty and credit risk in cross-border securities transactions, and can result in lower transaction costs and increase availability of short-term capital.

Master Agreements for Financial Contracts The use of master agreements for derivatives contracts began in the early 1980s in response to the growth of the swap-dealing market in which there was a need to reduce credit risk by allowing a nondefaulting counterparty to terminate its contractual obligations and to close out its position by netting against a defaulting or insolvent counterparty. These master agreements have reduced legal uncertainty by allowing more effective enforcement of swap and other derivatives contracts, which has allowed end-users (e.g., financial institutions) of derivatives contracts to hedge their credit exposure and to reduce transaction costs in cross-border securities transactions. In addition, the use of master agreements became extremely important for financial institutions and derivatives dealers in the 1990s as the Basel Committee agreed in 1994 to lower the regulatory capital charge for derivatives dealers based on the value of the credit exposure that they could close out by netting against a defaulting or insolvent counterparty. The use of standard master agreements has grown substantially in today's global capital markets and are used for a number of financial products covering many types of transactions that are applicable to parties in multiple jurisdictions.

The ISDA Master Agreement is probably the most often used financial agreement for derivatives and futures contracts. Two ISDA Master Agreements are used today: the Master Agreement published in 1992 and an amended version published in 2002. In the aftermath of the 1998 Asian financial crisis, the 1992 ISDA Agreement was seen to have major weaknesses, including ambiguous provisions regarding notice to defaulting

counterparties and no provisions dealing with the impossibility of contractual performance because of a supervening event or *force majeure.* As
Asian financial markets collapsed in 1998, legal uncertainty in these areas
contributed to what were already substantial losses. The 2002 ISDA Agreement sought to address these problems by clarifying the provisions
regarding notice in the event of default that allowed nondefaulting counterparties to use electronic communications to put defaulting counterparties on notice of a default event. The 2002 Master Agreement also adopted
provisions that more clearly defined what was meant by impossibility of
performance and *force majeure.* The 2002 Master Agreement has addressed
many of the ambiguities that had undermined legal certainty in the 1992
Agreement. This has produced significant benefits for the end users of
derivatives products in the form of lower spreads on counterparty obligations and reduced transaction costs in the negotiation and documen-
tation of these agreements. Today, market participants continue to use
both the 1992 and 2002 ISDA Master Agreements and their use has spread
beyond derivatives contracts to include many different types of financial
contracts.

*The Hague Convention and the Place of the Relevant Intermediary Approach
(PRIMA)* Another source of legal uncertainty in cross-border securities
markets involves the difficult choice of law issues surrounding the question of which law applies to the taking of property interests in securities
that are held in indirect holding systems. Traditionally, the trading of securities involved the exchange of physical certificates whose possession
or registration on a company registrar denoted ownership. Modern securities trading has moved away from this type of direct holding of securities to what is known as an indirect holding system in which the
ownership interests in the securities are recorded and transferred by way
of electronic bookkeeping entries between financial intermediaries (e.g.,
custodians or depositories) that hold accounts with other intermediaries,
often located in different jurisdictions. As a result, securities trading increasingly relies not on the physical exchange of certificates or the regis-
tering of interests in securities with a company registrar, but rather on the
crediting and debiting of securities accounts recorded and maintained by
custodians and depositories located in various jurisdictions. Indeed, most
securities are dematerialized and immobilized in the vaults of large financial intermediaries, such as Euroclear. The dematerialization and im-
mobilization of securities in indirect holding systems has substantially
reduced transaction costs in the borrowing and lending of securities, thus
increasing liquidity in international securities markets. However, it has
created legal risk regarding which law is applicable to the proprietary
interests in the securities.

   Legal uncertainty arises because lenders (collateral takers) that take
collateral interests in securities owned by borrowers (collateral providers)
are uncertain regarding which legal system's choice of law rules applies

to determine the law applicable to their collateral interests in the securities. The situation is complicated when the collateral takers and collateral providers are located in different jurisdictions. Generally, in most legal systems, the law of the place where the securities are physically located, or where they are recorded on the company registrar, determines which legal system's choice of law rules applies to determine the law applicable to the property interests in the securities. In global securities markets, however, where most ownership interests in securities are recorded electronically with custodians, depositories, and other intermediaries, it is very difficult for creditors to determine which jurisdiction's law applies for ascertaining and enforcing their legal rights as creditors. This legal uncertainty increases credit risk, thereby increasing the cost of lending, and sometimes results in lower levels of liquidity in financial markets. To reduce legal uncertainty in this area, the Hague Convention on Indirectly Held Securities was signed in 2003 and it adopts a uniform choice of law rule for determining which jurisdiction's law applies to the taking of collateral interests in securities held in indirect holding systems. The Convention adopts what is known as the place of the relevant intermediary approach (PRIMA), which requires the collateral taker to apply the law of the location of the intermediary that maintains the securities account for the collateral provider. This choice of law rule seeks to reduce legal risk for the lender by allowing it to ascertain where the relevant intermediary is located for purposes of determining which legal system's law applies to its interest in the securities. The Convention has been criticized on the grounds that its uniform choice of law approach will not be effective for most countries unless it is also accompanied by harmonization of substantive standards of property law for securities (Paech, 2002; Unidroit, 2004).

Although both of these legal approaches are important steps for reducing credit risk and legal uncertainty in cross-border securities transactions, there is little evidence to suggest that the effect of the ISDA master agreements or the Hague Convention will have a significant effect on systemic risk in global financial markets. Nevertheless, reform in this area will be of great interest to lawyers and market participants.

WHAT IS TO BE DONE?

The current approach to reform of the international financial architecture is increasing the homogeneity in behavior, fails in its policy proposals to take account of the interrelationship between microeconomic risk taking and macroeconomic performance, and is still trapped within the intellectual perspective of the nation state. In these circumstances, the likely consequences cannot be regarded with equanimity.

A satisfactory response to the economic losses imposed by the increasing volatility of financial markets should be to move in a rather different direction. Reforms should seek to increase liquidity by enhancing heterogeneity, should strengthen the forces underpinning stabilizing convention, should take full account of the possibilities of macroeconomic measures to reduce systemic risk, and should be conceived on an international scale.

So what is to be done?

First, we must deal with the need to increase heterogeneity. Faced with a collapse in liquidity in the 1930s, the policy response was to severely segment financial markets (e.g., Glass-Steagall Act), a market structure that was further reinforced by the Bretton Woods agreement. Controlled financial markets served the immediate postwar era rather well.

But is there no other way that doesn't involve the cry of "Forward to the 1950s!"?

There is. We can reap the benefits of an open international financial system if there is a far greater recognition of the risks imposed on society by individual risk-taking investors and if investors are made to bear a fairer proportion of the social costs of those risks. This would mean developing a far more powerful structure of international rules and charges associated with risk-taking investment. Recent proposals to impose bailout requirements on lenders and the IMF's SDRM proposal to permit repayment standstills in the face of financial crises were rejected on the grounds that they would increase the cost of funds. But this is what should happen, since too often funds are available today, and risks are taken, at well below their true social costs.

The failure of rules in the past has been primarily a result of their becoming outdated. What is necessary is that there should be an effective international policy function with the powers to develop a more flexible structure of rules and rule making. And, of course, there needs to be an appropriate surveillance and enforcement powers, applicable to all countries (not just those that need funding from the IMF).

Second, a powerful force in enhancing stabilizing convention in financial markets has been the lender of last resort and deposit insurance. There is no international lender of last resort providing liquidity without strings. If there were, it might enhance stability, but it would also create severe moral hazard, lifting the costs from exactly those shoulders on which the burden should most heavily fall. That is why improvements to the official provision of liquidity must be balanced by more powerful rules on risk taking. Regulation mitigates moral hazard.

Third, the new financial architecture should encompass macroeconomic concerns. This is particularly important for developing countries. They should be permitted to substitute macroeconomic controls for the resource intensive firm-level regulation that the IMF's current "one-size fits all" approach is imposing upon them.

Fourth, the rules need to make greater use of the new work on extreme, rare events,[14] and this, too, should be integrated with a macro view.

Fifth, it should be acknowledged that, in pursuing all these goals, efficiency requires that the domain of the regulator be the same as the domain of the market. None of the standard tasks of a financial regulator—authorization, the provision of information, surveillance, enforcement, and the development of policy—are currently performed in a coherent manner in international markets.

In 1998, Eatwell and Taylor recommended the establishment of a World Financial Authority, or WFA (Eatwell and Taylor, 1998). The role of the WFA was to create a framework of truly *international* regulation. The probability that a WFA would actually be established was not far from zero. But the prime objective in proposing the creation of a WFA was to test the regulatory needs of today's liberal financial markets. Whether or not WFA is created, the tasks that the model WFA should perform must be performed by someone if international financial markets are to operate efficiently.

This book builds on the idealized model of the WFA by setting forth a more practical institutional and legal framework to govern international financial policy. It does so by arguing that effective international financial regulation requires a multilateral treaty regime that combines legally binding principles of efficient regulation (i.e., capital adequacy and consolidated supervision) and a mechanism for developing nonbinding soft law codes (capital adequacy formulas and coordination of enforcement). Moreover, there should be defined rules of action for how central bankers will coordinate their actions regarding the lender of last resort function. The implementation of such binding and nonbinding international standards and rules will be the responsibility of the existing IFIs, but with expanded influence from developing countries. These institutional arrangements would be coordinated by a Global Financial Governance Council that would have representatives at ministerial or deputy ministerial level from most countries to facilitate the development of such norms and oversee their implementation. The Global Governance Council would delegate responsibilities for devising international soft law codes and formulas to existing international bodies, such as the BIS committees (with expanded membership), IOSCO, IAIS, and FATF. The treaty framework establishing the Governance Council must contain procedures to ensure that the decision-making and standard-setting process is accountable and legitimate for all stakeholder countries.

Today, an institutional structure of international financial regulation is emerging that embodies, albeit imperfectly, a few of the features of an idealized WFA.

- The authorization function is the responsibility of national regulators, with access to markets being determined by agreements specifying the terms of mutual recognition.
- The information function is performed by national regulators supplemented by the international financial institutions, particularly the BIS and World Bank.

- The surveillance function is performed by national regulators, supplemented now by IMF-World Bank sector programs.
- The policy function is in the hands of the Basel Committee, IOSCO, IAIS, FATF, the IMF, and national authorities.

This list of international regulatory activities has three major features:

1. If the same list were compiled ten years ago, most of the regulatory functions would lack any international dimension. Today, in all areas other than authorization, international bodies are taking up some of the regulatory tasks.
2. The list deals with major international regulatory developments and omits the growth of *regional* regulation, notably in the European Union.
3. Measured against the template of a WFA, the international regulatory structure is limited, patchy, even incoherent. It portrays a response to crises, rather than a coherent design to the international propagation of systemic risk.

CONCLUSION

The following principles should guide the design of the new international financial architecture:

- Full cognizance should be taken of the social costs of the externality of systemic risk, particularly its macroeconomic impact.
- Homogeneity of market behavior is a threat to liquidity, particularly at time of high volatility, when convention has broken down.
- Steps need to be taken to reinforce the stabilizing power of convention.
- Because financial markets are today international, policy formation and implementation should be international in scope, too.
- Finally, international decision making and standard setting should be effective in devising principles of efficient regulation, accountable in terms of transparency and clear lines of decision-making authority; and legitimate in so far as all countries should share a sense of ownership for the standards that are adopted.

On the basis of these principles, it would be possible to design a global governance structure for the efficient regulation of systemic risk in global financial markets that would maximize the social benefit of open financial markets for the entire world community.

Notes

Chapter 1

1. Others have addressed this issue within the context of strengthening the international financial architecture: Goodhart (2001); Giovanoli (2000); and the various reports of the Financial Stability Forum. See www.fsforum.org.

2. Allegret and Dulbecco (2003) raise this concern specifically in the case of the International Monetary Fund.

3. The main challenge of the principal-agent problem is seeking to align the interests of the principal with those of the agent. See discussion in chapter 10.

4. Great Britain had sought greater freedom of action for individual countries to adjust exchange rates without IMF approval, but the United States had resisted this proposal (Skidelsky, 2000).

5. The distinction between crises emanating from the microeconomy and those that are macroeconomically induced is worth further consideration. Though the second phase of the Great Depression was marked by the failure of the Austrian bank Credit Anstalt, much of the responsibility for the depression rests at the door of inappropriate macroeconomic policy—particularly adherence to the gold standard and domestic monetary policies associated with the gold standard (Temin, 1989). Similarly, the recent Korean crisis derived substantially from the decision of the Korean government to join the OECD and to accept the required liberalization of financial markets. This led private-sector firms to increase their foreign exchange exposure to excessive levels (Chang, Park, and Yoo, 1998). In both the 1930s and the 1990s, an inappropriate macroeconomic environment resulted in excessive risk taking by firms. In the 1950s and 1960s, macroeconomic crises were not associated with excessive private sector risk taking but with major macroeconomic imbalances.

6. Transparency in the context of the multinational financial conglomerate

would require full disclosure of the earnings and risk exposures of its entire international operations, including the financial groups of the conglomerate, parent companies, and its subsidiaries.

7. *Hartford Fire Ins. Co. v. California* 509 U.S. 764 (1993); *The Wood Pulp Case* [1988] E.C.R. 5193 (although not accepting the "effects doctrine").

8. The Financial Services Modernization Act (otherwise known as the Gramm, Leach, Bliley Act) allows U.S. and foreign banks to affiliate with insurance companies, eliminates the remaining restrictions of the Glass-Steagall Act on affiliations between banks and securities firms, and generally expands the scope of permissible financial activities. To engage in these broader financial activities, banks are required to apply for and obtain Financial Holding Company status. The Financial Services Modernization Act of 1999, Pub. L. 106-102, 113 Stat. 1338 (2000). For extraterritorial U.S. banking regulations, see Regulation Y, 12 C.F.R. Part 225 (2000).

9. Section 103 (requiring the Board to apply "comparable" capital and management standards to foreign banks with U.S. branches, agencies, or commercial lending companies, giving due regard to national treatment and equality of competitive opportunity).

10. U.S. Patriot Act 2001, section 312.

11. On the basis of these experiences, the G7 established, in 1999, the Financial Stability Forum, which has served as a forum to discuss issues of financial stability and to consider regulatory policy options, including improved international standards to regulate offshore financial centers and hedge funds.

12. This was the case with the U.S. savings and loan crisis of the 1980s, in which S&L managers were essentially protected from the downside of their risky investments because of limited liability and overly generous deposit insurance. It led to the biggest banking sector bailout in U.S. history, involving the creation of the Resolution Trust Corporation, which sold U.S. government-backed bonds that were used to finance a $800 billion bailout of the S&L industry and to payoff all depositors who lost money.

Chapter 2

1. Belgium, Canada, France, Germany, Italy, Japan, Luxembourg, the Netherlands, Sweden, Spain, Switzerland, United Kingdom, and United States.

2. The Bank for International Settlements was established in 1930 as an international organization primarily composed of member states and a few private shareholders. It was created to facilitate the war reparation payments of the German government to allied powers on the basis of the terms of the Treaty of Versailles. Its other major function was to hold the gold reserves of the world's major economies and to serve as a meeting place for central bankers. During World War II, its close involvement in acting, among other things, as a payment agent for the German Nazi regime resulted in proposals for its abolition at the end of the war. However, it began playing a new role in facilitating cross-border currency payments in postwar Europe. Its importance as a meeting place for technical discussions of central bank operations grew during the Bretton Woods era and culminated with the high-level policy meetings that began in the 1970s to deal with a number of financial crises that resulted from the collapse of par-value fixed-exchange-rate system. Today, it continues to provide a venue and administrative support for central bankers and financial regulators who hold numerous meetings

to discuss key issues related to banking, payment systems, and insurance regulation. In 2004, the BIS membership consisted of fifty member states. See www .bis.org.

3. See International Association of Insurance Supervisors (1999b).

4. In 1974, the G10 consisted of Belgium, Canada, France, Italy, Japan, Luxembourg, The Netherlands, West Germany, United Kingdom, and the United States. Today, it also includes Sweden, Switzerland and Spain.

5. The Core Principles Liaison Group remains the most important forum for dialogue between the Committee and systemically relevant non-G10 countries. Moreover, the BIS established the Financial Stability Institute to conduct outreach to non-G10 banking regulators by holding seminars and conferences on implementing international banking and financial standards.

6. In fact, a major obstacle in negotiations over Basel II has been the refusal of the U.S. Congress to apply Basel II to most U.S. banks. The Federal Reserve, which supports Basel II and has authority to apply it to financial holding companies, has stated that it will apply it to the ten largest U.S. financial holding companies, while all other U.S. credit institutions will continue to abide by existing U.S. law, which is based on Basel I (the 1988 Capital Accord). See Statement of Roger Ferguson, Vice Chairman of the Board of Governors of the Federal Reserve (December 13, 2003), available at www.frbny.org.

7. The 1988 Capital Accord was entitled "International Convergence of Capital Measurement and Capital Standards." It applied based on the principle of home country control to banks based in G10 countries with international operations (BCBS, 1988).

8. This defines a series of quantitative and qualitative standards that banks would have to meet in order to use their own system for measuring market risk.

9. In its 1999 report, the Committee states: "The Committee is proposing revisions to the existing approach to credit risk which would serve as the standardized approach for calculating capital charges at the majority of banks. Within this approach, the use of external credit assessments could provide a means of distinguishing some credit risks."

10. G10 bank regulators recently conducted the third Quantitative Impact Study 3 (QIS-3) on Basel II's impact on G10 banking systems, which was completed in May 2003. From October to the end of December 2002, more than 250 banks from fifty countries participated in testing the new rules. Many national regulators reported flaws in applying the standards that are similar to many of the criticisms in this book. The Committee intends to finalize the new Accord by December 31, 2003, and national governments will be encouraged to begin adopting the necessary legislation to implement the standards in January 2005 with a final deadline for the end of 2008.

11. The 1999 Consultation report states: "The Committee also believes that an internal ratings-based approach could form the basis for setting capital charges."

12. For instance, in 2001, Russia, South Africa, and Saudi Arabia proposed an alternative amendments to the Capital Accord that would provide a standard 9 percent capital-to-asset charge on all credit and market-risk assets.

13. As Lastra observes, the accountability of the bank regulator can be "amendatory," which might occur, for example, when the regulator is liable for loss caused to depositors because of inadequate supervision of banks. This issue has been particularly relevant in the case of *Three Rivers District Council v. Governor and Company of the Bank of England (No. 3)* [2000] 2 WLR 1220; HL (depositors'

damages claim against Bank of England for misfeasance in failing to supervise adequately the Bank of Credit and Commerce International [BCCI]).

14. Specifically, the Bank of England argued that under the Banking Act 1979, section 3.5 provided that supervisory responsibility lay with Luxembourg as the place of BCCI's incorporation.

15. Among the report's findings were these:

- All international banking groups and international banks should be supervised by a home-country authority that capably performs consolidated supervision;
- The creation of a cross-border banking establishment should receive the prior consent of both the host country supervisory authority and the bank's, or banking group's, home country supervisor;
- Supervisory authorities should possess the right to gather information from the cross-border banking establishments of the banks or banking groups for which they are the home country supervisor;
- If a host-country authority determines that any one of the foregoing minimum standards has not been met to its satisfaction, that authority could impose restrictive measures necessary to satisfy its prudential concerns consistent with these minimum standards, including the prohibition of the creation of a banking establishment. (BCBS, 1992)

16. We adopt the term "financial conglomerates" to describe multifunctional financial firms that often serve as holding companies for subsidiaries and affiliates that provide a wide range of financial service activities (Blumberg, 1993: 6–10).

17. In 1996, net international capital flows to developing countries exceeded \$235 billion; this amounted to 0.8 percent of world GDP, and more than 2 percent of developing country GDP (Fischer, 1997).

18. The Joint Forum has a mandate to continue the work begun by the Tripartite Group on the harmonization of standards for financial conglomerates.

19. Further coordination will be required regarding the implementation of pillar 3 market disciplines.

20. In some host jurisdictions, legal and regulatory requirements regarding capital adequacy and other supervisory issues will also apply to foreign bank branches. See discussion Scott and Wellons (2002).

21. The best example of this has been the Contact Group, an informal body of bank supervisors from western European countries that meet occasionally to exchange information, but not to adopt any formal or written statements. See comments of Keith Pooley, Groupe de Contact, Seminar at Christ's College, University of Cambridge (September 9, 2003).

22. These are known as mutual legal assistance treaties and are discussed in chapters 3 and 5.

23. For capital adequacy calculations for credit and market risk, the supervisor would have to agree with the bank on a particular measurement approach, such as the IRB, Foundation, or Standardized approaches, while deciding between the Standardized and Advanced measurement approaches for calculating capital for operational risk.

24. Under the by-laws, the presidents operate secretly at IOSCO meetings and "[o]bservers and special guests may not attend meetings of the Presidents' Committee unless invited by the Chairman with the concurrence of a majority of the members."

25. See IOSCO website, www.iosco.org, to view relevant IOSCO documents.

26. Rather, it was established by statute as a nonprofit organization by the Quebec Parlement in 1987 and its first secretariat was located in Montreal. See An Act Respecting the International Organization of Securities Commissions, ch. 143, 1987 S.Q. 2437 (Can.).

27. For example, the U.S. agencies represented are the Securities Exchange Commission, the Commodities Futures and Trading Commission (CFTC), and the Department of the Treasury.

28. The by-laws authorize the Presidents' Committee to exercise "all the powers necessary to achieve the purpose of the Organization."

29. Its membership includes the chairmen of the Technical and Emerging Markets Committees, nine ordinary members elected by the President's committee, and one ordinary member from each regional committee.

30. For example, the by-laws authorize the president's committee to operate secretly at IOSCO meetings with the requirements that visitors and observers can attend meetings only if invited by the chairman with concurrence of a majority of the committee.

31. By-Laws, 1999 pt. 2, ¶ 4. It goes on to state:

- "to exchange information on their respective experiences in order to promote the development of domestic markets;
- to unite their efforts to establish standards and an effective surveillance of international securities transactions;
- to provide mutual assistance to ensure the integrity of the markets by a vigorous application of the standards and by effective enforcement against offences."

32. For international accounting standards, see the International Accounting Standards Board (IASB), available at the IASB's Web site, www.iasb.com. For international auditing standards, see International Federation of Independent Auditors. See also IOSCO's accounting and auditing principles at 10.6, p. 4 (IOSCO, 2000c).

33. The IAIS was established as a nonprofit Illinois corporation by the U.S. National Association of Insurance Commissioners (NAIC).

34. The diverse membership includes regulators representing countries such as Albania, Bolivia, EU member states, the U.S. states, and Vanuatu.

35. IAIS, 1999b: 1.

36. Ibid., preamble. The IAIS has a small General Secretariat that is based at the Bank for International Settlements.

37. See International Association of Insurance Supervisors By-Laws, app. A [hereinafter IAIS By-Laws].

38. Ibid., pt. 4, ¶ 19.

39. Ibid., pt. 3, ¶ 10.

40. For instance, IAIS committees cover the following areas: Budget, Basic Market Data, Education, Directory, Emerging Markets, Supervision of Financial Conglomerates, Exchange of Information, and Conference Planning. Ibid., pt. 1, ¶ 2.

41. The IAIS has outreach programs for regulators in developing and emerging market countries that include training seminars for insurance regulators from emerging markets.

42. IAIS (2002b).

43. Principles on minimum requirements for supervision of reinsurers (October

2002). These principles provide supervisory requirements for two different areas: (1) where supervisory requirements differ for reinsurers compared to primary insurers; and (2) where supervisory requirements are the same for reinsurers and for primary insurers.

44. IAIS's by-laws emphasize its role in "promot[ing] liaison and co-operation," "facilitat[ing] the exchange of views," and "collect[ing] and dissemi-nat[ing] statistical and other technical information," as well as "arrang[ing] other information of a general or specific nature."

45. IAIS By-Laws, preamble.

46. Ibid.

47. In 1999, the U.S. Senate Subcommittee on Investigations estimated that money laundering had permeated the U.S. banking system through the use of correspondent accounts with U.S. banks. Similarly, the U.K. Financial Services Authority notes that money laundering in U.K. banks amounts to more than £ 3 billion annually and exceeds £700 billion worldwide (FSA, 2001).

48. The Basel Committee adopted, in 2003, very detailed rules and require-ments for banks to conduct customer due diligence background assessments and report suspicious transactions (Basel Committee, 2003). The European Union has adopted two antimoney-laundering directives that require member states, among other things, to implement "know your customer" regulations for financial insti-tutions, to make money laundering a criminal offense, and to require national authorities to exchange information in the investigation of financial crime.

49. The G-7 nations consist of Canada, France, Germany, Italy, Japan, the United Kingdom, and the United States. (FATF, 1990: Introduction).

50. Recommendation 1 requires that countries should criminalize money laun-dering on the basis of the requirements of the 1988 United Nations Convention Against Illicit Traffic in Narcotic Drugs and Psychotropic Substances (the Vienna Convention) and the 2000 United Nations Convention on Transnational Organized Crime (the Palermo Convention).

51. Recommendation 5 requires measures to be taken as follows: (1) Identifying the customer and verifying that customer's identity using reliable, independent source documents, data or information; (2) identifying the beneficial owner of accounts; (3) obtaining information regarding the intended purpose and nature of the business relationship; and (4) conducting ongoing due diligence on the busi-ness relationship.

52. Financial institutions should maintain, for at least five years, all necessary records on transactions, both domestic and international, to enable them to comply promptly with information requests by regulators and other authorities. Recom-mendation 10. This information should be immediately available for financial reg-ulators and for judicial and law enforcement authorities.

53. By January 2004, the FATF members included Argentina, Austria, Austra-lia, Brazil, Belgium, Canada, Denmark, Finland, France, Germany, Greece, Hong Kong, Iceland, Ireland, India, Italy, Japan, Luxembourg, Netherlands, New Zea-land, Norway, Portugal, Singapore, Spain, Sweden, Switzerland, Turkey, the United Kingdom, the United States, the Commission of the European Union, and the Gulf Co-Operation Council: thirty-one countries, two international organiza-tions, and fifteen countries or jurisdictions with observer status. See the FATF Web site, www.oecd.org.

54. The initial list included the following countries and territories: the Baha-mas, the Cayman Islands, the Cook Islands, Dominica, Israel, Lebanon, Liechten-

stein, the Marshall Islands, Nauru, Niue, Panama, the Philippines, Russia, St. Kitts and Nevis, and St. Vincent and the Grenadines. In June 2001, the Cayman Islands, Liechenstein, and Panama were taken off the list.

55. Indeed, U.S. Treasury Secretary Lawrence Summers welcomed the name-and-shame campaign by the FATF, calling it a "landmark step to limit the capacity of drug dealers, terrorists, organized criminals and corrupt foreign officials to launder their ill-gotten gains through safe havens" (James, 2000: 1).

56. Banks play an especially important role as financial intermediaries in developing countries, where capital markets are often underdeveloped and therefore most borrowing depends on bank-led finance.

57. The Tietmeyer Report was published in November 1998 under the leadership of Hans Tietmeyer, the then president of the Bundesbank.

58. Particular emphasis was placed, inter alia, on problems related to highly leveraged institutions, volatility of capital flows, interbank credit lines, unregulated financial institutions, corporate governance, lack of transparency, and lack of harmonized accounting standards and asset valuation systems (IAIS Newsletter, Issue 4, Second Quarter 1999: 1).

Chapter 3

1. Bowett defined international organizations as "created by a multilateral inter-governmental agreement [that] possess some measure of international personality" (1982: chapter 11).

2. The American Restatement of Foreign Relations Law describes international organizations as possessing "status as a legal person, with capacity to own, acquire, and transfer property, to make contracts" (sec. 223).

3. As discussed later, the GATS has important implications for a country's domestic regulation of its financial services industry.

4. The third Bretton Woods institution was the stillborn International Trade Organization. Although initially conceived at the Havana Conference of 1948 as one of the three Bretton Woods institutions to regulate international trade and supported by President Truman and his secretary of state, Dean Acheson, the proposed ITO never became operational because the U.S. Congress rejected it.

5. For instance, the Basel Committee's recommendations have been viewed as legally nonbinding (Giovanoli, 2000).

6. Statute of the International Court of Justice, articles 38 (a)–(d).

7. The U.S. House Financial Services Committee held hearings on the Basel Accord on February 17, 2003, and took testimony from the Comptroller of the Currency, John Hawke, who was critical of the proposed amendments to the Accord.

8. A member could adjust the value of its currency beyond a certain margin of 10 percent of par value only with the approval of the IMF.

9. Article VIII(2)(a) states in relevant part: "no member shall, without the approval of the Fund, impose restrictions on the making of payments and transfers for current international transactions."

10. The Second Amendment to the IMF Agreement (1979) amended Article XIV to make it more difficult for states not to assume the convertibility obligation. Article XIV(3) states in relevant part: "Any members retaining any restrictions inconsistent with Article VIII, sections 2, 3, or 4, shall consult the Fund annually as to their further retention." Further, the Fund may "make representations to any

member that conditions are favorable for the withdrawal of any particular restriction, or for the general abandonment of restrictions, inconsistent with the provisions of any other articles of this Agreement."

11. In the aftermath of World War II, this was necessary because many countries had maintained strict currency controls during the war and it was necessary to keep such restrictions in place after the war to prevent shortages.

12. Article IV, Obligations Regarding Exchange Arrangements.

13. Article IV, sections 2 and 3.

14. The IMF also publishes assessments of world capital markets with the International Capital Markets Reports, which analyze financial market data in both developed and emerging markets.

15. The economic basis of these staff reports as part of these consultations were published in a report entitled "Recent Economic Developments." The IMF began, in April 1999, to publish staff reports subsequent to consultations, and in 1999 the IMF began to release full staff reports.

16. Gold interpreted the amendment to Article IV (1) to mean that the Fund may now have some authority to regulate cross-border capital flows and, in certain circumstances, to insist that a country liberalize its capital account as part of an IMF conditionality program (Gold, 1981).

17. Article XXVI (2)(a) on compulsory withdrawal states in relevant part that "[i]f a member fails to fulfill any of its obligations under this Agreement, the Fund may declare the member ineligible to use the general resources of the Fund."

18. Article XXVI(2)(b)-(d).

19. 333 N.E. 2d 168 (1975).

20. *Banco do Brasil, S.A. v. Israel Commodity Co.*, 190 N.E. 2d 235 (1963). English courts have taken a similar approach. See *Wilson, Smithett, & Cope Ltd. V. Terruzi* [1976] Q.B. 683 (CA).

21. IMF quotas for member countries are determined by a formula on the basis of the size of the national economy, as measured by, for example, GDP and current account transactions.

22. Since the IMF was established, there have been twelve such reviews, and in eight reviews there was an overall quota increase along with some redistribution of quotas to reflect the changing economic positions of several states. The most recent change occurred in 1999, when the total quota was increased by 45 percent from S.D.R. 146 billion to 212 billion (approximately U.S. $291 billion, based on 1 $U.S. per S.D.R. $1.37494).

23. Since the 1960s, the IMF has had the authority to borrow additional resources in addition to its quotas from the G10 industrial countries under the so-called General Arrangements to Borrow (GAB). Under the GAB, the IMF may lend "to forestall or cope with an impairment of the international monetary system." The GAB was intended primarily to address financial problems in major reserve center countries such as the United Kingdom and the United States. This program was significant because it marked a change in the IMF's role from essentially that of a credit cooperative to that of a bank. The GAB was rarely used to support reserve currencies and was not used at all during the 1990s until the Russian bond crisis of July 1998. The IMF supplemented the GAB, in 1997, with a new lending mechanism that allows borrowing from advanced IMF member states. This "New Agreement to Borrow" was established in response to the 1997 Asian crisis in order to provide financial assistance to emerging economies in the event of a systemic crisis. Moreover, during the Asian financial crisis of 1997, the IMF, play-

ing the role of lender of last resort, adopted a new loan facility for countries experiencing financial problems called the Supplemental Reserve Facility (SRF), which is aimed at addressing abrupt reversals of confidence in a member's financial markets. Under the SRF, the IMF can lend much higher amounts than under its traditional programs to countries in financial distress but can charge a penalty rate of 300 to 500 basis points above the IMF's regular interest charge (Capie, 1998: 311–326).

24. The Report notes that "[l]iquidity loans would have short maturity, be made at a penalty rate (above the borrowers recent market rate) and be secured by a clear priority claim on the borrower's assets." Ibid.

25. The International Financial and Monetary Committee (IFMC) was then known as the "Interim" Committee.

26. The IFMC stated in relevant part that it "encouraged the Fund to continue its work on the appropriate pace and sequencing of capital account opening and, in particular, to further refine its analysis of the experience of countries with the use of capital controls, and to explore further issues related to the Fund's role in an orderly and well-supported approach to capital account liberalization."

27. The International Development Association was founded in 1960 to provide the poorest member countries with interest-free credits. The Multilateral Investment Guarantee Agency was established in 1990 to offer political risk insurance for private investors in member countries that were willing to invest in certain FDI projects in member countries that had signed investment agreements with MIGA. The International Finance Corporation was established in 1956 to provide loans for project finance for infrastructure development. The International Center for the Settlement of Investment Disputes was established in 1985 as an arbitration forum for signatory countries to the ICSID agreement and their private investors to resolve investment disputes regarding exporpriation and nationalization of foreign-owned property.

28. The African Development Bank, Inter-American Development Bank, and Asian Development Bank. These banks have become what later became known as the World Group Bank.

29. These structural and sectoral adjustment loans amounted in 2002 to more than 55 percent of Bank lending.

30. The Uruguay Round negotiations produced, in January 1995, the World Trade Organization Agreement that contained a new framework for regulating trade in services, the General Agreement on Trade in Services (GATS). The impetus for these negotiations occurred in the context of Uruguay Round of Multilateral Trade Negotiations under the auspices of the General Agreement on Tariffs and Trade (Croome, 1995: 122–30). For a balanced discussion of Uruguay Round negotiations, see Hoekman and Kostecki (2002).

31. Marrakesh Agreement, Article IX.

32. The Understanding on Commitments in Financial Services allowed members to designate certain financial sectors as subject to the national treatment principle.

33. Article I: 3(a)(i) and (ii).

34. GATS Annex on Financial Services, paragraph 5(a).

35. Ibid.

36. Paragraph 1(b).

37. Paragraphs 1(b)(i) and (ii).

38. Article 1:2.

39. Because subsidiaries are usually incorporated under host-state law and are therefore viewed as separate legal entities, they are more likely to be subject to more comprehensive regulation than branches.

40. Article II:1.

41. See Article V (allowing departure from MFN principle based on rules regarding economic integration).

42. Article II:2 (allowing departure from MFN for a member's listed exemptions). See GATS Annex on Article II Exemptions. An exemption may be extended for a member through a waiver process under Article XI:3 of the WTO Agreement.

43. Article III, III *bis*.

44. Article III:1.

45. Art. XVII:1

46. Art. XVII:2.

47. The six types of limitations that a member may not impose on a scheduled sector unless expressly listed in its schedule of commitments are limitations: (1) on the number of service suppliers; (2) on the total value of services transactions or assets; (3) on the total number of service operations or the total quantity of service output; (4) on the number of persons that may be employed in a particular sector or by a particular supplier; (5) that restrict or require supply of the service through specific types of legal entity or joint venture; (6) on the percentage participation of foreign capital, or limitations on the total value of foreign investment.

48. The GATT also contains provisions that address financial stability concerns regarding a member's right to derogate from liberalization commitments when it is suffering a severe balance of payments imbalances. See GATT Articles XII and XVIII:B.

49. Paragraph 3(a), Annex on Financial Services.

50. Paragraph 3(b).

51. These agreements would be recorded with the Trade in Services Division of the WTO Secretariat.

52. See WTO Doc. S/CSS/W/71, Communication from Switzerland (that prudential regulation should be interpreted according standards set by international bodies, i.e., Basel Committee), and WTO Doc.S/CSS/W/27, Communication from United States (that GATS obligations and commitments should not prejudice a member's prudential regulatory discretion).

53. See "U.S.-China Trade Relations Growing Steadily, Some Stumbling Blocks Remain," *Business Alert US*, Issue 12 (June 28, 2002) (discussing U.S. objections at a meeting of the WTO Council on Trade in Services on June 5, 2002, about discriminatory Chinese regulations that impose restrictive branching requirements for foreign nonlife insurance firms). www.tdctrade.com/alert/USabout.htm

54. The Annex on Financial Services provides that experts in the area of financial regulation and trade will be appointed as dispute panelists if a claim is brought under the Annex.

55. Moreover, the WTO has been criticized as lacking legitimacy because it adopts international rules and obligations to regulate trade which infringe the domestic authority of states to govern their economies (Woods and Narlikar, 2001).

56. The relevant provision in the GATS is Article XII, which requires the WTO to consult with the IMF regarding factual issues that concern a member's application to depart from its commitments on MFN, national treatment, or market access when it is having a serious balance-of-payments crisis or external financial difficulties (article XII(1)).

57. The WTO Appellate Body has addressed two cases involving the extent of the WTO's obligation to consult with the Fund regarding import restrictions taken by WTO members that were inconsistent with their GATT commitments. In Argentina, WTO members sought to justify import restrictions under the GATT because they were part of an IMF economic restructuring program; in another case, involving India, they sought to impose import restrictions under the GATT as part of a developing-country exception. The Appellate Body ruled that the GATT panel did not have to take into account the IMF's determination regarding India's status as a developing country. In the Argentina case, it held that, although Argentina had imposed certain surcharges on imports as part of a Fund restructuring program, Argentina was not excused under Article XV (2) of GATT because its import surcharge was not an express condition of the IMF program. Moreover, it held that the WTO dispute panel hearing the case had no legal obligation to consult and to take into consideration the factual findings of the IMF regarding Argentina's import surcharge.

58. EC Treaty, articles 52–58 (right of establishment), and articles 59–66 (freedom to provide services).

59. The Treaty of Rome (1957) established the European Economic Community (EEC). The EEC was one of three European Communities; the other two were the European Coal and Steel Community, established in 1951, and the European Atomic Energy Community, established in 1957. Each of the three European Communities has separate international legal personality. The Treaty of Maastricht of 1992 changed the name of the EEC to the European Community.

60. For instance, the EC has exclusive competence for issues related to fisheries and trade in goods, but it has shared competence with EU member states for telecommunications and trade in services (Aust, 2000). In these shared areas of competence, the EC and its member states can each become parties to the relevant agreement.

61. Articles 67–73, EC Treaty (Treaty of Rome) (1958).

62. See Second Banking Coordination Directive, 89/646/EEC, [1989] OJ L386/1; Own Funds Directive 89/299/EEC; Solvency Ratio Directive 89/647/EEC; Consolidated Supervision Directive 92/30/EEC, [1992] OJ L110/52; Prudential Supervision Directive 95/26EC, [1995] L168/7; Investment Services Directive, 93/22/EEC; Capital Adequacy Directive 93/6/EEC, [1993] OJ L 141/1(introduces capital requirements for market risk and extends harmonized solvency supervision to investment firms).

63. See First Banking Directive (1977), article 1; Second Banking Directive (1989), article 1(6).

64. This has become a major issue of concern for the ten new accession countries to the European Union (Masciandaro, 2004).

65. The euro was adopted on January 1, 1999.

66. See Article 105(2) of the Treaty establishing the European Community ("Treaty") and Article 3 of the Statute of the European System of Central Banks ("ESCB") and the European Central Bank ("ECB") recognizing oversight as a *basic* task of the Eurosystem. Article 105(2) of the Treaty and Article 3 of the Statute provide: "The basic tasks to be carried out through the ESCB shall be . . . to promote the smooth operation of payment systems." Further, Article 22 of the Statute provides: "The ECB and national central banks may provide facilities, and the ECB may make regulations, to ensure the efficient and sound clearing and payment systems within the Community and with other countries." The ECB's ca-

pacity to issue regulations in the area of payment systems has also raised the issue of the prudential role of the ECB vis-à-vis the national central banks.

67. Article 12.1(3), ESCB/ECB Statute.

68. Article 105(2), Treaty on European Union (TEU).

69. The ECB's field of competence also covers the minimum reserves for banks and financial institutions, the collection of statistical data, and the adjudication and imposition of sanctions. Article 19, ESCB Statute, and Regulation (EC) no. 2818/98 (ECB/1998/15).

70. Article 3, ESCB Statute (stating the same language as the Treaty's 105(5)).

71. Article 105(2), TEU, and Art 3.1 of the ESCB Statute.

72. Article 17, ESCB Statute.

73. Article 22, ESCB Statute.

74. Article 108, TEU, and Article 14.2 of the ESCB Statute.

75. Article 3, ESCB/ECB Statute.

76. Further information is available at http://europa.eu.int/comm. The European Commission adopted the Action Plan on May 11, 1999.

77. European Council Resolution of March 23, 2001, on more effective securities market regulation in the European Union, OJ L 138/1 of May 11, 2001, paragraph 3. The European Union's Economic and Finance Ministers appointed the Committee of Wise Men on the Regulation of European Securities Markets ("Committee of Wise Men") to devise a strategy for realizing and implementing the FSAP.

78. The EU FSAP is premised on the notion that the elimination of national regulatory barriers to cross-border trade in financial services will be the essential factor in achieving an integrated market for financial services (Avgerinos, 2002).

79. G. Hertig and R. Lee, "Four Predictions about the Future of EU Securities Regulation," *Journal of International Banking Law and Regulation* (January 2003).

80. Canada-Mexico-United States, 32 I.L.M. 289, *final draft revision* September 6, 1992, *entered into force*, January 1, 1995. NAFTA contains twenty-two articles and several annexes that runs to more than three thousand pages. See North American Free Trade Agreement Between the Government of the United States of America, the Government of Canada, and the Government of the United Mexican States (December 17, 1992).

81. NAFTA, article 1401(1)(a)–(c).

82. Article 1401(5) defines investors of another NAFTA country as being engaged in providing financial services in the territory of that Party.

83. It should be noted, though, that under article 1403(1), each state party recognizes the principle that investors of NAFTA states should be allowed to choose the juridical form through which they establish a financial institution in other NAFTA states, with the exceptions stated in article 1403(4)(a)–(b).

84. Article 1405(1) states in relevant part: "Each Party shall accord to investors of another Party treatment no less favorable than that it accords to its own investors, in like circumstances, with respect to the establishment, acquisition, expansion, management, conduct, operation, and sale or other disposition of financial institutions and investments in financial institutions in its territory."

85. If the regulatory standards of a NAFTA state party are not discriminatory de jure against foreign financial institutions, there will be compliance with the host country principle. De jure national treatment does not automatically mean de facto national treatment, however.

86. The NAFTA prudential exception provides broad authority for states to take regulatory measures that might depart from their obligations under Chapter

14 and under Part V of the Treaty. Part V covers trade in services, investments, monopolies, and temporary entry of employees.

87. Moreover, the requirements of NAFTA do not apply to nondiscriminatory measures taken by central banks or other public authorities in pursuit of monetary or related credit policies or exchange rate policies (art. 1410(2)).

88. NAFTA, article 1405.

89. The United States was very concerned that it should be able to continue its more stringent regulatory standards against the EU and that the principle of national treatment and MFN would prevail.

Chapter 4

1. See Article 38 (1)(a)–(d), ICJ Statute, in D. J. Harris, *Cases and Materials on International Law,* Appendix I (London: Sweet and Maxwell, 1991), pp. 990–1002. The traditional sources of public international law as stated in Article 38(1) are:

(a) international conventions, whether general or particular, that establish
(b) rules expressly recognized by the contesting states;
(c) international custom, as evidence of a general practice accepted as law;
(d) the general principles of law as recognized by civilized nations;
(e) . . . judicial decisions and the teachings of the most highly qualified publicists of the various nations, as subsidiary means for the determination of rules of law.

2. Oppenheim's *International Law* states that "custom and treaties . . . are the principal and regular sources of international law" (Jenning's and Watts, 1996, p. 24).

3. See "Military and Paramilitary Activities in and against Nicaragua (Nicaragua v. United States of America),"*ICJ Reports* (1986), p. 97, paragraph 183 (observing that to determine "rules of customary international law," the court must look "to the practice and *opinio juris* of states"). The *Lotus* case, Permanent Court of International Justice, series A, No. 10 (1927), p. 18 (emphasizing the voluntary or consent-based nature of *opino juris*); *North Sea Continental Shelf* cases, *IJC Reports* (1969), p. 3, paragraphs 71–72 and 78 (emphasizing the belief-based nature of *opino juris*).

4. The subjective element can generally be satisfied in two ways: (1) by the state's voluntary agreement or consent to be bound by the customary rule or obligation in quesiton, or (2) by the state's belief that its conduct is legally permitted or obligatory (Mendelson, 1995: 184, 195).

5. *The Lotus* case, Permanent Court of International Justice, Series A, No. 10 (1927). In fact, the Basel Accord and other international financial standards represent what Mendelson (1995) has called *opinio non-juris*, in which states expressly state that although they may act in a certain way, they do not consider their acts to be motivated by any legal obligation or that their behavior should serve as a precedent to restrict their future conduct (Mendelson, 1995: 198–201).

6. This view holds that international soft law principles and rules have converged at the international level and have filtered down to the national legal systems and domestic regulations of the world's leading states and thereby have produced certain general principles of public regulatory law that may have legal relevance as source of public international law.

7. Abbot et al. (2000) used the three elements of precision, obligation, and del-

egation to measure the degree of international legalization of a set of international rules or norms.

8. Wellens and Borchardt (1989), p. 270.

9. IMF CPAs have been conducted for over fifty countries, including recent ones for Argentina, Gabon, Turkey, and Uruguay. For example, in 2000, Angola affirmed its commitment to adhere to the Basel Capital Accord and Core Principles as part of a staff-monitored program (IMF, 2000c). In 2002, the Turkish government had a SDR 12.8 billion ($17 billion) standby arrangement with the IMF. In its Letter of Intent of June 19, 2002, Turkey committed itself to recapitalize its troubled banks in accordance with the Capital Accord and to adhere to other of the Core Principles. Uruguay's standby arrangement commits it to adopt a bank regulatory regime that complies with the Core Principles so that it may draw on a SDR 2.13 billion facility (IMF, 2004c).

10. Also, market participants are not allowed to use IFI assessments, because they cannot be published (except when the assessed country requests it).

11. The Federal Reserve Board shall also consider whether the foreign bank's home authority complies with international antimoney-laundering standards (i.e., FATF Forty Recommendations). See U.S. Patriot Act, Title III, section 327.

12. This would especially have implications for a state's obligations to liberalize access to its financial markets under the WTO General Agreement on Trade in Services.

13. FATF has extended its international institutional scope to include closer cooperation and coordination with regional antimoney-laundering bodies in investigations and exchange of information (FATF, 2001c: 9–11). These bodies include the Caribbean Financial Action Task Force, the European Commission, and the Financial Action Task Force on Money Laundering for South America. Moreover, the major international financial organizations (IMF and World Bank) and international supervisory bodies (e.g., Basel Committee and IOSCO) announced in 2001 that they had adopted the FATF's Forty Recommendations as their standards, as well.

14. An example of this is the detailed questionnaire circulated to each member (FATF, 1990). On the basis of the responses received, a "compliance grid" is prepared, providing an overview of members' adherence to the specific recommendations addressed.

Chapter 5

1. In 2003, FSF committees produced reports on offshore financial centers and highly leveraged institutions.

2. See generally Eatwell and Taylor, "The Future of Financial Regulation: World Financial Authority." Unpublished working paper, Cambridge University, 1999.

3. The Basel Committee has published *Guidelines to Banks and Bank Supervisors on Public Disclosures in Banks' Final Reports* (Basel, September 1998); see also *Enhancing Bank Transparency* (Basel, September 1998), and Basel Committee Paper, *Sound Practices for Loan Accounting, Credit Risk Disclosure and Related Matters* (Basel, July 1999).

4. The International Accounting Standards Board (IASB) was established in 1973 as the International Accounting Standards Committee with the objective of harmonizing accounting principles used by businesses and other organizations

for financial reporting. It is an independent, private-sector body composed of professional representatives from the accounting profession and does not represent any government agencies or international organizations. See www.iasc.org.uk. It therefore does not have the public legitimacy that the Basel Committee, IOSCO, and FATF have because its membership is not composed of government representatives or regulators but rather consists of experts from the accounting profession and from academia. The International Financial Auditors Committee (IFAC) is a private sector body that performs a similar function for auditors who audit banks and other financial institutions.

5. The International Accounting Standards have been approved by the European Community institutions and will take effect as a binding EU regulation in 2005 with direct effect on all EU member states.

6. Art. III: 5. Traditionally, cooperation and coordination between the Fund and the WTO applied in the case of Articles XII and XVIII:B GATT, which allows members to restrict imports when they experience severe current account imbalances. In deciding whether to allow a WTO member to depart from existing commitments regarding imports, the WTO Agreements expressly requires the WTO Committee on Balance of Payments to rely on the Fund's expertise in determining whether a member's import restrictions are justified.

7. Declaration on the Contribution of the World Trade Organization to Achieving Greater Coherence in Global Economic Policymaking, paragraph 5, WTO Legal Texts (1999).

8. For example, Article X states that: "The Fund shall cooperate within the terms of this Agreement with any general international organization and with public international organizations having specialized responsibilities in related fields." This provision authorizing cooperation between the Fund and other international organizations has provided a basis for the development of extensive cooperation between the WTO and the IMF that has taken the form of formal and informal staff contacts and joint involvement in various working groups and committees (Siegal, 2002).

9. Agreement Between the International Monetary Fund and the World Trade Organization, December 9, 1996. See WTO (WTO Legal Texts, 1999).

10. See Statement of Cooperation on the Exchange of Information for the Purposes of Consolidated Supervision, available at www.eurunion.org.

11. See E. Lomnicka, "Knowingly Concerned? Participatory Liability for Breaches of Regulatory Duties," *Company Lawyer* 21, no. 4 (April 2000): 121–126 (analyzing principles of third-party civil liability for breach of financial regulation).

Chapter 6

1. For further information, see the Suffolk banking system in the United States between 1820 and 1850 (Rolnick, Smith, and Weber, 1998; Calomiris and Kahn, 1996).

Chapter 7

1. Only a few decades ago, this risk was relatively low when the daily payment flow of foreign exchange transactions was roughly equivalent to the capital stock of a single large U.S. bank. However, recently the average daily turnover has exceeded the combined capital of the top one hundred U.S. banks.

2. TARGET is an acronym for Trans-European Automated Real Time Gross Settlement Express Transfer.

3. In 1974, *Bankhaus Herstatt*, a small German bank active in the forex market, went into liquidation after the German part of its trades was irrevocably settled but before the U.S. side was settled through CHIPS.

4. For further information, see *Settlement Risk in Foreign Exchange Transactions* (BIS, 1996); *Reducing Foreign Exchange Settlement Risk—Progress Report* (BIS, 1998); *Supervisory Guidance for Managing Settlement Risk in Foreign Exchange Transactions* (BIS, 1999).

5. Three alternative models have been identified under the DVP heading:

1. Gross simultaneous settlements of securities and funds transfers
2. Gross settlements of securities transfers followed by net settlements of funds transfer
3. Simultaneous settlement of securities and funds transfer.

6. Although there are many difficulties in Calomiris's argument, he suggests some solutions from the outset; for example, to avoid "cronyism" and collusion within a specific market, buyers of such subordinated debt would have to be outsiders, that is, foreign banks.

7. The net settlement systems CHIPS and FEYCS (Foreign Exchange Yen Clearing System) depend for final settlement on the gross settlement of the Fed and the Bank of Japan, respectively.

Chapter 8

1. Goldstein (1997) suggests that one of the causes of banking crises in developing countries is inadequate preparation for financial liberalization. Kaminsky and Reinhart (1996) confirm these results by reporting that the financial sector had been liberalized at some point during the previous five years in eighteen out of twenty-five banking crises in their paper.

2. *Chaebol* is the Korean term for a conglomerate made up of many companies clustered around one parent company. The companies usually hold shares in one another and are often run by one family.

3. The n lag period will be chosen separately for each country on the basis of the time when the liberalization process started in each country. Many studies have indicated that banking sector problems were preceded by strong credit growth (Pill and Pradhan, 1995).

4. Periods of distress in the banking sector were defined as crises when one of the following conditions were fulfilled:

1. The ratio of nonperforming assets to total assets exceeded 10 percent.
2. The cost of the rescue operation was at least 2 percent of GDP.
3. Extensive bank runs occurred, or emergency measure such as deposit freezes, prolonged bank holidays, or generalized deposit guarantees were enacted by the government in response to the crisis.
4. Banking sector problems resulted in a large-scale nationalization of banks.

5. This derivative shows that the rate of change in probability with respect to X involves both B and the level of probability from which the change is measured. This value is greatest when $P = .5$

6. The number of merchant banks rose from six in 1993 to almost thirty in 1996 (Jae-Kwon, 1998).

7. Scholes, Wilson, and Wolfson (1990) examined the recognition of securities gains and losses for a sample of mostly very large banks. They found evidence that banks with lower capital ratios are likely to have smaller recognized losses or larger recognized gains than banks with higher capital ratios. Carey (1995) examined securities sales from the investment portfolios and gains trading for a sample of more than six thousand commercial banks. He found that most gains trading is done to boost earnings or to smooth earnings. Relatively few banks appear to engage in gains trading to boost their capital accounts.

Chapter 9

1. Although there are many difficulties in Calomiris's argument, he suggests some solutions from the outset. For example, to avoid "cronyism" and collusion within a specific market, buyers of SD would have to be outsiders, that is, foreign banks. See Calomiris (1999).

Chapter 10

1. See OECD Principles of Corporate Governance, issued June 21, 1999, available at www.oecd.org.

2. For example, such incentive mechanisms may take the form of tying a portion of a manager's compensation to the company performance in the stock market through the use of stock options.

3. See, for example, Prowse (1995).

4. See Second Consultative Paper of the New Basel Accord (January 16, 2001) for more details on attempts to align regulatory capital with economic risk (Basel Committee, 2001a).

5. A. Mas-Colell, Whinston, M. and Green, J. (1995).

6. The International Accounting Standards Committee defines related parties as "controlling" parties that are "able to control or exercise significant influence." Such controlled relationships include (1) parent-subsidiary; (2) entities under common control; (3) associates; (4) individuals who through ownership have significant influence over the enterprise and close members of their families; and (5) key management personnel. See IASC, International Accounting Standard No. 24, Related Party Disclosures. www.iasb.co.uk.

7. Basel Committee on Banking Supervision, Consultative Document, *The New Basel Capital Accord*, April 2003, paragraph 400, pps. 77–78. It states in relevant part:

> All material aspects of the rating and estimation processes must be approved by the bank's board of directors or a designated committee thereof and senior management. These parties must possess a general understanding of the bank's risk rating system and detailed comprehension of its associated management reports.

8. Ibid., paragraph 401, p. 78.

9. Available at http://www.iosco.org/docs-public/1998-objectives-documents 03.html.

10. Ibid. at n.51.

Chapter 11

1. Although market failure in the financial sector can also arise because of the asymmetry of information between individual savers and market professionals, this is primarily a concern of consumer and investor protection and does not address the market failure manifest in systemic risk.

2. The problem for U.S. markets arose from settlement risk in forex dealings. Deutschmark legs had been paid but U.S. dollar pegs were unpaid.

3. Although the Committee has been influential in establishing international norms of banking regulation, its decision-making structure can be criticized on the grounds of accountability and legitimacy because it is dominated by the G10 countries. See chapters 2 and 4.

4. The most powerful convention of all is that imposed by governments. When the European System of Central Banks declared the exchange rate of the future euro-zone currencies prior to being irrevocably fixed on January 1, 1999, the markets rapidly converged on those rates.

5. Although capital controls do not today suffer the same opprobrium as they did before the Asian crisis, the link between micro and macro means of attaining the same objective is seldom made. The neglect of macromeasures is particularly puzzling given that microregulation tends to be quantitative and to some degree discriminatory, while Chilean-style macro controls are price based and nondiscriminatory—characteristics that might be expected to appeal to orthodox economic policymakers.

6. Even at the most simple level these interactions undermine the calculations of MPIs. For example, not only is the value of capital, and hence the capital adequacy ratio, directly affected by the revaluation of assets consequent upon a change in the interest rate, but declines in the level of activity can readily transform prudent investments into bad loans.

7. Regulatory standards, however, were not entirely abandoned: ". . . money center banks whose loans to heavily indebted countries exceeded their capital in the early 1980s were allowed several years to adjust—but there was no doubt that they would have to adjust" (Turner, 2000).

8. The 1981 Mexican crisis certainly threatened the stability of the U.S. banking system, but the origin of the crisis lay predominantly in the public sector (Mexico's public sector debt), though the liberalization of Mexico's import regime also played a significant part.

9. Alan Greenspan commented that he had never seen anything that compared to the panic of August–September 1998.

10. The IMF's new role in monitoring a country's private sector was made explicit on March 1, 2001, when the Fund established an International Capital Markets Department with a stated task "to enhance . . . surveillance, crisis prevention and crisis management activities." The new department's responsibilities will also include "the systematic liaison with the institutions which supply the bulk of private capital worldwide" (IMF, 2001).

11. For example, the IMF's "experimental" *Report on the Observation of Standards and Codes* (2000a) for Canada, prepared by IMF staff in the context of a FSAP, on the basis of information provided by Canadian authorities, produced "an assessment of Canada's observance of and consistency with relevant international standards and core principles in the financial sector, as part of a broader assessment of the stability of the financial system." The assessment covered (i) the Basel Core

Principles for Effective Banking Supervision, (ii) the IOSCO Objectives and Principles of Securities Regulation, (iii) IAIS Supervisory Principles, (iv) the Committee on Payment and Settlement Systems (CPSS) Core Principles for Systemically Important Payment Systems, (v) the FATF antimoney-laundering standards, and (vi) the IMF's Code of Good Practices on Transparency in Monetary and Financial Policies. "Such a comprehensive coverage of standards was needed as part of the financial system stability assessment for Canada in view of the increasing convergence in the activities of banking, insurance, and securities firms, and the integrated nature of the markets in which they operate" (IMF, 2000a).

12. Basel II has been critically examined by Persaud (2001) and Ward (2002b).

13. See *In re Bank of Credit and Commerce International S.A. (No. 10)* [1997] 2 W.L.R. 172, 178–79.

14. Professor Michael Dempster and his research team at the Centre for Financial Research at the University of Cambridge have produced cutting-edge research in this area (Dempster, 2002).

References

Books and Journal Articles

Abbott, K. W., R. O. Keohane, A. Moravcsik, D. Snidal, and A.-M. Slaughter. 2000. "The Legalization of International Soft Law." *International Organization* 54, no. 3: 401–419.

Adam, K. T. Jappelli, A. Menichini, M. Padula, and M. Pagano. 2002. "Analyse, Compare, and Apply Alternative Indicators and Monitoring Methodologies to Measure the Evolution of Capital Market Integration in the European Union." Centre for Studies in Economics and Finance, Department of Economics and Statistics, University of Salerno.

Adams, G. 1999. "The Regulation of Financial Conglomerates." *Journal of Financial Compliance* 5, no. 3: 215–217.

Agosin, M. 1998. "Capital Inflows and Investment Performance: Chile in the 1990s." In R. Ffrench-Davis and H. Reisen (eds.), *Capital Flows and Investment Performance: Lessons from Latin America*. Paris: Organization for Economic Co-operation and Development.

Alexander, K. 2001. "The Need for Efficient International Financial Regulation and the Role of a Global Supervisor." In E. Ferran and C.A.E. Goodhart, *Regulating Financial Services and Markets in the 21st Century*. Oxford: Hart.

———. 2002. "Extraterritorial U.S. Banking Regulation and International Terrorism." *Journal of International Banking Regulation* 3, no. 4: 307–326.

Alexander, K. 2000. "The Role of Soft Law in the Legalization of International Banking Supervision," a paper distributed on the occasion of the Advisory Committee Meeting of 21–23 January 2000 at Queen's College, Cambridge University on the "World Financial Authority Project," p. 2.

Alexander, K., and J. Ward. 2004. "How Voluntary is the Basel Accord?—the Accord as Soft Law." CERF Discussion Paper, Cambridge: Cambridge Endowment for Research in Finance, University of Cambridge, www.cerf.cam.ac.uk

Allegret, J. P., and P. Dulbecco. 2002. "Global Governance versus Domestic Governance: *What Role for International Institutions?" European Journal of Development Research* 14, no. 2: 173–192.

————. 2003. "Why International Institutions Need Governance. The Case of the IMF." Paper submitted at the conference "Economics for the Future: Celebrating 100 Years of Cambridge Economics," Cambridge, England, September 17–19, 2003.

Allen, F., and D. Gale. 2000. *Comparing Financial Systems.* Boston: MIT Press.

American Law Institute. 1987. *Restatement of the Law (Third).* Vol. 1, *The Foreign Relations Law of the United States.* St. Paul, MN: West.

Andenas, M., and C. Hadjiemanual (eds.). 1998. *European Banking Supervision.* London: Kluwer Law.

Arup, C. 1999. *The World Trade Organization Agreements.* Cambridge: Cambridge University Press.

Attanasio, J., and J. Norton. 2001. *A New International Financial Architecture: A Viable Approach.* London: British Institute of International and Comparative Law.

Aust, A. 2000. *Modern Treaty Law and Practice.* Cambridge: Cambridge University Press.

Avgerinos, Y. 2002. "Essential and Non-Essential Measures: Delegation of Powers in EU Securities Regulation." *European Law Journal* 8(2): 269–289.

Axelrod, R. 1984. *The Evolution of Cooperation.* New York: Basic Books.

Bank for International Settlements (BIS). 1988. "Report of the Committee on Banking Regulations and Supervisory Practices, International Convergence of Capital Measurement and Capital Standards." Basel: Basel Committee on Banking Supervision.

————. 1990. "Report of the Committee on Interbank Netting Schemes of the Central Banks of the Group of Ten Countries" (Lamfalussy Report). Basel: Basel Committee on Banking Supervision.

————. 1992. *62nd Annual Report.* Basel: Basel Committee on Banking Supervision.

————. 1994. *65th Annual Report.* Basel: Basel Committee on Banking Supervision.

————. 1995a. "The Supervision of Financial Conglomerates." Basel: Basel Committee on Banking Supervision.

————. 1995b. *66th Annual Report.* Basel: Basel Committee on Banking Supervision.

————. 1996. *67th Annual Report.* Basel: Basel Committee on Banking Supervision.

————. 1998. *69th Annual Report.* Basel: Basel Committee on Banking Supervision.

————. 2001a. *72nd Annual Report.* Basel: Basel Committee on Banking Supervision.

————. 2001b. "Marrying the Macro- and Micro-Prudential Dimensions of Financial Stability." BIS Papers No.1. Basel: Basel Committee on Banking supervision.

Bank of England. 1998. "The Development of a U.K. Real-Time Gross Settlement System." *Bank of England Quarterly Bulletin* 34: 163–168.

Bank of Thailand. 1997. *Supervision Report 1996/97.* Bangkok: Bank of Thailand.

Basel Committee on Banking Supervision (BCBS). 1975. "Report to the Governors on the Supervision of Banks' Foreign Establishments." Basel: Bank for International Settlements.

————. 1983. "Principles for the Supervision of Banks' Foreign Establishments" ("Revised Concordat"). Basel: Bank for International Settlements.

——. 1988. "International Convergence of Capital Measurements and Capital Standards" (amended in 1995). Basel: Bank for International Settlements.

——. 1992. "Minimum Standards for the Supervision of International Banking Groups and Their Cross-Border Establishments." Basel: Bank for International Settlements.

——. 1995. "An Internal Model–Based Approach to Market-Risk Capital Requirements." Basel: Bank for International Settlements.

——. 1999a. "Proposed Revisions to the Basel Capital Accord." Basel: Bank for International Settlements.

——. 1999b. "Enhancing Corporate Governance for Banking Organizations." Basel: Bank for International Settlements.

——. 2000a. "Principles for the Management of Credit Risk." Basel: Bank for International Settlements.

——. 2000b. "Supervisory Guidance for Managing Settlement Risk in Foreign Exchange Transactions." Basel: Bank for International Settlements.

——. 2001a. "The New Basel Capital Accord." Basel: Bank for International Settlements.

——. 2001b. "Recommendations for Public Disclosure of Trading and Derivatives Activities of Banks and Securities Firms." Basel: Bank for International Settlements.

——. 2003. *The New Basel Capital Accord.* April.

Basel Committee on Banking Supervision and the IOSCO Technical Committee. 1995. "Joint Report: Framework for Supervisory Information about the Derivatives Activities of Banks and Securities Firms." Basel: Bank for International Settlements.

Basel Committee on Banking Supervision Joint Forum on Financial Conglomerates. 1999. "Capital Adequacy Principles." Basel: Bank for International Settlements.

Bingham, L. J. 1992. Bingham's Report on BCCI, Inquiry into the Supervision of the Bank of Credit and Commerce International. London: HMSO, Oct. 1992.

Blumberg, P. I. 1993. *The Multinational Challenge to Corporation Law.* Oxford: Oxford University Press.

Board of Governors of the Federal Reserve System. 1990. Letter SR 90-23 (FIS) from the Federal Reserve Associate Director of Supervision (July 3).

Bordo, M. D., and H. James. 1999. "The International Monetary Fund: Its Present Role in Historical Perspective." Report prepared for the U.S. Congressional International Financial Institution Advisory Commission, Washington, DC.

Borio, C., J. C. Furfine, and P. Lowe. 2001. "Procyclicality of the Financial System and Financial Stability: Issues and Policy Option." Bank for International Settlements Papers no. 1 (March).

Bowett, D. 1982. *The Law of International Institutions.* 4th ed. London: Stevens.

Brown, G. 1999. Prepared speech before the Council on Foreign Relations, New York, September 16.

Buria, A. (ed.). 2003. *Challenges to the World Bank and IMF.* London: Anthem Press.

Buchheit, L., and G. M. Gulati. 2002. "Sovereign Bonds and the Collective Will." Paper No. 138, LSE Financial Markets Group, London School of Economics.

Bull, H. 1977. *The Anarchical Society.* Basingstoke: Macmillan.

Cabral, I., F. Dierick, and J. Vesala. 2002. "Banking Integration in the Euro Area." ECB Occasional Paper No. 6. Frankfurt: ECB.

Calem, P., and R. Rob. 1996. "The Impact of Capital-Based Regulation on Bank Risk Taking: A Dynamic Model." U.S. Board of Governors, Finance and Economics Discussion Series, No. 96-12, 1–44.

Calomiris, C. 1999. "Building an Incentive Compatible Safety Net." *Journal of Banking and Finance* 23: 1499–1519.

Calomiris, C., and C. Kahn. 1996. "The Efficiency of Self-Regulated Payment Systems: Learning from the Suffolk System." National Bureau for Economic Research Working Paper 5442.

Calvo, G., and C. Reinhart. 1994. "The Capital Inflows Problem: Concepts and Issues." *Contemporary Economic Policy* 12: 54–66.

Canals, J. 1997. *Universal Banking, International Comparisons and Theoretical Perspectives.* Oxford: Oxford University Press.

Capie, F. 1998. "Can There Be an International Lender of Last Resort?" *International Finance* 1, no. 2.

Caporaso, J. 1993. "International Relations Theory and Multilateralism: The Search for Foundations." In G. Ruggie, *Multilateralism Matters.* New York: Columbia University Press.

Caprio, G. 1998. "Banking Crises: Expensive Lessons from Recent Financial Crises." Paper prepared for the Development Research Group. Washington, DC: World Bank.

Caprio, G., and D. Klingenbiel. 1996. "Dealing with Bank Insolvencies: Cross-Country Experience." Working paper. Washington, DC: World Bank.

Carey, M. 1995. "Partial Market Value Accounting, Bank Capital Volatility, and Bank Risk." *Journal of Banking and Finance* 19: 607–622.

Chakravorti, B. 1996. "Dynamic Public Goods Provision with Coalitional Manipulation." *Journal of Public Economics* 56: 143–161.

Chang, H.-J., H.-J. Park, and C. G. Yoo. 1998. "Interpreting the Korean Crisis: Financial Liberalization, Industrial Policy, and Corporate Governance." *Cambridge Journal of Economics* (November).

Chang, R., and A. Velasco. 1998. "Financial Crises in Emerging Markets: A Canonical Model." Working paper. Atlanta: Federal Reserve Bank of Atlanta.

Claessens, S., and T. Glaessner. 1998. *The Internationalization of Financial Services in Asia.* Policy Research Paper 1911. Washington, DC: World Bank.

Claessens, S., and M. Jansen (eds.). 2000. *The Internationalization of Financial Services: Issues and Lessons for Developing Countries.* Hague: Kluwer Law.

Committee of Wise Men. 2000. "Initial Report on Regulation of European Securities Markets." Brussels: European Union.

Crane, D. (ed.). 1995. *Global Financial System: A Functional Perspective.* Boston: Harvard Business School.

Cranston, R. 1996. *Principles of Banking Law.* Oxford: Oxford University Press.

Crockett, A. 2000. "Why Is Financial Stability a Goal of Public Policy?" Working paper. Basel: Bank for International Settlements.

Croome, J. 1995. *Reshaping the World Trading System: A History of the Uruguay Round.* The Hague: Kluwer Law International.

Cull, R. J. 1997. "Financial Sector Adjustment Loans: A Mid-Course Analysis." World Bank Working Paper No. 1804.

Dahlman, C. 1979. "The Problem of Externality." *Journal of Law and Economics* 22: 141–162.

Dale, R. 1984. *The Regulation of International Banking* Oxford: Blackstone.

———. 1992. *International Banking Regulation.* Oxford: Blackstone.

Dalhuisen, J. "Liberalisation and Re-Regulation of Cross-Border Financial Services," Parts 1–3. *European Business Law Review.* London: Kluwer Law International.

——. 2000. *International Commercial, Financial and Trade Law.* Oxford: Hart.

Davies, H. 2002. "A Toxic Financial Shock: General Insurance Companies May Be Taking on Risks That Are Hard to Quantify." *Financial Times,* January 30.

Demirguc-Kunt, A., and E. Detragiache. 1997. "Financial Liberalization and Financial Fragility." Paper presented to the Annual World Bank Conference on Development Economics, Washington, DC, April.

Demirgu A., C. Kunt, and R. Levine. 1996. "Stock Market Development and Financial Intermediaries: Stylized Facts." *World Bank Economic Review* 10.

Dempster, M.A.H. (ed.). 2002. *Risk Management: Value at Risk and Beyond.* Cambridge: Cambridge University Press.

Dhumale, R. 2000. "Capital Adequacy Standards: Are They Sufficient?" Center for Business Research Working Paper Series, No. 165.

Dine, J. 2000. *The Law of Corporate Groups.* Cambridge: Cambridge University Press.

Dobson, W., and P. Jacquet. 1998. *Financial Services Liberalization in the WTO.* Washington, DC: Institute for International Economics.

Dornbusch, R. 1976. "Expectations and Exchange Rate Dynamics." *Journal of Political Economy* 27: 192–234.

Dow, James. 2000. "What Is Systemic Risk? Moral Hazard, Initial Shocks, and Propagation." *Monetary and Economic Studies* 21: 1–24.

Drazen, A. 2002. "Conditionality and Ownership in IMF Lending: A Political Economy Approach." *IMF Staff Papers* 49 (special issue): 36–67.

Duncan, G. 1994. "Clearing House Arrangements in the Foreign Exchange Markets." Speech at the International Symposium on Banking and Payment Services. Washington, DC: Board of Governors of the Federal Reserve System.

Eatwell, J., and L. Taylor. 1998. "International Capital Markets and the Future of Economic Policy." Paper prepared for the Ford Foundation project *International Capital Markets and the Future of Economic Policy.* New York: Center for Economic Policy Analysis; London: Institute for Public Policy Research.

——. 1999. *The Future of Financial Regulation: A World Financial Authority.* Unpublished working paper, Cambridge University.

——. 2000. *Global Finance at Risk.* New York: Free Press.

——. 2002 (eds.). *International Capital Markets: Systems in Transition.* New York: Oxford University Press.

Eatwell, J., and M. Milgate (eds.). 1983. *Keynes's Economics and the Theory of Value and Distribibution.* London: Duckworth.

Economist. 1997. "Survey of Banking in Emerging Markets." April 12.

Edison, H. J., R. Levine, I. Ricci, and T. Slok. 2002 "International Financial Integration and Economic Growth." *Journal of International Finance* 21, no. 6: 749–776.

Edwards, F. 1996. *The New Finance: Regulation and Financial Stability.* Washington, DC: AEI Press.

Eichengreen, Barry. 1999. *Toward a New International Financial Architecture.* Washington, DC: Institute for International Economics.

Eisenbeis, R. 1995. "Private-Sector Solutions to Payment Systems Fragility." *Journal of Financial Services Research* 9: 327–349.

English, W. 1996. "Inflation and Financial Sector Size." Finance and Economics Discussion Paper Series No. 16. Washington, DC: Federal Reserve Board.

European Central Bank. 2002. "European Integration: What Lessons for other Regions? The Case of Latin America." Working Paper Series. Frankfurt: ECB.

European Commission. 1999. "Financial Services: Implementing the Framework for Financial Markets: Action Plan." COM 232 (11/05/99).

———. 2001. "Decision Establishing the European Securities Committee." COM 2001. 1493 final, June 6.

———. 2003. "Tracking Financial Integration in Europe." Commission Staff Working Paper, May 26, 2003.

European Council. 1999. "Decision 1999/468/EC Laying Down the Procedures for the Exercise of Implementing Powers Conferred on the Commission." OJ L184/23, July 17.

European Monetary Institute. "Lamfalussy Report on Settlement and Payment Systems." 1992. Frankfurt: EMI.

European Parliament. 2002. "Report on the Implementation of Financial Services Legislation" ("von Wogau Report"). A5-0011/2002 final, January 23.

European Shadow Financial Regulatory Committee. 2001. "The Regulation of European Securities Markets: The Lamfalussy Report" (Statement No. 10). Madrid, March 26.

European Union Economic and Finance Ministers. 2000. "Initial Report of the Committee of Wise Men on the Regulation of European Securities Markets" (Lamfalussy Committee). Brussels: EU Economic and Finance Ministers.

———. 2001. "Final Report of the Committee of Wise Men on the Regulation of European Securities Markets" (Lamfalussy Committee). Brussels: EU Economic and Finance Ministers.

Evans, O., A. Leone, M. Gill, and P. Hilbers. 2000. "Macroprudential Indicators of Financial System Soundness." IMF Occasional Paper 00/192. Washington, DC: International Monetary Fund.

Faulhaber, Philips, and A. Santomero. 1990. "Payment Risk, Network Risk and the Role of the Fed." In D. Humphrey (ed.), *U.S. Payment Systems: Efficiency, Risk, and the Role of the Federal Reserve.* Boston: Kluwer.

Federation of European Securities Commissioners. 2000. "Market Abuse: FESCO's Response to the Call for Views from the Securities Regulators under the EU's Action Plan for Financial Services." COM 1999. 232, Fesco/00-961 (June 29).

Federation of European Securities Exchanges. 2001. "Second Report and Recommendations on European Regulatory Structures." January.

Ferran, E. 2004. *Building an EU Securities Market.* Cambridge: Cambridge University Press.

Financial Action Task Force. 1990. "Directorate for Financial, Fiscal and Enterprise Affairs, Organization for Economic Cooperation and Development, Financial Action Task Force on Money Laundering Report." Sections 2(B), 3(A)–(D). Paris: Organization for Economic Cooperation and Development (OECD). www.fatf_gafi.org

———. 1995. "Directorate for Financial, Fiscal and Enterprise Affairs, Organization for Economic Cooperation and Development, Financial Action Task Force on Money Laundering, Annual Report 1994–1995."

———. 1996a. "International Anti-Money Laundering Recommendations." Paris: Organization for Economic Cooperation and Development.

———. 1996b. "Directorate for Financial, Fiscal, and Enterprise Affairs, Organization for Economic Cooperation and Development, Financial Action Task

Force on Money Laundering, FATF VII Report on Money Laundering Typologies."

———. 1996c. "FATF Statement about the Lack of Anti-Money Laundering Law in Development." September 19, 1996.

———. 2000a. "Financial Action Task Force on Money Laundering 2000–2001, Twelfth Annual Report," p. 1. Available at www.oecd.org.fatf/.

———. 2000b. "Report on Non-Cooperative Countries and Territories." June 7, 4–7.

———. 2000c. "Report on Non-Cooperative Countries and Territories." February 14.

———. 2001a. "Report on Compliance with Forty Recommendations by Non-Cooperative Jurisdictions."

———. 2001b. "Special Recommendations, Terrorist Financing."

———. 2001c. FATF Annual Report 2001–2002.

———. 2002. "Guidance for Financial Institutions in Detecting Terrorist Financing."

———. 2003. "The Forty Recommendations." With explanatory note.

Financial Crimes Enforcement Network (FinCEN). 1992. "International Cooperation against Money Laundering Gains Momentum." Washington, DC: Financial Crimes Enforcement Network, U.S. Treasury Department.

———. 1993. "Guidance Notes for Mainstream Banking, Lending and Deposit Taking Activities." London: FinCEN.

———. 1996. "FinCEN Advisory: Enhanced Scrutiny for Transactions Involving the Seychelles." March.

Financial Services Authority. 2001. "Money Laundering Theme—Tackling Our New Responsibilities."

Financial Stability Forum. 2000. "Report of the Follow-Up Group on Incentives to Foster Implementation of Standards." www.fsforum.org

Fischer, S. 1997. "How to Avoid International Financial Crises and the Role of the International Monetary Fund." October 14. Available at www.imf.org/external/np/sec/mds/1997/mds101497.htm

Fitch Ratings, database resources, various years. www.fitchratings.com

Folkerts-Landau, D., and P. Garber. 1992. "The ECB: A Bank or Monetary Policy Rule?" In M. Canzoneri, V. Grilli, and P. Masson (eds.), *Establishing a Central Bank: Issues in Europe and Lessons from the U.S.* Cambridge: Cambridge University Press.

———. 1996. "Payment System Reform in Formerly Centrally Planned Economies." *Journal of Banking and Finance* 18: 33–48.

Folkerts-Landau, D., and M. Khan 1995. "Effect of Capital Flows on the Domestic Financial Sectors in APEC Developing Countries." In M. Khan and C. Reinhart (eds.), *Capital Flows in the APEC Region.* Occasional Paper No. 122. Washington, DC: International Monetary Fund.

Folkerts-Landau, D., and I. Takatoshi. 1995. "International Capital Markets Developments, Prospects, and Policy Issues." IMF Working Paper No. 135. Washington, DC.

Follak, K. P. 2000. "International Harmonisation of Regulatory and Supervisory Frameworks." In M. Giovanoli (ed.), *International Monetary Law: Issues for the New Millenium.* Oxford: Oxford University Press.

Fox, Merritt B. 1997. "Securities Disclosure in a Globalizing Market: Who Should Regulate Whom." *Michigan Law Review* 95.

Freeland, C. 1994. "The Work of the Basle Committee." In R. C. Effros (ed.), *Current Legal Issues Affecting Central Banks,* vol. 2. Washington, DC: International Monetary Fund.

Freis, J. 1996. "An Outsider's Look into the Regulation of Insider Trading in Germany: A Guide to Securities, Banking, and Market Reform in Finanzplatz Deutschland." *British Columbia International and Comparative Law Review* 19: 1, 11.

Freixas, X., C. Giannini, G. Hoggarth, and F. Soussa. 1999. "Lender of Last Resort: A Review of the Literature." *Financial Stability Review.* London: Bank of England.

Galbis, V. 1993. "High Real Interest Rates under Financial Liberalization: Is There a Problem?" IMF Working Paper No. 7. Washington, DC: International Monetary Fund.

Garber, P., and Weisbrod, R. 1992. *The Economics of Banking, Liquidity, and Money,* Lexington: D.C. Heath.

Garegnani, P. 1970. "Heterogeneous Capital, the Production Function and the Theory of Distribution." *Review of Economic Studies* 13: 28–39.

———. 1983. "Notes on Consumption, Investment and Effective Demand." In J. Eatwell and M. Milgate, *Keynes's Economics and the Theory of Value and Distribibution.* London: Duckworth.

General Accounting Office. 1994. "International Banking: Strengthening the Framework for Supervising International Banks." Washington, DC: GAO.

Gilmore, W. 2002. "International Initiatives." In T. Graham, *International Guide to Money Laundering Law and Practice.* London: Butterworths.

———. 2003. *Dirty Money.* Strasbourg: Council of Europe Publishing.

Giovanoli, M. 1994. "The Role of the BIS in Monetary Cooperation and Its Tasks Relating to the ECU." *Current Legal Issues Affecting Central Banks* 1: 39.

———2000. *International Monetary Law: Issues for the New Millennium.* Oxford: Oxford University Press.

———. 2002. "Reflections on International Financial Standards as 'Soft Law.' " In J. J. Worton and M. Andenas (eds.), *International and Monetary Law upon Entering the New Millennium—A Tribute to Sir Joseph and Ruth Gold.* London: British Institute of International and Comparative Law.

Godley, W.A.H., W. Nordhaus, and K. Coutts. 1978. "Industrial Pricing in the UK," Working Paper, Department of Applied Economics, Cambridge University, WP 26.

Gold, J. 1977. "International Capital Movements under the Law of the International Monetary Fund." Pamphlet Series No. 21. Washington, DC: International Monetary Fund.

———. 1979. *Legal and Institutional Aspects of the International Monetary System: Selected Essays.* Washington DC: International Monetary Fund.

———. 1981. "Transformation of the International Monetary Fund." *Columbia Journal of Transnational Law* 20: 227.

———. 1982. "Developments in the International Monetary System: The International Monetary Fund and International Monetary Law since 1971." *Recueil des Cours.*

———. 1996. *Interpretation and the Law of the International Monetary Fund.* Dordrecht: Kluwer.

Goldstein, M. 1997. *The Case for an International Banking Standard.* Washington, DC: Institute for International Economics.

Goodhart, C.A.E. 2001. *The Organisational Structure of Banking Supervision.* London: Financial Markets Group.

―――. 2003. *A Framework for Assessing Financial Stability.* London: Financial Markets Group.

―――. 1992. *EMU and ESCB After Maastricht.* London: Financial Markets Group.

Goodhart, C., P. Hartmann, D. Llewellyn, L. Rojas-Suarez, and S. Weisbrod. 1998. *Financial Regulation: Why, How, and Where Now?* London: Routledge.

Gorton, G. 1988. "Banking Panics and Business Cycles." *Oxford Economic Papers* 40: 221–255.

Graham, G. 1996. "Seychelles Condemned over 'Money Launders' Charter." *Financial Times*, February 2.

―――. 1996. "Seychelles to Face Critics on New Law." *International Herald Tribune*, January 31.

―――. 1996. "Seychelles Foreign Investment Law Draws More Fire." Reuters, February 1, available in LEXIS, News Library, Reufin file.

Graham, T. 2002. *International Guide to Money Laundering Law and Practice.* London: Butterworths.

Griffith-Jones, S., and A. Persaud. 2003. "The Political Economy of Basel II and Implications for Emerging Economies." Paper prepared for the Economic Commission of Latin America.

Group of Ten. 1996. "The Resolution of Sovereign Liquidity Crises." Washington, DC. www.bis.org

―――. 2001. *Report on Consolidation in the Financial Sector.* Basel: Bank for International Settlements.

Group of 22. 1998. "Report of the Working Group on International Financial Crises." Washington, DC. www.bis.org.

Haas, E. B. 1980. "Why Collaborate? Issue-Linkage and International Regimes." *World Politics* 32: 357, 358.

Hawkins, J., and P. Turner. 2000. "International Financial Reform: Regulatory and Other Issues." Unpublished paper presented at conference in Washington, DC (3–4 February, 2000).

Helleiner, E. 1994. *States and the Reemergence of Global Finance.* Ithaca, NY: Cornell University Press.

Herman, B. (ed.). 1999. *Global Financial Turmoil and Reform.* New York: United Nations University Press.

Hilbers, P., R. Krueger, and M. Moretti. 2000. "New Tools for Assessing Financial System Soundness." *Finance and Development* (September) 4: 13–19.

Hoekman, B. M., and M. M. Kostecki. 2001. *The Political Economy of the World Trading System.* Oxford: Oxford University Press.

Holder, W. E. 1999. "Fund Jurisdiction over Capital Movements. Comments, Panel on Preventing Asian Type Crises: Who If Anyone Should Have Jurisdiction Over Capital Movement?" *ILSA Journal of International and Comparative Law* 5 (spring): 407–415.

Honohan, P., and J. Stiglitz. 1999. "Robust Financial Restraint." Paper presented at a workshop titled "Financial Liberalization: How Far? How Fast?" presented by the Development Research Group, World Bank, Washington, DC (September).

House of Commons, 1994–95. Memorandum Submitted by Interpol and Reproduced in House of Commons, Home Affairs Committee, Organized Crime, H.C. Paper 18–11.

Hudec, Robert. 1999. *Essays in International Trade Law*. Boston: Cameron May.

Humphrey, D. 1989. "Market Responses to Pricing Fedwire Daylight Overdrafts." *Federal Reserve Bank of Richmond Economic Review* 75: 2–41.

Hupkes, E.H.G. 2004. "Insolvency—Why a Special Regime for Banks?" In *Current Developments in Monetary and Financial Law*, vol. 3. Washington, DC: International Monetary Fund.

Independent Task Force, Council on Foreign Relations. 1999. Safeguarding Prosperity in a Global Financial System. Washington, DC: Institute for International Economics.

International Association of Insurance Supervisors (IAIS). 1994. *Annual Report*. Basel: IAIS.

———. 1995. "Recommendation Concerning Mutual Assistance, Cooperation, and Sharing of Information." Basel: IAIS.

———. 1997a. *Annual Report*. Basel: IAIS.

———. 1997b. "A Model Memorandum of Understanding." Guidance paper 2. Basel: IAIS.

———. 1997c. "Report on Global Standards for Insurance Supervisors." Basel: IAIS.

———. 1999a. "Executive Committee Reports on 1999 Activities." IAIS Newletter. 4th Quarter, Issue 6, pp. 1–2.

———. 1999b. *Annual Report*. Basel: IAIS.

———. 1999c. IAIS Newsletter, Issue 3.

———. 1999d. IAIS Newsletter, Issue 5.

———. 2002a. "Principles on Capital Adequacy and Solvency." Basel: IAIS.

———. 2002b. "Supervisory Standard on the Evaluation of the Reinsurance Cover of Primary Issuers and the Securities of Their Reinsurers."

———. 2002 (October). "Principles on Minimum Requirements for Supervision of Reinsurers."

———. 2003a. *Annual Report* (covering October 2002–September 2003).

———. 2003b. "Insurance Core Principles, Comparison of Previous and New ICPs."

———. 2003c. "IAIS Expands Core Principles for Insurance." Press release.

International Financial Institutions Advisory Committee to the United States Congress 2000. *Meltzer Report*.

———. 2004. "Guidance Paper on Investment Risk Management" (October 2004).

International Monetary Fund. 1997a. *International Financial Statistics*. Washington, DC: IMF.

———. 1997b. Communiqué of the Interim Committee of the Board of Governors of the International Monetary Fund, April 28. Washington, DC: IMF.

———. 1998. *International Capital Markets: Developments, Prospects, and Key Issues.* Washington, DC.: IMF.

———. 2000a. *Report on the Observance of Standards and Codes: Canada.* Washington, DC: IMF.

———. 2000b. *Experimental Reports on Observance of Standards and Codes (ROSCs).* Washington, DC: IMF.

———. 2000c. Memorandum of Economic Policies of the Government of Angola (April 3, 2000).

———. 2001a. IMF Information Notice 01/41 (April 29).

———. 2001b. "IMF Establishing International Capital Markets Department." News Brief No. 01/24 (March 1).

———. 2004a. "IMF Statement on New IMF Stand-by Arrangement for Turkey" (October 13, 2004).

———. 2004b. "IMF Completes First Review Under Gabon's Stand-by Arrangement and Approves US \$20 Million Disbursement" (Sept. 20, 2004).

———. 2004c "IMF Completes Fifth Review of Uruguay's Stand-by Arrangement" (August 27, 2004).

International Organization for Securities Commissioners (IOSCO). 1986. IOSCO Resolutions, Resolution Concerning Mutual Assistance ("Rio Declaration"). Available at www.iosco.org/resolutions/resolutions.html.

———. 1989a. *Annual Report*. Madrid: IOSCO.

———. 1989b. "Technical Committee Report on Capital Adequacy Standards for Securities Firms" (August). Madrid: IOSCO.

———. 1994. "Operational and Financial Risk Management Control Mechanisms for Over-the-Counter Derivatives of Regulated Securities Firms." Available at IO IOSCO website, www.iosco.org

———. 1996. "Report on International Standards for Regulation of Securities Markets." Madrid: IOSCO.

———. 1998a. "Methodologies for Determining Minimum Capital Standards for Internationally Active Securities Firms Which Permit the Use of Models under Prescribed Conditions." Report of IOSCO Technical Committee (May). Madrid: IOSCO.

———. 1998b. IOSCO Resolution 18; "Risk Management and Control Guidance for Securities Firms and Their Supervisors." IOSCO Consultation Paper 2 (March). Madrid: IOSCO.

———. 1998c. Technical Committee, "Principles for Memoranda of Understanding," released at the 16th Annual Conference. Available at www.iosco.org/publ-docs/d . . .-1991-principles-of-memoranda.html.

———. 1999. *Annual Report*. Madrid: IOSCO.

———. 2000a. By-Laws of the International Organization of Securities Commissions, pt. 2, sec. 2. Madrid: IOSCO.

———. 2000b. *Annual Report*. Madrid: IOSCO.

———. 2000c. "Objectives and Principles of Securities Regulation." Madrid: IOSCO.

———. 2003. Annual Report. Madrid: IOSCO.

———. 2004. "IOSCO Moves to Strengthen International Capital Markets against Financial Fraud." Press release.

International Swaps and Derivatives Association. 2002. ISDA Master Agreement. London.

Jackson, P. 1999. "Capital Requirements and Bank Behaviour: The Impact of the Basel Accord." Basel Committee on Banking Supervision Working Paper No.1. www.bis.org.

———. 2000. "Amending the Basel Capital Accord." Unpublished paper, Cambridge Endowment for Research in Finance Seminar, January 22.

Jae-Kwon, O. 1998. "Managing the Crisis: The Case of Korea." Paper presented at the ADB seminar on International Finance, Tokyo, November.

Jennings, R., and Watts, A. (eds.). 1996. *Oppenheim's International Law*. Vol. 1, *Peace*. London: Longman.

Jorion, P. 2002. *Fallacies in the Effects of Market Risk Management Systems*. Mimeo. University of California at Irvine.

Kahane, Y. 1977. "Currency Options as Theoretical and Practical Instruments in

Hedging the Exchange Rate in Excess of Loss Reinsurance." Working Paper, Institute for Economic Research, Tel Aviv University.

Kahler, M. 1995. *International Institutions and the Political Economy of Integration.* Washington, DC: Brookings Institute.

Kahler, M. (ed.). 1998. *Capital Flows and Financial Crises.* Ithaca, NY: Cornell University Press.

Kahn, C. 1996. "Payment System Settlement and Bank Incentives." Federal Reserve Bank of Atlanta Working Paper Series 96-10. Atlanta: Federal Reserve Bank of Atlanta.

Kalecki, M. 1939. *Essays in the Theory of Economic Fluctuations.* London: Allen and Unwin.

Kaminsky, G., and C. Reinhart. 1998. "The Twin Crises: The Causes of Banking and Balance of Payment Problems." Mimeo. Washington, DC: Board of Governors of the Federal Reserve System.

Kaplow, L. 1992. "Rules versus Standards: An Economic Analysis." *Duke Law Journal.*

Kapstein, E. 1989. "Resolving the Regulator's Dilemma: International Coordination of Banking Regulations." *International Organization* 43: 327–328.

———. 1994. *Governing the Global Economy,* Cambridge, MA: Harvard University Press.

Karmel, R. S. 1991. "The Second Circuit Role in Expanding the SEC's Jurisdiction Abroad." *St. John's Law Review* 65: 743.

Kasman, B. 1992. "A Comparison of Monetary Policy Operating Procedures in Six Industrial Countries." Federal Reserve Bank of New York *Quarterly Review* 17.

Kenen, P. B.. 2001. *The International Financial Architecture: What's New? What's Missing.* Washington DC: Institute for International Economics.

Keohane, R. 1984. *After Hegemony: Cooperation and Discord in World Political Economy.* Princeton, NJ: Princeton University Press.

Keohane, R., and J. Nye. 2001. *Power and Independence* (2nd ed.). London: Longman.

Key, S. 1997. "Financial Services in the Uruguay Round and the WTO." G-30 Occasional Paper 54. Washington, DC: Group of Thirty.

Key, S., and H. Scott. 1991. *International Trade in Banking Service: A Conceptual Framework.* Washington, DC: Group of Thirty.

Keynes, J. M. 1936. *The General Theory of Employment, Interest and Money.* London: Macmillan.

———. 1973. *Collected Economic Writings.* London: Macmillan.

Kim, D., and A. Santomero. 1980. "Risk in Banking and Capital Regulation." *Journal of Finance* 32: 87–113.

King, R., and R. Levine. 1993. *Finance and Growth: Schumpeter Might Be Right.* Policy Research Working Paper. Washington, DC: World Bank.

Koehn D., and A. Santomero. 1980. "Modelling the Banking Firm: A Survey." *Journal of Money, Credit and Banking* 16: 576–616.

Kono, M., and L. Schuknecht. 1998. "Financial Services Trade, Capital Flows, and Financial Stability." Working paper. Geneva: World Trade Organization.

Kono, M., P. Low, M. Luanga, A. Mattoo, M. Oshikawa, and L. Schuknecht. 1997. "Opening Markets in Financial Services and the Role of the GATS." Working paper. Geneva: World Trade Organization.

Koskenniemi, M. 2004. "Global Governance and Public International Law." *Vierteljahresschrift fur Recht und Politik Jahrgang* 37(3): 241–254.

Kurz, M. 1987. "Myopic Decision Rules." *The New Palgrave: A Dictionary of Economics.* London: Macmillan.

Lastra, R. M. 1996. *Central Banking and Banking Regulation.* London: Financial Markets Group.

Lastra, R. M., and H. Shams. 2001. "Public Accountability in the Financial Sector." In E. Ferran and C.A.E. Goodhart (eds.), *Regulating Financial Services and Markets in the 21st Century,* pp. 165–188. Oxford: Hart.

Lastra, R. M., and H. Schiffman (eds.). 1999. *Bank Failures and Bank Insolvency Law in Economies in Transition.* The Hague: Kluwer Law.

Liechtenstein, C. C. 2000. "International Jurisdiction over International Capital Flows and the Role of the IMF." In M. Giovanoli (ed.), *International Monetary Law: Issues for the New Millennium.* Oxford: Oxford University Press.

———. 1991. "Bank for International Settlements: Committee on Banking Regulation and Supervisory Practices." Consultative Paper on International Convergence of Capital Measurement and Capital Standards, 30 I.L.M. 967, 969.

Lindgren, C., G. Garcia, and M. Saal. 1996. *Bank Soundness and Macroeconomic Policy.* Washington, DC: International Monetary Fund.

Litan, R., and J. Rauch. 1997. *American Finance for the 21st Century.* Washington, DC: U.S. Treasury Department.

Lo, A. 1987. "Logit versus Discriminant Analysis: A Specification Test and Application to Corporate Bankruptcy." *Journal of Econometrics* 31: 151–178.

Lomnicka, E. 2000. "Knowingly Concerned? Participatory Liability for Breaches of Regulatory Duties." *Company Lawyer* 21(4): 121–126.

Long, M., and D. Vittas. 1992. "Changing the Rules of the Game." In D. Vittas (ed.), *Financial Regulation: Changing the Rules of the Game.* Washington, DC: World Bank.

Lucatelli, A. 1997. *Financial and World Order, Financial Fragility, System Risk, and Transnational Regimes.* Westport, CT: Greenwood Press.

Mann, F. A. 1992. *The Legal Aspect of Money.* 5th ed. Oxford: Oxford University Press.

Marchetti, J. A. 2003. "What Should Financial Regulators Know about the GATS?" Unpublished paper prepared for the World Trade Organization.

Martin, L. 1993. "Credibility, Costs, and Institutions: Cooperation on Economic Sanctions." *World Politics* 45 no. 3: 418.

Mas-Colell, A., M. Whinston, and J. Green. 1995. *Microeconomic Theory.* Oxford: Oxford University Press.

Masciandaro, D. (ed.). 2004. *Financial Intermediation in the New Europe.* Cheltenham: Edward Elgar.

McFadden, D., S. Wu, and M. Balch. 1973. *Essays on Economic Behavior under Uncertainty.* Amsterdam: Oxford University Press.

McKinnon, R. 1973. *Money and Capital in Economic Development.* Washington, DC: Brookings Institution.

Mearsheimer, J. J. 1994–95. "The False Promise of International Institutions." *International Security* 19(3): 5–49.

Medova, E. A., and M. N. Kyriacou. 2002. "Extremes in Operation Risk Management." In M.A.H. Dempster (ed.), *Risk Management: Value at Risk and Beyond.* Cambridge: Cambridge University Press.

Mendelson, M. 1996. "The Subjective Element in Customary International Law." *The British Yearbook of International Law,* pp. 177–208.

Miller, M., and P. Luangaram. 1998. *Financial Crisis in East Asia: Bank Runs, Asset Bubbles and Antidotes.* Working paper, Centre for the Study of Globalization and Regionalization, University of Warwick, November.

Millspaugh, P. 1992. "Global Securities Trading: The Question of a Watchdog." *George Washington Journal of International Law and Economics* 26: 355–374.

Mishkin, F., 1996. "Understanding Financial Crises: A Developing Country Perspective." National Bureau for Economic Research Working Paper No. 5600, Cambridge, MA.

Moggridge, D. (ed.). 1973–1980. *Collected Writings of John Maynard Keynes,* vols. 14, 25, and 26. Cambridge: Cambridge University Press.

———. 1992. *Maynard Keynes: An Economist Biography.* London: Routledge.

Nasution, A. 1997. "The Meltdown of the Indonesian Economy in 1997–1998: Causes and Responses." *Seoul Journal of Economics* 11: 447–482.

Neild, R. R. 1963. *Pricing and Employment in the Trade Cycle.* Cambridge: Cambridge University Press.

Newburg, A. 2000. "The Changing Roles of the Bretton Woods Institutions: Evolving Concepts of Conditionality." In M. Giovanoli (ed.), *International Monetary Law: Issues for the New Millenium.* Oxford: Oxford University Press.

Norman, P. 1988. "Capital Ratio Is Set by Banks of 12 Nations." *Wall Street Journal,* July 12, p. 3.

North, D. C. 1990. *Institutions, Institutional Change and Economic Performance.* New York: Cambridge University Press.

Norton, J. 1995. *Devising International Bank Supervisory Standards.* Dordrecht: Kluwer.

———. 2000. *Financial Sector Law Reform in Emerging Economies.* London: British Institute of International and Comparative Law.

O'Brien, R., Goetz, A. M., Scholter, J., and Williams, M. 2000. *Contesting Global Governance.* Cambridge: Cambridge University Press.

Organization for Economic Cooperation and Development. 1996a. "Financial Action Task Force on Money Laundering Condemns New Investment Law in the Seychelles." OECD Press Release, February 1.

———. 1996b. "Financial Action on Task Force on Money Laundering Welcomes New Anti-Money Laundering Law in Turkey." OECD Press Release, December 12.

———. 1997. "Regulatory Reform in the Financial Services Industry: Where Have We Been? Where Are We Going?" *OECD Financial Market Trends* 67: 32, 41.

———. 1999. "Cross-Border Trade in Financial Services: Economics and Regulation." *Insurance and Private Pensions Compendium for Emerging Economies,* Book 1, Part 1:6. www.oecd.org

———. 2000. "Financial Action Task Force on Money Laundering Welcomes Proposed Austrian Legislation to Eliminate Anonymous Passbooks." OECD press release, June 15.

Overseas Development Institute. 2000. "Conference Report on International Standards and Codes: The Developing Country Perspective." London: Department for International Development.

Passacantando, F. 1991. "Central Banks' Role in the Payment System and Its Relationship with Banking Supervision." *Giornale degli Economiste e Annali di Economia* 51: 453–491.

Pecchioli, R. M. 1983. *Internationalization of Banking: The Policy Issues.* Oxford: Oxford University Press.

Peek, J., and E. Rosengren. 1996. "The Use of Capital Ratios to Trigger Intervention in Problem Banks: Too Little Too Late." *New England Economic Review* (September–October) 13: 123–172.

Persaud, A. 2000. *Sending the Herd Off the Cliff Edge: The Disturbing Interaction between Herding and Market-Sensitive Risk Management Practices.* State Street Bank. Available at www.cerf.cam.ac.uk

———. 2001. *Liquidity Black Holes.* State Street Bank. Available at www.cerf.cam.ac.uk

———. 2003. (ed.). "Liquidity Black Holes: Understanding, Quantifying and Managing Financial Liquidity Risk." In A. Persaud (ed.), *Liquidity Black Holes.* London: KPMG.

Peterson, W., and M. Wall. 1998. "Monetary Instability and Economic Growth." University of Minnesota Economic Development Center Bulletin No. 98/6.

Pill, H., and M. Pradhan. 1995. "Financial Indicators and Financial Change in Africa and Asia." IMF Working Paper No. 2. Washington, DC: International Monetary Fund.

Prowse, S. 1995. "Should Banks Own Shares?" World Bank Policy Paper 1481, Washington, DC.

Rahman, Z. 1998. "The Role of Accounting and Disclosure Standards in the East Asian Financial Crisis: Lessons Learned." Mimeo. Geneva: United Nations Conference on Trade and Development, Washington, DC.

Reisen, H. 1998. *Domestic Causes of Currency Crises: Policy Lessons for Crisis Avoidance.* Technical Paper No. 136. Paris: OECD Development Centre.

Richards, H., 1995. "Daylight Overdraft Fees and the Federal Reserve's Payment System Risk Policy." *Federal Reserve Bulletin* 81: 42–61.

Robinson, J. 1951. *The Rate of Interest and Other Essays.* London: Macmillan.

Rolnick, A., B. Smith, and W. Weber. 1998. "Lessons from a Laissez-Faire Payments System: The Suffolk Banking System (1825–58)." *Quarterly Review.* Minneapolis: Federal Reserve Bank of Minneapolis.

Rosenau, J. N. 1995. "Governance in the Twenty First Century." *Global Governance* 1(1): 13–43.

———. 1997. *Along the Domestic-Foreign Frontier: Exploring Governance in a Turbulent World.* Cambridge: Cambridge University Press.

Ruder, D. 1991. "Effective International Supervision of Global Securities Markets." *Hastings International and Comparative Law Review* 14: 317–327.

Santos, J. 1998. "Commercial Banks in the Securities Business: A Review." Working Paper No. 56. Basel: Bank for International Settlements.

Schachter, Oscar. 1977. "The Twilight Existence of Non-Binding International Agreements." *American Journal of International Law* 71: 295–304.

Schnadt, N. 1994. "The Discount Rate of Bank Bills on the U.K. Money Market." Mimeo. London: London School of Economics.

Scholes, M., S. Wilson, and M. Wolfson. 1990. "Employee Stock Ownership Plans and Corporate Re-Structuring: Myths and Realities." *Financial Management* 19: 12–28.

Schotter, A. 1981. *The Economic Theory of Social Institutions.* Cambridge: Cambridge University Press.

Scott, H., and K. Wellons. 2002. *International Finance* (5th ed.). Boston, MA: Foundation Press.

Scott, H., and S. Iwahara. 1994. *In Search of a Level-Playing Field: The Implementation of the Basle Committee Accords in Japan and the United States*. Washington, DC: Group of 30.

Seidl-Hohenveldern, I. 1979. "International Economic 'Soft Law.' " *Hague Recueil:* 169–246.

Shaw, E. 1973. *Financial Deepening in Economic Development*. New York: Oxford University Press.

Shleifer, A., and R. Vishny. 1997. "A Survey of Corporate Governance." *Journal of Finance* 52: 737–783.

Siegel, D. E. 2002. "The Legal Aspects of the IMF/WTO Relationship: The Fund's Articles of Agreement and the WTO Agreements." *American Journal of International Law* 96: 561–609.

Singh, A. 1999. "Corporate Financial Patterns in Industrializing Economies: A Comparative International Study." Paper, Department of Applied Economics, University of Cambridge.

Skidelsky, R. 2000. *John Maynard Keynes: Fighting for Britain*. Basingstoke: MacMillan.

Smith, G. 1991. "Competition in the European Financial Services Industry: The Free Movement of Capital versus the Regulation of Money Laundering." *University of Pennsylvania Journal of International Business Law* 13: 101–130.

Spencer, P. D. 2000. *The Structure and Regulation of Financial Markets*. Oxford: Oxford University Press.

Stiglitz, J. 1994. "The Role of the State in Financial Markets." In *Proceedings of the World Bank Conference on Development Economics 1993*. Washington, DC: World Bank.

———. 1999. "The World Bank at the Millennium." *Economic Journal* 109: F576–F597.

———. 2002. *Globalization and Its Discontents*. London: Penguin/Allen and Lane.

Stultz, R. 1999. "Financial Structure, Corporate Finance, and Economic Growth." Revised mimeo. Available at www.osu.edu/finance/papers.

Summers, B. 1994. "The Payment System." IMF Working Paper 94/36. Washington, DC: IMF.

Temin, P. 1989. *Did Monetary Forces Cause the Great Depression?* New York: Norton.

Tirole, J. 2002. *Financial Crises, Liquidity, and the International Monetary System*. Princeton, NJ: Princeton University Press.

Trachtman, J. P. 1995. "Trade in Financial Services under GATS, NAFTA, and the EC: A Regulatory Jurisdiction Analysis." *Columbia Journal of Transnational Law* 34: 37–105.

Truell, P., and L. Gurwin. 1992. *False Profits: The Inside Story of BCCI, The World's Most Corrupt Financial Empire*. Boston: Hougton Mifflin.

Tung, Ko-Yung. 2003. "The Rule of Law: From Rule Based to Value Based Paradigm." Unpublished paper, The London Forum, March 12.

Turner, P. 2002. "Procyclicality of Regulatory Ratios." In J. Eatwell and L. Taylor (eds.), *International Capital Markets: Systems in Transition*. New York: Oxford University Press.

United Nations Convention against Illicit Traffic in Narcotic Drugs and Psychotropic Substances, opened for signature December 20, 1988, UN Doc. E/CONF.82/15, 28 I.L.M. 497.

U.S. Congress. 1994. The Anti-Money Laundering Act of 1993: Hearings on S.1664 before the Senate Committee on Banking, Housing and Urban Affairs. 103d

Cong. 38 1994. Statement of R. K. Noble, Assistant Secretary for Enforcement, U.S. Treasury Department.

Van Zandt, D. E. 1991. "The Regulatory and Institutional Conditions for an International Securities Market." *Virginia Journal of International Law* 32: 47–78.

Vital, C. 1994. "An Appraisal of the Swiss Interbank Clearing System." Speech before the IBC International Payment Systems Conference, London (April).

von Furstenberg G. M. (ed.). 1997. *Regulation and Supervision of Financial Institutions in the NAFTA Countries and Beyond.* Norwell, MA: Kluwer.

Walker, G. A. 2001. *International Banking Regulation: Law, Policy, and Practice.* New York: Kluwer International.

Wall, L., and G. Peterson. 1996. "Managerial Rents and Regulatory Intervention in Troubled Banks." *Journal of Banking and Finance* 20: 331–335.

Ward, J. 2002a. *The New Basel Accord and Developing Countries: Problems and Alternatives.* Working Paper No. 4. Cambridge Endowment for Research in Finance. Available at www.cerf.cam.ac.uk

———. 2002b. *The Supervisory Approach: A Critique.* Working paper 2, Cambridge Endowment for Research in Finance. Available at www.cerf.cam.ac.uk

Wellens, K.C., and G., M. Borchardt. 1989. "Soft Law in European Community Law." *European Law Review* 14: 267–321.

White, W. 2000a. "Recent Initiatives to Improve the Regulation and Supervision of Private Capital Flows." Working paper no. 92. Basel: Basel Committee on Banking Supervision.

———. 2000b. "What Have We Learned from Recent Financial Crises and Policy Responses?" Working paper no. 84. Basel: Basel Committee on Banking Supervision.

Woods, N. 2001. "Making the IMF and the World Bank More Accountable." *International Affairs* 77: 83–100.

Woods, N., and A. Narlikar. 2001. "Governance and the Limits of Accountability: The WTO, the IMF, and the World Bank." Paper available at www.globaleconomicgovernance.org

World Bank. 1997. *Guidelines for Financial Sector Development.* Mimeo. Washington, DC: World Bank.

———. 1998. *Global Development Finance.* Washington, DC: World Bank.

World Trade Organization. 1994. *International Legal Materials.* GATS, Annex on Financial Services (April 15, 1994), WTO Agreement, Annex 1B, p. 33.

———. 1999. "An Introduction to the GATS." October. Geneva: WTO Secretariat.

———. 1999. *The WTO Legal Texts.* Cambridge: Cambridge University Press.

Young, O. 1990. *International Governance: Protecting the Environment in a Stateless Society.* Ithaca, NY: Cornell University Press.

Legal Documents and Instruments

Treaties

Articles of Agreement of the International Monetary Fund. 1993 (April). Washington, DC: IMF. 22 July, 1944. 60 stat. 1401, 2 UNTS 39 as amended through 28 June 1990. Reprinted March 2000.

North American Free Trade Agreement between the Government of the United States of America, The Government of Canada and the Government of the United Mexican States, December 17, 1992. Chapter 14, "Financial Services."

Treaty of Rome (1957) (EC Treaty).
Treaty on European Unioin (1993).
Treaty of Amsterdam (1997).
Treaty Establishing a Constitution for Europe.
United Nations Convention against Transnational Organized Crime. Vienna, 3 March 2000. *International Legal Materials* 40: 335.
World Trade Organization Agreements: Marrakesh Agreement Establishing the World Trade Organization and its substantive agreements (April 15, 1994); The Legal Texts (1999) (World Trade Organization). *International Legal Materials* 33: 1143.
World Trade Organization Charter (Marrakesh Agreement) (1994).
General Agreement on Tariffs and Trade, Annex 1A to the WTO charter. (1994).
General Agreement on Trade in Services, Annex 1B to the WTO charter. (1994).

Statutes

Financial Services Modernization Act of 1999, Pub. L. 106–102, 113 Stat. 1338 (2000).
North American Free Trade Agreement Implementation Act (1993), Chapter 14, "Financial Services."
"The Uniting and Strengthening America by Providing Appropriate Tools Required to Intercept and Obstruct Terrorism" (USA Patriot Act), Title III, Pub. L. 107–56, 115 Stat. 272 (2001).

Judicial Decisions

Caixa-Bank France v. Ministère de l'Economie, des Finances et de l'Industrie, European Court of Justice, C-442/02 (2004).
Hartford Fire Insurance v. California 509 US 764 (1993).
Pulp Wood case [1988] E.C.R. 5193.
In re Bank of Credit and Commerce International S.A. (No. 10) [1997] 2 W.L.R. 172.
Banco do Brasil, S.A. v. Israel Commodity Co., 190 N.E. 2d 235 (1963).
Long Term Capital Holdings, et al., v. United States of America, 330 F. Supp. 2d 122 (U.S. D. ct. Conn., 2004).
J. Zeevi and Sons Ltd. v. Grindlays Bank (Uganda) Limited, 333 N.E. 2d 168 (1975).
Peter Paul and Others v. Federal Republic of Germany, European Court of Justice, C-222/02 (2004).
Regulation Y, 12 C.F.R. Part 225 (2000).

Regulations and Supervisory Notices

Federal Reserve Board Supervisory Letter SR 02-8 on implementation of Section 327 of the U.S. Patriot Act (March 20, 2002).
Supervisory Letter SR 00-13 on framework for supervision of financial holding companies (August 15, 2000).
Lotus Case (France v. Turkey) (1927) PCIJ Rep. Series A, No. 10, Permanent Court of International Justice.
Case Concerning Military and Paramilitary Activities in and against Nicaragua (Merits) (1986) (*Nicaragua v. United States*) ICJ Rep. p. 14.
North Sea Continental Shelf Cases (Federal Republic of German v. Denmark; Federal Republic of Germany v. the Netherlands) (1969) ICJ Rep. p. 3.

Three Rivers District Council v. Governor and Company of the Bank of England (No. 3)
    [2000] 2 WLR 1220 HL.

WTO Cases

Panel Report, Mexico. Measures Affecting Telecommunications Services (adopted
    April 2, 2004). WT/DS204R.
Panel Report, Argentina. Measures Affecting Imports of Footwear, Textiles, Ap-
    parel and other Items (adopted April 22, 1998). WT/DS56/R (November 25,
    1997).
Appellate Body Report, Argentina. WT/DS56/AB/R and Corr. 1, DSR 1998: 111,
    1033.
Panel Report, India. Quantitative Restrictions on Imports of Agricultural, Textile
    and Industrial Products (adopted September 22, 1999). WT/DS90/R (April 6,
    1999).
Appellate Body Report, India. WT/DS90/AB/R, AB-1999-3.

Conference Presentations

Norgren, K. 2003. "The Financial Action Task Force: Complying with the Rec-
    ommendations." Economic Crime Symposium, Jesus College, Cambridge
    (September 11), Cambridge, UK.
Footer, M. 2004. "The World Trade Organization and International Law." The
    Changing Face of International Law, University of Warwick School of Law
    (March 4), Coventry, UK.

Index